The Collected Lyrics
of
Háfiz of Shíráz

Some secrets may the poet tell,
For the world loves new ways;
To tell too deep ones is not well–
It knows not what he says.

From Matthew Arnold's
Stanzas in Memory of the Author of 'Obermann'

The Collected Lyrics
of
Háfiz of Shíráz

Translated by Peter Avery

This first edition published in 2007 by
Archetype
Chetwynd House, Bartlow
Cambridge CB1 6PP, UK
www.archetype.uk.com

Publisher's acknowledgements:
Grateful acknowledgement for their invaluable support is given to
The British Institute of Persian Studies, The Centre for Promotion
of Persian Language and Literature, and Dr M. A. Mannish.
Printed in association with the Iran Heritage Foundation.

ISBN 10 digit 1-901383-26-1   (cloth)
ISBN 13 digit 9781901383263   (cloth)

ISBN 10 digit 1-901383-09-1   (pb)
ISBN 13 digit 9781901383096   (pb)

British Library Cataloguing in Publication Data
A catalogue record for this book is available from
The British Library

Book design by Shems Friedlander

Typeset by DL Graphics, London

Printed and bound by St Edmundsbury Press,
Bury St. Edmunds, UK.

CONTENTS

Translator's Dedication:
I dedicate this book to Eric Hewett without whom it might never have happened.

Translator's Acknowledgements:
My considerable indebtedness to the amanuensis who took down these translations in the first place is acknowledged in the Dedication of this book. There remain others to whom I wish to express profound gratitude for the meticulous work with which they have helped me by carefully going through the manuscript. Principal among them is Mr Jesse Billett. He has devoted time while a graduate student in King's College, Cambridge, to ensuring that the manuscript is as correct as possible. In this he has been helped by Mr Julian Hendrix, also of my College. To them I am deeply indebted, as I am to my publisher, Patricia Salazar. Her faith and enthusiasm for this work has ensured its being eventually presented to the public.

As it represents the thoughts and efforts of many years, it is only natural that in its production Iranian friends and mentors should have been in my mind. It is to them I owe most. Principal among them mention must be made of the late Sayyid Sádiq Goharín and the late Dr Parvíz Nátíl Khánlarí. Over the years they constantly encouraged me in my studies of Persian poetry and especially that of Háfiz. I have used Dr Khánlarí's admirably edited edition of Háfiz's *Díván* for my translations.

INTRODUCTION

HÁFIZ is the *takhallus*, penname, of Khwájeh Shamsu'd-Dín Muhammad, and means "one who knows the Koran by heart". Throughout the centuries the poet has been known by the name he used for himself in his poems, Háfiz. His date of birth has been ascertained as *c.*726/ 1325–6, but the years 1317–18 and 1320 have also been suggested.[1] He died in 1389–90. What seems incontrovertible is that he was born in Shíráz. His fondness for his native city withstood disappointments there and the extremely troubled times through which he lived. Poem CCLXXIV is a paean of praise for what he describes as a city with a peerless situation. Evidence of his affection for Shíráz is supported by his reluctance ever to leave it, in spite of the attraction of patrons elsewhere. His animadversion is hostile to the only other city, Yazd, where he made an unhappy and unfruitful sojourn.[2] There is a legend-like account of his having set out, perhaps for India, and been so dismayed by the roughness of the sea off the southern coast of Iran that he immediately landed and returned to Shíráz.

There are numerous references to him in the "Memorials of the Poets" *tazkhirehs*. They go back to times near his own. The early popularity and fame of his verses throughout the 14th-century

7

Persian-speaking world is shown by frequent citations from them in near-contemporary historical annals. There is reason to believe that, even very shortly after their first utterance, in the court or some garden at Shíráz, his poems were widely repeated. In his own time they were known in places as distant as Tabríz and Baghdad, to say nothing of claims that his surpassing skill was recognized as far away as Bengal.

He himself suggests that a welcome might have awaited him at the court of the Jalayarid Sultan in Mesopotamia and Western Iran,[3] but it cannot for certain be deduced from these references, or from that in Poem ccxviii to Bengal, that the rulers thus alluded to actually intimated readiness to welcome him. Rather, he may have mentioned them when despairing of the vagaries of the patronage of his masters at home. He may have been making a kind of threat to local patrons: if their kindness failed, as it sometimes did, he had alternatives.

A number of the lyrics and "Memorials of the Poets" hint that, even from his long-time patron Sháh Shujá' (r. 1358–1385 AD), he was an object of contumely and envy; Sháh Shujá' fancied himself as a poet. Háfiz was eventually banned from Sháh Shujá's court. It was then, sometime between 1372 and 1374, that he may have been prompted to try his luck in Isfahán, but instead of going there, he made his unfortunate journey to Yazd, where he stayed no longer than was necessary to find money to return to his beloved city. After the death of Sháh Shujá', he appears to have lived as a recluse under the next two rulers, Zainu'l-'Ábidín, who reigned from 1384 to 1387, and Sháh Yahyá, who reigned from 1387 to 1388. Háfiz was rehabilitated by Sháh Mansúr, who reigned from 1388 to 1392, when, after Háfiz's death, the Muzaffarid family was destroyed by Timúr (Tamburlane).

The Muzaffarids were in power in central and southeastern Iran throughout most of Háfiz's life. The dynasty's founder, Mubárizu'd-Dín Muhammad (r. 1353–58) in 1353 ousted the court at which it is clear that Háfiz had found great happiness. This was the court of the Shaikh Abú Isháq Ínjú, who flourished with a love of luxury and a nonchalance that eventually cost him the throne of Shíráz, which he occupied from 1343 until the cruel advent of Mubárizu'd-Dín in 1353. Abú Isháq was executed by his conqueror three years later in Isfahán whither he had fled. For Háfiz his and his benign *vazír's* days were halcyon.

Mubárizu'd-Dín was a fanatically orthodox Sunni Muslim. When Háfiz uses the word *muhtasib*, censor or policeman of morals, he is taken to have been referring to this austere prohibitor of wine-drinking and other activities frowned upon by the orthodox. The poet welcomes the accession of Mubárizu'd-Dín's son, Jalálu'd-Dín Abu'l-Faváris Sháh Shujá', after the latter had deposed and blind-ed his father in 1358. Life in Shíráz was never peaceful for long under a dynasty whose brothers, nephews and uncles were con-stantly at war with each other. Sháh Shujá' himself had to go into exile for three years between 1363 and 1366. There are poems in which Háfiz virtually documents this exile, and gladly greets news of his patron's return. Thus the remark of a respected mentor,[4] that it must not be forgotten that Háfiz, too, was "a political animal", seems appropriate: so much of the political turmoil under the Muzaffarids is reflected in the poems. At this stage, however, discussion of the history of Háfiz's times must be cut short. Books mentioned in the Bibliography furnish plenty of information on this history, not least the excellent Introduction to Gertrude Bell's *Poems from the Divan of Hafiz*.[5] Now must be addressed the much disputed question of how far Háfiz's compositions were secularly "political", and how far the expression of spiritual aspiration.

Chaucer died in 1400, some ten years after Háfiz's death. Dante died in 1321. While Chaucer was practically Háfiz's contemporary, Dante predeceased him by over sixty years, but all three breathed the air of medieval Christendom and Islam. They shared an ethos in which the dichotomy between the secular and the spiritual did not, and certainly not for poets, exist to the same degree as in the West it has done since the Reformation. Dante's *Divine Comedy* is full of allusions to the political climate in which he lived and suffered, but remains a great spiritual poem. Háfiz lived in the last two centuries of the development of Iranian Sufism, a development which ended in 1492 with the death of the poet Jámí. The more one reads the poetry of Háfiz, the more perceptible become two things. Firstly, living under the dome of the Ptolemaic conception of the universe, but believing in the possibility of escape to the Empyrean beyond, to the Divine Overseer of all, he was fatalist in so far as he believed that the imprisoning dome exercised a malign influence on sub-lunary affairs. Secondly, that the hope of release from this influence, through spiritual devotion, inspired his utter-ance. He emerges from his *Díván* steeped in a Sufism which he counted as genuine, in sharp contrast to the pretensions of those hypocritical, false Súfís whom he frequently castigates. That he was a Súfí seems incontrovertible, unless, and this is hard to accept, he used the imagery of an already well established Súfí poetic tradition simply for the purpose of praising and cajoling wayward patrons.

The problem remains that the poems frequently and sometimes critically, as well as eulogistically, do refer to patrons, rulers and their chief ministers and law officers. How, if the context is ultimately spiritual, can these apparently mundane allusions be explained? One explanation is that Persian panegyrists' praises of the powerful were often two-edged. If the beloved who figures in the poem in a manner which warrants spelling the word with a capital rather than a small "b", that is to say, as God, seems in the end to have been a Sháh Shujá' or Mansúr, or a benevolent *vazír*, is it to be assumed that such personages are being treated as divine? Well, in a world in which the divine and the terrestrial were, in a manner difficult for the modern mind to grasp, indissolubly blended, the answer could be yes. And if the ruler, God's shadow upon earth, did not come up to the mark, there was all the more reason why, in the guise of flattery, he should be shamed by constant reminders of conduct proper to his position. At the same time the poet, especially one apparently born of an impoverished family and who seems to have remained impoverished all his life, needed a living. Hence most of the poems conclude with what can be described as "passing round the hat" verses: hints at the expected bounty. Nevertheless, it is difficult to deny that these lyrics have a spiritual message.

Indeed, the last couplet of the very first of them seems to point the way towards the Sufism of those *illuminati* associated with the name of Suhrawardí. This influential teacher was Amirak Muhammad ibn Shiháb al-Dín known as the Shaikh al-Ishráq, Master of Illumination, and, due to the circumstances of his death, or martyrdom, in 1208 AD, Maqtúl, the Slain. He was born near Zanján in northwestern Iran, probably in 549 AH/1170 AD. What in Háfiz's poem immediately brings Suhrawardí to mind is his reference to the "Presence":

If it's Presence you want, do not be absent from Him. (Poem 1, verse 7)

The word translated "Presence" is *huzúrí.* This is the term used in Suhrawardí's marriage of rationality with spiritual detachment, for the absorption of the self in the all-pervading Divine Light. It is thus, incidentally, that Suhrawardí answers the question often asked about whether or not in Sufism the self is considered to be completely annihilated in the Divine. Suhrawardí's contention is that ultimately the Divine is always, as it were, implicit in the Self, and once the latter is released from entrammelment with mundane matter, it then becomes part of the realm of the Divine Light. (It is interesting to note the age-old Iranian preoccupation with Light, in the ancient Iranian faith, the seat of goodness in opposition to Darkness, the abode of evil. Those who are acquainted with Iranians will have noticed how, on entering a darkening room at, for example, twilight, they will immediately ask to be permitted to put on lights; the Iranian desire for light is still endemic.) The Suhrawardian theory of Light may be traced under "Presence" in Mehdi Aminrazavi's *Suhrawardi and the School of Illumination,* especially pp. 91 and 110.[6] While it might be pressing the matter too far positively to suggest that Háfiz was himself a follower of Suhrawardí, it seems more than likely that he was attracted to the school of the *illuminati,* and that this aspect of Súfí practice should not be ignored in any attempt to define Háfiz's spiritual-Sufistic position.

In the context of the return to spirituality, although not of a kind Háfiz would necessarily have welcomed, inaugurated by the 1979 Iranian Revolution, it is interesting that Háshim Jávíd, in a recently published work on the poems of Háfiz,[7] has, in Part One of his book, produced an ingenious series of essays, playing on the fact that Háfiz was a professional Koran-reciter and exegete, to demonstrate how a whole *ghazal* can verse by verse be explained with reference to verses in the Sacred Koran. This effort continues a type of Persian Háfiz criticism which began in his own period and seeks to exculpate him from apparent lapses into unorthodoxy, if not blasphemy.

Such an explanation has to be borne in mind but need not be emphasized. Háfiz has been known through the ages, since his works became as venerated as it seems they were already while he was still alive, as the *Lisánu'l-Ghaib,* "Tongue of the Invisible". This fact does nothing to destroy the thesis that each verse of a number of his compositions might subtly echo passages in the Koran. Open allusions to the Koran are frequent, and the suggestion not absent that, unlike others, the poet does not knavishly exploit the Sacred Text. The tradition of attempts at Háfiz's, so to speak, desecularisation, shows how long the problem of the secular versus the spiritual in his oeuvre has been recognized. Part of the problem was that the beauty of his compositions appealed equally to the orthodox and the unorthodox.

The orthodox still seek an excuse for loving, as all Iranians literate and illiterate do, Háfiz's poems. The unorthodox, on the other hand, have insisted that he was, indeed, political. The axe they grind is that of Iranians who are legitimately conscious that they and their compatriots for hundreds of years have been subjected to the intolerable oppression of tyrants, with the apparatus of informers and secret police haunting the lives of innocent citizens. Those who comment on Háfiz as "a political animal" are apt to cite verses where the poet remarks that the "wily bird" does not go to a certain coterie or party because snares are laid there for the unwary. That Háfiz was a member of a coterie is impossible to gainsay. That the coterie was of a certain Order of Súfís is also plausible. No doubt some of the Muzaffarid princes to whom he alludes, especially Sháh Shujá', could have patronised a "lodge" to which Háfiz was affiliated, although they were probably of an inconsistent allegiance in accordance with what they considered expedient. In one poem Háfiz suggestively mentions the "expediency of the moment".[8]

When all is said and done, and in this instance the doing must be perusal of the poems, what strikes the reader is that Háfiz was genuinely concerned with the Spiritual Path as the way to the realization of love in release from the distractions and turmoil of this world. To paraphrase Pascal, he believed that God is "perceptible to the heart but not to reason".[9] As for religion, surely like Dante he was inspired by the overriding power of love. Religious he was; but not tied to any particular orthodoxy or rite, or concerned with theological minutiae. These aspects of his position are emphasized by his repeated references to the Magian: to a Guide *outside* the Islamic Faith. This does not mean that profound respect for the Holy Koran was precluded, or that Háfiz did not insist on its sanctity being preserved.

To be dogmatic about a poet whose verses lend themselves to interpretation on more than one level, and as the individual reader might wish, is impossible. This introduction is deliberately cursory.

The intention is that the imagination should be free so to receive Háfiz's astonishingly adroit imagery that auditors or readers might draw their own conclusions. Although the themes, among which chief is love, remain the same, the poems' genius lies in how in each lyric, stock images are constantly but startlingly introduced in a fresh setting.

However, no introductory remarks on the poetry of Háfiz can fail to mention the interesting parallel between his, both in themes and style of expression, and the poems of the English poet Sir Thomas Wyatt (1503–42). So it happens that the latter is mentioned in Robert Briffault's *The Troubadours*[10] where he quotes Arthur Quiller-Couch[11] as having said that it was Wyatt who introduced "the flame of lyrical poetry to England, the flame of the Petrachists, caught from the Troubadours". Thus is introduced another parallel between the "Courtly Love" theme of Háfiz's lyrics and the work of poets remote from him in time and space.

It is not possible here more than to allude to the Troubadouresque reminiscence that must strike the Western reader of Háfiz's *ghazals*. The subject is complex and awaits further exploration.[12] But the Troubadours' debt to Hispano-Arabic poetry is now generally recognized among scholars, as, indeed, is that of European lyrical poetry in general. Háfiz was himself heir to the Islamic civilization to which the Spanish Arab tradition belonged.

In the context of Háfiz, two things come to mind. First the fact that, as in the Troubadour etiquette, he does not always refer to his principal Royal Patrons by their names. The point is that he is not without examples of the Provençal "courtesy" of not referring to the Patron/Patroness explicitly by name. He uses such indications of who such Patrons might have been by references to "the Lord of Knights", "the descendant of Turks", etc. This, although a few patrons are mentioned and were princes, but not sovereigns.

Secondly, and more importantly, is the fact that, like the Troubadours, Háfiz lived in times characterized by brutality and violence,and in which the memory of the Mongols'devastation of northeastern Iran in the beginning of the 13th century would still be fresh. It is not without significance that the late Muhammad Mu'ín opens his discussion of the times of Háfiz with a description of the Mongol invasion.[13] Hence, as in the case of the Troubadours, it is fair to claim that his poetry extolled a delicacy, spirituality, and refinement of sentiment conspicuously lacking in his political and social environment. His poems lifted what might have been the songs and rough bardic ballads of the camp to the level of the greatest literature mankind has known. This too is a feature of the poetry of the Troubadours. It is as if he and they saw the poet's role as keeping alive in an age of darkness the flame of high cultural aspiration, and the replacement of lust by a passion of love devoted to God as He is manifested in human beauty and in gardens of delights that are earthly replicas of the Elysian Paradise[14] promised the righteous in the Koran.

Cambridge, 2007   Peter Avery

1. See Jan Rypka, *History of Iranian Literature,* English version ed. by Karl Jahn (Dordrecht, Holland, 1968), p. 264.
2. See Poem xii.
3. See, for example, Poems clviii and cccclxiii, where the name of Shaikh Uvais the Jalayarid is mentioned, and Poems xlii, clxxxv, ccxlv and cccclxiii, with references to, in the first, Baghdad and Tabríz, the two Jalayarid capitals, and in the other three, to Baghdad.
4. The late Professor Vladimir Minorsky, who made this remark to the writer in 1947.
5. London, 1928.
6. London, 1997. See also Art. "Suhrawardi" in Encyclopaedia of Islam[(2)] Vol. ix, pp. 782–784.
7. Háshim Jávíd, *Háfiz-i Jávíd,* "The Eternal Háfiz", (Tehran, 1375 Iranian Solar Year/1995–6 AD), pp. 3–26.
8. Poem cccclxxv, verse 5.
9. Pascal, *Pensées,* ed. Ernest Havet, Paris, 1881, p. 420.
10. Briffault, Robert, *The Troubadours,* Bloomington, in, 1965, pp. 194–195.
11. Quiller-Couch, Sir Arthur, *On the Art of Writing,* Cambridge, 1916, Lecture ix.
12. Reference might be made to J. W. Draper's article, 'The Early Troubadours and Persian Poetry', in the *Rivista di Letterature Moderne e Comparate,* Anno x, N. 3–4, 1957, pp. 149–259. I am indebted for this reference to Mr Ovidio Salazar. It might be said that it raises more questions than it answers, but is a useful research pointer.
13. Muhammad Mu'ín, *Háfiz-i Shírín Sukhan* "Háfiz of the Sweet Discourse", (Tehran, 1370/1991), Vol. i, pp. 31 sqq.
14. "Paradise" is in fact derived from an ancient Persian word signifying a place enclosed against the encroachment of desert sands, and made into a cool space adorned with flowers and shaded by trees. For the Koranic Paradise in the after-life, see Koran xxx, 14, xxxvii, 39, xxxviii, 50, xl, 16, and lii, 17, also xviii, 307 and xxiii, 11, in which the word *firdaus* is used. This word, like *paradise,* is derived from the old Persian *pairidaeza, firdaus* in modern Persian.

A NOTE ON THE TEXT
AND TRANSLATION

The translations offered here are of the *Diván-i-Háfiz*, Volume i, The Lyrics (*ghazals*),edited by Parvíz Nátíl Khánlarí,published in Tehran 1362/1983–4. It is generally accepted that, besides being among the most recent, Dr Khánlarí's edition is of unquestionable reliability. Before its publication, among a number of 20th-century editions of the complete works of Háfiz the most reliable was generally conceded to be that of Qásim Ghaní and Mirzá Muhammad Qazvíní, Tehran, 1940.

E. G. Browne's *Literary History of Persia*, Vol. iii, (Cambridge, 1928), pp. 271–319, and A. J. Arberry's *Classical Persian Literature* (London, 1958), pp. 329–363, provide useful accounts of Háfiz translations into European languages, as well as references to editions of his collected works in Persian. It can now be noted that Volume xi of the *Encyclopaedia Iranica* (Encyclopaedia Iranica Foundation, New York, 2003) has been published and, see pp. 461–507, includes detailed articles on Háfiz, with (pp. 498–501) a section entitled *Translations of Háfez in English*. Attempts to translate all Háfiz's lyrics into English have generally speaking been rare, but selections less so. Arberry's useful *Fifty Poems of Háfiz* (Cambridge 1947, 1953, and reprints up to 1977), besides including his own, has translations by several others.

They do not include Fitzgerald, celebrated for his quatrains of Omar Khayyám: "transmogrifications", as he himself preferred to call a series of inspired renderings in English that are gems of English literature. Of Háfiz, Fitzgerald, in a letter dated 12th March 1857, two years before he published his Khayyám quatrains, remarked that "Háfiz and old Omar Khayyám ring like true Metal". In the same letter, most interestingly, he says of Háfiz that Háfiz's "*best* is untranslatable because he is the best Musician of Words". Thus Fitzgerald's unerring literary sense prompted him correctly to recognize Háfiz as the "best Musician of Words". He was not far wrong in declaring that this quality made Háfiz "untranslatable".

In this volume translations of Háfiz's lyrics are offered in English prose. Wilberforce Clarke published the entire *diván* (collected works) in prose in 1891, in Calcutta. Payne's versified *The Poems of Shamseddin Muhammad Háfiz of Shiraz* was published ten years later. Payne's version of Háfiz has been described as "certainly not lacking in sentimentality", and Clarke's as "curious rather than reliable". But in this field any pioneering attempt deserves respect.

Like the *Thirty Poems from Háfiz*, published by John Heath-Stubbs and myself in 1952 and reissued in 2006 by Archetype, Cambridge, what has been attempted in the following translations is to present Háfiz in an English that reflects the hard directness and colloquialism characteristic of the originals. A major feature of the great Persian poet's achievement was the use of everyday language lifted to the level of high poetic diction, but without the primary simplicity of common speech being obscured. Translations in verse tend to conceal the original's fibrous colloquialism. The result can be at worst jingles and at best verses that, because of the inimitability of Persian prosody, veil the enamel-like hardness of the Persian.

Háfiz composed in a language that by his time was already sufficiently well established to remain the Persian of Iran today; a language that has changed less since the 9th century AD than English has since the times of Chaucer and Shakespeare. There must have been a long and powerful oral tradition of poetry, or minstrelsy, before the 9th century. It is from this century that the first fragments known emerged in writing.

P W A

POEMS

POEM I

Hey, boy, pass the bowl round and offer it;[1]
At first love seemed easy, but snags have cropped up.

In desire of the pod of musk the eastern breeze[2] might at last open,
From the twist of his musky tress[3] how much blood has flooded hearts!

Stain the prayer-mat with wine, if the Magian Elder tells you:
The traveller won't be ignorant of the road and of how to behave at the halts.

At the darling's alighting-place, what scope have we for making love when
Every moment the bell clangs, "Strap up the camel-litters"?

Dark night, the waves' terror, so dreadful a whirlpool,
How might the lightly-burdened on the shore know our condition?

Through self-gratification all my actions have led to disrepute. Yes, indeed,
How, gossip-parties being held about them, can secrets stay secret?

Háfiz, if it's Presence you want, do not be absent from Him:[4]
When you meet what you long for, bid the world farewell and let it go hang.

1. See the periodical *Yádgár* (Vol. 1. number 9, pp.69–78); Mirzá Muhammad Qazvíní rebuts the Turkish Háfiz commentator Súdí's (d. 1598) suggestion that the opening hemistich in Arabic is a *tadhmín*, "borrowing", from a poem, which has not been found, attributed to the Umayyad Caliph Yazíd ibn Mu'áwiya (d. 683 AD). Háfiz seems to be echoing an Arabic verse in a lyric of his compatriot Sa'dí, see the sixth verse in poem number 586 in Furúghí's edition of Sa'dí's complete works, Tehran in 1363/1984–5, pp. 629.
2. "eastern breeze", *sabá*, or, *bád-i sabá*, the messenger breeze between lover and the Beloved; the Beloved's intimate, for the breeze has access everywhere, and so might give news of the Beloved to the suitor, even if only by blowing aside the Beloved's tress.

3. "tress", *zulf*, a frequently employed symbol for the plurality of creation which veils the face of Unity. Thus Shabistarí (Gulshan-i Ráz, *The Mystic Rose Garden*, the Persian text with an English translation and notes, ed. and tr. by E. H. Whinfield, London, 1880, p. 74 and text p. 45), in a work written in 1317 describes the tress as "the chain for binding the love-crazed lovers". He ends by saying that

    ... the heart is put in turmoil on account of His tress,
    Because in burning fire it withholds the heart from His face.

    The tresses were the trellis that obscured the refulgent glory of the Divine Countenance. The lover entangled in the tress or the tresses, caught in the trellis in his longing, is the same lover who in the following poems is frequently described as the captive at the *ástáneh*, the threshold of the Beloved. The lover also perceives the line of down, *khatt*, the newly sprouted beard on the face of a youth, as the margin of the Glory, a Glory which cannot be "bordered" save that it was revealed in the lines of the holy Koran; *khatt*, besides meaning "line", also means "writing". Háfiz's imagery itself is a trellis-work of symbols, all of which are meshed together to form both the continuing sub-text to the poems and their adornment. They are the setting and the jewels placed within it. Háfiz describes the everlasting quest for the elusive realization of the self-manifesting and, as it were, coyly self-concealing Divine, the origin of all, but only fitfully to be apprehended. It may be in the saucy eye of the wine-boy, or in the caprices of a patron-prince.

4. In the first hemistich of verse 7, Háfiz juxtaposes absence and presence. Presence is the heart's presence with the Divine in the realization of "intuitive faith" (*yaqín*). But though this is to reflect Súfí terms' resonances, on a more mundane level Háfiz could have been alluding to exclusively devoting oneself to a patron.

POEM II

What has asceticism to do with derelict me?
See the contrast in the Way from that to this!

What has debauchery to do with godliness and devotion?
Where listening to sermons? Where the note of the rebeck?

My heart's sick of the hermit's cell and cloak of hypocrisy:[1]
Where the Magian Temple, where unadulterated wine?

Gone—its memory stay sweet!—the day of union;
Where indeed has gone that fetching eye? That rebuke?

From the face of the friend what might the enemy divine?
Where the burnt-out lamp, where the candle of the sun?

Have no eye for the dimple in the chin:[2] it's the pitfall in the way.
Where, heart, are you going so hastily? Where?

The dust of your threshold's like collyrium for our eye.
Where else should we go? Say, from this doorway where?

From Háfiz, friend, seek no repose or sleep.
What is repose? Which the patience? Where sleep?[3]

---

1. The *khirqa*, the patched gown worn by Súfí *pírs*, elders. Háfiz is, of course, allud-
   ing to false dervishes.
2. The word play is on *cháh-i zanakhdán*, the pit or dimple in the chin: the word for
   "pit", *cháh*, is transposed to the context of the Way, its "pitfall". For the hastening
   heart there must be no attention to externals; but more likely, in view of the refer-
   ence to "repose" etc. in the last verse, the allusion is to the stillness required in the
   Súfí experience in order to reach comprehension of the Divine.
3. The morning call to prayer, the *idhán*, can include the words, *as-salát khair minu'n-
   naum*, "Prayer is better than sleep". Háfiz could, therefore, be taken as alluding to
   prayerful vigils; although a "profligate", he too is, in his own way, a devotee.

POEM III

If that Shírází Turk captures our heart,
For his Hindu dark mole[1] I would forgive Samarqand and
    Bukhara![2]

Pour out the last of the wine, boy, because in Paradise you'll
    not find
The banks of Ruknábád's stream and the rose garden of Musallá.[3]

Alas that these saucy, jesting, city-ravishing gypsies
Should, as Turks do the spoil's feast, pillage patience from the
    heart.[4]

Of our imperfect love the friend's beauty has no need:
What needs the beautiful face, of lotion, colouring, patch, pencil?

Talk of minstrels and wine, and probe less the secret of the sphere.
No one by intellectual reasoning has solved this riddle, nor ever
    will.

I have known that daily-waxing beauty Joseph had
So that from behind chastity's veil passion could draw Zulaikha.[5]

You spoke ill of me and I do not mind. God forgive you! You
    spoke well:
The bitter answer is becoming from sugar-crunching ruby lips.

Listen to advice, my dear, for well-blessed youths hold
Dearer than life the Wise Elder's counsel.

A lyric have you composed and pearls threaded, so, Háfiz, come
    and bravely sing:
The firmament over your verse scatters the necklace of the
    Pleiades.

---

1. The mole is the point of Unity, the hidden *huwiyyat*, "ipseity", the single He-ness,
    a dot, but, like the pupil of the eye, capable of embracing a wide spectrum, in the
    case of the symbol of the mole, inclusive of all phenomena. Shabistarí (op. cit.

p. 77) says in Whinfield's translation,

On that cheek the point of His mole is single,
It is a centre which is the basis of the circling circumference.
From that centre is drawn the circle of the two worlds,
From that centre Adam's heart and soul ...

It might be added that in Canto xxvIII, LL. 41–42 of the *Paradiso*, Dante makes Beatrice explain to him that:

Da quel punto
depende il cielo, e tutta la natura,

Which might be rendered "From that point hangs heaven and all nature".

2. Legend has it that when Tímúr invaded Fárs for the first time in 1387, two years before Háfiz's death, he took exception to this offer of his "customary abodes and capitals" for the mole on a Shírází Turk's cheek, but Háfiz's adroit answer dispelled the conqueror's wrath. For several reasons, the story, attributable to Dawlatsháh's *Memorials of the Poets*, cannot be considered authentic. See Browne, *Literary History of Persia* (Cambridge, 1928), Volume III, pp. 188,189, and 282, and Dawlatsháh's *Tadhkiratu' Shu'ará*, edited by Browne, London and Leiden, 1901, pp. 305–6.

3. The stream flows from uplands north of Shíráz to irrigate the city. Its banks are still a popular picnic area. The Musallá, literally "oratory", is a suburb of Shíráz and, in addition to the tomb of the poet, still contains gardens. Both would be the resorts of "well-blessed youths" like those referred to in the penultimate verse of the poem.

4. Najm al-Dín Rází, Dáya, *Mirsád al-'Ibád*, ed. Muhammad Amin Ríyáhí, Tehran, 1972 and 1986, p. 49, has the couplet, "Were the heart to be seething in desire for a gypsy / And you to offer it a hundred Turks, it would take no notice", (see Hamíd Algar's translation, "The Path of God's Bondsmen...", Delmar, New York, 1982, p. 74). The context is God's sustaining love of Man and Man's commitment to assume the burden of the Trust he accepted from his Lord in the primordial Covenant (see Koran xxxIII, 72), so that God has a love-traffic with Man, His creature *par excellence*, such as He has with none other. See also, *ibid*, text p. 59, translation pp. 88–89, for the stanza which it seems most likely Háfiz had in mind, as he seems so often to have had verses from the Mirsád:

Love came and plundered Intelligence.
O heart take this happy news to the soul!
Know love is a Persian Turk,
For in the Turk plundering is not strange.
Intelligence was desirous of bringing into a trope
His cheek's description by way of metaphor.
His cheek's light thrust out a tongue of fire:
It burnt both Intelligence and trope.

(In the context of "Intelligence", see the reference to *hikmat*, intellectual reason, in the fifth verse.) The whole poem seems to have the Mirsád in the background. The *'ajamí Turk*, as Professor Algar explains (note 41), could mean a Turk imported as a slave and not yet fully assimilated to the ethos into which he has been brought, but as *'ajamí* means non-Arab and therefore came to mean "Persian" (someone who, for Arab ears, does not speak Arabic correctly), this is the meaning given to it here, as it is seen as parallel to the "Shírází Turk", one already resident in Shíráz, though still a Turk in manners, morals, and appearance. Meanwhile it should be remembered that, most notably in the works of Rúzbihán Baqlí (1128–1209 AD), by Háfiz's time it had become a convention to refer to the Beloved (or beloved) as a *Turk*. Háfiz's fellow townsman Sa'dí (d. 1292 AD) has a verse which contains the words *Turk-i Shírází* where he says:

> No one experiences as much cruelty from a Khitayan Turk
> As I at the hands of a Shírází Turk

5. For the story of Zulaikha's passion for Joseph see Koran XII, 23–24.

POEM IV

Breeze, please say to that dappled gazelle:
"You've thrown us into the mountains and deserts".

Why doesn't the sugar-seller—may his life be long—
Enquire after the sugar-gnawing parrot?

Is it, rose, that beauty's pride didn't allow you
To make some enquiry about the lovesick nightingale?

It's by courtesy and kindness that men of insight might be
    captured.
Not by gins and snares is the wise bird caught.

When you sit and measure out wine with the beloved,
Think of lovers measuring the wind.[1]

It's beyond me why the dark-eyed, moon-faced cypress form
Sports not a single blush of recognition.

Only to this extent can your beauty be faulted,
That the handsome face has no sign of love and constancy.

There's no wonder if, at the words of Háfiz, in the heavens
Venus's[2] ecstasy makes the Messiah dance!

---

1 To measure the wind: a metaphor for being destitute, bankrupt.
2. Venus, *zuhra*, is the guardian of music and musicians. There is controversy about
which of the heavens Jesus was halted in, because he had with him a pot as well
as, in some versions, a broken comb, relics of material existence, but some
Koranic commentators, notably Tabarí, place him in the third. Venus's abode was
also said to be the Third Heaven. However, Rúmí in the *Masnaví* (Cambridge for
the E.J.W. Gibb Memorial Trust, 1937, with the commentary), Book 1, verse 649,
and Nicholson's comment on the same, places him in the Fourth Heaven, as do
many other poets. In any event, music, illicit in the eyes of strictly orthodox
Muslims, was associated with Christians and so, naturally, with their "dancing"
Messiah; dancing and singing in ecstasy and joy were, of course, part of Súfí
practice, as in the *samá'*, "audition". The dance was itself an enactment of the
harmonious dance of the Cosmos.

POEM V

Men of piety, for God's sake, my heart's going wild.
Ah the pity that the hidden secret will be divulged!

We are storm-wracked mariners. Let a fair wind arise.
Let it be that we see the familiar friend[1] again.

A ten-day-stretch of the wheeling heaven's kindness is guile
    and vanity.
Goodness towards friends count a boon, O friend!

Last night, in the circle of the rose and wine, sweetly sang the
    nightingale.
Fetch the morning cup! Hey drunkards, get up!

A bowl of wine is the mirror of Alexander. Look,
So that it might display to you the state of Dara's kingdom.[2]

O Lord of Grace, in gratitude for security,
Spare a glance one day for the penniless poor.

Of both worlds the well-being is these two sayings' commentary:
"To friends kindness. To foes civility".

I have no access to the street of good repute.
If you can't approve, change fate's decree!

The daughter of the grape the ascetic called the
    "Mother of Iniquities"
Is more pleasant to us than virgins' kisses, and more sweet.

In days of penury, go for revelry and drunkenness,
Because this elixir of existence might make a beggar a Korah.[3]

Persian-speaking beauties are life-bestowers.
Boy, give the old men of Fárs the good news!

Háfiz did not of himself don the wine-stained gown.
Clean-skirted[4] Shaikh, hold us forgiven.

1. There is a pun on the word translated "familiar", *áshná*: it can also mean "swimming"; "fellow swimmer"?
2. Dara: Darius, the last Achaemenid Emperor, defeated and his empire overrun by Alexander the Great in 331 BC; thus the "state" of his empire was one of ruin. Alexander was reputed to hold a magic mirror which foretold future events and reflected what had gone before.
3. The Qárún (or Croesus) of the Koran. Chapter XXVIII, 76, alludes to his treasure.
4. The idiom "of the clean skirt" alludes to how those who pray and wish to appear pure take care to keep the hem of their garment clean.

POEM VI

Who's going to take this prayer to the Sultan's aides:[1]
"In gratitude for sovereignty do not drive the beggar from sight"?

From the demonic rival, I take refuge in my own God;
For the sake of God, that gleaming star might grant some help.

If your black eye-lash has our blood in its sights,
Think of his guile, my dear, and make no mistake.[2]

When you set your cheek[3] alight, you burn up the heart
    of a world;
What do you gain from this, that you display no courtesy?

All night I'm in the hope that the dawn breeze
Might indulge the friend with the friends' message.

What is the doom, my darling, that you've shown lovers?
Hearts and souls your face's sacrifice, reveal the cheek[3] to us.

For God's sake, give dawn-rising Háfiz a single draught,
That an early morning prayer[4] might have some effect on you.

---

1. Háfiz must have had in the mind the opening of a famous and moving *qasida* of
    Jamálu'd-Dín Isfahání (d. 1192). It begins, "Who is it who'll take my message to
    the city of Shirván / Who'll carry a word from me to that man of eloquence?".
    The reference is to the poet Kháqání, who died in 1121–2 AD, and was a Shirvání.
    See *Diván-i Ustád Jamál al-Dín*, ed. Vahíd-i Dastgirdí, Tehran, 1320/1941–42 and
    1362/1983–4, pp. 85 ff.
2. The Sultan-Patron will repent of the true lover's being ousted and cease to
    favour the false rival.
3. The "cheek", *'izár* (also *rukh*): Shabistarí (op. cit. p. 76 and Persian text p. 46)
    defines the cheek as the stage on which the Divine Beauty is revealed. The cheek
    is the *jamál*, the beauty of God, the vestibule to God's *jallál*, His Glory and
    Power. The cheek is the Divine Essence manifested in its names and qualities.
4. I.e. this poem?

POEM VII

Because the bowl holds a clean mirror, come, Súfí,
To look into the purity of ruby coloured wine.

Ask of drunken wastrels the secret behind the veil:
The Súfí of High Degree doesn't know this state.

The 'Anqa[1] is not for being caught. Fold the net up,
Because in this instance the snare's forever void.

Labour to enjoy pleasure that's to hand, because, when no joy
    remained,
Adam quit the garden of the Abode of Peace;

At the banquet of revolving time, drain a bumper or two
    and be gone.
In other words, do not expect everlasting union.

Ah heart, youth's done with and you from life have plucked no
    rose!
For old age's sake make a virtue of modesty and repute.

For service at your threshold we're owed many a due;
O master, look once more with compassion on the slave.

Háfiz is the wine-bowl's disciple. Go breeze,
And from the slave convey homage to the Shaikh of Jám.[2]

---

1. The *'Anqá* or *Símurgh*, the mythical bird of fortune and the aura of power in Arabic and, where it most likely originated and really belongs, Persian folklore, though the *Símurgh* of Iran has Chinese and shamanistic associations too.
2. The reference, as the 17th-century Turkish commentator, Súdí, suggests, might be to the famous and powerful Shaikh'ul-Islam Ahmad Námaqí Jámí of Jám in Khurasan (1049/50 – 1141/42). The pun is on the place name, Jám, and the word, *jám*, meaning wine-bowl or cup. The eminent Shailkhu'l-Islám of Jám was known as the *Zhandah Píl*, "The Great Elephant". The legend of his conversion describes how he was inspired to pour away all the wine he had in his vats, and then told, no, but to give it to his waiting guests. When they drank of it, it turned out to be no longer wine, but honey. Prior to his conversion, he had been a wine-bibbing, convivial youth. He was changed, at the age of twenty-two, to become in

his day an extremely influential and, although capable of individual acts of kindness, intransigent upholder of canonical law at its most puritanical. His correspondents included the Saljúq Sultan Sanjar (d. 1157 AD), and when the Shaikh died, he left a large following in northeastern Iran, including the Herat region of what is today Afghanistan, whence his influence was felt in India. It is interesting that the Khurasanian mystic, and, in prose and poetry, biographer of eminent Súfís, 'Attár (d. 1220) never mentions this Great Elephant. (See Súdí, the Persian translation of his Commentary by Sattárzáda, Tehran, 1341/1962–3, Vol. 1, p. 63, and Jámí, *Nafahátu'l-uns*, edited by Mahmud 'Abidi, Tehran 1370/1991–2, pp. 363–373. The articles, under Ahmad-i Jám, in both the *Encyclopaedia of Islam* (2) and *Iranica* merit perusal.)

POEM VIII

O wine-boy, jump up and hand round the bowl:
Put the sorrows of the days to shame.

Put a cup of wine in the palm of my hand, while
I snatch this dark blue gown[1] from my breast.

Although to the pundits it is infamy,
It is neither honour nor shame we want!

Dispense the wine. How much more of this empty conceit?
Dust and ashes on pointless pride!

The smoke of the sighs from my grieving heart
Has scorched these ice-cold raw ones.

Privy to the secret of my love-crazed heart
No one do I see, from either the high or the low;

My mind is in bliss with a comforter of hearts
That from my heart comfort has entirely stolen.[2]

Whoever's seen this silver-limbed cypress
Won't look again at the cypress in the meadow.

Bear patiently, Háfiz, the hardship of days and nights:
In the end one day you'll find satisfaction.

---

1. The dervish's gown, *khirqeh*, but that it is blue in colour suggests the colour of mourning; the darkness of the physical ("sorrows of the days") as contrasted with the spiritual world.
2. See *Mirsád al-'Ibád*, op. cit., p. 45, translation, op. cit., p. 69:

    Love it is that steals the delight of youth. Love it is that steals eternal joy.
    Although love is the heart's Water of Life,
    Yet from the heart it steals the Water of Life.

POEM IX

Again the garden has the lustre of the time of youth:
Glad news of the rose comes to the sweet-voiced nightingale.

Should you, breeze, once more blow over the youngsters of the
     meadow,
Convey our greetings to the cypress, the rose, the sweet-basil.

When such radiance the wine-seller's child reveals,
I make the eye-lashes a broom for the wine-shop's doorway.

O you who across the moon draw a hockey-stick of purest amber,
Do not make head-spinning me distracted!

I fear the party that scorns those who drain the barrel
Might make religion obsessed with the business of the tavern.

Be the ally of men of God because, in Noah's ark,
There's a speck of dust that wouldn't buy the deluge for a
     water-drop.

Whoever's last resting place is nothing but a fistful of earth,
Ask, "What is the need for you to raise a portico up to the
     heavens?"[1]

Escape from the domicile of the wheeling dome and seek no
     sustenance,
Because in the end this black bowl slays the guest.

My moon of Canaan, Egypt's chief seat is yours:
It is time now for you to say farewell to prison.[2]

Háfiz, drink wine, play the rapscallion and be joyful, but
Do not, as others do, falsify the Koran.

---

1.   Háfiz's earliest and, at least in retrospect, much loved royal patron was Abú Isháq
     Injú, ruler of Fárs until ousted and put to death by the founder of the Muzaffarid
     Dynasty, Mubáriz al-Dín (d. 1357) in 1353. Abú Isháq in his last days of rule, with

apparent insouciance, ordered the construction of a luxuriously ambitious palace. 'Ubaid-i Zákání, the great satirist and then a fellow poet with Háfiz at the Injuid court, commented on this ill-timed royal project, as did the traveller Ibn Battuta (see H.A.R. Gibb's translation, Vol. II pp. 3o6 sqq.). 'Ubaid in a *qasida*, in praise of Abú Isháq and his *ayván*, "portal" or "palace", has the line,

> The spirit is worthy the builder of your edifice
> Noah is fitting to be your palace's carpenter.

(*Díván-i 'Ubaid-i Zákání*, edited by 'Abbás Iqbál, Tehran, 1332/1952, p. 22.)

2. See Koran, XII, 3 sqq, for the story of Joseph and his imprisonment.

POEM X

Last night our Elder went out of the mosque to the wine-shop,
So now, comrades of the Way, what must be our strategy?[1]

Let us, too, be fellow-lodgers in the Magian's tavern:
In the Covenant of Eternity without Beginning thus our fate befell.

How might we novices turn our faces towards the Ka'ba when
Our Guide has fixed his on the wine-shop?

Does our ardent sigh, the searing nightly cry,
One single night ever touch your stony heart?

If reason knew how joyous the heart is in the fetters of his tresses,
Men of reason would go crazy in pursuit of our chains!

The breeze blew over your locks. For me the world turned black.
In the passion for your tresses our fulfilment is no more than this.

For the heart's bird the quarry of composure had fallen
    into the snare.
You loosened a tress from our net. Our prey was gone!

Out of grace your fair face revealed a sacred verse to us.
Hence in our exegesis there is nothing but grace and beauty.[2]

The arrow of our sigh shoots beyond the revolving heavens.
    Be quiet, Háfiz.
On your own soul have mercy: watch out for our arrow!

---

1. The poet Saná'í (d. 1130–1 AD), who might be called the father of the mystical
    ghazal, has several poems on the theme of neglecting the mosque for the tav-
    ern. One opens with the words:

    O my Ka'ba is in your mansion
    For me body and soul and heart are on your behalf.

2. The word translated "sacred verse" is *áyatí*, the term used for a verse of the
    Koran, so the word for "exegesis", *tafsír*, in the next hemistich follows naturally.

POEM XI

Saqi, make our bowl glow with the light of wine.
Minstrel, sing how the world has gone our way.

You, unaware of our constant drinking's sweetness,
In the bowl we have seen the reflection of the friend's cheek!

What price the ogling and hip-swaying of forms erect
When in splendour our pine-strutting cypress arrives?

He never dies whose heart is alive with love:
Our persistence is recorded in the register of the Cosmos.

Come the Day of the Questioning, I fear the Shaikh's lawful bread
Will have nothing on our unlawful waters!

Being drunk with the eye of our heart-enthralling beauty is bliss.
This is why we have been committed to drunkenness.

Should you, breeze, pass over the rose garden of the beloved,
Take care you present the loved ones our message.

Say, "Why deliberately obliterate our name from memory?
When there'll be no memory of our name, that will come about
    of itself."

Go on, Háfiz, scattering the grain of tears from your eyes;
It might be that the bird of union will make for our snare.

The green ocean of the firmament and the boat of the new moon
Are surely drowned in the bounty of Hájjí Qavám![1]

---

1. Hájjí Qavámu'd-Dín Hasan , the *Tamghachí* or "Keeper of the Seal", is not to
   be confused with Qavámu'd-Dín Muhammad ibn 'Alí, also mentioned in poems
   of Háfiz. The latter was Sáhib 'Ayyár, Chief Assayer, and minister to Sháh
   Shuja', the Muzaffarid ruler of Fárs from 1357 until 1384, for whose comfort this
   Qavám became too powerful. He was put to death. Hájjí Qavám was counsel-
   lor and intendant of finance to Abú Isháq-i-Injú during the halcyon days of the

latter's reign, 1343 to 1353. In this year, on the eve of the Muzaffarids' conquest of Fárs and deposition and execution of Abú Isháq, this benign minister died. He was a celebrated patron of learning and literature, and in particular of Háfiz, for whom he is said to have founded a Koran school. Ibn Battuta apparently conversed with him when in Shíráz, probably in 1347. He obtained from Hájjí Qavám first-hand information about the Injuid revenues. (See *The Travels of Ibn Battuta*, translated by H.A.R. Gibb, published for the Hakluyt Society by Cambridge in 1962, Vol. II. p. 307.) The verse in which his name and the reference to his magnanimity occur is not included in the version of this poem found in a manuscript collection written between 813 and 814 AH, 1410 and 1411 AD. In Tehran in 1957–8, Dr. Khánlarí published the Háfiz *ghazals* the manuscript contains. Since they were copied within twenty-one or twenty-two years of the poet's death, they constitute the oldest known copies of Háfiz *ghazals*. They are included in a sort of pocket library of poetry and prose compiled for 'Umar Shaikh, ruler of Fárs on behalf of his uncle, Sháh Rukh Sháh (1404–1447), the son of Timur the Lame. 'Umar Shaikh rebelled and was put to death in 1414. In this manuscript, described in Rieu's *Catalogue of the Persian Manuscripts in the British Museum* (Add. 27, 261, Vol. II. p. 868), of the Háfiz selection this poem comes first, but *does not have* the final verse in which the patron and his bounty are mentioned: the preceding verse is the "signature verse", and it is certainly unusual for Háfiz to have two final *baits* in the first of which he gives his name, generally reserved for the poem's last verse. Questions have been raised about these "signing-off *baits*", and whether or not they were later additions. Some appear undoubtedly to be so, lacking the soundness of the preceding verses and thus seeming jejeune.

POEM XII

Light of the moon of beauty from your shining face,
Paragon of beauty due to the dimple in your chin,

O Lord, when might this intention come about, that
Our concentrated heart and your scattered locks are joined?

The soul on the verge of departure has the purpose of seeing you.
Is it to go back or come forward? What is your command?

When you pass our way, lift the skirt free of the
    dust and blood:
In this road many are slain, your sacrifice.

The heart wreaks havoc. Alert the sweetheart.
Look out, friends, for my soul and your lives.

From your eye's revolving no good turn of fortune's been
    enjoyed by anyone:
To those drunk on you, you'd better not sell abstinence.

Would our drowsing luck be awakened,
Were the sight to be struck by your shining lustre?

Along with the breeze send a bunch of roses from your cheeks;
Perhaps I might sniff a fragrance from your garden's soil.

May life and success reward the wine-servers at Jamshíd's feast,
Even though in your rounds no wine fills our cup.

Listen, Háfiz is uttering a prayer; say an "Amen" to,
"May our daily bread be your sugar-shedding ruby lip."

Breeze, tell the people of the city of Yazd,
"The ball in your swishing stick is the skull of the ungrateful!"

Far off are we, but from the carpet of proximity ardour
    is not far:
We're your ruler's slave and singer of your praises.

Well-starred King of Kings, for God's sake, one generous act—
That I, like the rolling heavens, might kiss the dust of your portico.[1]

---

1. In the delicate issue of when Háfiz is being, so to speak, "spiritual," and when "political", or when he is, as it were, using one stone to kill both birds, this poem hits the reader as being decidedly personal and, in a sense, political. He is expressing disappointment at having gone to Yazd, to the court of Sháh Yahyá, the nephew of Sháh Shujá' at Shíráz, with whom Háfiz was temporarily at outs, and received no favour from the ruler of Yazd. Sháh Yahyá had been appointed there in 1361–2 by his uncle, to obviate the designs on Yazd of another uncle, Mahmúd, the governor of Isfahán desirous of adding the revenues of Yazd to those of the latter city. In a short ditty, a *qit'a*, the poet directly alludes to Sháh Yahyá's notorious meanness when he says that the ruler of Hormuz, whom he had not seen, had shown him kindnesses, but that Sháh Yahyá, whom he had seen, had not. (For this, see Khánlarí's *Diván*, p. 1066, *qit'a* 10, and see also Mu'ín, *Háfiz-i Shirín Sukhan*, Tehran, 1370/1990–1, Vol. 1, pp. 152 sqq. and *passim*). Háfiz, as the poem suggests, also resented the short shrift he had received at Yazd from Sháh Yahyá's courtiers and officials. Háfiz rarely left his beloved Shíráz and was so impecunious that he had difficulty in returning there from the unfortunate trip to Yazd, a place he never forgave.

POEM XIII

Dawn is breaking, but the sky's been curtained with clouds.
Comrades, the morning cup! the morning cup!

Dew-drops drip on the tulip's cheek.
Beloved ones, wine! Always wine!

The breeze of paradise is blowing from the meadow.
Forever drink your fill of unclouded wine!

In the field the rose has set up an emerald throne.[1]
Look for the fiery ruby-like wine!

They've shut the wine-shop again.
Come conqueror, open the doors![2]

It's surprising that at such a season
They should have been in a hurry to close the tavern.

---

1.   Cf. Shelley, *Ode to a Skylark:*

>   Like a rose embower'd
>   In its own green leaves.

2.   In Háfiz's time when fanaticism prevailed its predominant sign was closure of the taverns in wine-loving, and wine-producing, Shíráz. During his four-year rule in Shíráz (1353–1357),the first Muzaffarid ruler, Mubáriz al-Dín, was particularly rigorous in this respect, until he was blinded and deposed by his son Sháh Shujá'. The latter inaugurated a less repressive regime so far as the pleasures of wine and song were concerned. The poem is interesting: a coded message to an expected and hoped-for conquering prince, asked to come and restore more relaxed times; the word translated "conqueror" also means "opener", hence "opener" of the wine-shop's shutters. Interestingly, the reference to the Elysian breeze in verse 3 might have put Muslim auditors in mind of, for example, Koran xxx, 14, speaking of a "meadow" in which those who have believed would be rejoiced in the afterlife.

POEM XIV

The morning of prosperity's dawning—where's the sun-like bowl?
When a better chance than this? Hand out the bowl of wine!

A house at ease, the wine-boy the friend, a minstrel the singer
    of witty ditties,
It's the season of revelry and passing round the cup; the time
    of youth.

In pursuit of the disposition's pleasure and the decking out
    of beauty and joy,
Let the golden mixture of bowl and melted ruby be good!

Wine's goodness in mind, the ingenious bride-attirer of nature
Nicely secretes rose-water in the rose-petal's very heart.

The beloved[1] and the minstrel clapping hands, and drunken ones
    dancing,
The wine-boy's enticing look has stolen sleep from
    wine-worshippers' eyes.

May that moon be purchaser of Háfiz's pearls, when
The sweet rebeck note rings constantly in Venus's ear.

---

1.   *Sháhid*, here translated "beloved", can also mean "darling", "sweetheart", but
    primarily means "witness": "the true witness of divine beauty" or, rather, the
    evidence for it, but see Schimmel, *Mystical Dimensions of Islam* (Chapel Hill,
    NC, 1975) p. 291.

POEM XV

I said, "O Sultan of Beauties, on this stranger have mercy."
"In the heart's pursuit the poor stranger loses the way." he replied.

I asked him to stay awhile. He begged to be excused.
How should the pampered of the Household cope with
    sorrow so strange?

Reposing on royal ermine, what concern might the spoilt have,
If of thorn and stone the outsider makes his bed and pillow?

You in whose tresses' fetters are the souls of many an
    acquaintance,
Happily has the musky mole fallen on a cheek so rarely
    coloured!

On your moon-like face's complexion the wine's reflection shows
As curiously as a petal of the Judas tree[1] on the surface of the
    wild rose.

Strangely enough has that ant-line of down[2] girdled your cheek,
Not that in a fine picture gallery[3] dark etching's out of place.

I cried, "You whose night-black tresses are the stranger's supper,
If at dawn this stranger laments, take heed."

He answered, "Háfiz, friends are at the stage of confusion;[4]
It would not be out of the way if the stranger sat wounded and
    in distress."

---

1.   The Judas tree, the *arghván* (*Cercis siliquastrum*; cf. redbud) frequently alluded
    to in the context of red wine.
2.   This is a reference to *khatt* (see Poem 1, note 3), the "ant-line of down". Shabistarí
    (op. cit, Persian text p. 46) defines *khatt* as "the margin of the Almightiness". His
    Persian commentator, Láhíjí, describes the down as being the world of those
    pure spirits nearest to divinity. Shabistarí says that

       The line has become the verdant field of the world of the spirit,
       For this reason it has been called the Water of Life.

Thus

> From His down seek the Fountain of Life.

But, as noted elsewhere in these translations, on the mundane level the newly-sprouting beard of a youth was considered attractive; the possibility that Háfiz was using his symbols in a mundane as well as a spiritual sense has to be borne in mind.

3. The word for "picture gallery" used here is *nigáristán*, literally the place where beauties abound, and the name given the gallery of fine paintings created by the Iranian heresiarch Mani (d. 273 or 274 AD).

4. The "stage of confusion", *maqám-i hairat*, a Súfí term for the state when the seeker of gnosis has progressed through the seven stages of the Way to the point of being on the verge of gnosis and is enveloped in a "cloud of unknowing" as reason is outreached in a total spirituality beyond reason's scope. Hence the state of amazement, *hairat*, into which the seeker falls. See *Kashfu'l Mahjúb of Hujwirí*, ed. by R. A. Nicholson (London, 1936) p. 275.

POEM XVI

O hallowed beauty, who might unfasten your veil?
Alas, bird of the celestial garden, who should your seed and water
    supply?

Sleep has shunned my eyes in this heart-harrowing thought that,
In whose arms have you found a perch and place to sleep?

You do not ask after the dervish; I fear you've
No mind for forgiveness and providing reward.

That wine-languid eye has on the road waylaid the hearts
    of lovers;
From this fetching glance that your wine is lethal is evident.

Because of a wink, by mistake the arrow you shot landed
    on my heart,
So what next will your "true" perception think up?

You heard none of my cries and complaints.
Ah sweetheart, that your threshold is lofty is clear.

Water-holes are far apart in this desert. Beware
Lest the desert demon lead you astray with mirages.

So, on old age's path, by what rule do you proceed, O heart?
Yes, your youth's days in error were spent.

O heart-enkindling palace, as you are the abode of love,
May the Lord not let the evil of the days destroy you!

Háfiz is not a slave who runs away from the master.
One kindness do: come back, since by your repudiation I am
    devastated.

POEM XVII

The curve which your pert eyebrows have bent in a bow,
Was bent in aim at the life of afflicted, helpless me.

Wine taken and sweat dripping, when did you enter the meadow,
That your face's lustrous drops sprayed the Judas tree with fire?

By one single glance your eye toutingly shot,
Your eye's deceit launched endless trouble into the world.

In shame at him who compared it to your face,
With the help of the breeze the jasmine threw dust into the
    mouth.

The violet was crinkling its curling tress—
The morning breeze threw the legend of yours into the midst!

Out of piety before this I was shunning wine and song.
The desire for Magian children has thrown me into both.

I wash the gown of piety now in liquid ruby wine—
There's no divesting oneself of what Eternity Without End
    apportions!

When there was the design of love, there was no stain of the two
    worlds:
Not in this time did Time cast the mould of love.[1]

Perhaps Háfiz's opening was in this ruin,
When Eternity Without End's bestowal threw him into the
    Magian wine.

The world is going my way now: the wheeling of Time
Has tumbled me into the service of the World's Master.

---

1. The meaning is that "love", here *ulfat*, "intimacy", but for Háfiz the equivalent
    of *'ishq*, spiritual love, was coeval with Eternity Without End, not a temporal

phenomenon. In the second hemistich, for "love" the word used is *muhabbat*, the love of Man for God and God for Man, according to the Koran, ii, 160, iii, 29, where the mutuality of this love is evident: "if you love Alláh, Alláh will love you"; cf. v, 59. In relation to this verse Wordsworth might be recalled:

> ...the pervading grace
> That hath been, is, and ever shall be.

(*Prelude,* Book iii, lines 38–39)

POEM XVIII

Yearning for the beloved, my breast burnt with the fire
    of the heart;
In this house there was a blaze that burnt down the nest.

My body was melted through distance from the sweetheart.
In the fire of love of the darling's cheek my soul burned.

Whoever the dangling chain of your tress on your fairy face
    beheld,
His love-stricken heart burned for love-crazed me.

See the heart's burning when, because of my tears' blazing fire,
Last night on account of love the heart of the candle moth-like
    burned for me.

It is not strange that an acquaintance's heart burns for me:
That when I was beside myself, a stranger's heart burned:

The waters of the tavern stole my ascetic's cloak.
The fire of the wine vaults burnt the abode of my reason.

When in the repentance I made, the crucible of my heart broke,
For lack of wine and cup my liver was branded like the tulip petal.

Let bygones be bygones and come back, because for me the
    pupil of the eye
Has torn from over my head and gratefully burned the ascetic's
    gown.[1]

Leave off fables, Háfiz, and drink wine a while,
Because at night we did not sleep and the candle burned
    to no avail.

---

1. This verse has been the subject for several centuries of much discussion
among commentators. What is here translated as "bygones" refers to the term,
májará, that among Súfís means a kind of falling-out, quarrelsomeness, not
uncommon in religious Orders, but changed to reconciliation by an Order's
Superior. Because he has abandoned the garb of the hypocrisy (false Sufism),
that presumably had caused the rift between him and the beloved, Háfiz here

45

pleads for reconciliation and calls the comrade back to him. The reference to the "pupil of the eye" alludes to the weeping that separation occasioned. But it also evokes the idea of the eye as mirror of the beloved's beauty, beholding which has made Háfiz cast off hypocrisy and false asceticism, again to become a sincere devotee. Burning the Súfí gown in the path of love brings to mind the story of the Shaikh of San'án, as described in 'Attar's *Mantiqu't-Tair*. A model of formal pious orthodoxy, the Shaikh falls madly in love with a Christian girl and abandons Islam, and burns his gown while even repudiating the Koran. It might be assumed that Háfiz intended a reminiscence here of the Shaikh's moving story. This story, besides containing allusions to alchemy (fire and colours), is pregnant with other references that would not be lost on its original auditors. The reference to the eye is subtly resumed in the final verse below, in the phrase "we did not sleep". The eye wept itself dry while the candle "burned in vain".

POEM XIX

May the festival's coming be blessed for you, O wine-boy,
And those promises you made not slip from your memory.

I am surprised that during the time of the days of absence,
You took heart from rivals and the heart was letting you.

Convey homage to the daughter of the vine. Say, "Come in,
For our incantations and concentrated zeal have freed you from
    captivity."

The joy of the assembly is in your step and coming;
May all those hearts be the home of grief that do not desire the
    joy of you!

God be thanked that from this autumn wind
Your garden of jasmine, cypress, rose and box-tree has suffered
    no breach!

May the evil eye be far off, since, from this separation,
Renowned destiny and mother-born luck have happily brought
    you back.[1]

Háfiz do not lose the company of this ark of Noah,[2]
Otherwise the storm of events might destroy your foundations.

---

1. There could be a twofold intention in the use of epithets like "renowned" and
    "mother-born". The high destiny of the wine is to gladden hearts with a capacity
    owed to its mother, the vine. But if the poem is taken to refer to Sháh Shujá' and
    his ousting of his fanatical wine-prohibiting father, Mubáriz al-Dín, in 1357,
    besides alluding to the 'id al-fitr, the festival when the month of fasting and
    abstinence ends, the use of an epithet like "mother-born" would signal reference
    to Sháh Shujá', whose distinguished maternal ancestry stemmed from the Qara
    Kitayan dynasty (1222–1303) of the Qutlugh Sháhs of Kirmán.
2. I.e. the wine-bowl.

POEM XX

The red rose has burst into bloom, the nightingale into
    drunkenness:
The call to merriment, O time-watching Súfís![1]

Those foundations of repentance that in their firmness seemed
    like stone,
See how marvellously a crystal goblet[2] smashed them!

Fetch the wine, because at the court of self-sufficiency,[3]
What's the difference between doorman and sultan, the drunk
    and the sober?

In this two-doored caravanserai since departure is unavoidable,
What does it avail if the portico and arch of your abode be low
    or lofty?

The stage of felicity is not attainable without pain's trial;
Yes, it was with the sentence of being tested that the Primeval
    Pact[4] was sealed.

Do not fret the heart with being and non-being and rest content:
Being nought is the end of every perfection that there is:[5]

An Ásaf's[6] splendour, the wind its steed, and knowledge of the
    speech of the birds,
Vanished on the wind, the possessor having nothing profited
    from them.

On wings and plumes do not soar off the path. The flying arrow
Rides the air awhile, but it's in the dust that it settles.

What thanks,[7] Háfiz, does the tongue of your reed give
For your speech's utterance being passed from hand to hand?

---

1.   "Time", *vaqt*, for the Súfí signifies the time when the heart is concentrated and
    has no thought of time past and time to come, but only of a present time suffused
    with the One Reality when that Reality manifests itself. For this the mystic must

keep himself prepared: he must keep space for a realization which comes fleetingly and at no bidding of his, in a matter in which he has no volition. He awaits time, which comes like "a cutting sword" to eradicate past and future time, to leave room only for the Eternal Present. There is an *hadíth* in which the Prophet said, "I have a time with God in which not any angel of those closest nor any prophet of those sent has access to me." But this witnessing of the Holy alternates between manifestation and concealment: "He shows Himself and snatches Himself away". Thus the "time-observing" Súfí can be taken to refer to this waiting on an epiphany. But "time-observant" can also have the pejorative meaning, of "opportunist". Such phrases as *ibnu'l vaqt*, "son of time", and *vaqt parast*, "time-worshipper", stand for "time-server". As Khánlarí suggests (*Díván-i Háfiz*, pp. 1238, 1239) there might well be a typically Háfizian double entendre here, although the poem is full of Súfí references. Some perhaps more squeamish copyists have left manuscripts which have *bádeh parast*, "wine-worshipping", instead of the more ambiguous qualifier.

2. A *bait* by Salmán-i Sávají (d. 1376), Háfiz's contemporary, comes to mind:
   Did you see how one glass of wine smashed
   That stony repentance of mine?

   Repentance, *taubeh*, is the first step on the Súfí Path and one of the most important; if it is adhered to, salvation may be attained. The verse is pregnant with spiritual overtones. The word for "crystal" is *zajájí*, which brings to mind the remarkable verse 35 in the Koran, Chapter xxiv: "Alláh is the light of the heavens and the earth: His light is like a niche in which is a lamp, the lamp in crystal and the crystal glass like a brilliant star, lit from a blessed tree, an olive of neither the East nor of the West, whose oil would give light even though no fire did touch it; light upon light." The light in Hafiz's crystal cup is that of wine.

3. "self-sufficiency", *istighná*, see Koran LXIV, 6, "Alláh showed himself independent of them" (the unbelieving rejectors of His message): Alláh is above all need.

4. The Covenant, the Primeval Covenant between God and Man, often called the Covenant of *alast* from the fact that Koran VII, 171, contains the covenant in the form of God's question to Adam, *alastu birabbikum*, "Am I not your Lord?", in reply to which Adam sealed the covenant in answering *balá*, "Yes". But this Arabic affirmative lends itself to punning on the Persian word *balá*, meaning "catastrophe", "calamity", "trial", "testing". It is in the last meaning that the word has particular significance for the Súfí as "the probation of the bodies of God's friends by diverse troubles and sicknesses and tribulations". (—Hujvírí, *Kashfu'l Mahjúb*, op.cit, pp. 388–389).

5. To be called to mind in connection with this verse might be Koran XVIII, 88, "... everything perishes but His countenance." Cf. LV, 27.

6. Ásaf, Solomon's *vazír*, who was blamed for lack of diligence in finding Solomon's stolen signet ring. For the knowledge of the speech of birds, see Koran XXVII, 16; cf. XXI, 81. Háfiz makes Ásaf participator in the gifts granted his master, and, as the great one of Solomon's entourage, the symbol of the latter's magnificence. He might have had reasons for not, in the context of vanishing, bootless pomp, mentioning King Solomon by name, and for referring instead to the minister. (Cf. Poem XXIV, note 3.)

7. There is here an orthographical pun, *jenás-i emlá'i*: the word translated "thanks" is *shukr* which is the only word the metre of the poem allows, but the fact that the three letters which spell this word are the same as those that spell the Persian for "sugar", *shakar*, would not be lost on Hafiz's audience, especially in the context of a "reed".

POEM XXI

Ask not for obedience, trust-keeping nor righteousness from
    drunken me:
On the Day of the Covenant[1] for wine-bibbing I became the talk
    of the town.

The very moment I made my ablutions at the spring of love,
I at once four times acknowledged God's greatness for all that
    exists.[2]

Give wine that I might give you news of the secret of the Divine
    Decree,
Telling through whose face I became a lover and on whose
    fragrance drunk.

In this the waist of a mountain is slenderer than an ant's:[3]
Do not, wine-worshipper, despair of compassion's door.

Other than this inebriate eye—may the Evil Eye be far from it!—
Nobody rests happy beneath this turquoise dome.

May the soul be the sacrifice of your mouth because in the
    sight's garden,
The Meadow-Adorner of the World has fashioned nothing more
    fair than that rose-bud.

Through the boon of love for you Háfiz has become a Solomon.
In other words, through union with you he gained nothing but a
    handful of wind![4]

---

1.   *rúz-i alast*, the Day of the Covenant (see Poem xx, note 4) when Adam
    acknowledged God as his Lord, see Koran VII, 171. Implicit in this poem seems
    to be allusion to the Trust which God reposed in Man, a trust which (Koran
    XXXIII, 72) the heavens, mountains and earth refused to bear, but Man accepted,
    though he fell into ignorance and disobedience.
2.   Literally, "I uttered four *takbírs*": four times said *"Alláhu Akbar"*, "God is Greatest".
3.   For the ant's encounter with Solomon and his host see Koran XXVII, 17–19. (Cf. 1
    Kings IV, 33.) The ant here symbolises God's compassion and His communicating
    wisdom even to the most minute of His creatures. The ant impressed Solomon and
    participated in the mercy and wisdom which God granted Solomon.
4.   An allusion to Solomon's riding the wind, but used here, sarcastically perhaps,
    to indicate that Háfiz gained nothing from being united with the one he loved.

POEM XXII

Tress awry, sweating, laughing-lipped, drunk,
Shirt in shreds, lyric-lisping, wine-cup in hand,[1]

His eyes spoiling for a fight, lips complaining,
In the middle of last night he came and sat by my pillow.

He brought his head down to my ear and in an aggrieved voice
Said, "O ancient lover of mine, can you be asleep?"

A mystic to whom a night-stealing cup such as this is given,
Would be a heretic to love if he were not a worshipper of wine!

Go away, ascetic, and stop picking on the drainers of dregs:
On the Day of the Covenant this was the only gift conferred;

We have imbibed what He poured into our cup,
Were it the nectar of Paradise[2] or the wine of intoxication.

The wine-bowl's laughter and the idol's knotted tress,
How many a repentance like Háfiz's have they shattered!

---

1. This type of epithet-strung opening is a feature of Persian poetry and known
   in rhetoric as *husn-i matla'*, "beauty of introducing".
2. Koran xxxvii, 44–47 speaks of the cup "from a spring" which is passed round in
   Paradise and gives pleasure without impairing the senses. Paradisial "rivers of
   wine" are mentioned in xlvii, 16, and, in lii, 23, the denizens of Paradise are
   said to pass to each other a cup.

POEM XXIII

Into the Magian's temple stepped my friend, wine cup in hand,
Drunk with wine and the wine-bibbers drunk with his drunken
  eye.

The shape of the new moon appears in his steed's hoof,
By his tallness the height of the pine is brought low.

After all, how can I say, "There is he," when I've no news of
  myself?[1]
And why should I say, "He is not," when my gaze is fixed on him?

When he got up, the heart's guttering candle sank down,
And when he sat down, up went the cry of would-be eye-catchers.

If the blend of perfume is sweet smelling, it's been entwined in
  his tresses.
If the eye-black proves a bow-drawer, his eyebrow's been
  tinctured with it.

Come back so that Háfiz's spent life may come back,
Even though the bolt shot from the thumb-stall never does.

---

1. A Tradition, *hadíth*, sometimes attributed to the Prophet's son-in-law 'Alí, is
   implied here: He who knows himself, knows his Lord; see Firúzánfar, *Ahádíth-
   i Masnaví*, Tehran, 1324/1944–5 p. 167.

POEM XXIV

By the life of the Master[1] past dues and the keeping of promises,
I swear the solace of my day-break is prayer for your prosperity.

My tears, that out-do Noah's flood,
Could not wash out your love's engraving from the tablet of the
    breast.[2]

Do a deal and purchase this shattered heart:
For all its brokenness, it's better value than a hundred thousand
    pure gold coins.

Do not blame me for being dissolute: love's Guide
Consigned me to the tavern the First Day.

The tongue of the ant reviled Ásaf and it is right:
The Master let Jam's ring go astray and did not go after it.[3]

O heart, do not stop desiring the boundless kindness of the
    friend.[4]
As you boast of love, smartly at one fell swoop risk your head.

On your account I've become a wild man in the mountains and
    deserts,[5]
Yet still you have not the compassion to loosen the belt of chain.

Do not torment yourself, Háfiz, nor in snatchers of hearts seek
    any sense of shame.
Is it the garden's fault if this tree doesn't thrive?[6]

---

1. The commentator Súdí suggests that this is a reference to Hájjí Qavám al-Dín
    Hasan (see Poem XI, note 1).
2. It is as if the lover were branded on the breast like a slave.
3. Ásaf ibn Barkhía, Solomon's *vazir* (cf. Poem XX). Alluded to is the loss of Solomon's
    magic ring; for Jamshíd, Jam, the ancient legendary king of Persia, read Solomon.
    The king had removed the signet ring while he performed ablutions. He gave it by
    mistake to a *dív* disguised as his valet. The *dív* ascended the throne and ruled forty
    days as Solomon, until, the king having been reduced to fish-mongering, Ásaf and
    the ladies of the royal harem realized what had happened. The *dív* fled and threw

the ring into the sea. God made a fish swallow it. The fish was netted and brought to Solomon, who found his seal of power in its belly. Thus was Solomon restored to all his glory. This is the tale as told in Abú Isḥaq Ibráhím Níshábúrí's *Qisas al-Anbíyá*, "Tales of the Prophets" ed. by, Habíb Yaghmá (Tehran, 1961) pp. 204–206.

4. Sa'dí has the couplet in Arabic, in *Gulistán*, Book XVII:

    Don't despair, brother, over misfortune:
    The Compassionate holds hidden kindnesses.

5. The allusion is to Farhád, Shírín's unrequited lover.
6. In addition, a suggested argument for this poem might be that it was composed in perturbation, perhaps because the patron, possibly Hájjí Qavám al-Dín, had appeared to take offence at the poet.

POEM XXV

The fast's over now and 'Íd[1] has come and hearts risen.
In the vault the wine has fermented and wine must be demanded.

Bigotted asceticism-mongers' turn has passed:
The time of roistering and revellers' music-making has taken
    its place.

What blame should be his who imbibes wine like this?
What is wrong in this intemperance and what its error?

A wine-drinker in whom there's neither deviousness nor hypocrisy
Is better than the vaunter of abstinence in whom there are both.

We are not false piety's men nor friends of pretence.
He Who is the knower[2] of secrets is witness to this state.

We perform God's commandment and do no one ill,
And what they say is impermissable, we do not say is lawful.

What would it matter if you and I drank a few cups of wine?
Wine is of the blood of vines: it's not from your blood.

What harm is there that there will be some breach because of
    this erring?
And if there is, still what does it matter? Where is the man
    without fault?

---

1.   *'Id*, the *'id al-fitr*, the festival which marks the end of *Ramazán*, the annual
     Muslim month of fasting from sunrise to sunset.
2.   Koran L, 15: "We have created man and We know what his own self whispers
     to him and We are closer to him than the jugular vein." Also, XXVII, 76: "And
     verily your Lord knows what their breasts conceal and what they reveal."

POEM XXVI

When you hear the speech of people of the heart,[1] don't say,
  "It's wrong."
You are not a connoisseur of speech, my dear. In this is the error.

My head bows neither to this world nor the next;
Allah be praised for these dissents that are in our head.

I don't know who it is inside heart-wounded me,
That I should be silent while he's in an uproar.

Where are you, minstrel? My heart's got out of tune.[2]
O strike up a lament: our business is in tune with this mode.

I have never had any truck with the world's strife,
So beautifully in my sight does your cheek set it in order.

Because of the vain fancies I concoct, many a night I have not
  slept:
I've a hundred nights' hangover. Where's the wine-shop?

So bespattered has the cell become with the blood of my heart,
If you were to wash me in wine,[3] you'd be doing right.

It's for this that in the Magian Temple they hold me dear,
That a fire which never goes out is forever in my heart.

What was the tune that last night the minstrel strummed,
So that life departed, and my brain stayed filled with desire?

Last night the call of love for you was planted within me:
Out of passion my breast is still resounding with its echo.

---

1. *Ahl-i dil*: the people of the heart, i.e. Súfís, people of spirituality.
2. "got out of tune", which is to take the word *pardeh* (*purdah*, "veil", "curtain") in its mean-
    ing "tune" or "musical mode", but the pun could give the translation: "My heart's come
    out from behind the veil." Hafiz's auditors would, of course, be aware of this pun and
    its implication that the love-stricken state of the heart has become public knowledge.
3. Cf. Manúchihrí's celebrated hymn to wine, with the line *rafíqán-i maná*: "Oh my noble
    friends, when I die / With the reddest of wine my body wash." (*Díván* edited Dabirsiyaqi,
    Tehran, 1326/1947–8, p. 63, Poem 32.)

POEM XXVII*

O breeze of the morning, where is the resting place of the friend;
Where the setting place of that vagabond, lover-slaying moon?

The night is dark[1] but the way to the blessed vale lies in front:[2]
Where the fire of Sinai? Where the promise of seeing?[3]

Whoever has come to the world bears the imprint of ruin:
Do not in the tavern's shambles ask where the sober are.

The one who knows the mystic sign[4] is of the people of the good
    news;
The mystical subtleties are many. Where's the one with access
    to them?

Every hair-tip of mine has a thousand preoccupations with you—
What have we to do with the blamer with no preoccupations at all?

Reason has gone mad. Where is that musky chain?
The heart has taken leave of us. Where are the heart-keeper's
    eyebrows?[5]

Wine, minstrels, roses, all are set out ready, but
No pleasure's present without the friend. Where is the friend?

Because of the autumn blast in the cosmic meadow, be not
    discomfited Háfiz;
Deign to think it out sensibly; where the rose without the thorn?

---

*This poem has been said to lament the demise of Abú Isháq Ínjú.

1. But *tár*, "dark", can also mean "string" as of a stringed instrument.
2. The blessed vale: see Koran XXVIII, 30, when Moses sees the fire on the Mount and,
   approaching it, hears the voice of God. Cf. Koran XX, 12 sqq., and Exodus XXIV, 17.
3. See Exodus XXXIII, 12 sqq., and Koran VII, 138 sqq., Moses asks to be allowed to
   look upon the Lord. His request was not granted, but he saw the mountain pul-
   verised at the revelation of the glory of God.
4. The inner truth (*ishárat*) explained to the adept without the intervention of words.
5. The purpose of this verse is twofold: (a) the chain to confine the lunatic reason,
   and (b) the arch of the eyebrow of the heart-keeper into the shadow of which
   the heart has retired from us.

POEM XXVIII

Heart and religion have deserted me and the heart-snatcher
    risen in reproach.
He said, "Do not sit by us,¹ because by you safety's been banished."

Who have you heard sit at this banquet happy a moment,
Who, when the party's over, has not risen without remorse?

If with its tongue the candle boasted of that laughing cheek,
In the presence of your adorers, many a night has it stood in
    payment of the fine.

In the meadow the breeze of spring along the rose and cypress
    border
Has arisen in desire of that cheek and erect form.

Drunk you passed by, and at the sight of you
Among the intimates of the Kingdom of Heaven a Doomsday
    tumult rose.

Before your gait the proud cypress that in pride of height and
    form exulted,
Out of shame has not lifted a foot.

Háfiz, throw away this tattered gown; perhaps you'll save your soul,
For from the heaped-up harvest of hypocrisy's "miracles" a blaze
    has sprung.

---

1. See *Mirsád al-'Ibád*, op. cit., p. 81, and the English translation, op. cit., pp. 108–109,
for the inspiration of these verses and the thinking behind this *ghazal*. In the
Mirsád (p. 81) the verse occurs:
    Love is happier that is accompanied by blame:
    He who is accompanied by safety is the false ascetic.
Also:
    Rather, may my woollen cloak be completely torn to tatters
    For your sake, O nimble free-booting friend.
    Be alone in love: why bother with men?
    You have the beloved: dust be on the head of the world!
This last quatrain is brought to mind by the final verse of this *ghazal*. The
context in the *Mirsád* is that of Adam, with the tongue of the spirit addressing the
Majestic Presence and saying, "Upon the shoulder have we lifted the burden of
the Trust by the rope of blame, and sold safety to buy reproach."

POEM XXIX

The image of your face is our companion on the Way.
The breeze from your hair, the link to our awakened soul.

In spite of contentious prohibiters of love,
Our just proof is your face's beauty.

See what the dimple in your chin proclaims:
"A thousand Josephs of Egypt have fallen into our pit."

If our hand fails to reach your lengthy tress,
It is the fault of dishevelled luck, and of our short arm.

Tell the door-keeper of the royal palace's private apartments:
"In the dust of our portal is so-and-so, one of the
    world-renouncers."

If one year Háfiz were to knock on the door, open it;
Many a year has he been longing for our moon-like face.

Though outwardly He is veiled from our sight,
Always is He in the sight of our contented heart.

POEM XXX

That Night of Power,[1] which the people of seclusion[2] say is
    tonight,
O Lord, in which constellation does this turn of fortune lie?

That the hands of the unfitting[3] may not reach your tresses,[4]
Every heart in a ringlet of them is repeating,[5] "O Lord! O Lord!"

I am one of those slaughtered by the dimple in your chin, as,
    from every side,
The necks of a hundred thousand souls are beneath the collar[6] of
    the chin.

My knightly king,[7] to whose face the moon is mirror-holder,
The crown of the lofty sun is dust beneath his horse's hoof.

See the shine of the sweat on his cheek, for the hot-paced sun,
So long as it is, in desire for this sweat is in a fever all day.

I will not abandon the ruby lips of the friend, nor the wine bowl;
Ascetics, hold me excused, for this is my religion.

He who from beneath a half-closed eye shoots arrows at my heart,
The nourishment of Háfiz's soul is in the smile of his half-
    closed lip.

The water of life drips from its eloquent beak—
What, in the name of God, an exalted liquor is the black crow
    of my pen!

---

1.   See Koran xcvii, the "Chapter of Power": "Lo, We have sent it down on the
    night of power," a verse in which "it" is taken to mean the Holy Koran. Háfiz
    might also have had in mind xliv, 22, with its reference to the "blessed night"
    on which "We have sent it down". This night is also known in Persian as the
    "Night of Power". What is apparently referred to is in fact an especially holy
    night when prayers are most likely to be accepted, good deeds recognized, and
    angels abound on earth; a night such as befits the one on which the Prophet
    received his first Revelation (Koran liii, 1–18). For the Súfí devotee, the Night of
    Power is every night, as Háfiz suggests.

2. For the Súfi seclusion with God is the state of having lost all consciousness of the self.

3. The unfitting are contrasted with the people of seclusion.

4. The Prophet Muhammad was reputed to have two locks which fell from the crown of his head down to his shoulder. Such an allusion as this would not be lost on Háfiz's audience.

5. "repeating" stands for the Súfi technical term *zikr*, remembrance of God, but a remembrance induced by and manifested in constant repetition in praise of Him, of such expressions as are exemplified here by the phrase "O Lord". *Zikr* is an essential part of a Súfi's discipline. It is intended to achieve concentration on God to the exclusion of all else.

6. Cf. Poem xxix, verse 3. The collar, *tawq*, suggests enslavement: the collar of a villein or the ring in a slave's ear. The fleshy part of the chin, the jowl or dewlap, was considered alluring in those of beauty.

7. The words "cavalier" or "knight" allude to the Muzaffarid ruler of Fárs who was a patron of Háfiz's, Sháh Shujá' (1357–1384). He was known as Abú'l-Faváris, Father of Knights, in allusion to his maternal ancestry as a descendant of Nusrat al-Dunyá wa'l-Dín Abú'l-Faváris Qutlugh Sultán Buráq Hájib, who ruled over Kirmán from 1222 to 1234.

POEM XXXI

How with the image of you can we pay attention to wine?
Tell the wine jug to look to itself, because the pothouse is reeling.

Though it were the wine of Paradise, spill it,
Because without the friend, every sweet sip you give me is vilest
    torment.

It's a pity that the heart-stealer has gone away, for, in weeping eyes,
The portrayal of the image of the down on his cheek is writing
    on water.

Awake, O eye, because there is no safety
From this ever-swelling flood that is in this abode[1] of sleep.

The sweetheart passes by you plain to see, but
Is looking at others, so that the veil is drawn close.

As soon as on your flushed cheek the rose saw the grace of
    moisture,
In the fire of envy through the grief of its heart it drowned in
    rose-water.

What way is your way that, out of the extremity of awe,
The surrounding ocean of the firmament is nothing but its mirage?

Don't look for wisdom in the inner chamber of my brain:
This chamber is full of the rumour of the harp and the rebeck.

What does it matter if Háfiz is a lover, a rogue with a roving eye?
In the time of youth, many strange gyrations are not to be avoided.

---

1. The eye.

POEM XXXII

Your tress in one single lock of hair has confined a thousand hearts.
To a thousand panacea-peddlers it has closed the way in all four
    directions.

That at the breath of a breeze all might surrender the soul,
He opened a musk pod, but closed the door of desire.

I went mad because of this, that my darling, like the new moon,
Revealed an eyebrow and preened himself, but veiled the face.

The wine-boy poured multi-coloured wine into the cup,
See these patterns, how beautifully in the cup enclosed![1]

O Lord, what a sweet sound the long-necked flask[2] made, when
    the vat's blood
In its gullet it held with a gurgling note.

What mode has the minstrel struck, that, in the dervish
    congregation's chanting,
He has closed the door of "Him and He"[3] on the people of
    ecstasy and holy states?

Háfiz, whoever has craved for union but not practised love,
Without ritual ablution has donned the pilgrim garb for processing
    round the Ka'ba of the heart.[4]

---

1. Implied metaphors here are derived (a) from the additional connotation of *rang*,
    "colours", as "seduction", "desire", "trick", and (b) from the fact that it was common
    for wine bowls to have verses and pictures engraved on the inside of the metal.
    Here, however, *rang's* primary meaning, "colour", is the operative one, with the
    shifting play of colours in a cup gently twisted in the hand; the shifts of the fate
    meted out to Man in the primeval Covenant between God and Man, when God
    asked Adam, "Am I not your Lord?", and Adam answered, "Yes," (Koran VII, 171).
2. The *ibríq*, a long-necked flask.
3. In the "congregation", *Samá'*, of Súfí dervishes, ecstasy is induced by, not only
    dancing, but the chanting of *Há* and *Hú*, "He", "He" in reference to the only
    real "He", God.
4. The allusion is to the ceremonies of the Pilgrimage at Mecca, which include the
    processing round the Ka'ba, *tauf*, after donning the *ihrám*, the pilgrim's seamless
    shirt. Since this word can also mean "being unlawful", Háfiz is punning. What
    was unlawful was, of course, performing this rite without having carried out the
    prescribed ablution.

POEM XXXIII

God, when He fixed the shape of your heart-opening eyebrows,
Tied the opening of my affair to your fetching glances,

He stole comfort from the heart of me and from the bird of the
    field,[1]
As soon as He wove the narcissus's brocade and your tunic.

The rose-breeze untied many a knot from our perplexity and the
    rose-bud's heart
When it bound the heart to desire for you.

The wheeling of the sphere made me content with your bonds,
But to what purpose, when the end of the thread it attached to
    your pleasure?

Do not like a musk pod knot up my musky heart
When it's concluded a Covenant with your knot-loosening
    tress-tips.

You, O time of union, were indeed another life—
See the error when the heart conceived hope of your fidelity!

Because of your tyranny I declared: "I will leave the city."
Laughing, he replied: "Go, Háfiz. Who's stopping you?"

---

1.   The bird of the field: the nightingale forever longing for the beloved.

POEM XXXIV

What need of the show-booth has he who has chosen seclusion?
What need is there of the wilderness when there is the street of
   the friend?

O darling, for the need that you have with God,
Ask at least once what need is ours.

O king of beauty, for God's sake we have burned!
Ask at last what is the beggar's need.

Need is our patrimony, but without the language of begging:
What need is there of asking in the presence of the generous?

If it is our life you are after, there's no need for any preamble.
When the goods belong to you, what need is there for plundering?

The world-revealing cup[1] is the friend's luminous heart.
What then is the need for disclosing my want?

Gone the time when I was under the weight of obligation
   to the seaman:[2]
Once the pearl is netted, what need is there of the sea?

O beggar-lover, when the soul-conferring lip of the friend
Recognizes you, what is the need for claiming daily rations?

Go, O false claimant! I have nothing to do with you.
Loved ones are present. What is the need of importunate rivals?

Háfiz, stop speaking now: skill becomes manifest of itself.
Where is the need of quarrelling and vying with the contender?

---

1. The magic cup (reminiscent of Alexander the Great's legendary mirror) pos-
   sessed by the ancient Iranian mythical king Jamshíd, in which he could view
   the past, present, and future.
2. A reference to the pearl fishers of the Persian Gulf. See next line.

POEM XXXV

Your threshold is the gateway to the vision of my eye.
Show kindness and alight here: the house is your home.

You have stolen the heart of gnostics with the charm of a mole and
    line of down[1] —
Marvellous are the subtleties beneath your grain[2] and net!

O nightingale of the dawn, may your heart be gladdened by union
    with the rose,
For in the meadow the amorous warbling is all yours.[3]

Assign to your lip the cure for the fainting of the heart:
That exhilarating ruby is in your treasury.

In the body I am deficient in the felicity of waiting upon you,
Yet the essence of my soul is the dust of your threshold.

I am not the one to give my heart's coin to every cheeky fellow.
The treasury's door is under your seal and your stamp.

And you, what a trickster you are, O sportive cavalier,
Under whose whip an unbroken colt like the firmament is tamed!

Where do I come in when the juggling sphere slips
Because of these tricks that are in your excuses' store?[4]

The singing in your assembly makes the heavens dance now
That the poetry of sweet-tongued Háfiz is your ditty.

---

1. The newly sprouting beard of a youth.
2. The mole of the cheek of the beloved is likened to a grain: according to Muslim
   belief it was a grain, not an apple, which Adam was tempted to eat.
3. The rose is silent and still. It is the nightingale that sings.
4. The, perhaps indigent, poet plays on the words which are here translated
   "treasury" and "store", *khazáneh* and *anbáneh*.

POEM XXXVI

Get about your business, sermonizer. Why this protesting?
For me the heart has gone astray. What has gone astray for you?

Until, as it does the reed, his lip makes me attain my desire,
In my ears the world's counsel is as wind.

His waist, which God has created from nothing,
Is a subtlety that none created has unlocked.

The beggar in your street is in no need of Paradise's eight degrees:
The captive in your bonds is free of both worlds.

Although love's intoxication has ruined me, yet,
Due to that ruin, my being's foundations are good.

O heart, do not complain of the friend's injustice and cruelty,
    because the friend
Made this your apportionment and it is just.

Go, stop reciting parables and breathing spells,[1] Háfiz:
Of these fables and incantations I have many by heart.

---

1. Blowing on knots was practised to induce magical spells. See Bess Allen
    Donaldson, *The Wild Rue* (London, 1938) pp. 13–14 for the story of a female
    opponent of the Prophet Muhammad attempting to bring calamity upon him
    by tying seven knots in a piece of rope and blowing on them.

POEM XXXVII

Come, for the foundations of the mansion of hope are most
  unsound.
Bring wine: life's foundations are on wind.

I am the slave of the resolve of him who, under the azure wheel,
Is free of all that accepts the hue of attachment.

How might I tell you what glad tidings, of the world of the
  unseen, Surúsh[1] the angel gave me,
When last night in the tavern I was dead drunk?

It said: "O soaring-visioned royal falcon of the Lote Tree,[2]
Your nest is not this corner of the city of woe.

From the battlements of the throne they are whistling you.
I know not what in this place of snares has befallen you."

I will give you a piece of advice. Remember and apply it,
For this saying is learnt of the Elder of my Way:

"Seek no word-keeping from the world built on sand.
This old hag's the bride of a thousand wooers."

Suffer not the world's grief and erase not my advice from the
  memory,
For this subtlety of love I learnt from a traveller on the Way:

"Be content with what is given and smooth the furrows from the
  forehead,
Since neither to you nor to me has the door of choice been
  opened."

In the smile of the rose there is no sign of troth and constancy.
Lament, lover nightingale. There is occasion for lamenting.

Why, sloppy-versed poetaster, do you envy Háfiz?
The heart's acceptance and speech's charm are gifts from God.

1. Surúsh, cf. Shraosha, one of the "Beneficient Immortals" among the Avestan Amesha Spentas. With Ahura Mazda, on whom they attended, these angels made a sevenfold Divine Directorate for the welfare of the world. Shraosha later became associated with death and was an archangelic type of spirit which assumed guardianship over good souls during the three days after expiry when these souls hover near the body. The souls of the wicked were taken over by an evil spirit. Since etymologically the word *shraosha* can be traced to the noun for "obedience", Shraosha acquired the sense of discipline and was closely allied to Mithra in the latter's role as guardian of contracts. In Islam Surúsh retains the sense of Guardian Angel, intent upon keeping the faithful obedient to the Divine Law.

2. The Lote Tree, the *Sidra tree* of Koran LIII, 14, 16, where the Sidra tree "at the boundary, which is near the Garden of the Abode", is mentioned in the context of Muhammad the Prophet's seeing "one of the signs of his Lord, the greatest". This tree, on the boundary between terrestial and celestial worlds, is peculiarly holy as marking the site where the Archangel Gabriel delivered God's Revelation to the Prophet. The name "Háfiz" means one who knows the whole Koran by heart.

POEM XXXVIII

As soon as your tresses fell into the wafting of the breeze,
The passion-wrecked heart fell into two halves with grief.

Your sorcery-working eye itself is the delineation of magic,
But there is this, that this prescription has turned out ineffectual.

Do you know what that mole in the curve of your tress is?
It is the ink-blob that has topped the letter "j".[1]

Your musky tress in the rose garden of the cheeks,
What is it? A peacock that has dropped into the Garden of
    Paradise!

Out of desiring your fragrance my heart, O comforter of the soul,
Is the dust that has fallen on the road in the wake of the wind.

Like dust, this body of dust cannot rise
From the corner of your street, so deeply has it fallen.

The shadow of your cypress, O Jesus-breathed,
Is the reflection of the soul fallen on putrid bones.

He whose seat was only the Ka'ba, I found, on account of
    remembering your lips,
Had become an habitué of the door of the tavern.

O dear one, in grieving for you the lost Háfiz has
The uniting bond that was cast in the Primeval Covenant.[2]

---

1.   The allusion is to the letter *jím* of the Arabo-Persian alphabet which has a dot
     in the centre. It stands for the letter "j". Háfiz has "the ink-blob that has
     dropped into the ring of the letter *jím*".
2.   I.e. The covenant of *Alastu*, see Koran VII, 171. This beautifully knitted together
     poem fittingly ends with reference to the Covenant between God and Man on
     the latter's creation, because the whole poem seems to be about Man's coming
     into the material from the spiritual world. It might be added that the penulti-
     mate verse appears distinctly to allude to the story of Shaikh San'án in 'Attár's
     Mantiqu-t-Tair. Cf. poem LXXIX, verse 6, note 1.

POEM XXXIX

Without the sun of your face, my day is bereft of light,
And of life, only darkest night is left me.

Patience is the cure for me for separation from you, but
How can patience be born when no strength is left?

At the time of farewell to you, from the excess of the weeping
    that I made
Far from your cheek, in my eye no light was left.

Departed your image from my eye, and the eye was crying:
"Alas for this corner left untilled!"

Being united with you used to keep the angel of death far from me.
Now, because of the dominion of separation from you, far he is
    no longer.

That moment has approached when your rival might say,
"Far from your door, that wounded rejected one is no more".

After this, what might it profit if the friend takes the trouble
    of a step,
When of life in a stricken body not a last breath is left?

In separation from you, if there were not a waterdrop left
    in my eyes,
Say: "Shed the blood of the liver because no excusing's left."

Háfiz through grief from weeping did not engage in laughter:
The mournful has no petitioning of the festive board left.

POEM XL

What need of cypress and pine has my garden? Less than whom
    is my home-grown boxtree?
O flirtatious boy, what religion have you taken up, that our blood
    should be more lawful to you than mother's milk?

Since you from afar behold the imprint of sorrow, drink wine:
We have made the diagnosis and the treatment is infallible.

Why should I shun the Magian Elder's threshold?
Good fortune is in this mansion, and opening in this door.

Yesterday he gave me promise of union, but wine had gone to
    his head.
See what he says today and what is now in his head!

In our Way only the broken-hearted is bought—
The market of the swaggerer is on the other side.

Love's sorrow is but one story, but this is the marvel,
That from everyone that I hear it, it is never the same.

Shíráz and the water of Ruknábád and this sweet blowing of the
    breeze,
Do not decry them. They are the beauty-spot on the cheek of the
    Seven Climes.

There is a distinction between the water of Khizr, which is in
    darkness,
And our water, the spring of which is the Alláhu Akbar.[1]

We do not betray the honour of poverty and contentment;
Tell the king that our daily bread is pre-ordained.

Háfiz, what a wonder! Your reed is a piece of candy,
Of which the fruit is more delightful to the heart than honey
    and sugar.

1. *Khizr*, the "Green Man" of Muslim legend and folklore, the keeper of the Water of Life, which was situated in a place of darkness to which only he knew the way. *Alláhu Akbar* refers to the Northern Gate into Shíráz, which bears this name because on reaching it travellers would call "God is great" in God's praise and gratitude to Him for the safe accomplishment of their journey. The Ruknábád stream flows down from the plain north of Shíráz, to enter the city near this gate.

POEM XLI

Thanks be to God that the wine-shop's door is open,
Considering that I have a longing face turned towards it.

The jars are all bubbling and clamorous with drunkenness—
And this wine that's there is real, not metaphorical.[1]

On its part, all intoxication and overweeningness and pride;
And on ours, all hopelessness, helplessness and need.

The secret we have told no other nor will tell,
Let us tell the friend, because he's the one secrets are told.

The description of the curls in the tress, curve within curve, of
    the beloved,
Cannot be made short, because this affair's a long one.

The burden of Majnún's heart and the curl of Layla's[2] tress,
Is the cheek of Mahmúd and the sole of the foot of Ayáz.[3]

Like the hawk I have hooded my eyes from all the world,
So much is my eye open to your beautiful cheek.

Everyone who enters the Ka'ba of your street,
Through the qibla[4] of your eyebrow is rightly directed in prayer.

O comrades of the assembly, the burning heart of humble Háfiz
Inquire of the candle that's engrossed in burning and melting!

---

1. "metaphorical", *majáz*, but an orthographical pun is involved here: if the short
    vowel on *majáz* is changed to short "u", *mujáz*, the word would mean "permissible".
2. Majnún and Layla, celebrated lovers of ancient romance; *majnún* means "mad".
3. Mahmúd the Gaznavid Sultan (r. 998–1030 AD), whose love for his Turkish slave,
    Ayáz, was celebrated and became one of the paradigms of love frequently
    alluded to by Súfí poets.
4. Literally "anything opposite"; it is the direction in which all Muslims must pray,
    that is, towards Mecca. (See Koran II, 136–145.)

POEM XLII

Although the wine is joy-bestowing and the breeze rose-sifting,
Do not drink wine to the twanging of the harp, because the censor
    is sharp.

Should a bowl and a companion be at hand for you,
Drink in reason, because the times are dire.

Hide the cup in the sleeve of the ragged gown,
Because, like the eye of the flagon, the times are blood-letting.

We wash away patched gowns' wine-stains with tears,
Because it is the season of abstinence and time for caution.

The sphere raised aloft—is it not a sieve, blood-spattering,
The drops of which are the head of Khusrau and the crown of
    Parvíz?[1]

Do not seek sweet life from the wheeling of the
    up-turned heavens:
The clear at the top of this wine-jar is all muddied with dregs.

'Iráq and Fárs you, Háfiz, have captured with your sweet verse.
Come, it is the turn of Baghdad and time for Tabríz![2]

---

1. Háfiz uses the term "Khusrau" (Caesar) as the general term for (pre-Islamic) Persian rulers, and the name Parvíz for a particular one, the Sassanid Khusrau II, who ruled from 590 to 628 AD. That *Parvíz* also means "sieve" affords an opportunity for word-play.
2. By 'Iráq Iranians of Háfiz's and later times meant and mean central and western Iran as well as Mesopotamia. Fárs of course was Háfiz's native province, capital Shíráz. The allusion to Baghdad and Tabríz is to the winter and summer capitals of the Jaláyirids (1336–1411), who ruled northwestern Iran and Mesopotamia contemporaneously with the Muzaffarid rulers of Fárs (1313–1393). Háfiz in the first verse of this poem has already alluded to the first Muzaffarid, Mubáriz al-dín Muhammad (1313–1357), whose extreme orthodoxy made him close the wine-shops and prohibit religiously illicit pleasures. Hence he was alluded to as the *muhtasib*, "censor", the policeman of weights, measures, and morals; in this translation the word "censor" translates the word *muhtasib*. The Jaláyirids were celebrated for patronage of poetry and the arts; Háfiz is threatening to accept, or expressing the desire for, their invitation that he should leave the Muzaffarid patronage for the Jaláyirid.

POEM XLIII

The desire is mine, to tell you the condition of the heart;
It is my desire to hear news of the heart.

See the crude wish, that the notorious tale
It should be my desire to hide from rivals!

A "Night of Power",[1] so dear and so holy—
To sleep with you till day is my desire.

Alas, that such a delicate pearl-grain
It is my desire to pierce in the darkness of night![2]

O easterly breeze, this night vouchsafe me help,
For come the dawn it is my desire to break into flower.

For the sake of glory, with the tip of the eye-lashes
The desire is mine to sweep up the dust of your path.

Like Háfiz, in despite of the disputatious
It is my desire to utter a licentious poem.

---

1. See Poem xxx, note 1.
2. See Poem iii, verse 9: the reference is, among other things, to the conceiving of
   a poem. But see the preceding verse with the allusion to the coming down of
   the Koran, as described in Koran xcvii, 1, "Lo, We have sent it (the Koran) down
   on the Night of Power."

POEM XLIV

The arena of the garden is relish-imparting and the company of
    friends delightful.
May the time of the rose be lovely, because with it the
    wine-drinkers' day is joyous:

By the morning breeze each breath of our soul's sense of smell is
    sweetened:
Yes, yes, the sweet breeze of lovers is good.[1]

Unopened, intending departure, the rose has arranged the veil;
Nightingale, sob the lamentation: the note of the sore of heart
    is good;

May the night-singing bird have the glad news that, in the way
    of love,
It is in tune with the dirge of those keeping a vigil for the sake of
    the friend.

In the world's market-place there is no happy heart, but if there
    were,
The flirting of licentiousness and the libertinism of vagabonds
    would be fine!

Háfiz, the way of the happy heart is abandoning the world,
So do not suppose the state of world-possessors happy!

---

1.   The breeze (*sabá*) which blows from the street of those who have love.

POEM XLV

Now that in the palm of the rose's hand rests the bowl of pure
    wine,
In a thousand tongues the nightingale is busy praising it.

Seek a book of poems and get out into the fields.
What time is this for school and disputation on commentaries
    on the "Commentary"?[1]

Cut out people and apply the measure of the 'Anqá bird,[2]
Because the honking of the recluses goes from Qáf to Qáf.

The School's jurisprudent was drunk last night and issued a
    decree,
That, "Wine is unlawful, but better than the revenue from
    endowments"!

Demanding either the dregs or the filtered wine is not for you.
    Just drink up:
Whatever our wine-dispenser pours is the essence of favours.

The utterance of rivals and the fancies of colleagues
Are the same as the stories of gold-lace sewers and those of the
    weavers of mats.

Quiet, Háfiz! Keep these subtleties like you would pure gold,
Because the town's counterfeiter is its money-changer.[3]

---

1. Alluded to is the famous Arabic commentary on the Koran, the *Kashsháf*, of
    Zamakhsharí (1074–1143 AD).
2. The *'Anqá*, or, in Persian, *Símurgh*, a fabulous bird that lives in solitude on the
    Mount of Qáf; the Phoenix of Arabic and Persian lore. Qáf is the legendary
    mountain that bounds the world.
3. See Poem XI, note 1, with its reference to Qavámu'd-Dín Muhammad ibn 'Alí,
    the Chief Assayer.

POEM XLVI

In these times the friend who is free from blemish
Is a flask of clear wine and a book of songs.

Travel light, because the passage to safety is narrow.
Seize the cup, because precious life has no going back.

Not I alone in the world am plagued by lack of works:
The vexation of doctors of religion too is from theory minus
    practice.

In this tumult-filled way, to the eye of reason
The world and its business are without permanence and settling
    place.

My heart entertained high hopes of union with you,
But on life's way death is hope's highwayman.

Catch hold of the curl of the moon-cheeked one and do not
    repeat the fable.
That good luck and ill are from the effect of Venus and Saturn;[1]

At no revolution will they find him sober,
Because it's on the wine of eternity that our Háfiz is drunk.

---

1.   Cf. Poem LXXIII, verse 6.

POEM XLVII

Rose in the bosom, wine in the hand, and the beloved going my
    way,
On such a day the Sultan of the world is a slave to me.

Say, "Fetch no candles for this gathering, because tonight
In our assembly the moon of the cheek of the friend is full."

In our religion wine is lawful, but,
Without your countenance, O rose-limbed cypress, forbidden.

In our assembly mix no perfume, because we
Every moment from your locks have fragrance sweet to smell.

My ear is concentrated on the voice of the reed and melody of
    the lute;
My eyes, on the ruby of lips and the circulation of the bowl.

Say nothing about the taste of candy, and not a word about sugar,
For the simple reason that my desire's gratification is in your
    sweet lip.

So long as the treasure of yearning for you abides in my ruined
    heart,[1]
The corner of the tavern will forever be my abode.

What is it you say of shame, when I enjoy repute because of shame?
What is it you ask of repute, when I have the shame of repute?

We are wine-bibbers and giddy and rogues and lewd oglers—
And who is the one in this city not like us?

Don't fault me to the policeman of morals,[2] because he too
Is always in search of never-ending pleasure, as are we.

Háfiz, sit not a moment without wine and the darling,
For it is the time of the rose and jasmine and the Festival after
    the Fast.[3]

1. Ruins, of which there are many in a land as ancient as Iran, were popularly supposed always to have treasure beneath them since, when a city was sacked, as in Iran's long history they so often have been, people buried their treasure under the cellar floor.
2. The *muhtasib*.
3. The *'Idu'l-Fitr*, the festival at the end of *Ramazán*, the Muslim month of fasting from sunrise to sunset.

POEM XLVIII

In the street of the wine-shop every wayfarer who knew the way
Considered that to knock at another door would be to
    contemplate ruin.[1]

Whoever found a way to the threshold of the tavern,
In the brimming bowl of wine knew the secrets of the mystics'
    hospice.

Time gave the crown of profligacy only to him who
In this Tatar cap[2] perceived the Cosmos's highest degree.

Seek not from us anything but madmen's submissiveness,
Because the Shaikh of our rite knew reasonableness to be sin.

Whoever has read the secret of the Two Worlds in the bowl's
    inscription,[3]
Has known the riddles on the cup of Jamshíd[4] to be pictures of
    the dust of the path.

My heart has sought no safety in the wine-boy's eyes:
It knew the blandishments of that black-hearted Turk.

On account of the tyranny of the star of destiny, at dawn my eyes
Wept so much that Venus saw and the moon knew.

Happy that vision which in the rim of the bowl[3] and the wine-boy's
    face
Realised both the crescent moon of one night and the
    fourteenth's moon too.

Háfiz's tale and the cup he secretly quaffs—
What place the policeman's and the watchman's? The king knew—

A kingly loftiness of rank which knew the sphere's nine domes
As the model of the curve of the arch of its portal.

1. But in the terminology of this kind of poetry, of course, the wine-shop or tavern was often referred to as *kharábát*, literally "ruins", since such places were in deserted and often ruined parts of a town (cf. Poem XLVII, note 1).

2. "Tatar cap"; although *kulah* can mean, in addition to "cap", "crown", "diadem", etc., here Háfiz alludes to his patron, Sháh Shujá', whose mother was the last of the Qara Khitayan line which, in the person of Buráq Hájib, comprised the Qutlugh Khanid dynasty of Kirmán (1222–1303 AD). "Tatar cap" implies Central Asian origins. The last two verses of the poem mention "king" (*sháh*), and "kingly" (*sháhí*): here is further indication of to whose ears these verses were meant to be attuned (cf. Poem XXX, note 7).

3. See Poem XXXII, note 1.

4. See Poem XXXIV, note 1.

POEM XLIX

Through the sparkle of wine the Súfí comprehended the hidden
    mystery:
This ruby is the touchstone for the substance of everyone.

Only the bird of the morning knows the worth of the clustered
    petals of the rose:
Not everyone who has read a page has realized its meaning.

O you who from the book of reason would learn the verse[1] of love,
I fear that by research, you will not be able to know this subtlety.

Bring wine, because anyone who has known the rapine of the
    autumn wind
Makes no boast of the rose in the garden of the world.

To my much-tried heart I have offered both worlds;
Other than your love, inconstant it knew the rest.

Whoever has known the value of the Yemenite breeze,[2]
Through felicity of vision makes stone and clay ruby and carnelian.

The time has passed now when I would worry about public
    contempt:
The censor of morals also knew this secret pleasure.

His grace did not regard our comfort seasonable,
Otherwise on our part he would have recognized an expectant
    heart.

Háfiz knew this threaded pearl he's teased from the mould[3]
To be the stamp of the patronage of the Second Ásaf.

---

1.   Here Háfiz uses the word *áyat*, the term for verses of the Koran.
2.   There is an allusion here to the mysterious ascetic, Uvais-i Qaraní, whose saint-
    liness is said to have inspired the Prophet to say, "Lo, I feel the breath of the
    Merciful from the direction of Yemen." (See Jalálu'd-Dín Rúmí, the *Masnaví*,

Book II, verse 1203, and IV, 1826 sqq.; the *Kashf al-Mahjúb* of al-Hujwírí, Nicholson's translation (London, 1936) pp. 83–84; and the *Tadhkirat al-Awliya* of 'Attár, ed. R. A. Nicholson (London and Leiden 1905) vol. I, pp. 15–24.

3. Since Háfiz is playing on the idea of seals and stamps, and bearing in mind the fact that Hájjí Qavám al-Dín Hasan was called the *Tamgháchí* or "Keeper of the Seal" (see Poem XI, note 1), and is the most likely *persona* intended by "the Second Ásaf", the word *tab'* in this verse has been translated in one of its primary meanings, "mould", to connect it with the reference in the second hemistich to the "*stamp* of the patronage of the Second Ásaf". But *tab'* can also mean "nature", "temperament", "genius".

POEM L

The garden of the Highest Paradise is the Dervishes' private
    retreat.
The essence of exaltation is the service of Dervishes.

In the compassion of the glance of Dervishes is the unlocking
Of the treasure of glory, that has wondrous talismans.

The Elysian Palace, of which Rizván[1] went as doorkeeper,
Is a belvedere in the Dervishes' meadow of delights.

By the light of that through which counterfeited alloy turns
    to gold,
Is an alchemy that reposes in the company of Dervishes.

That before which the sun lays down the crown of pride,
Is the grandeur that is in the entourage of Dervishes.

From one boundary to the other is the army of tyranny, but
The Dervishes' moment is from Eternity before and after Time.

The good fortune that mayn't suffer the pain of decay,
Listen, there is no doubt about it, is the blessed fortune of
    Dervishes.

The stored wealth of Qárún,[2] that is still sinking below because
    of the wrath,
Represents a blow on behalf of the jealousy of Dervishes.

O rich man, brag no more of all this pomp, because for you
The head and the gold are in the safe-keeping of the devotional
    zeal of Dervishes.

The sought-after face that kings seek with prayer,
The place where it is visible is the mirror of the faces of Dervishes.

Be respectful here, Háfiz, because Sultanship and dominion
Are both in bondage to the majesty of Dervishes.

I am the slave of the Ásaf of the age,[3] because in this authority
    of his,
There is the outward form of lordship, but the character of
    Dervishes.

1.   The name of the gardener of Paradise.
2.   Qárún, the Korah of the Old Testament. See Nicholson's edition of the
    Masnaví, Book 1, verses 1712–13, and his lengthy note on verse 1733. The
    Dervishes, as men of God whose souls have been utterly purified, participate
    in the divine jealousy of God and of His devotees. They can brook no object of
    devotion other than God. Qárún made wealth the object of his worship. For
    this he was punished. The story of Qárún is told in Koran xxviii, 76–84, where
    it is described how Alláh sank Qárún and his household into the earth.
3.   Another allusion to Hájjí Qavám al-Dín Hasan (see Poem xi, note 1).

POEM LI

My afflicted heart has entangled itself in the snare of your tresses.
Kill it with an amorous look. This is its very own desert.

If at your hands the desire of our heart might be attained,
Make haste: goodness finds its home.

The puckered rose is not in need of the musk of China and Chigil:[1]
Its musk pods stem from the cords of its own coat.

By your soul, O sweet idol of mine, like a candle,
Dark nights my desire is its own annihilation.

When you purposed love, I said to you, "O nightingale,
Don't, for that self-willed rose is for itself."

Do not visit the home of the ungenerous masters of the age,
Because the treasure of well-being is in one's own abode.

Háfiz burned, but according to the convention of love-play,
He is still sticking to his own faith and constancy.

---

1. Chigil is situated to the southwest of Lake Issyk'kul'.

POEM LII

The juicy ruby, thirsty for blood, is the lip of my beloved,
And after seeing it, surrendering life is my duty.

With that dark eye and those long lashes, shame be theirs
Whoever beheld his heart-ravishing, but disapproved of me!

Camel-driver, do not take my chattels to the city's exit, because it
    is this street corner
That is the high road where my heart-holder's alighting-place is.

I am the slave to my own stars, because in this dearth of fidelity,
My constancy is love for that drunken gypsy vagrant.

A tray of attar of roses and an ambergris-scattering jewelbox
Are the brimming over of a single portion of my perfumer's
    sweet odour.

Gardener,[1] do not drive me away, like a passing breeze, from the
    garden gate,
Because the watering of your rose bed is from my pomegranate
    tears.

His eye prescribed a candy draught and rose-water from my
    friend's lips,
For it is my sick heart's physician.

He who taught Háfiz the knack of constructing lyrics,
Is my friend of the sweet tongue and rare gift of speech.[2]

---

1. See Poem L, note 1.
2. Sháh Shujá' is known to have tried his hand at versification, a fact to which
   Háfiz might here be (very) flatteringly alluding, but, while the allusion to Sháh
   Shujá' need not be ruled out, Háfiz might indeed have had some notable poet
   in mind, perhaps the poet Auhadí of Marágheh (d. 1338). But cf. the first
   hemistich of verse 4 of Poem LIII below.

POEM LIII

It's the time when my religion is madness for idols;
This affair is joy to my grief-stricken heart.

To see your ruby, a spirit-perceiving eye is needed,
But how should this be the status of my world-seeing eye?

Be my comrade, because the ornament of the firmament and
    adornment of eternity
Are from your moon-face and my Pleiades-like tears.

From the time your love granted me tuition in composition,
People have the perpetual office of praise of you and approbation
    of me.

O God, grant me the fortune of poverty,
For this favour is the source of splendour and dignity.

O Lord, whose is the sought-after spectacle-displaying Ka'ba,
That the desert thorn bushes on its way are roses red and white?

Tell the preacher in the Lieutenant Governor's pocket not to
    brag of this grand position,
Because the home of the Sultan is the heart of wretched me.

Háfiz, of Parvíz's[1] pomp recite no more the tale,
Because his lip is my sweet Khusrau's wine dispenser.

---

1.   See Poem XLII, note 1. Khusrau's skull has become a wine receptacle.

POEM LIV

I am he whose dervish hospice is a corner of the wine-bothy.
Prayer for the Magian Elder is my dawn litany.

Though to the morning harp no singing is mine, what does it
    matter?
My dawn music is my sighing petition for forgiveness.

I am free of king and beggar, God be praised!
The least beggar at the door of the Friend is my king.

My goal from mosque and wine-shop is union with you.
I have no thought other than this, as God is my witness.

From that moment when I laid my face on this threshold,
My resting place is above the throne of the sun.

Perhaps with the Sword of Death I might strike camp, otherwise,
To run away from the door of good fortune is not my style.

Although the fault was no choosing of ours, Háfiz,
For the sake of decent manners, make an effort and say,
    "The fault is mine."

POEM LV

Because of weeping, the pupil of my eye is ensconced in blood.
Behold what the state of people is in seeking for you!

With the memory of your ruby lip, lacking your drunken,
     wine-hued eye,
The ruby-coloured wine I drink is blood from the bowl of sorrow.

If from the east of the end of the lane, the sun of your countenance
Should rise, my fortune is auspicious.

The tale of Shírín's lips is the discourse of Farhád;[1]
The curl of Layla's tresses is the dwelling of Majnún.

Seek out my heart, because your cypress-like form is
     heart-ravishing.
Utter speech, because your talk is gracious and metrical.

From the passing round of the cup bring comfort to the soul,
     wine-boy,
Because the torment of my heart is due to the tyranny of the
     circling of the heavens.

From that time when the darling boy slipped from my grasp,
The hem of my garment is like the river Oxus.[2]

How might my sorrowful heart turn joyous
With a choice that is beyond choosing?

Out of madness, Háfiz is seeking the friend
As a bankrupt might be craving the treasure of Korah.

---

1.   Two celebrated lovers of the type of Layla and Majnún (see Poem XLI, note 2).
2.   There is a pun here on the word *rúd*, which means "river", but also "boy",
     which is the meaning in the first line of the couplet.

POEM LVI

The curl of your tress is the snare of both Unbelief
    and of the Faith:
From its busy workshop this is one small whiff.

Your beauty is a miracle of fairness, but
The tale of your glance is clear magic!

Whose life can be spared from your saucy eye,
When it is perpetually lying in wait with its bow?

May there be a hundred blessings on that dark eye,
That in the slaying of lovers is the inventor of sorcery.

The science of the cosmology of love is an amazing study,
Because to it the eighth heaven is lowly earth in the seventh
    degree.[1]

Do not suppose that the speaker of evil has gone but saved
    his soul:
His reckoning is with the two Recording Angels.[2]

Háfiz, from the snare of the tresses of him who has stolen
The heart and now intends entrapping the Faith, do not
    become safe.

---

1.   Love is beyond the degrees of heaven and earth, in other words, in the path of
    love, the highest exaltation is the lowest degradation.
2.   See Koran LXXXII, 10–11, "But over you the two guardians / Noble, writing." Háfiz
    alludes directly to the Koranic phrase *kiráman kátabína*, "the noble, two
    recorders". Cf. Nakír and Munkír, who visit the grave and, the soul revived for
    the ordeal, subject the newly-interred dead to rigorous questioning. (See Bess
    Allen Donaldson, *The Wild Rue*, op. cit., pp. 73 sqq.)

POEM LVII

Our willing head and the presence of the friend's threshold—
Whatever passes over our head is his will.

I have not seen the equal of the friend, even though of the moon
and the sun
I have placed mirrors in front of the friend's cheek.

What exposition should the morning breeze give of the state of
our straitened heart
That, like the fold of a rose-bud's petals, is fold upon fold?

I am not the only cup-drainer in this wastrel-burning temple:
O, in this workshop how many heads are clay for pots!

Is it that you have combed your ambergris-scattering locks,
And that the wind has become perfume-diffusing and the earth
fragrant with ambergris?

Every rose-petal that is in the meadow is the strewing of your face;
The sacrifice to your stature is every cypress tree lining the bank
of the stream.

The image of your cheek has entered my heart. I shall gain my
wish,
Because the happy state is behind the happy omen.

Not at this time is the heart of Háfiz in the fire of longing,
Because like the wild tulip it is the brand-bearer of Eternity
without Beginning.

In describing our passion for you the tongue of eloquence is
dumb;
So what of the reed with its nonsense-scribbling cleft tongue?

POEM LVIII

On the friend's part I have hope of some kindness.
I have committed a crime, but my hope is for pardon.

So much did I weep that everyone who passed,
When they looked at my flowing tears asked, "What rivulet
    is this?"

I know that he might overlook my sin, because,
Although he is like a peri, yet he is of the nature of an angel.

Heads like hockey balls have we played at the end of your street,
No one was knowing what the ball was and which the street.

Without any question or answer your tress was attracting the
    heart;
Who with your heart-alluring tress has the face to argue?

That mouth, of which I see no trace,[1] is nothing.
That waist is a hair and I do not discern what hair it is.

It is a lifetime since I scented fragrance from your tress;
Of that perfume in my heart's sense of smell the scent still
    lingers.

I wonder at how the picture of the vision of him has not dropped
From my eye, when its unremitting occupation is washing and
    cleansing.

Háfiz, your distracted condition is bad, but,
With the hope of the tress of the friend, your distraction is good.

---

1. Smallness of the mouth was hailed as exceedingly attractive.

POEM LIX

That one of the dark skin with whom the sweetness of the world is,
With whom there are the wine-dark eye, laughing lips, joyous
    face, joyous cheek,

Although the sweet-mouthed are kings, yet
He is the Solomon of the Age because with him is the seal.[1]

Like the sweet mole that is on that wheaten cheek
Is the secret of that grain which was the waylayer of Adam.[2]

My sweetheart has set off on a journey. For God's sake, comrades,
What can I do with a wounded heart when the salve is with him?

He is comely of countenance, of perfect virtue and unsullied;
Inevitably, the devotion of the pure of both worlds is with him.

To whom can this subtlety be told, that the stony-hearted one
Slew us, yet the breath of Jesus[3] son of Mariam is with him?

Háfiz is of the believers. Hold him dear,
For remission of many a noble soul is with him.

---

1. *Khátim*, "seal": there is an allusion here to the Prophet Muhammad as the Seal
   of Prophecy, but the allusion to Solomon's magic seal-ring and the fact that he
   was the supreme ruler of his age is also suggested.
2. See Poem xxxv, note 2.
3. Jesus's breath brought people back to life.

POEM LX

The pavilion of his love is the heart,
The holder of the mirror to his countenance, the eye.

I who do not bow to either of the two worlds,
My neck is under the burden of obligation to him.

You and the paradisial Túbá tree,[1] and we, and the form
    of the friend—
Everyone's idea is commensurate with their devotion.

What is the loss if I am stained?
The whole world is witness to his innocence;

Who am I in that sanctuary where the morning breeze
Is the curtain-holder of his chastity's sacred precinct?

The time of Majnún[2] has passed and it is our turn—
The turn of everyone is five days.

The realm of being a lover and the treasure of merriment,
All that I have is owed to the felicity of his good fortune.

Do not regard the outward poverty, because Háfiz's
Breast is the treasure-house of love for him.

---

1. *Túbá* literally means "good things", "the best of anything", as in Koran xiii, 28,
    but commentators have averred that it is a blessed tree in Paradise, the Elysium
    promised to the devout.
2. The archetypal lover.

POEM LXI

Gentle wind, should you chance by the country of the friend,
Bring a fragrant air from the ambergris tresses of the friend.

By his soul would I in gratitude shed life,
If towards me you brought a breeze from the breast of the friend.

If it so stands that to that presence no access is yours,
To these two eyes fetch some dust from the threshold of the friend.

I a beggar and, ah the woe, begging for union with him!
How might I in the eye behold the sight of the image of the friend?

My pine-cone heart is trembling like the willow
In passion for the figure and pine-tree tallness of the friend.

Although the friend would purchase us for nothing,
I for a world would not sell a hair of the head of the friend.

What difference would it make if from the bondage of grief his
   heart were freed,
When sweetly singing Háfiz is the slave and servant of the friend?

POEM LXII

This renowned messenger[1] who has arrived from the land of the
  friend,
And brought the life-protecting charm in the musky writing of
  the friend,

Joyfully conveys the sign of the beauty and glory[2] of the friend,
So that in seeking, the heart becomes hopeful of the friend.

As a tip for bringing good news, I gave him my heart,
  but felt ashamed
Of this false money of mine that I dispensed for the friend.

God be thanked that with the aid of consenting luck,
In tune with desire are all the deeds and impositions[3] of the
  friend.

What choice have the progression of the sphere and the turning
  of the moon?
They are wheeling in dependence on the choice of the friend.

If the wind of discord knocked both worlds together,
Still there would be us, the lamp of the eye and the way of
  expectation of the friend.

O breeze of the morning, bring me collyrium mixed with pearl
From that happy dust that was the trodden path of the friend.

If the enemy were to speak against Háfiz's life, why fear?
Thanks be to God that I am not ashamed of the friend.

---

1. The allusion is to the Archangel Gabriel who was God's messenger to
   Muhammad the Prophet and delivered the Koran to him; but this, of course, is,
   as it were, to sanctify what could be a purely secular allusion. Háfiz, however,
   was above such dichotomies.
2. The beauty, *jamál*, and the glory, *jallál*, are names of God. They denote His
   grace and His power.
3. "deeds and impositions" translates what is also treated as a compound, *kár o
   bár*, "action", "business", etc.

POEM LXIII

Welcome messenger to those who long! Deliver the message of
   the friend,
So that in desire I might sacrifice the soul, in the name of the
   friend.[1]

Woeful and forever distracted, like a nightingale in a cage, is
My parrot-nature, because of yearning for the sugar and
   almonds[2] of the friend.

His curls are a snare and his mole the grain in it, and I,
In hope of a grain, have toppled into the snare of the friend.

Not till Resurrection Day morning do any leave off drunkenness,
Who, like me, in Eternity without Beginning drank a draught
   from the cup of the friend.

I was telling a small part of the description of my passion, but
I am anxious no more than this to importune the friend.

If the chance were granted, as tutty to the eyes would I apply
The dust of the road that has been honoured by the steps of
   the friend.

My leaning, towards unity; his intention, separation:
My inclination I have forgone, to achieve the purpose of
   the friend.

Go on burning, Háfiz, in grief for him and put up with lack of a
   cure,
Because there is no remedy for the unremitting longing for
   the friend.

---

1. To say, "I am your sacrifice" is still an epistolatory convention.
2. Sugar, lips; almonds, the eyes.

POEM LXIV

No one has seen your face, but you have a thousand watchers.
Still in the bud, but you have a thousand nightingales.

Although I am far from you—far from you may no one be!—
Yet I have the hope of early union with you.

If I came to your street, it would not be all that strange;
Like me, in this country there are strangers by the thousands.

Who became a lover whose state the loved one did not observe?
O Sir, there is no pain and, were this not so, there is a physician!

In love there is no difference between the Súfí hospice and the
    tavern:
Wherever it is, there is the ray of the face of the beloved.

The place where the cloister's business is given lustre,
There is the chantry[1] of the monk and the name of the cross.

The warbling of Háfiz is, after all, not complete nonsense:
It is both a strange tale and a wonderful event![2]

---

1.   Háfiz is punning here: the world translated "chantry", *námús*, can also mean
    "law", "principle", but "fraud", "deceit", as well.
2.   But the word he uses for "event", *hadíth*, also means "dictum", a traditional say-
    ing attributed to the Prophet or to those close to him and referred to, with the
    Koran and the Prophet's example, as a source of Islamic law.

POEM LXV

Although parading learning in front of the friend is not good
    manners,
The tongue silent, but the mouth is full of Arabic![1]

The peri cheek hidden, yet a demon at beauty's fetching glances!
Reason was burnt up in astonishment, crying, "What Father of
    Marvels is this?"

Ask not the reason why the wheeling sphere turned a cherisher
    of wastrels.
Its conferring of gratification is a nonsense without any reason.

No one in this field has gathered a thornless rose. Yes,
The lamp of the Prophet with the sparks of an Abú Lahab![2]

Not for half a groat would I buy the portal of the Súfí hospice
    and lodgings:
I am the one for whom the tavern is the portal, the foot of the
    wine vat, the pavilion.

The daughter of wine's beauty is the light of our eye, only
It is in a crystal veil and the curtain of the grape.

Seek you now physick for your pain from the exhilarating elixir
That is within the Chinese porcelain flask and goblet of
    Aleppan glass.[3]

Bring wine because, like Háfiz, my calling for help is forever
In dawn-weeping and midnight craving.

---

1. As a *háfiz*, "one who knows the Koran from memory", and as a teacher of
Koranic exegesis, Háfiz would, of course, be exceedingly well versed in Arabic.
2. Abú Lahab (literally, "Father of the Flame") was the Prophet Muhammad's half-
uncle. He became the Prophet's implacable foe in opposition to the preaching
of Islam. Sura cxi of the Koran names him and says that he will roast in Hell,
his wife carrying the fuel.
3. Aleppo, a great East–West entrepôt city under the Mamlukes from the 13th to
the 16th century AD, was an exporter of glass, which was made elsewhere, but
brought to market in Aleppo.

POEM LXVI

What is better than enjoyment, conversation, a garden, and
 Spring?
Where is the wine-boy? Explain, why the waiting?

Every happy time vouchsafed count a boon.
Nobody has any inkling of what the outcome of the affair is.

The link of life depends upon a single hair. Watch out!
Harbour your own sorrow. What is Fate's sorrow?

What is the meaning of the Water of Life and the
 Garden of Iram[1]
But the bank of the stream and nice-tasting wine?

The abstainer and the drunkard both belong to one tribe.
To whose ogling shall we give the heart? What is the choice?

Of the secret behind the curtain, what do the Heavens know?
Quiet, O pretender to knowledge! What is your quarrel with the
 keeper of the curtain?

If the remissness and mistake of the slave have any credence,
What is the meaning of the grace and the mercy of the
 Omnipotent?

The ascetic sought the fountain of Kawthar,[2] but Háfiz, the cup.
Now, what between the two is the Creator intending?

---

1. See Koran LXXXIX, 6, for "Iram of the Pillars", a city which God laid low because of its
   inhabitants' wrong-doing. But in legend Iram is cited as a great lost city, and a city built
   in imitation of Paradise, the builder of which, Shaddád ibn 'Ád, was destroyed for his
   presumption. Shíráz boasts a Garden of Iram, a celebrated resort.
2. The fountain of Kawthar: Koran CVIII, 1, "We have given you abundance"; the word
   kawthar means "abundance", but it is in the meaning for it which has become tradi-
   tional, that of the sacred pond in Paradise, that it is used here; the pond the waters of
   which are reserved for the righteous.

Lament, nightingale, if you've a mind for comradeship with me,
Because we are both lamenting lovers: to lament is our business.

In the land where the breeze blows from the curls of the friend,
What place has boasting of the musk pods of Tartary?

Bring wine for us to stain the gown of hypocrites:
We are drunk in the cup of pride, but sobriety is the name.

No work for the inept, the conjuring up of your tresses' image;
Going beneath the chain is the way of the cunning.

It is a hidden mystery love rises from,
Of which neither the ruby lip is the name, nor the line of
    rust-coloured down.

Not the eye is a person's beauty, nor the face, nor the cheek, nor
    the sprouting beard:
In this there are a thousand subtleties and a load of invasions of
    the heart.

The stripped on the Path would not for a half-penny buy
The satin tunic of the man void of virtue.

It is with difficulty your threshold can be reached. Yes,
The ascent to the heaven of mastery is pressed with hardship.

At dawn I was watching your eyes' glances in my dream.
Good! The time of sleeping is better than the time of being awake!

Háfiz, vex not his heart with lamentation. Apply the seal,
Because eternal salvation lies in less vexation.

POEM LXVIII

O Lord, from whose pavilion is this heart-illuminating candle?
It has burnt our soul. Ask, "Of whom is he the beloved?"

Now he is the ruiner of the pavilion of my heart and my religion.
Splendid! Whose arms is he in, and whose fellow-lodger?

The wine of the ruby of his lips—may they not be far from mine!—
Is wine for whose soul, and the replenisher of whose cup?

The luck of companionship with that candle of the light of bliss,
Again for God's sake ask, "For whose moth is it?"

Everyone is breathing a spell, but it is as yet unclear
To whose incantation his coquettish heart will incline.

O Lord, that kingly, moon-faced, Venus-browed,
Whose unequalled pearl is he? The incomparable jewel of whom?

I have uttered a sigh from the love-crazed heart of Háfiz
    lacking you.
He, lisping and cracking a smile, asked, "Who's he mad for?"[1]

---

1.   When verses occur in which Háfiz treats himself as the third person, the sup-
position might be made that these *ghazals* were sung or chanted by a profes-
sional singer. In the verse to which this note refers, the singer is made to say
that he has uttered a sigh from the love-crazed heart of Háfiz, in response to
which the sought-after patron smirked and asked who Háfiz was mad for.

POEM LXIX

This week my moon left the city, but in my eyes it is a year.
What do you know about how hard a state is the state of
    separation from you?

By favour of his cheek, in his cheek the pupil of the eye
Saw its own reflection and took it for a black mole!

From his sugar-like lips milk still drips,
But in darting, winning glances, his every eye-lash is a slayer.

Although in every city notorious for generosity,
Alas that towards strangers your negligence should be a marvel!

After this, I have no doubt respecting the incomparable gem.
On this point, your mouth is sweet proof.

Good tidings were given, that you will be coming our way.
Do not alter the good intention: it's a blessed portent.

With what wiles does the mountain of your separation's grief
    stretch
The stricken Háfiz, so that through lamenting his body's
    like a reed?

POEM LXX

There is no one who has not fallen for that twisted tress.
Whose path is it in which this calamitous snare is not?

Is it perhaps that your face is the mirror of Divine Grace?
Yes, by God, such it is, and in this there's no hypocrisy and
    doubting.

On your face the ascetic cautions me. What insolence!
Does he have no respect for God and no shame before your face?

Do not for God's sake trim the tress. No night is ours
Without a hundred tangles with the morning breeze.

Come back! Without your face, O heart-lighting candle,
At the comrades' feast there's no sign of light and pure enjoyment.

Care of strangers is the cause of fair mention.
Is it that this, O my dear one, is not the custom of your town?

Yesterday he was going away and I, saying, "O idol, keep your
    word!"
He replied, "You're wrong, Mister. In this age there's no keeping
    of promises"

As your eye steals recluses' hearts,
To be after you is no sin on our part.

Were the Magian Elder to be my guide, what difference would it
    make?
There is no head in which there is no secret from God.

To tell the sun, "I am the source of light",
Great ones[1] know is unworthy of a Suhá.[2]

In the cell of the monk and the seclusion of Háfiz,
There is no prayer-niche[3] save the curve of your eyebrow.

1. The *buzurgán*, literally, "great ones", but in Súfí circles used for those eminent as exemplars of the Mystic Way; see the reference to the Elder and Guide in the preceding verse.
2. An obscure star in the Lesser Bear.
3. The reference is to the *mihráb*, the niche in the wall of a mosque which faces Mecca and towards which the congregration faces in prayer.

POEM LXXI

The pupil[1] of our eye looks only at your cheek.
Our bewildered heart says the litany for no one but you.

My tears weave the pilgrim garb[2] for the circumambulation of
    your sacred precinct,
Although not a moment are they unsullied by a sore heart's blood.

May the Sidra Bird[3] like a bird that is wild be kept in a cage
If it is not on the wing in quest of you.

If it is false coin the bankrupt lover has scattered for you,
Do not blame him. Legal tender is not in his power.

In the end that tall cypress might be within the grasp
Of all whose zeal in seeking you does not fall short.

In front of you I will say nothing about Jesus's spirit-inspiring:
In enlarging the soul, it is not expert like your lips.

I who in the fires of yearning for you never heave a sigh,
How can it be said, "He cannot put up with my heart-branding"?

The first day I saw your tress-tip, I said,
"This chain's distraction has no ending."[4]

Not Háfiz's heart alone harbours desire for attachment to you:
Who is there in whose heart there is no wish for union with you?

---

1.   The pupil of the eye, "the man in the eye", *insánu'l'ain*, is "the instrument of
vision" (Nicholson, *Masnaví*, Commentary Book, 1, 1004, cf. IV, 762). It stands in the
same relation to the eye as does the Perfect Man to God. It is through the Perfect
Man that God sees His own works, as if the Perfect Man were the eye whereby
God beholds His Creation and ceases to be, since that Creation is the reflection
of Him, "a hidden treasure". A useful explanation of the mystical significance of
the eye may be found in Shabistarí, *Gulshan-i Ráz*, op. cit., beginning at verse 138

with footnote 2, in which Láhijí, Shabistarí's commentator, points out that "Man is the eye of the world, whereby God sees His own works"; and footnote 4 where from the same source is derived the comment, "My servant draws nigh to me by pious works till I love him, and when I love him, I am his eye, his ear, his tongue, his foot, his hand, and by me he sees, hears, talks, walks, and tastes". (The translations are those of E.H. Whinfield.)

2. The *ihrám*, the pilgrim's shirt, which, see next hemistich, must be ritually spotless. For both the *ihrám* and the circumambulation see Poem xxxii, note 4.

3. The Sidra tree, or Lote Tree (See Poem xxxvii, note 2). The bird of the Sidra is the Archangel Gabriel, God's messenger to Muhammad the Prophet.

4. Cf. Poem xc, verse 9.

POEM LXXII

The ascetic worshipper of externals is uninformed of our
    condition.
Whatever he says about us is no reason for constraint:

In the way of the mystic, whatever confronts the wayfarer is his
    blessing;
On the Straight Road,[1] O heart, nobody goes astray.

We will move a pawn whatever game the rook plays;
On the chessboard outsiders have no chance of mating the
    Sháh.

What is this lofty ceiling, void of a host of images?[2]
Of this enigma no sage in the world is informed.

For the Lord's sake, what are this utter disdain and this puissant
    judge,[3]
That all these wounds are suppressed and no scope left for
    sighing?

You would say our Chancellor of the Exchequer is ignorant of the
    Reckoning:
The seal of his official documents lacks the sign, "God's is the
    accounting".[4]

Whomsoever desires, tell, "Come", and to whatsoever needs, say,
    "Ask":
In this Court there is no haughtiness, shilly-shallying, chamberlain,
    or doorman.

Whatever it is, it is due to our awkward and ill-proportioned body;
Otherwise your robe of honour would not be too short for the
    tall fellow.[5]

The choice of those of our complexion is to go to the tavern door;
Otherwise, those who would palm themselves off have no access
    to the wine-seller.

I'm slave to the Elder of the inn whose kindness never fails,
While that of the Shaikh and the preacher sometimes is and
    sometimes is not.

If they sit Háfiz down in the seat of the Mighty, sublime longing
    is the reason;
The dregs-draining lover is in no bondage to riches and rank.

---

1.   *Sirátu'l-Mustaqím* ("straight road"), frequently mentioned in the Koran as the right way of religion, obedience to Alláh and His Revelation. Traditionally, it has come to mean the hair-breadth bridge to be crossed by the dead, the righteous passing over it, sinners falling off into the blazing abyss.

2.   The stars are erased by the light of the sun.

3.   "utter disdain" alludes to God's having no needs, while "puissant judge" translates the words *qádir* and *hákim*, both names of God.

4.   The sign *hisbatan l'láh*, "God's is the Reckoning", echoes "the Reckoning", i.e. the Day of the Resurrection in the preceding hemistich. *Hisbatan l'láh* is the phrase which in pre-Pahlavi times invariably appeared on official documents and on coins of the realm. It was a sign of humility before God and is derived from Koran xxxix, 39: "in God is my sufficiency, in Him do the trustful trust." Háfiz is not only impugning the Chancellor's piety, but his lack of generosity: the sign of the *hisbatan l'láh* appears on those coins of which none appear under the hand of this Chancellor. In other words, the petitioner goes unrewarded. Háfiz might have been suggesting the contrast between the Minister to Abú Ishaq Ínjú, Hájjí Qavám al-Dín Hasan, and the chief revenue officer under Sháh Shujá' the Muzaffarid, Qavám al-Din Muhammad ibn 'Alí. (See Poem xi, note 1).

5.   The scanty robe of honour also implies lack of munificence.

POEM LXXIII

The road of love is a way that has no limit.
There is no help on it but to surrender the soul.

Any moment that you give your heart to love is auspicious:
Doing what is right calls for no auguries of the favourable time.

Seize the opportunity the path of licence offers. It is a trail,
Like those to treasure troves, not obvious to all.

Do not frighten us with reason's prohibition but bring the wine.
That prefect has no business in our jurisdiction.

Him, like the new moon, the clear eye can discern;
Not every eye is the abode of the splendour of that sliver of moon.

Ask of your eye, "Who is it who is slaying us?"
Ah, my dear, it is not the sin of fate nor the fault of the stars!

Háfiz's weeping has had no effect on you whatsoever.
I am amazed at that heart which is no less hard than rock.

POEM LXXIV

No sight is not lighted from the radiance of your face,
No eye not beholden to the salve of your threshold's dust.

Men of insight are observant of your countenance.
There is no head from which the mystery of your curl is absent.

What wonder is it if, yearning for you, my tears have come out red?
There is no curtain keeper not ashamed of the duty he's performed.

Lest the breeze should leave a speck of dust on your tress,
No pathway is not a torrent-bed flowing from my eyes

That it might not boast all over the place of supping your tress-tip,
There is no dawn that I miss engaging the breeze in conversation.

I am in distress at this mixed fortune, but were it not so,
There is no one else sharing your street's end who is not.

From the bountiful rain of your sweet lips, O mouth of the beloved,
No one is left who, wet through with water and sweat, is not a
    piece of sugar.

The water of my eye, on which lies the boon of your door's dust,
Leaves the dust of no door not covered in gratitude for it.

Of my existence scant name or trace remains.
Were it not so, due to weakness there would be no effect on it
    that would be lacking.

In the wilderness of your love, the lion becomes a fox—
Alas for this way in which there is no danger that is missing!

Letting out the secret from behind the veil is not expedient.
If it were, in the licentious gathering no rumour would be left
    unspread.

Apart from the point that Háfiz is discontented with you,
In the whole of your being there is no virtue not to be found.

POEM LXXV

The products of the factory of the universe all amount to nothing.
Bring in the wine, because the trappings of the world are all
    nothing.

From heart and soul the longing is for the honour of nearness to
    the beloved.
That's all and were it not, heart and soul would be all nothing.

Do not for the sake of shade be under obligation to the Lote[1]
    and Túbá tree:[2]
When well you look, O shimmering cypress, Paradisial gardens
    are all nothing.

The five days you are spared in this stopping place,
Rest easy awhile: the time is not all that much.

O wine-boy, we are expectantly waiting on the shore of the ocean
    of annihilation:
Consider any chance between lip and mouth to be none at all.

The suffering of me, woefully grievously burnt—
Obviously all this needs no reciting and explanation.

Ascetic, don't feel safe: watch out for envy's tricks;
The distance is not all that much from the oratory to the Magian
    Temple.

Háfiz's name has got a very good mark indeed, but
Among freebooters, the profit and loss of this is all nothing.

---

1.   See Poem xxxvii, note 2.
2.   See Poem lx, note 1.

POEM LXXVI

Save your threshold, in the world no refuge is mine.
Except this door, my head has no place of repose.

When the enemy draws the sword, I throw the shield away:[1]
Our only arrow is sighs and lamentation.

Why should I desert the street of taverns
When in the world no better rite or way than this is mine?

If Time sets fire to my life's harvest, say,
"Burn it up. It's not a blade of grass to me!"

I am the slave to that erect form's saucy eye,
From which out of the wine of his pride no one is spared a glance.

Do whatever you wish, but do not pursue cruelty.
In our Law[2] there is no sin other than this.

O king of the land of beauty, go with your horse reined in,
Because on no highway is there not a justice-seeker.

Much as in every direction I see snares in the path,
Better than your tress's defence no sanctuary is mine.

Don't give the treasury of Háfiz's heart to black curls and moles;
Such matters as this are not within the compass of all that's dark.

---

1. Cf. Francis Thompson, *The Hound of Heaven*:

    Naked I wait Thy love's uplifted stroke!
    My harness piece by piece Thou hast hewn from me.

2. Háfiz uses the word *sharí'a*, the word meaning the Law of Islam.

POEM LXXVII

Now that the breeze of Paradise is blowing from the garden,
Here I am with joy-bestowing wine and a friend of the houri sort.

Today why isn't the beggar boasting of sultanship,
When a cloud is the tent's shade and the banquet hall, the edge
    of the field?

The meadow is telling the tale of the month of Spring.
He who buys credit for cash is not privy to divine mysteries.[1]

Seek no constancy from the enemy. He gives no light,
While you kindle the candle of the mystics' cell
    from the unbeliever's temple lamp.

Restore the soul with wine, because this derelict world
Is bent on this, that it should fashion a brick out of our dust.

Do not throw the Book at drunken me;
Who knows what the Divine Decree has inscribed on its bowl?[2]

Do not begrudge attendance on Háfiz's funeral bier:
Though immersed in sin, he is bound for Paradise.

---

1.   In other words: "Take present joy and do not await promised bliss in the here-
    after."
2.   See Poem XXXII, note 1.

POEM LXXVIII

Do not, puritanically disposed ascetic, censure the depraved:
The sin of others will not be recorded against you.

Whether I am good and whether bad, you go and test yourself!
In the end everyone harvests what he has sown.

Everyone, if sober or drunk, is in quest of the Friend:
Every place is the house of love, whether mosque or temple.

My head in submission and the brick of the wine-shop's door;
If the disputer doesn't understand this, say, "Beat your head
    against the wall".

Do not make me hopeless of Eternity without Beginning's erst-
    while kindness.
What do you know who behind the veil is good and who bad?

Not only have I tumbled out of the secluded abode of piety:
My father[1] also let Paradise slip from his grasp.

If your mind is on all this, fine for the mind!
And if your nature is on all this, good for a good nature!

O Háfiz, if the Day of Doom you raise a cup,
From the street of the tavern go at once straight to Heaven.

---

1.   Adam.

POEM LXXIX

A nightingale had in its beak a rose-petal of beautiful colour,
But for that blessing set up a clamour of bitter lamentations.

I asked it, "Why at the very moment of union this crying and woe?"
It answered, "The beauty of the beloved has reduced me to this."

If the friend does not sit down with us, there is no reason to object:
The king was well off; beggars shamed him.

On the beauty of the friend our pleading and gentle supplication
    have no effect;
He is happy who enjoys good luck from the capricious!

Get up so that for that limner's pen we may sacrifice the soul,
Because he has all this marvellous imagery in a compass's twirling.

If you are a novice on the way of love, do not think about ill repute;
Shaikh-i San'án[1] pawned the gown of piety at the shop of the vintner;

Happy the time of that gentle wandering Dervish who in the
    byways of the voyage
Kept the litany of the prayer beads wearing the pagan's girdle!

Beneath the vault of the palace of him of the houri-nature,
    Háfiz's eyes
Keep the custom of the Elysian Gardens[2] through which the
    rivers flow.

---

1. Most appropriately Háfiz, as he is speaking of love, remembers the story of the pious
Shaikh who, with his large band of disciples, went in obedience to a dream and
toured Christian Byzantium until he saw a Christian girl at her window, and fell
hopelessly in love with her. He gave up his shaikhliness, burnt his gown, lay among
the dogs in the street before her house, until she eventually noticed him and, in order
that he might gain her favour, commanded that he should abjure Islam, put on the
Christian's girdle, the *zonnár*, drink wine, and herd swine. All this he did, and even-
tually won his beloved, but, led by a devoted member of his flock, his disciples
returned from Mecca and regained him for the fold. The girl pursued him, became
a Muslim, and died a blessed death in his arms. The story is one of the great love sto-
ries of the world and is recorded in full by 'Attár in the *Mantiqu't-Tair*, "The Speech
of the Birds". (See the present translator's translation (Cambridge, 1998) pp. 108–143).
2. Koran xxii, 23. The gardens Alláh gives for the enjoyment of those who have believed
and performed righteous deeds. Háfiz quotes the Koranic phrase almost literally.

POEM LXXX

Did you see how the friend had no intention but violence and
    oppression?
He broke his word and was not in the least grieved by our grief.

O Lord, do not call him to account, although my dove-like heart
He's thrown away and slain, without respecting prey hunted in
    the Sacred Precinct.[1]

My own luck visited cruelty upon me. Were it not so,
God forbid that the friend lacked courtesy and the knack of
    being kind!

For all this, any who have not suffered humiliation from him,
Wherever they have gone, they have had no honour.

Wine-boy, bring wine and tell the critic,
"Do not disavow us, for Jamshíd[2] had no cup like this!"

Every wayfarer who has not accomplished the journey into the
    Sacred Enclosure,
The poor wretch has traversed the valley but found no access to
    the sanctuary.

Háfiz, you carry off the ball of bliss because the false claimant
Has no finesse at all nor any inkling either.

---

1.   In the holy precinct of Mecca it is forbidden to hunt and, if any prey is taken,
    compensation is exacted.
2.   See Poem xxxiv, note 1.

POEM LXXXI

At dawn-break, the bird of the meadow said to the newly
    blossomed rose,
"Prank less: in this garden many like you have bloomed."

The rose laughed saying, "Truth does not hurt us, but
No lover has spoken harshly to the beloved.

If you desire ruby wine from the jewelled cup,
Pearls and carnelians must be pierced by your eye-lashes."

Eternity without End the perfume of love may not touch the
    sense of smell
Of any who have not brushed away the dust of the wine shop's
    door with their cheeks.

In the garden of Iram[1] last night when by the favour of gentle
    airs,
The hyacinth's tress was ruffled by the breeze of dawn,

I said, "O throne of Jamshíd, where is your world-seeing cup?"
It replied, "A pity that that vigilant fortune has slept!"

Talk of love is not that which comes to the tongue.
Give wine, wine-boy, and cut this dialogue short.

Háfiz's tears have flushed sense and patience out into the sea.
What should he do? The searing of the sorrow of love cannot be
    concealed.

---

1.   See Poem LXVI, note 1.

POEM LXXXII

That peri-cheeked Turk who last night passed us by,
What wrong did he see that he took the road to China?[1]

As soon as for me that world-seeing light went out of sight,
Nobody can imagine what tears flowed from my eyes.

Last night, from the fire of the heart's passing, from no candle
    has arisen
That smoke which with the heart's burning rose over our head.

Far from his cheeks, every moment from the spring of my eyes
A torrent of tears has flowed and a storm of affliction risen.

When the grief of separation struck, we fell down;
When the remedy was lost, we were left in pain.

The heart said, "By prayer union with him can again be found."
It is a lifetime that all my life has been passed saying prayers!

Why put on the pilgrim shirt when that cynosure of prayer
    is not here?
Why in striving do we toil when from the Ka'ba purity has departed?

Yesterday out of concern when he saw me, the physician said,
"Alas, your sickness is beyond the canon of healing."[2]

O friend, put a foot forward to ask how Háfiz is,
Before they say, "He's left the abode of perishing."

---

1. "China", *khitá*, and "wrong", "mistake", "error", *khatá*: Háfiz is punning. The
pun depends on the change of the short vowel from "a" to "i". *Khitá* is "Cathay".
The idea of taking the wrong road is implied; in Persian, "to take the road to
Turkestán" is used to the same effect.
2. "canon of healing", *qánún-i shifá*: Háfiz is alluding to the great medical treatise by
Ibn Síná (Avicenna) (980–1037 AD). This work was called the *Qánún*, "Canon" or
"Law". Háfiz also alludes to another of Avicenna's works, the *Shifá'*, literally, "The
Healing". This work treats of physics, mathematics, and metaphysics, while the
Qánún "superseded all previous works on medicine". See Cyril Elgood, *A Medical
History of Persia*, Cambridge, 1951, p. 195. Cf. E. G. Browne's translation of 'Arúzí's
Chahar Maqála, "The Four Discourses" (Cambridge, 1921) pp. 79–94, and xxvii, 10.

POEM LXXXIII

If on account of your musky tress wrong has been done,
    it's been done,
And if because of your black mole oppression has come,
    it has come.

If the lightning flash of love burns the harvest of the wool-clad,[1]
    it's burnt it.
If the tyranny of a blissful Sháh[2] has hurt a beggar, it has hurt him.

Vexation has come about through rumour-mongers, but,
When any impropriety has arisen among comrades, it's been
    passed over:

In the Way[3] there can be no riling of the heart. Bring wine:
All the impurities you see, once purity has come, have gone.

The game of love requires patience. Keep firm, heart!
If there has been irritation, it's been, and if error happened,
    it's happened.

Say, "Sermon-preacher, chide not Háfiz because he's left the
    dervish hospice."
The feet of the free are not for binding. If he's gone somewhere
    else, he's gone.

---

1.   "wool-clad": the Súfí, whose sobriquet, *súfí*, is derived from his garb; *súf* in
    Arabic means "wool".
2.   The "tyranny of the Sháh" refers to the tyranny of sovereign love. The figure of
    speech is of the category of metaphor (*tamsíl* or *tanvír*); but, of course, the allu-
    sion need not only be metaphorical, especially in view of the following verse!
3.   *taríqat*, a technical term: the Path of Love, the Way of the Mystic.

POEM LXXXIV

Wine-boy, fetch the wine: the month of fasting[1] is over.
Pass the cup: the season of caution has passed.

Precious time has been lost. Come so that we can make up for
A lifetime that without the presence of the cup and bowl has
    passed.

How long can one burn like aloes-wood in the flames of
    repentance?
Give wine because life has been wasted in a pointless madness.

Make me so drunk that, in unconsciousness, I might not know
Who across the field of fancy has come and who has gone.

In the hope of this that a draught from your cup might reach us,
In the tavern morning and night prayers have gone up to you.

For the heart that had died, a life reached the soul
As soon as a scent of the whiff of wine reached its nose.

The ascetic had pride: he did not reach salvation.
By the way of supplication, the debauched reached the
    Home of Peace.

What heart's cash I had went on wine.
It was counterfeit coin. Consequently it went on the unlawful.

Admonish Háfiz no more, No one who has strayed,
Has found the way once pure wine has filled his mouth.

---

1.   See Poem xxv, note 1.

POEM LXXXV

Not a sip have we tasted from his ruby lip and he's gone!
We have not seen enough of his moon-picturing face and he's
    gone!

You would say that he got extremely bored by our conversation;
He's packed his traps and before we caught up with him, he'd
    gone.

However much we recited the Fátiha[1] and the Hirz-i Yamání,[2]
And in his wake breathed the Chapter of Ikhlás,[3] he's gone.

He was offering beguilement saying, "We'll never leave the street
    of reproach."
Did you see how in the end we bought such deceit and he went?

Swaggering he went in the meadow of beauty and elegance, but
In the garden of union with him we did not presume to walk,
    and he's gone.

Like Háfiz, we wept and wailed every night,
Saying, "Ah the pity! We didn't get to his farewell and he's gone."

---

1. The opening chapter of the Koran which is recited in each posture of the
   prayer ritual and also for departed souls, and as a kind of Paternoster on
   occasions of need and distress, or in the hope of mercy. For the Súfí, the
   Fátiha contains the whole essence of the Koran, as the cheek of the beloved
   is the manifestation of the seven names of God; the *Fátiha* chapter of the
   Koran itself contains seven verses.
2. A prayer for protection which Muhammad the Prophet taught his son-in-law
   'Alí when he sent him as an envoy to the Yemen.
3. Koran cxii. Like the *Fátiha* it is recited in the daily prayer. It is the "Prayer of
   Exclusivity" (*ikhlás*) or of "Unity" (*tawhíd*) reminding the devout of God's exclu-
   sive Oneness and undivided Eternity.

POEM LXXXVI

Wine-boy, come because the friend has lifted the veil from
   the cheek;
The lamp of the recluses has started to give light again;

The retrimmed candlewick has again lit its face,
And this old man of many years has achieved renewed youth.

Love has so played the coquet that piety's gone astray,
And the friend has granted that favour which has put the enemy
   on the alert.

Beware of these sweet and deceptive words!
You would say your lips have dipped speech into sugar.

When the burden of sorrow had wounded our heart,
God sent one of Jesus's breath and he snatched it up.

Every houri-type that was parading beauty before the moon and
   the sun,
Took to other work when you arrived.

The seven domes of heaven are filled with the echo of this tale—
Regard as short-sighted him who took the matter lightly.

From whom, Háfiz, did you learn this prayer, that luck
Has made an amulet of your verse and taken it for gold?

POEM LXXXVII

Your beauty combined with callow down[1] has conquered the world.
Yes, by combining the world can be taken.

The candle wanted to spread abroad the secret of our seclusion.
Thank God it has caught the secret of the heart in the flame of
    its tongue.

With this fire that is hidden in my breast,
The sun that is in the heavens is but a torch.

The rose was wanting to boast of the colour and scent of the friend.
Out of jealousy the breeze stopped its breath in the mouth.

On the edge at rest, I was like the compass.
In the end the twisting of Fate took me into the middle,
    like the point.

That day, love of the wine cup burnt my harvest,
When the fire reflected from the wine-boy's cheeks set it alight.

I will go to the street of the Magian flapping my sleeves in joy,
Out of these discords that these last days the skirt has picked up.

Drink wine, because whoever has seen how the world's affair ends,
Has immediately abandoned sorrow and seized a bumper.

On the rose-petal they have written in the blood of the tulip,
"He who has matured has taken wine that is as red as the Judas
    tree."

Seize the opportunity, because when anarchy fell upon the world,
The Súfí took to the cup and from despair took his leave.

Háfiz, since the water of grace drips from your verse,
How can the envious take exception?

Cf. John Dryden's "the callow down began to shade my chin" (*Virgil's Aeneis*, Book VIII,
lines 214–215).

POEM LXXXVIII

I have heard the good words the old man of Canaan[1] spoke:
"Separation from the friend does not do what can be told";

The frightful narrative of the Day of Resurrection told by the
   town preacher
Is a metaphor for what he said of the Day of Separation.

Of whom might I get the truth of the sign of the friend on the
   journey gone,
When whatever the message-bearing breeze has reported it has
   garbled?

Alas that that unkind moon, loving the enemy,
Has so easily addressed himself to deserting his friends!

Henceforth it is I and the station of acquiescence, and it is
   thanks to the rival
That the heart has got used to pining for you, and abandoned
   any remedy.

Don't tie a knot in the wind, although it is blowing your way,
Because this is what as a proverb the wind told Solomon:

"For the brief respite that the sphere grants you, do not stray
   from the path;
Who has told you that this old hag[2] has given up spinning
   yarns?"

With old wine keep the ancient sorrow at bay,
Because this is the seed of happiness of heart, as the old squire
   has said.

Ask no why's and wherefore's because the happy slave,
Heart and soul has accepted every word the beloved has spoken.

Who said Háfiz had repented of thinking of you?
I've never said this. He who has, told a lie.

1. Jacob, who often figures in Persian verse mourning for his lost son Joseph. Hence Jacob is a symbol of bereavement.

2. The word used for "old hag" is *zál*, but Zál happens also to be the name of the father of the hero of the Iranian national epic, Rustam. Zál is the "Zál-i Dastán" of legend. Háfiz uses the word *dastán*, which means "tale", "fable", etc., where this translation has "yarns". Háfiz carries on the punning reminiscence of Firdawsí's *Sháhnáma*, "Book of Kings", to the next verse when he introduces a *dehqán*, here translated "squire"; a landed proprietor or farmer. The epic refers to the "old *dehqán*" as a source for the tales of Iran's ancient times: the "squire" is seen as a man of wisdom who is versed in ancient lore.

POEM LXXXIX

What a benison it was when suddenly the stroke of your pen
Ascribed to your generosity the dues owed us for service.

With the nib of the writing-reed you have indited greetings to us.
May the firmament of Fate not lack citation of you!

I do not say that you remembered heart-lost me through
    inadvertence:
In wisdom's accounting, no inadvertence stems from your pen.

Do not humble me in gratitude for this settlement:
Everlasting riches keep you dear and respected.

Come, for I will promise by the tip of your tress
That if my head goes, still I won't move it from your feet.

Your heart may be informed of our state, but at the moment
When the tulip is blossoming out of the mould of the slain in
    yearning for you.

The morning breeze has spread to every rose news of your locks:
When did the doorman grant the informer access to your private
    apartments?

What concern have you for the hearts of the wounded when
    forever
You are being given the wine of Khizr[1] from the cup of Jamshíd?

My heart is abiding at your door. Treat it with respect
In thanks for this, that God has kept you respected.

O Jesus-breeze, may your times always be happy,
For by your breath Háfiz's wounded soul has come alive.

---

1.   "The wine of Khizr", that is to say, the Water of Life, to which Khizr (the Green
    Man) has access. See Poem XL, note 1.

POEM XC

O Lord, devise some means whereby my friend might in safety
Come back and release me from the bondage of reproach.

Please bring the dust of the road of that journeying friend,
That I might make the world-seeing eye[1] its permanent abode.

Help! In six directions my path has been barred—
That mole, the down of the new sprung beard, the tress, the face,
 the cheek and the posture.

Today, when I am at your command, show some pity.
Tomorrow, when I have turned to dust, what use your repentant
 tears?

O you who in disquisition and explanation talk of love,
May peace and prosperity be yours,[2] I have nothing to say to you.

Dervish, do not raise a clamour because of the swords of darlings:
This tribe takes blood-money for the slain.

Set fire to the gown, because the curve of the wine-boy's eyebrow
Smashes up the niche the prayer-leader faces.

God forbid I should bewail your violence and tyranny:
The injustice of the lovely is all kindness and beneficence!

May Háfiz not cut short talk about the tip of your tresses:[3]
These chains have been linked as far as the Day of Resurrection.[4]

---

1. I.e., the eye of the poet.
2. The phrase stands for "Goodbye to you".
3. See Poem xxx, note 4.
4. Cf. Poem lxxi, verse 8.

POEM XCI

O hoopoe of the eastern breeze, I am sending you to Sheba![1]
See whence and where I am sending you!

It is a pity, a bird like you in the dustbin of sorrow.
From here to the heaven of fidelity I am sending you.

On love's route, there is no near and far stage:
I see you clearly and am sending you greeting.

Every morning and evening a caravan of good wishes
I am sending you, in the company of the northern and eastern
    breezes.

That the army of grief for you should not lay waste the kingdom
    of the heart,
For a geld my own precious soul I am sending you.

Come, wine-boy, because last night the voice of the Unseen told
    me as good news,
"Bear the pain patiently, because I am sending you medicine."

O you invisible to sight, who have become the heart's companion,
I am saying prayers for you and sending you salutation.

In your own face enjoy the handiwork of God,
For a God-revealing mirror[2] I am sending you.

That minstrels might give news of my passion for you,
A song and a lyric with instruments and voices I am sending you.

Háfiz, the chanting of our assembly is the recitation of your
    goodness.
Hurry up! A horse and robe of honour I am sending you!

---

1. Koran XXVII, 20–28: the *hudhud*, hoopoe, is sent by Solomon to the queen of
    Sabá (Sheba) with a letter.
2. "God-revealing mirror": his heart, purified so that it might reflect the Divine.

POEM XCII

O absent from view, I am entrusting you to God.
You have burnt up my life, yet with the soul I love you.

Until I trail the shroud's skirt beneath the surface of the earth,
Do not believe that I will lift my hand from your skirt.

Show the prayer-niche of your eyebrow, so that at dawn
I might perform my prayers and put my hand round your neck.

Even if it is necessary for me to go to Hárút of Babel,[1]
A hundred kinds of magic I'll perform to fetch you.

I want, O faithless physician, to die in front of you.
Ask after the sick man, because I am on the lookout for you.

I have revetted a hundred conduits of water from the eye,
In hope that I might sow the seed of love in your heart.

Háfiz, wine, dalliance with beauties, depravity are not your style;
In short, you do these things, but I take no notice of you.

---

1. Hárút is mentioned with Márút in Koran ii, 96: what actions uttered and the magic they taught the people with "what had been sent down to the two angels in Babel, Hárút and Márút", did not prevail with Solomon who refused to disbelieve. In Persian folklore (see Donaldson, op. cit., p. 81), Hárút and Márút are the two angels sent down to Earth to see whether they could resist human temptations. They were unable to do so and sinned. As a punishment they are said to have been hung head downwards in a well near Babylon, where they still are, ever ready to teach mankind sorcery.

POEM XCIII

For that heart-caressing friend I have thanks with complaint—
If you are a knower of the subtleties of love, listen closely to
    this tale.

Every service I have rendered was without reward or
    acknowledgement.
May no one, O Lord, receive service without a present!

Nobody gives the parched-lipped drunks a cup.
You'd say those who appreciate the sincere[1] have deserted this
    realm.

Although you have robbed me of my honour, I'll not turn my
    face from your door:
Oppression from the friend is pleasanter than courtesy from
    the rival.

Do not tangle with his lasso-like tresses, because there
You will see heads severed, guiltless and without crime.

Your eye with a glance drank our blood, but did you approve?
Ah my dear, for the shedder of blood no defence is permissible.

In this dark night, the way to my desire has been lost.
From a corner, O guiding star, shine out!

From every direction I went, my terror only increased.
Beware of this desert and this never-ending road!

How might an end to this road be conceived,
When it has more than a hundred thousand staging posts
    at its start?

Love might answer your cry for help if you yourself, in the style
    of Háfiz,
Recite the Koran in all the fourteen traditions of reciting.

1. The word translated, "sincere" (or "associate"), *valí*, can, besides meaning "servant", mean "someone especially favoured", as by God, i.e. a saint, but Háfiz is not arrogating saintliness to himself. What he seems really to be doing is to play on the words *valí* and *viláyat*, "realm", both derived from the same Arabic verbal root.

POEM XCIV

The breeze from the curls of your locks keeps me drunk all the
    time.
The sorcery of your magic eye destroys me from moment to
    moment.

After all this waiting, O Lord, might a night be known,
When we light the candle of seeing in the prayer-niche of your
    eyebrows?

The black disk in the eye I hold dear because
For the soul it might be a model of the image of your black mole.

If at a stroke you want forever to enhance the world,
Ask the breeze to lift the veil from your face a moment.

And if you wish to clear the mode of the world's being ephemeral,
Ruffle each hair of yours for a thousand souls to pour down.

I and the eastern breeze wretched: both in hopeless despair—
I from your eye's spell intoxicated, it, from the scent of your
    tresses—

Ah the wonderful zeal Háfiz has, that of this world and the next,
Nothing but the dust from the top of your street should reach
    his eye!

POEM XCV

Desiring the face of Farrukh,[1] my heart
Was as tangled as Farrukh's hair.

Apart from the Indian slave of his tresses, no one
Might be partaking of Farrukh's countenance:

It is the lucky black servant who always
Can be the fellow-marcher and shoulder-to-shoulder with Farrukh.

Like a trembling willow the orchard's cypress would be,
Were it to see the stature of this heart-winning Farrukh.

Give the crimson wine, wine-boy,
For a toast to the bewitching eye of Farrukh.

My body has become as curved as a bow,
With longing as unbroken as the eyebrows of Farrukh.[2]

The breeze of Tartary musk was put to shame
By this Farrukh's ambergris-scented tress.

As the heart of everyone inclines in a certain direction,
My heart's inclination is in the direction of Farrukh;

I am slave of the heart of him who, like Háfiz, is
Servitor and Indian slave-boy to Farrukh.

---

1. *Farrukh* is the rhyme word of this poem. Literally it means the fortunate or aus-
   picious or glorious, so that Háfiz could be saying "the fortunate or glorious face
   or countenance", but it is also a proper name. (It has been suggested that it was
   the name of someone by whom Háfiz was attracted. Several other suggestions
   have also been made, relating to the Prophet Muhammad and those in whom
   the world is blessed.)
2. To have eyebrows joined together was considered a mark of beauty.

POEM XCVI

Yesterday the wine-selling Elder—may his mention be good—
Said, "Drink wine and the heart's regret banish from memory."

I replied, "Wine would cast my reputation to the wind."
He answered, "Accept what has been said and let what will be be."

Profit, loss, and capital, since they'll be lost,
Say, "For the sake of this transaction, be not sorry and be not glad."

If you put your heart on trifles, you will have nothing to show,
On a stage where the throne of Solomon goes by the wind.

Háfiz, if the advice of the wise is a bore to you,
Let us cut the tale short with, "May your life be long!"

POEM XCVII

What are wine and pleasure in secret? No use at all;
We have joined the rank of the licentious and what will be, will be.

Relax the knot of the heart and ponder not on the heavens:
The mind of no geometer has undone such a knot as that.

Do not wonder at the revolution of Time, because the wheel
Has a repertoire of thousands upon thousands of tales of this sort.

Take the cup as etiquette requires[1] because its composition
Is of the dust of Jamshíd, of Bahman and Qubád[2] too.

Who knows where Káús and Kai have gone?[3]
Who's aware of how the Throne of Jam[4] went by the wind?

I still see that from his yearning for the lip of Shírín,
The tulip blossoms with the blood of the tears of Farhád.[5]

Is it that perhaps the tulip knew Time's inconstancy,
That from flowering to fading it never put the wine-bowl down?

Come, come, that a while we may be destroyed by wine;
We might perhaps in this city of ruin hit upon some treasure;

The airs of Musallá and the water of Ruknábád[6]
Do not grant me leave for travelling and wayfaring.

Like Háfiz, do not take the cup except to the twanging of the harp,
Because the happy heart has been tied to joy's silken strings.

---

1. See Edward Fitzgerald's *Rubá'iyyát* of Omar Khayyam, xxxvi:

> For I remember stopping by the way
> To watch a Potter thumping his wet clay:
> And with its all-obliterated Tongue
> It murmur'd — 'Gently, brother, gently, pray!'

2. Ancient Persian kings, legendary and historical. See also those mentioned in the following verse.

3. This verse brings to mind a quatrain, attributed to Omar Khayyam, which the traveller R. B. M. Binning found carved on a stone in the ruins of Persepolis, *A Journal of Two Years' Travel in Persia, Ceylon, etc.* (London, 1857), Vol. II, p. 20, and which Fitzgerald quoted in a letter dated 13 January 1859. The verse may be translated:

> That palace which lifted its pillars up to the wheeling dome,
> At its portal kings used to lay down their face;
> We saw that on its battlements a dove
> Was uttering the cry: "Where, where, where, where?"

The Persian word used for "where" is *kú*, hence *kú, kú, kú, kú?*, an onomatopoeia for the cooing of the dove.

4. See Poem XCVI, verse 4. Solomon and Jamshíd are often equated in Persian legend. Jam is short for Jamshíd.

5. See Poem LV, note 1.

6. See Poem III, note 3.

POEM XCVIII

Last night the wind gave news of the friend gone journeying.
I too gave my heart to the wind—whatever there might be,
    so be it.

My affair has reached such a pass that my confidants I make,
Every evening, the lightning flash, and each morning, the breeze.

In the crinkle of your forelock my unguarded heart
At no time did not say, "May the habitual abode be remembered."

Today I saw the value of the dear ones' advice.
O Lord, through You may our counsellors' soul be joyful!

Remembering you, my heart was stricken every time that in the
    meadow
The wind was tearing open the rose-bud's fastening.

My feeble life had been given up.
Come the morning, the breeze with hope of union with you life
    to me restored.

Háfiz, your right intention achieves your wish;
May souls be the sacrifice of men of good disposition!

POEM XCIX

May the day of union with friends be remembered!
May those times be remembered, be remembered.

My mouth has turned poisonous with the bitterness of sorrow.
May the wassail of the happy wine-bibbers be remembered!

Although the friends do not bother to recollect me,
On my part memories by the thousand are theirs.

I have become afflicted in these trials and tribulations;
May the attentiveness of those payers of dues be remembered!

Although continuously a hundred rivulets are in my eyes,
Still may the Zindeh Rúd and the Garden of Kárán be
    remembered.[1]

Háfiz's secret has remained unspoken after this.
O the pity! May the confidants be remembered!

---

1. The Zindeh Rúd is the river which flows through Isfahán. The Bágh-i Kárán,
    Garden of Kárán, was one of the pleasances established by the Saljúq Sultan
    Maliksháh (1072–1092) when he selected Isfahán as his capital. (See Rávandí,
    Ráhat-us-Sudúr, ed. by Muhammad Iqbal, Leiden, 1921, p. 162.) The absent
    beloved whom Háfiz is remembering appears to have left Shíráz for Isfahán.
    This poem might be an early composition related to the capture of Shíráz by the
    Muzaffarid Mubáriz al-Dín Muhammad in 1353, and the flight to Isfahán of the
    defeated ruler of Shíráz, Abú Isháq Ínjú, Háfiz's apparently much-loved early
    patron. Abú Isháq was finally executed in 1357.

POEM C

May his beauty be the sun of every sight.
Than handsomeness may his face be more handsome.

May the Humá[1] of his falcon-feathered tress
Have the hearts of the kings of the world beneath its wing.

May he who is not bound by his locks,
Like his tresses be agley and topsy-turvy.

May the heart that does not fall in love with his face,
Be forever drowned in the blood of sorrow.

O idol, when your glance scatters arrows,
May my wounded heart be the shield against them!

When your sugary ruby grants a kiss,
May the taste of my soul be filled with sugar from it.

Of you every moment I have a fresh love —
May you every moment have a new comeliness.

By his soul Háfiz is longing for your face;
May you have an eye for the state of the longing!

---

1. The Humá is the fabulous bird of good omen: kings who have been blessed by
    being under the shadow of its wing are the possessors of an auspicious royal
    grace.

POEM CI

Should the Súfí drink wine to a certain extent, may it do him good!
But if not, may forgetfulness of anxiety over this practice be his.

But he who can spare a single draught of wine,
May the hand of the desired beauty be in his grasp.

Our Elder said, "No error crept into the Pen of Creation."
May his pure, sin-disregarding eye be praised![1]

The king of Turks was listening to the word of calumniators;
May some shame be his for the wronging of Síyávush.[2]

My eye became one of the mirror-holders to his line of down and
  his mole;
May my lips be snatchers of kisses on his breast and back!

Although because of haughtiness not a word to poor me did
  he say,
May life be a sacrifice to his sugary, silent pistachio nut.[3]

His drunken, caressing, people-arresting eye,
Though in a cup it quaffs the blood of the lover, may the cup do
  him good!

Háfiz through servitude to you has become world-famous;
May your tress's slave-ring be in his ear!

---

1. Commentators have discussed this verse extensively in terms of the theologi-
    cal debate on whether or not Man has freedom of will, and, if he has, how can
    the belief in God's omnipotence (e.g. Koran xxxvii, 94: "Alláh has created you
    and that which you perform") remain unimpaired? The school named after Al-
    Ash'arí (d. 935–6) propounded a subtle compromise solution to the problem.
    God alone created all, but Man was endowed with the power to "acquire" his
    acts for himself, so that while God created both good and ill, God was above
    their actual practice. On this latter consideration seems to rest what, the sug-
    gestion might be ventured, is to be inferred from this verse of Háfiz's, the sense
    of which is Sufistic or mystical, rather than in the realm of theology (kalám).
    God and Love are above the concepts of good and evil, belief and unbelief. The

achieved mystic's immediate realization of God lifts him out of the order in which good and evil, faith and no faith, count, and this is the purport of 'Attár's story of Shaikh San'án (see Poem LXXIX, note 1), who was transported into the realm of a self-abandonment that included his leaving behind belief and disbelief, good and evil. It is a story certainly paradigmatic for Háfiz. The second hemistich of this verse alludes to the lover's "achieved mysticism" in the reference to his "pure, sin-disregarding eye".

2. Síyávush was the disaffected son of Kai Káús (see Poem XCVII, verse 5), from the effects of whose weakness and folly the champion Rustum had to rescue Iran in the face of attacks from Afrásíyáb, the king of Turán, "King of the Turks". Kai Káús listened to the calumniators of his son, who, however, exculpated himself in an ordeal of fire. He later deserted his cruel father for service with Afrásíyáb, whose daughter he married, to beget Kai Khusrau. The latter later slew Afrásíyáb in revenge for this tyrant's murder of his father, Síyávush. Háfiz was doubtless alluding to royal inability to resist the prompting of jealous slanderers against people such as an apprehensive tyrant's own sons and kinsmen, or against the poet himself. Hence the "King of the Turks" stands for Sháh Shujá' (see Poem XLVIII, note 2).

3. See Poem LVIII, note 1.

POEM CII

May your body not be in need of the physician's soothing,
Your delicate frame not be hurt by sickness.

The health of all horizons is in your well-being;
May your person not be pained by any ailment.

When Autumn's plundering comes into this meadow,
May it not find the way to the lofty erect cypress form.

In that arena where your beauty begins to reveal splendour,
May there be no scope for the pessimist's and ill-wisher's gibes.

The perfection of form and substance is from your security and
    health,
So may your outward appearance not be ravaged nor your heart
    dejected.

Everyone who looks at your moon-like face with the eye of evil,
May his eye be naught but wild rue[1] for your fire.

Seek a cure from Háfiz's sugar-scattering utterance,
That you may not have need of the rose-water and sugar-candy
    treatment.

---

1. Burnt to ward off the effects of the Evil Eye. (See Donaldson, op. cit., p. 20 and
    passim.)

POEM CIII

May your beauty be forever on the increase,
Your face every year tulip-coloured,

And in my head, may the dream of your love
Every day there is, be augmented.

May the height of all the world's heart-ravishers
In service to your stature be bent down;

Every cypress that appears in the field
Be like an "n" before the "alif"[1] of your figure.

May the eye that is not stormed by you,
Be an ocean of blood from the pearls of tears.

For the snatching of hearts may your eye
Be in the working of magic a master of skills.

Wherever there is a heart, through longing for you
May it be impatient, restless, and without peace.

May anyone who has no head for separation,
Be excluded from the circle of union with you.

Your ruby, that is the very life of Háfiz,
May it be far from the lip of all the sordid avaricious.

---

1. *Alif*, the first letter of the Arabo-Persian alphabet, shaped as "l".

POEM CIV

O Khusrau, may the ball of the firmament be in your hockey-
    stick's crook,
May the arena of the cosmos be your playing field.

The tress of the Lady of Victory is infatuated by your spear-tip's
    tassel;
May the eye of eternal victory be in love with your dashing
    manoeuvres!

O you of whose majesty Mercury's[1] composition is the description,
May the Holy Spirit be the servant of the cypher-engrosser[2] in
    your Chancellery;

Your cypress-like form became an affront to the show of the
    Túbá tree;[3]
May your portico's expanse be the envy of Eternal Paradise.

Not only animals, vegetation, minerals—
May whatever is in the world of command be at your behest.

---

1.   Mercury was the planetary patron of writers as Venus was of musicians, Mars of
    fighters, Jupiter of doctors of law.
2.   The allusion is to the engrosser of the royal seal and sign manual affixed to
    regal documents and decrees, and generally models of the art of the calligra-
    pher.
3.   See Poem LX, note 1.

POEM CV

It is a long time since the heart-holder has sent no message,
Not written a word nor sent any greeting.

I have sent a hundred letters, but that king of knights
Has dispatched no courier and sent no message;

The way of feral-like, reason-deserted me,
He has not sent a single gazelle-bounding partridge-strutting.

He knew that the bird of the heart will elude me,
Yet of that chain-like line of down no snare has he sent.

Woe that that sweet-lipped, intoxicated dispenser of wine
Knew I was hung-over, yet sent no cup!

Much as I have vaunted works of grace and stages of the Way,
No news has he sent me at all of any stage whatsoever!

Háfiz, be politely restrained because there is no calling to account,
If the Sháh has sent no word to a slave.

POEM CVI

In old age love for a youngster fell into my head,
And that mystery I had hidden in the heart tumbled out.

From the track of seeing, the bird of my heart went soaring into
    the air;
O eye, look and see into whose snare it has fallen.

O the pain, that because of that dark-eyed musky gazelle,
As in the musk bladder, so much my heart's blood has fallen into
    the spleen.

From the path of the dust of the top of your street was
Every musk pod that fell into the hand of the breeze of dawn.

As soon as your eye-lashes drew the world-conquering blade,
Many living hearts slain, upon each other fell.

Much have we experienced how in this temple of retribution,
Whoever fell out with drainers of the dregs fell down.

Even were the black stone[1] to give its life, it would not become
    a ruby:
What can it do? Given its original nature, it's turned out base.

Háfiz, whose leash was the tip of idols' locks,
It is a most novel scamp he's now taken a fancy to.

---

1.   The "black stone": having the Black Stone in the Ka'ba in Mecca in mind, the
commentator might regard this verse as unconscionably blasphemous. It is
noteworthy that commentators have tended not to draw attention to a possible
inference implied by this verse.

POEM CVII

When your face's reflection fell onto the mirror of the wine-bowl,
Because of the wine's laughter the mystic fell into raw desire.

Beneath the veil, on the Day of Eternity without Beginning your
    cheek displayed a splendour:
All these images fell onto the mirror of illusions;

All this reflection in wine and these contrasting figures that have
    appeared,
Are a single light fallen into the bowl from the wine-boy's cheek.

Love's jealousy has silenced the tongue of all the nobles,
Because of how the mystery of its sorrow fell into the commoner's
    mouth.

I did not of myself lurch out of the mosque into the wine-booth:
This fell out my allotted end from the Primeval Covenant.[1]

Since like the compass they do not swivel in the traces of the
    turnings, what are they to do
Who've fallen inside the perimeter of Time's revolving?

Beneath the sword of sorrow for him one must go dancing,
Because the end of him who has been slain for him has turned
    out good.

From the well of the chin, my heart was suspended in the curl of
    your tress.[2]
Ah that it came out of the well, but fell into the trap!

O master, the day has passed when you'll see me again in the
    cloister:
My affair has fallen in with the wine-boy's cheek and the lip of
    the bowl.[3]

Every moment for heart-burnt me He has another favour;
See this beggar, how deserving of reward he has proved!

Súfís are all of one cloth and of the roving eye, but
From their midst heart-afflicted Háfiz has turned out notorious.

---

1. See Poem XXI, note 1. This verse has been cited by certain commentators as indicative of Háfiz's predestinarianism or fatalism; but due to its complexity the matter will not here be discussed. Any asseveration on this question in the context of Háfiz ought perhaps to be regarded as dubious.
2. See Koran XII, 10, 15, and 19, for Joseph's brothers putting him in a well out of which the water-drawer of a caravan drew him. Háfiz subtly alludes to Joseph in this verse.
3. Cf. verse 5 above.

POEM CVIII

He who gave your cheek the hue of the rose and eglantine,
Might give poor me some patience and composure.

He who taught your locks contumely,[1]
His kindness might also grant desolate me redress.

I that very day gave up hope for Farhád,
When he gave the reins of a lovesick heart to the lips of Shírín.[2]

There might not be the goldsmith's stock. Contentment's corner
  remains.
He who gave that to kings, gave this to beggars.

By way of appearance, the world's a fine bride, but
Whoever linked up with her, his own life the dowry gave.

Henceforth it'll be my hand and the skirt of the cypress and the
  lip of the stream,
Especially now, when the breeze has given the good news of April.[3]

In the hands of the ordeal of wheeling Time, Háfiz's heart has
  turned to blood,
Complaining, O Khwájeh Qavám al-Dín,[4] of your countenance's
  remoteness.

---

1. Háfiz has *tatávul*, "arrogance", "insolence", "tyranny", etc., but from the Arabic
    root *tál*, *túl*, "to lengthen", "grow long"; as the commentator Súdí observes, in
    the context of locks of hair, Háfiz's choice of word is apt.
2. See Poem LV, note 1.
3. "April", *Farvardín*, the first month of the Persian solar year. The year begins at
    the spring solstice, 21/22 March. Illustrative of the continuity of imagery in
    Persian poetry is Háfiz's reminiscence here of the poet Mas'úd Sa'd, who
    died *c*.1121–22, some 268 years before the death of Háfiz. Of the month of
    Farvardín (*Díván*, ed. by Rashíd Yásamí, Tehran, 1318/1939, p. 664) he says:

    > It's Farvardín and the season of Farvardín
    > Inspires mirth and song;
    > Ah your two lips like wine give me,
    > For this is the custom of the time of Farvardín!

4. See Poem XI, note 1.

POEM CIX

The violet last night spoke to the rose and gave a delicate hint,
That, "My frizzled curls, the ringlets of so-and-so have given the
    world".

My heart was a treasury of mysteries, and the hand of Fate
Sealed its door and gave the key to the stealer of hearts.

As one broken, I came to your gate for the physician
To show to me the liniment of your kindness.

He passed by wretched me and remarked to rival suitors,
"Alas, what a soul my poor lover's given up!"

May the body be fit and heart joyful with good fortune,
Of him who has granted help to the weak, and friendship.

Go, dispense your own particular remedy, O admonisher
To whom wine and a sweetheart have been obnoxious.

POEM CX

The Humá[1] of the zenith of felicity would fall into our net,
If passing by our dwelling should you befall.

Like a bubble I would throw the cap aloft with joy,
If a reflection of your face fell into our wine-bowl.

The night when the moon of desire comes up over the horizon,
May it be that a beam of light might fall onto our roof.

When kings do not have access to kissing the dust of this door,
When might the favour of an opportunity for our salaam befall?

When life became the ransom for your lip, I conceived the notion
That a drop of its pure liquor might fall into our mouth.

The beguilement of your tresses said, "Do not make life the price:
For this, abundant prey falls into our snare".

Do not go from this door in despair. Take an omen.[2]
It may be that the lucky lot falls out in our name.

Whenever Háfiz speaks of the dust of your street,
A breeze from the rosebed of the soul wafts onto our sense
of smell.

---

1. See Poem C, note 1.
2. As people do from the *Díván-i Háfiz: sortes Háfizianae* c.f. *sortes Virgilianae*; bibliomancy. The word for "omen" in this context is *fál*.

POEM CXI

Plant the tree of friendship so that it might bear the fruit of the
    heart's desire.
Uproot the sapling of enmity that bears countless troubles.

When you're the guest in the tavern, be respectful towards the
    revellers,
Because, my dear, if drunkenness produces a hangover, you'll
    suffer a headache.

Treat the night of companionship as precious because after our
    time,
The sphere will make many a revolution, bring many nights and
    days.

The bearer of Layla's[1] palanquin, who has the cradle of the moon
    in his keeping,
O God, put it into his mind that he makes a detour in the direction
    of Majnún.

Desire, O heart, life's spring-time, but if not, every year this
    meadow
Flourishes a hundred flowers like the wild-rose, and brings a
    thousand like the nightingale.

For God's sake, as my sore heart has closed a deal with your tresses,
Command your sweet ruby to bring its state to rest.

If God wishes, it may be that the grey-haired Háfiz
Again in this garden might sit by the bank of a stream and pull a
    cypress-form to his breast.

---

1.   See Poem XLII, note 1.

POEM CXII

The person who keeps his eye on the beauty of the friend's line
    of down,
It is certain that he has the harvest of true discernment.

Like the reed upon his command's inditing, the head of obedience
We have positioned. It might be that he will have his sword
    uplifted.

A person through union with you has comprehended the candle-
    like decree,[1]
When beneath your blade he presents another head.

The person has attained the kissing of your feet when he,
Like the door-step, at this door always has the head.

I am fed-up with dry asceticism. Bring the pure wine,
That the scent of wine might keep my brain forever fresh.

Though you gain nothing from wine, is not this enough
    that for you
One moment is kept ignorant of reason's prompting?

The person who has not put a foot outside the door of piety,
Now intent on the wine-shop has a mind for travel.

The broken heart of Háfiz will take to the grave
The tulip-like brand of licentious singing he has welded on the
    heart.

---

1. "decree", "royal decree", "rescript", "writing"; Háfiz has a *jeu de mot* here. He
uses the word *parváneh* which, in addition to having the meanings listed above,
also means, "moth", especially in the context of the candle that draws the moth
to destruction. As the candle presents a new "head" every time it is snuffed, so
here the devotee has a fresh head always ready to be severed by the sword of
the beloved.

POEM CXIII

In the season of your face our heart has no time for the meadow,
Because, like the cypress, its feet are bound, and, like the tulip, it
  has a brand.

Our heart is not lowered beneath the arch of the
  eyebrows of anyone,
Because the heart of hermits has no time for the world.

A dark night, how can I accomplish the road of his tresses' twists
  and turns,
Unless the reflection of his face holds a lamp to my way?

I am vexed with the violet that boasted of its locks—
See you what airs the slave of little value has!

I and the candle burning at dawn, it is fitting that
  we weep together:
We have burned, but our idol has no time for us.

Háfiz's painful heart has a fancy for the lesson of love,
Because it has no mind for show nor longing for the garden.

Stroll in the meadow and look at the throne of the rose,
  when the tulip
Resembles the Sháh's intimate, who holds a bowl on the palm of
  the hand.

POEM CXIV

The heart that reveals the invisible and has the cup of Jam,
What worry has it over a signet ring gone missing a moment?[1]

Do not entrust the treasury of the heart to the down and moles
    of beggars:
Give to the hand of a king-like one who has respect.

Not every tree might endure the cruelty of autumn;
I am the slave of the determination of the cypress that has this
    fortitude.

That season's arrived when, for merriment like the drunken
    narcissus,
Whoever's got six dirhams puts them to service the cup.

Gold for the price of the wine like the rose do not now begrudge,
When of vices by the hundred Universal Reason holds you
    suspect.

My heart that used to boast of unattachment, now,
Because of your tresses' scent, has a hundred concerns with the
    morning breeze.

From whom might I seek the heart's desire when there is no
    sweetheart
Who has the beckoning look and the art of kindness?

No one is acquainted with the secret of the Invisible. Tell no
    moral tales –
Which initiate of the heart has access to this sacred place?

From the pocket of Háfiz's gown of patches what profit is to be
    gained
When we have sought the Most High, yet he has an idol?

---

1. The reference is to Solomon's magic ring, stolen by a devil for a while. See
    Poem XXIV, note 3.

POEM CXV

He who has got the cup in his hand,
Forever has the sovereignty of Jamshíd.

The water from which Khizr[1] found life,
Seek in the tavern, because it has the cup.

Consign the tip of life's thread to the cup,
Because this thread owes its stringing to it.

Us and the wine, and the devout and abstinence –
Let's see which the friend has a liking for.

Other than from your lip, O server of wine,
There is not in the revolving world anyone who has satisfaction.

The narcissus all the guiles of drunkenness
From your merry eye has on loan.

Memorizing your face and tress is for my heart
The litany it performs night and morning.

For the scarred breast of the pain-stricken,
Your ruby has the perfect saltiness.

In the pit of the chin, O beloved,
Your beauty has two hundred slaves like Háfiz.

---

1.   See Poem XL, note 1.

POEM CXVI

I have an idol who has a shade of hyacinth round a rose:
The Spring tide of his cheek has a line in Judas tree blood.

The dust of the line has clothed the sun of his face; O Lord,
Grant him eternity everlasting, for he has everlasting beauty.

When I was becoming a lover, I said, "I have borne off the
    sought-for pearl".
I did not know what blood-tossing waves this ocean has.

There's no snatching away the soul from your eye, because on all
    sides I see
It has made an ambush in corners and has an arrow in the bow.

Do not deprive my eye of your heart-winning cypress-form;
Seat it in this fountain-head that has sweet flowing water.

If you would fasten me onto the saddle-strap, for God's sake,
    quick, make me the quarry.
There are hardships in delay, and it is loss to the seeker.

When he shakes the snare of the tress free of the dust of the
    hearts of lovers,
To the tale-bearing wind he says, "It keeps our secret hidden".

When the rose laughs in your face, do not fall, O nightingale,
    into her trap,
For, though she holds the world's loveliness awhile, the rose is
    not reliable.

Save me from fear of separation if you've the hope
That God may keep you in safety from ill-wishers' evil eye.

Sprinkle a draught on the dust and inquire of the state of the
    mighty,
Because it has many a tale of Jamshíd and Kai Khusrau.

For God's sake, O governor of the gathering, extort my due from
    him,
Because he's drunk wine with others and is bored with me.

What excuse can I utter for my luck when that city-disrupting
    elusive rover
Has murdered Háfiz with bitterness, yet has sugar in the mouth?

POEM CXVII

Everyone who has a collected heart and an obliging friend,
Bliss has become his companion and he has luck going his way.

The sanctuary of love has a portal far more lofty than reason.
The person may kiss that threshold who wears his life on his
    sleeve.

Is it that your sweet small mouth is the seal of Solomon,
That the design of its ruby signet keeps the world in thrall to a
    ring?

The ruby lip and dusky line, how has he this and not that?
I revel in my heart-snatcher, because his beauty has that and this!

While you are on the surface take advantage of power to act:
Those with none have ages enough beneath the sod.

Do not you, the affluent, look with contempt on the weak and
    the lean:
The chief seat in the assembly of esteem the roadside beggar has.

The heart and soul's evading of calamity is the prayer of the
    wretched;
Who sees good from the harvest who is ashamed of the gleaner?

Convey a sign, breeze, of my love to that king of beauties,
Who holds a hundred Jamshíds and Kai Khusraus the meanest
    of slaves.

If he responds, "I do not want a lover stony-broke like Háfiz",
Tell him that dominion and beggary go together.[1]

---

1.   An allusion to kingship's requiring the collection of revenue for State purpos-
es, but also, in Súfí terms, to the fact that the beggar who is deprived of all
earthly attachment enjoys the "dominion" of association with the Divine. Cf.
the sixth verse of this poem. Háfiz exemplifies how he can be interpreted in
both spiritual and mundane terms.

POEM CXVIII

Whoever keeps an eye on the purlieus of the people of fidelity,
May God in every state preserve him from disaster.

If you entertain the desire that the beloved should not break the
　　pact,
Keep hold of the end of the thread, so that he'll be observant.

I'll not tell the tale of the friend's pain except to the friend,
Because the friend respects the word of one known.

My head, my gold, my heart and soul, the offering for that beloved,
Because he esteems dues of association and bond-keeping.

If, breeze, you find my heart in that tress-tip,
Out of kindness tell it to stand fast.

O heart, live in such a way that, if the foot slips,
The angel might uphold you with both hands in prayer.

He has not regarded our heart and has no time for suffering;
What arises from the hand of the slave, God perceives.

Where is the dust of your path, for Háfiz
To keep as a memento of the dawn breeze?

POEM CXIX

Love's minstrel has a wonderful song and tune;
The theme of every chord he's struck finds a home.

May the world never be empty of lovers' wailing,
For it has a secret note and a joy-imparting echo.

Our dreg-draining Elder, though he lacks gold and power,
Has a happy knack of goodly bounty and overlooking sin.

Hold my heart in respect: this sugar-worshipping fly,
Once it started flying after you, has the glory of the Humá.[1]

It would not be far from justice if a king who has
A beggar as a neighbour, were to ask how he was!

I showed bloodied tears to the doctors. They said,
"It is the pain of love, but it has a medicine: the burning of the
    heart".

Do not from the fetching glance learn tyranny, because in love's
    religion,
Every action has a price and every deed, its retribution.

That Christian, wine-worshipping child idol put it well:
"Partake of the gladness of the face of one who possesses purity".

O Khusrau, Háfiz, the sitter at the door, has recited the Fátiha,[2]
But from your tongue craves a prayer.

---

1. See Poem C, note 1.
2. See Poem LXXXV, note 1.

POEM CXX

He of whose hyacinth ringlets a pot-pouri might writhe in envy,
Again has flirting and peevishness for the lost of heart.

From the head of his own slain, he passes swiftly like the wind.
What can be done? He is life and in a hurry!

From behind the veil of the tress his sun-revealing moon
Is a sun that has a cloud in front.

If the Water of Life is that which the lip of the friend has,
This is clear, the portion Khizr[1] has is a mirage.

My eyes have set up a flowing torrent of tears in every corner,
So that your erect cypress may with water be kept fresh.

Your saucy ogling inadvertently sheds my blood.
May it take its chance, because this judgement has a point;

Your drunken eye, on account of my heart, is after the vitals:
The Turk is drunk. No doubt he fancies a kebab.

The boldness of questioning you is not for my ailing soul;
Ah, fortunate is the wounded who gets an answer from the friend!

When might be offered a glance at Háfiz's wounded heart
By your drunken eye, that has a ruin in every corner?

---

1.   See Poem XL, note 1.

POEM CXXI

He's no beauty who has hair and a waist:
Be in thrall to the appearance of him who has that something
    special.[1]

The style of the houri and of the peri is nice and elegant, but
Loveliness and elegance are not what so-and-so has.

Seek out, O laughing rose, the fountain of my eye;
In hope of you, it has a full flowing stream.

The curve of your eyebrow, in the art of shooting arrows
Disarms all those who have a bow.

Who snatches the ball of beauty from you, when in this, the sun
Is not a rider that has the reins in his control?

Agreeable to the heart my speech became as soon as you accepted
    it –
Ah yes, yes, the speech of love has a distinctive mark.

In the path of love no one with certainty has become privy to the
    mystery:
Everyone has a notion according to the understanding.

With the haunters of taverns, do not boast of grace-conferred
    powers:
Every issue has a time and every subtlety a place.

The wise bird doesn't go into the meadow trilling its notes aloud
Every spring that has an autumn in tow.

Tell the disputant, "Do not sell Háfiz conceits and pithy sayings".
Our reed too has a certain perspicuity, and a tongue.

---

1.   "that something special", *ání*: in his edition of Rúmí's *Díván-i Kabír*, in the glos-
    sary of rare terms *Kulliyát-i Shams yá Díván-i Kabír* (Tehran, 1345/1966–7) vol. v,
    pp. 185–6. Furúzánfar says that in the Súfí context the word *án*, "that", alludes

to a state that is "not utterable, but understandable: a beauty... that cannot be defined, but can be perceptible to the inner sense of comprehension (*zauq*)". From the *Díván* among examples which he cites are:

> That one who has no sign of you,
> Though he were the sun, would not have that something,

And,

> On all sides there is a beauty:
> Súfí, look to see which has that something special.

And,

> O a royal eye and lamp –
> By God, for God's sake how have you that something special?

And also quoted may be the poet Saná'í (d. 1130-1):

> Than Joseph more sweet because in beauty
> You have that something special, but Joseph has it not.

See Khurramsháhí: *Háfiz-Náma* (Tehran, 1987) vol. 1, p. 510.

POEM CXXII

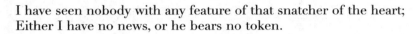

The soul lacking the beauty of the beloved has no fondness for
    the world,
And that person who has not that, in reality has no soul.

I have seen nobody with any feature of that snatcher of the heart;
Either I have no news, or he bears no token.

In this path every drop of dew is a hundred blazing oceans.
O the torment that this conundrum defies description and
    elucidation!

There is no giving up the station of contentment:
O camel-driver, alight, because this road has no limit.

Without the friend life has not all that much relish,
Such that in the friend's absence, life has no delight.

The crooked-shaped harp summons you to pleasure:
Listen, because there's no harm for you in old men's counsel.

What happened to the treasure of Korah,[1] that Time cast to the
    wind,
Repeat to the rose-bud so that she will not keep gold hidden.

Nobody in the world has a single slave like Háfiz,
Because no one in the world has a king like you.

---

1.   See Poem v, note 3.

POEM CXXIII

The moon has not the brightness of your face.
Before you, the rose has the not the lustre of grass.

The corner of your eyebrow is my soul's abode;
The Pádsháh has no privacy more pleasant than this.

I looked, but that black hearted eye you possess
Spared not a glance in any acquaintance's direction.

Give me, O disciple of the wine-shop, a hefty bumper,
A Shaikhly merriment the dervish-hostelry lacks.

So, what has the smoke of my heart to do with your cheek?
Do you know a mirror that can put up with a mist of sighs?

Swallow sorrow's bitterness and hold your peace, because that
    tender heart
Cannot stand cries for help from those who seek justice.

Not I alone suffer the tyranny of your tress;
Who is there who does not bear this black one's[1] brand?

See the cheekiness of the narcissus that's broken into flower in
    front of you;
The shameless eye observes no etiquette.

Say, "Go and wash your sleeves in the blood of your heart,
Whoever has no access to this threshold".

If Háfiz has prostrated himself to you, find no fault;
The infidel of love, O idol, commits no crime.

---

1. The allusion is to a black slave, placed, as they often were, in positions of high
    authority by masters who trusted them more than they could their freedmen.

POEM CXXIV

There is no beauty in the town who steals our heart:
If luck befriends me, it'll take my chattels away from here.

Where is an amiable, drunken comrade, to whose kindness
The heart-scorched lover might pronounce the name of desiring?

O keeper of the garden, I find you unaware of autumn;
Alas for that day when the wind blows your gorgeous rose away!

Time's highwayman has not dropped off to sleep. Do not feel
    safe from him:
If he's not got you today, he will carry you off tomorrow.

In the imagination I am playing all these games by way of fantasy –
It could be that a perceptive master might find them worthy of
    interest.

The learning and accomplishment that in forty years I have gathered,
I fear that that Turkish narcissus will snatch as plunder.

The lowing of a calf, what sound does it emit? Don't be taken in:
Who is Sámirí[1] that he should prevail against the White Hand?[2]

The multi-hued crystal bowl of wine bars the way of the heart's
    straitening;
Do not let go of it lest the torrent of sorrow carry you away.

Although the Way of Love is the place for bowmen's ambush,
Whoever proceeds with his wits about him will outstrip enemies.

Háfiz, if the drunken glance of the friend seeks life,
Clear the house of all else and leave it for him to take.

---

1.   The allusion is to Koran xx, 90, where the people of Israel are described as having
    been tempted in Moses's absence by the calf which Sámirí produced and which
    lowed, and which he told them was their and Moses's god (see Deuteronomy ix, 9,
    Hosea viii, 5,6).
2.   Koran xx, 23, in which God commands Moses to press his hand to his side
    whereupon it will turn out white, as one of the signs which God conferred on
    Moses as His servant.

POEM CXXV

If no wine clears the heart's grief from our memory,
The terror of what might happen will wrench up our foundations.

If in drunkenness reason doesn't drop the anchor,
How will it carry the ship through this maelstrom of calamity?

Alas that the Firmament played with everyone by hidden proxy,[1]
So that there is nobody who gets the upper hand over this deceit!

The passage is through the realms of darkness.[2] Where is a Khizr
    for the way?
Let it not be that the burning of deprivation[3] steals our honour.

The feeble heart for this draws me towards the meadow,
That through the fitful weakness[4] of the breeze of morning, it
    may snatch the soul from death.

I am love's physician. Drink wine, because this electuary
Produces forgetfulness of care and erases wrong suspicion.

Háfiz was burning and nobody reported his condition to the
    friend.
Perhaps, for God's sake, the gentle gale will take a message?

---

1. The allusion is to a partner in chess being prompted by a hidden accomplice
   so that he is able to checkmate his opponent.
2. Where the spring of the Water of Life is situated, and to which only Khizr
   knows the way. (When composing this poem, Háfiz seems to have had in mind
   Koran XVIII, 59-81).
3. Deprivation of the Water of Life.
4. Arab and Persian poets likened the fitfulness of the morning breeze to the
   weakness and restlessness of the sick, but Háfiz is making this "sick" breeze the
   attendant on his sick heart.

POEM CXXVI

At dawn the nightingale related to the breeze,
"What things love of the face of the rose has done to us!"

It blew away the rose's veiling and hyacinth tresses:
Undid the fastening of the bud's leafy mantle.

In all directions, the lover-nightingale in lamentation;
In the midst, the morning breeze having a good time.

Through the colour of that cheek, it has cast sorrow into my heart,
And because of this rose garden, has afflicted me with thorns.

May that morning breeze be pleasant to him
Who has physicked the pain of vigil-keepers!

I will not ever complain against strangers:
Whatever it did to me the known one did.

If I entertained hope of the Sultan, it was a mistake.
And if I sought constancy from the sweetheart, it was cruelty he
    committed.

I am the slave of the resolution of that gracious one
Who did good works with no dissembling or hypocrisy.

From the notables of the city, fidelity to me
The Perfection of Grace and Faith,[1] Abú'l-Vafá kept.

Take the good news to the wine-sellers' quarter,
That Háfiz has repented of false asceticism.

---

1. "The Perfection of Grace and Faith", but here these words translate the name,
    Kamál u'd-Dín Bú'l-Vafá, Perfection of Faith, Father of Fidelity. This was the
    name and titles of a saintly man of Shíráz in the time of Háfiz. His shrine is
    situated on the northwestern edge of the city. Little is known about him except
    that he was a Sayyid, a descendant of the family of the Prophet, and was deeply
    revered by the poet. See Mu'ín, *Háfiz-i Shírín Sukhan* (Tehran 1370/1990–1) Vol. 1,
    pp. 289 and 405.

POEM CXXVII

Come because the Turk of the firmament has overturned the
    table of the Fast:[1]
The new moon of the Festival has signalled circulation of the bowl.

That one has carried off the reward for abstinence and the valid
    pilgrimage,
Who made the visitation at the door of the wine-shop of love.

Our proper dwelling is the nook in the tavern.
May God bestow blessings on him who made this habitation.

In the arch of those prayer-niche resembling eyebrows,
He offers prayers who has made his ablutions in the blood of the
    heart.

What is the price of ruby-like wine? The jewel of reason.
Come, because he who has made this transaction has creamed
    off the profit.

The pity that the furtive eye of the city Shaikh today
Has looked upon the dregs-drainers with contempt!

Hear the news of love from Háfiz, not from the preacher,
However much art in rhetoric he has deployed.

---

1.   See Poem xxv, note 1 and/or Poem lxvii, note 3.

POEM CXXVIII

In the luminous liquid of wine the mystic made ablution
In the morning, when he made a visitation[1] to the wine-shop.

As soon as the sun's golden bowl became hidden,
The new moon of the festival of the Fast's end urged circulating
    the cup.

O happy the prayer and petition of the person who out of pain
Has made his ritual cleansing in tears and the blood of the heart!

Look upon the face of the friend with a recognitive eye,
That has performed the function of seeing with insight.[2]

My heart with his tresses' curl bought tumult at the price of the
    soul;
I do not know what profit he saw who made this bargain.

If Friday's Imám issues the bidding today,[3]
Give notification that Háfiz has made his ablutions in wine.

---

1. As in verse 2 of the preceding poem, "visitation", translates *ziyárat*, "visit",
    used in the sense of a visitation of a shrine or sanctified place.
2. An allusion to the *'árif*, translated "mystic", in the first hemistich of verse 1
    above. It also means "gnostic".
3. Friday is the Muslim Sabbath when the faithful are enjoined to attend the
    congregational mosque in which the local imám leads the prayers.

POEM CXXIX

The Súfí laid a snare and took to playing tricks –
Laid the foundations of deceit against the guileful Firmament!

The sphere's ball smashed the egg he'd got up his sleeve,
Because he tried sleight of hand on people in the know.

Come, wine-boy, because the Súfí's lovely darling
Has come again in splendour and started flirting.

Where is this minstrel from, who has struck up the 'Iráqian mode,
But made the return in the tune of Hejáz?[1]

Come, O heart, that we may take refuge in God
From that which the short in the sleeve but long in the arm has
    done.[2]

Use no artfulness, because whoever's unchastely played at love,
Love has shut the door of true meaning in the his heart's face.

Tomorrow, when the Court of the Truth is opened,
The wayfarer will be ashamed who has practised profanity.

O nicely-strutting partridge, where are you off to? Halt.
Don't be taken in because the ascetic's cat has prayed.[3]

Háfiz, do not castigate reprobates, because in Eternity without
    Beginning
God created us without the need of the affectations of asceticism.

---

1. Two modes of music, that of 'Iráq and of Hejáz, are being alluded to, in the con-
   text of the playing of cunning tricks, those of the false ascetic, who might reside
   in west-central Iran, the area called 'Iráq with Isfahán, Rayy, Hamadán, and
   Qazvín as its principal cities, but who as a religious man, would constantly have
   his eyes set on the Hejáz, and the Holy City of Mecca. The terms, 'Iráq and
   Hejáz, refer to musical modes here, but are also susceptible to being read in
   their primary geographical meaning. (Cf. Khurramsháhí, op. cit., pp. 545-47).
2. "Short in the sleeve" means the Súfí whose woollen gown had short sleeves.

"Long in the arm", the same, but a Súfí of a rapacious, intrusive and oppressive demeanour – the fraudulent Súfí mentioned in the first verse of the poem as the layer out of snares.

3. The historian Khwándamír in his work *Habíb'al-Siyar* (see the edition published in Tehran in 1333/1954-5, vol. III, p. 315), a work written some 132 years after Háfiz's death, has an allusion to this verse. Khwándamír says that at the court of Sháh Shujá' there was a certain 'Imádu'd-Dín Faqíh (d. 1371-2). 'Imádu'd-Dín Faqíh was a jurist, but also the head of a Súfí *khángáh*, a Súfí hospice, and was renowned for his holiness. He was a panegyrist of the Muzaffarid rulers of Shíráz, who, like himself, hailed from Kirmán. His poetry was of no mean order and quite voluminous. But Háfiz probably saw him not so much as a rival in the composition of verses, in, incidentally, a style not dissimilar to Háfiz's own, but as sufficiently in the good graces of Sháh Shujá' for Háfiz to wish to warn his patron against a charlatan, rather than simply to excoriate a literary competitor. Khwándamír recounts how, to impress the ruler with his powers as a miracle-monger, 'Imádu'd-Dín taught his cat to imitate him in performing the postures of prayer. As, however, Sháh Shujá' appears to be the model for the strutting, over-confident partridge, it seems clear, as the late Mujtabá Mínuví suggested, that Háfiz had in mind a story in *Kalíla o Dimna*, known also as "Bidpay's Fables", an ancient collection of moral tales. The apposite story here is that of the partridge and the hare. The hare expropriates the (presumably chukar) partridge's nest in the ground. When the partridge returns from a period of absence and asserts his claim to his abode, the hare pleads squatter's rights. Hearing of an extremely pious, fast-keeping, prayerful cat, they go to him as one most likely to be a just arbitrater. The cat assumes a high and sanctimonious moral tone. He exhorts the two litigants to draw closer, and he preaches a homily, on the evil of material attachments, in the style of a mullah. He so fascinates the hare and the partridge that spell-bound by his sermonizing, they go nearer and nearer to him and are put off their guard. Then, he suddenly pounces, grabs them both, and slays them. See Mínuví, editor, *Kalíla wa Dimna* (Tehran 1343/1964-5) pp. 406-408, and p. 408, footnote 7, where the learned editor points out that Háfiz's verse about the praying cat "is apparently related to this story".

POEM CXXX

The nightingale drank sorrow's blood, but gained a rose.
The wind of envy splintered his heart with a thousand thorns.[1]

The parrot in the thought of a morsel of sugar had a gladsome
    heart.
Suddenly the torrent of annihilation made the image of hope void.

The light of my eye, that fruit of the heart, may he be
    remembered,
That himself passed easily away, but made my life hard.

Camel-driver, my load has slipped off. Some help, for God's sake;
The hope of a helping hand made me this camel-litter's travelling
    companion.

Do not hold in contempt my dust-spattered face and the dew of
    my eye;
The turquoise wheel has built a pleasure dome out of this dust
    and straw.

Sighs and cries that, because of the jealous eye of the sphere's
    moon,
In the tomb, the moon of the bow of my eyebrow has taken up
    his abode.

You did not castle and the chance has passed, Háfiz.
What can I do? Time's play made me inattentive.

---

1. This poem is reputed to be Háfiz's elegy (*marthíya*) on the death of his infant
   son. The nightingale (*bulbul*), the bird of song, is of course the poet, as is the
   parrot (*túti*) of the next verse.

POEM CXXXI

Like the breeze I shall set out for the top of the street of the friend.
I will make the breath musk-raining with his sweet odour.

All the esteem that through learning and religion I have gathered,
I will make the sprinkling on the dust of this idol's path.

Without wine and the beloved, life is frittered away in trifles.
Enough of my sloth! From today I will work.

Where is the breeze, because this life, blood-clotted like the rose,[1]
I would make a sacrifice to the perfume of the friend's curls.

At the time of dawn, as with the candle, it became clear to me
    that for love of him
I shall spend life in devotion to this affair;

With the memory of your eye I shall destroy myself;
I will confirm the foundation of the Ancient Covenant.[2]

Hypocrisy and pseudo-abstinence do not, Háfiz, bestow purity of
    heart:
I shall choose the way of debauchery and of love.

---

1. Besides being an allusion to the red rose in full bloom and ready to drop, there
   is a veiled reference here to Koran xcvi, 1–2:

   > Recite in the name of thy Lord who created,
   > Created man from clotted blood.

2. See Poem xx, note 4.

POEM CXXXII

He stole my heart, but hid the face from me.
For God's sake, with whom can this game be played?

At dawn my loneliness was bent on slaying the soul,
Imagining him perform kindnesses that had no limit.

Why should I not be of a heart like the blood-coloured tulip,
When his narcissus-eye has disdained me?

How can I say that, in spite of this soul-burning pain,
The physician intended taking my feeble life?

He made me burn like a candle so that for me,
The flagon wept and the lute lamented.

Breeze, if you've a remedy, now is the time,
Because the torment of longing has attempted my life.

Among the kind, how can it be told,
That my friend spoke like this, but acted like that?

An enemy would not have done that to the life of Háfiz,
Which the arrow of that eyebrow bow has done.

POEM CXXXIII

There can be no reaching into that bent tress's ringlet:
No relying on your promise and the eastern breeze![1]

What effort there is, in seeking you I make it;
This is the decree to which there can be no changing of fate.

Through a hundred harrowings of the heart the skirt of the friend
    came within reach.
For all the spite the enemy tries, there can be no letting go.

His cheek cannot be compared to the moon in the sky:
There can be no relating the friend to anything headless and
    footless.

The moment my tall cypress embarks on the self-ridding song
    and dance,[2]
What rating the coating of the soul which cannot be torn apart?

The problem of love is not within the compass of our knowledge:
There can be no solving this subtlety with this flawed thinking.

What can I say when you have the winningness of a disposition
To such a degree susceptible[3] that there can be no praying gentle
    enough?

The pure vision can see the cheek of the beloved:
Other than with polished purity, in the mirror there can be no
    seeing.

Envy has slain me because you are the beloved of the world, but
There can be no quarrelling night and day with the creatures of
    God.

Apart from your eyebrow there is no prayer-niche for the heart
    of Háfiz;
In our rite there can be no devotion to other than you.

1. The true Súfí belief is that any spiritual attainment must be God-given: it cannot be due to the volition of the *sálik*, the wayfarer.

2. The Súfí *samá'*, literally "audition", "hearing", by extension means the gathering in which the seeker loses consciousness of the self by hearing or himself chanting *zikrs*, prayers, songs, and in some circumstances, by dancing; hence the "Whirling Dervishes".

3. "susceptible" used here to translate the word *latíf*, "delicate", "gentle", etc., and one of the names of God.

POEM CXXXIV

Did you see, O heart, what love's sorrow has done once more,
When the heart-snatcher departed, and what he did to the faithful
    friend?

O what a game that magic-working narcissus spurred on!
Alas for what that wanton drunkard has done to sober men!

Because of the friend's unkindness, my tears took the hue of
    sunset's glow.
See what in this affair merciless destiny has dealt!

At dawn a lightning flash from Layla's abode streaked out.
Woe for what it did to the harvest of Majnún of the wounded
    heart.[1]

O wine-giver, pour me a bowl of wine, for it will not be known
What mysteries the hidden artist has limned behind the veil.

No one knew what he who cast this azure circle full of images
In the twirling of the compass accomplished.

Thought of love the fire of grief in Háfiz's heart was kindling –
See you what the lover of old did to the friend!

---

1.   For Layla and Majnún see Poem XLI, note 2.

POEM CXXXV

Friends, the daughter of the vine has repented of being veiled:
She went to the magistrate and got the business licensed.

She's come from behind the curtain into the assembly. Cleanse
    her of the sweat of shame,
So that she'll tell comrades why she kept her distance.

It is fitting that she be caught in the knot of union –
Such a drunken girl as this, who went in for all that bashful veiling.

Give the reward, O heart, for the good news, that again love's
    minstrel
Has struck the inebriate note and fixed the remedy for the
    drunkard's aching head.

If my nature's rose has blossomed, no wonder that because of
    her fragrant bouquet,
The night-singing bird's warbled joy for the petal of the red rose.

Not with the prescribed seven dippings[1] nor in a hundred fires
    will the stain go
That the wine of the grapevine has dropped on the ascetic's gown.

Háfiz, do not lose humility, as the envious
Did house and home, wealth, heart and religion, out of the
    prompting of pride.

---

1. Under the rules of the Sháfi' School of Law, articles that have become ritually
   impure, *najis*, must be dowsed in clean water seven times.

POEM CXXXVI

Years the heart was seeking Jamshíd's cup from us:
That which it itself possessed, it was desiring of a stranger.

A pearl that is outside the shell of time and place,
From the lost in the ocean main it was seeking.

Last night I took my problem to the Elder of the Magians,
Because with the help of vision he was for solving the riddle.

I found him smiling and heart-elated, wine-cup in the hand,
In that mirror, enjoying a hundred varieties of spectacle.

I asked, "When did the All-Wise give you this world-seeing cup?"
He replied, "The day He was fashioning this azure dome".

He said, "That comrade because of whom the gallows became
    exalted,
His crime was this, that he was divulging the mysteries.[1]

If again the Angel Gabriel's divine grace from God were to deign
    help,
Others might do that which the Messiah was doing."[2]

I asked, "What are the chain-like tresses of idols for?"
He replied, "Háfiz has been complaining because of a heart dis-
    tracted."[3]

---

1. He who by being executed hallowed the gallows was Mansúr al-Halláj, the great
    mystic who in 922 AD in Baghdad was hung, drawn, and quartered, and worse,
    allegedly for having declared *ana'l-Haqq*, "I am God". Reference should be
    made to the article *Al-Halláj* in (*Encyclopedia of Islam*).
2. A paraphrase to reflect the inference that Gabriel's communication of God's
    Revelation, the Koran, to Muhammad is being alluded to in this hemistich.
3. A disturbed heart for the concentrating of which the tresses of the beloved
    ones are intended.

POEM CXXXVII

You can contemplate the secret of the cup of Jamshíd the time
When you're able to make the wine-shop's dust collyrium for
   the eye.

Do not be without wine and minstrel because, beneath the arch
   of heaven,
With this song you can rid the heart of sorrow.

The rose of your desire that time lifts the veil
When, like the breeze of the morning, you can salute her.

In setting out for the staging-post of love, put a foot forward:
You might make gains if you can make this journey.

Come, because the remedy of tasting the Presence[1] and composing
   affairs
You can make with the grace-bestowing of the visionary.

The beauty of the beloved has neither veil nor curtain, but
Lay you the dust so that you can see—

You who do not make an exit from the mansion of nature,[2]
How can you make your way up the street of the Way?

Mendicancy within the tavern is a marvellous elixir—
If you try this, you can turn dust into gold!

O heart, if you gain consciousness of the light of discipline,[3]
Like a candle, with a laughing tongue you can forfeit the head,

But so long as it is the darling's lips and the wine-bowl you're after,
Do not expect that you can achieve anything other.

If, Háfiz, you heed this royal advice,
You will be able to travel on the highway of true realization.[4]

1. See Poem I, note 4, and the Prophet's dictum, *hadíth*, "There is no prayer except with the presence of the heart". (this verse harks back to the third verse.)
2. God is always to be realized if we know how to realize Him. (See also Poem CCLX, verse 9.)
3. *riyázat*, the discipline whereby the adept may free himself of carnal sin and bodily desires. See *Kashfu'l-Mahjúb*, op. cit. in R. A. Nicholson's translation, pp. 196, 202.
4. *haqíqat*, the True, the way to which is *taríqat*, translated in verse 7 above, "the Way". In this poem, Háfiz employs both these Súfí technical terms. For *haqíqat*, "man's dwelling in the place of Union with God...", see *Kashfu'l-Mahjúb*, op. cit., pp. 384,383. *Taríqat*, the way; *haqíqat*, the reality.

POEM CXXXVIII

May he be remembered who when travelling did not remember us:
Who did not gladden our grief-stricken heart with a word of
    farewell.

That one of promising fortune who would dash off rescripts of
    benevolence and approval,
I do not understand for what reason he did not release the old
    slave from bondage.

The petitioner's paper shirt[1] let us wash in tears of blood, because
    the Firmament
Has not offered me guidance to the foot of the flag of justice.

The heart, in the hope that an echo might perhaps penetrate as
    far as you,
Raised lamentations in these mountainous places that Farhád did
    not raise.

From the time you withdrew your shadow from the meadow, the
    bird of the dawn
Has not made its nest in the fold of the box tree's curl.

It would be fitting if the messenger breeze learnt its business
    from you,
For the reason that no wind has moved quicker than this.

The decker-out of creation's pen will record no gratification
For any who have not acknowledged this God-given beauty.

O minstrel, turn the key and strike the Hejáz mode,[2]
For by this route the friend went and did not remember us.

The ghazals of 'Iráqí[3] are the song of Háfiz –
Who has heard this heart-kindling mode and not cried out?

The petitioner's paper shirt[1] let us wash in tears of blood, because the Firmament
Has not offered me guidance to the foot of the flag of justice.

The heart, in the hope that an echo might perhaps penetrate as far as you,
Raised lamentations in these mountainous places that Farhád did not raise.

From the time you withdrew your shadow from the meadow, the bird of the dawn
Has not made its nest in the fold of the box tree's curl.

It would be fitting if the messenger breeze learnt its business from you,
For the reason that no wind has moved quicker than this.

The decker-out of creation's pen will record no gratification
For any who have not acknowledged this God-given beauty.

O minstrel, turn the key and strike the Hejáz mode,[2]
For by this route the friend went and did not remember us.

The ghazals of 'Iráqí[3] are the song of Háfiz –
Who has heard this heart-kindling mode and not cried out?

188

1. It was customary for those seeking redress or mercy from rulers, to present themselves clad in a paper shirt.
2. It appears that the friend went on the Pilgrimage to Mecca. For "Hejáz mode" see Poem CXXIX, note 1.
3. This is a significant reference to a great exemplar of the mysticism of love expressed in both verse and prose: Fakhru'd-Dín 'Iráqí (d. 1289), an obvious paradigm for Háfiz, both for his exquisitely "heart-enrapturing" poetry expressive of love, and for the concept that "in every beautiful face or object, a reflection, as in a mirror, of the Eternal Beauty" may be seen. See E. G. Browne, *Literary History of Persia* (Cambridge 1928) vol. III, p. 124, where the words in quotation marks above occur, and the *Encyclopedia of Islam*, article *'Iráki*; Cf. the end of the dialogue between Socrates and Diotima in Plato's *Symposium*.

POEM CXXXIX

I laid my face on his path, but he did not pass my way.
I expected a hundred kindnesses. He never spared a glance.

Our flood of tears did not wash away the rancour from his heart –
The rain-drop made no impression on hard stone.

Preserve, O Lord, this brave youth,
Because he has taken no precaution against the arrows of the
    solitary.

Last night neither fish nor fowl slept on account of my laments,
But look at that cheeky-eyed who never raised his head from sleep!

I was ready to go out like a candle at his feet.
Not like the morning breeze did he ever blow by us.

O soul, who is the dull of heart and the inept,
Who against the striking of your sword has not made life the
    shield?

The reed of Háfiz's sharp tongue, in the assembly
So long as its nib was not pared away, told your secret to no one.

POEM CXL

The heart-stealer went and did not tell the heart-lost,
Did not remember either the town comrade or the travelling
   companion.

Either my luck has quit the path of gallantry,
Or he did not pass along the high road of the Way:

I standing, to make my life, like a candle, a sacrifice to him,
He, like the morning breeze, did not pass by us.

I said, "Perhaps I may soften his heart by weeping".
On the form of rock, a drop of rain left no impression.

Although because of yearning the wings and feathers of my heart
   were broken,
It did not rid its head of the frenzy of a lover's trap.

Everyone who saw your face, kissed my eye:[1]
What our eye did, it did not do without expectation.

---

1.   As a mark of favour.

POEM CXLI

I do not know what the drunkenness is that has waylaid us –
Who was the wine-server, and whence did he bring this wine?

What mode is this well-versed minstrel striking,
Who in a song's midst introduces word of the friend?[1]

You too get hold of wine and take off into the wilderness,[2]
Because the melodious singing-bird has brought music of a
    happy note.

May the coming of the rose and eglantine be auspicious and glad;
The violet has come joyous and pretty. The jasmine's added
    brightenness.

With good news the breeze is Solomon's hoopoe,
That brought tidings of joy from Sheba.

O heart, do not like a rose-bud complain of business unresolved:
The morning airs have brought a knot-loosening breeze.

The treatment for our heart's debility is the wine-boy's inviting
    look;
Lift up your head, because the doctor has come, and brought the
    medicine.[3]

I am the disciple of the Magian Guide. Do not, O Shaikh, rail at
    me.
Why? Because you gave a promise, but he fulfilled it!

I preen myself on the narrow eyes of that soldierly Turk,
Who assaulted me, a dervish with only a single cloak.

The Firmament performs Háfiz's service with obedience now,
Because he has taken refuge at the door of your good fortune.

1. Poetry was used frequently, especially in Háfiz's time when princes like Sháh Shujá' resorted to it for this purpose, as a cypher in which to convey messages, while diplomatic exchanges in verse were also a feature of the time.
2. Cf. Omar Khayyam in Fitzgerald's translation, quatrain XII,

> A Book of Verses underneath the Bough,
> A Jug of Wine, a Loaf of Bread – and Thou
> Beside me singing in the Wilderness –
> O, Wilderness were Paradise enow.

3. The wine of Paradise.

At dawn-time the breeze was bringing a scent from the tresses of
the friend.
It was setting my crazy heart beating afresh.

I uprooted that pine-shape from the garden of the breast,
Because every rose that out of sorrow for it blossomed, was
bringing affliction.

In dread of his love's devastation, I let go the heart in blood,
But it was spilling blood and attracting notice to this proceeding.

From his palace roof I was seeing clearly the splendour of the
moon,
Out of shame at which the sun was hiding its face in despair.[1]

In season and out, from the voice of minstrel and wine-boy I
went outside,
Because by that tedious road the courier with difficulty might be
bringing some news.

The bounty of the beloved was entirely the way of kindness and
benevolence,
Whether he was handling Muslim prayer-beads or bringing the
pagan's girdle.[2]

Last night I was marvelling at Háfiz,
But I didn't argue: it was as a Súfí that he was bringing the cup
and bowl.

God forgive his eyebrow's frown, although it has disabled me
With a glance that was also bringing a message to the sick man's
head.

---

1. The idiom is *rú bedívár ávardan*, literally, "to bring the face to the wall" or "turn
   the face to the wall", in other words, to be confused or in despair, to give up hope.
2. The *zonnar*, the girdle worn by Zoroastrians and used by them in praying, and,
   as a distinguishing mark, by Christians and Jews. Háfiz is saying that the char-
   ity of the beloved is above any specific religious allegiance; above belief and
   disbelief. (See next verse).

POEM CXLIII

Last night the postman breeze informed me
That the time of affliction and grief was heading for curtailment.

Let us yield the minstrels of the morning a garb rent with joy
At this happy news that the dawn wind has brought.

By courtesy of the friend, let us be off to Shíráz.
Splendid, the companion for the road that luck has brought!

Come, come, because Rizván[1] has brought you, a houri of
    Paradise,
Into this world for the sake of the heart of a slave.

Strive to piece our heart together, because this felt cap[2]
Has brought many a battering to kingly crowns.

What wailings ascended to the halo of the moon from my heart
When it revived memories of that down-haloed moon's cheek!

The standard of Mansúr[3] was lifted to the heavens, Háfiz,
When he took refuge on the side of the King of Kings.

---

1. See Poem L, note I.
2. The "felt cap", as worn by Turks, probably alludes to Sháh Shujá'. See the next note.
3. Háfiz puns on the name "Mansúr", and the epithet "mansúr", which means
   "conquering" or "victorious". He is praising Mansúr, a prince who was always a
   favourite with Háfiz, for having joined his uncle Sháh Shujá', with a contingent
   of the tribes whom he had brought to order in the region south of Kirmán and
   who provided the reinforcement that Sháh Shujá' needed to regain Shíráz
   from his brother, Mahmúd. Mahmúd had usurped the sovereignty of Shíráz
   and ousted Sháh Shujá' in 1364. It took Sháh Shujá' until 1366 to regain his
   capital after an exile of two perilous years which ended with his making
   Kirmán his base. News of Mansúr's decision to join his uncle and pave the way
   for the latter's triumphant return to Shíráz is celebrated in this poem, as com-
   mentators have recognized from early times. See Qásim Ghaní (*Táríkh-i 'Asr-i
   Háfiz*, Tehran) 1321/1942, p. 229.

POEM CXLIV

When my friend takes the wine-cup in hand,
The market of the idols is bankrupted.

I have fallen abjectly at his feet.
May it be that he lifts me up.

Like a fish I am fallen into the sea,
That the friend might hook me.

Everyone who saw his eye said,
"Where's the policeman to arrest the drunk?"

Happy the heart of him who, like Háfiz,
Takes a bowl of the wine of the First Covenant![1]

---

1.   See Poem xx, note 4.

POEM CXLV

No other rite does my heart accept but love of moon-faced ones.
By every opening do I render it observance, but it doesn't work.

For God's sake, exhorter, tell the tale of the wine-boy's line of down,
For no image more fetching than this grips our imagination!

Secretly I'm carrying off a cup of clear wine, but people think it
    a book!
Marvellous if the fire of this hypocrisy were to take hold of the
    book!

One day I want to burn this parti-coloured patched gown
That the Elder of the vintners won't take for a cup.

It is for this reason that the comrades have pure delights with
    the wine of your ruby,
That apart from truthfulness in this jewel no picture is reflected.

The heart of the admonisher of the licentious, who is at war with
    the pre-ordained,
I see very straitened. Perhaps he doesn't take to the cup?

In the midst of weeping I am laughing, because, like the candle,
    in this gathering
Mine is the fiery tongue, but it doesn't have any effect.

One day, Alexander-like, I take that mirror[1] in hand
Whether for a while this fire takes effect or whether it does not.

How well you have made my heart a prey! I'm proud of your
    drunken eye,
Because nobody more successfully than this lures wild birds into
    the net.

The theme is our need and the beloved's disdain –
What use, O heart, incantation when on the heart-ravisher it
    won't work?
O benefactor, for the Lord's sake, show a little compassion,

because the dervish on your street
Knows no other door, follows no other path!

With this fresh, sweet poetry I wonder at the Sháhansháh,
As to why he doesn't cover Háfiz from head to foot in gold.

---

1. Alexander's world-seeing mirror is here used as a metaphor for the all-seeing wine-bowl. See Poem v, note 2

POEM CXLVI

If a wine-boy in this manner were to pitch wine into the bowl,
He would plunge all the mystically knowing into perpetual
    drinking.

And if he placed the tress's curve over the grain of a mole,
Ah, many the wise bird would he plunge into the snare!

O happy the state of that drunkard who at the feet of the darling,
Doesn't know, of the head or the turban, which he is throwing
    away.

By day, strive in the acquisition of virtue, because wine-drinking
    by day casts
The mirror-like heart into the tarnishing of darkness –

That time is the moment for morning-bright wine when night
Throws the veil of evening round the pavilion of the horizon.

The raw ascetic who disallows wine
Gets cooked when on wine unadulterated he casts an eye.

Do not, Háfiz, swig wine with the city policeman:
He drinks your wine, but throws stones at the cup.

POEM CXLVII

A moment spent in sorrow isn't worth the whole world.
Sell our gown for wine, because it's worth no better than this;

In the wine-sellers' street, they won't take it for a single cup!
What, a prayer-mat of piety that isn't worth a glass of wine!

My watchful rival took to reviling me saying, "Turn the face away
 from this door".
What's gone wrong with this head of yours, that it doesn't merit
 the doorway's dust?

The glory of a Sultan's crown, in which fear of life is contained,
Is an alluring head-gear, but not worth losing the head.

In hope of profit, toiling in the sea sounded very easy at first.
I was wrong. This flood is not worth a hundred pearls.

For you this were better, that from those full of longing you keep
 your face hidden,
Because the joy of world-conquering is not worth the trouble of
 an army.

Like Háfiz, strive for contentment and let the base world go by:
One grain of obligation to the despicable isn't worth a hundred
 tons of gold.

POEM CXLVIII

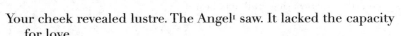

In Eternity before Time, the light of your beauty boasted of the
   glorious epiphany;
Love appeared and set the whole world on fire.

Your cheek revealed lustre. The Angel[1] saw. It lacked the capacity
   for love.
Out of jealousy of this, it turned into a fountain of fire and struck
   Adam.

Reason was wishing to light a lamp from this flame.
The lightning of jealousy shot forth and smote the world into
   confusion.

The Adversary[2] wanted to reach where the mystery might be
   observed.
The Invisible Hand came and smote the breast of the one
   excluded from the secret.

Others cast the lot of fate on living the good life;
It was our sorrow-witnessing heart that drew the lot of yearning;[3]

The high-aspiring soul possessed the desire for the dimple in
   your chin.
It struck out the hand into the ring of those curls of enmeshed
   tresses.

Háfiz wrote the song-book of your love that day
When the pen cancelled out the encumbrances of a cheery heart.

---

1. i.e. the angel: the angels lacked the capacity to love which was granted Adam,
    but see the following note for the reference, and verse 5 for further elucidation
    of this point.
2. "adversary", *Iblís*, "Satan": in the context of this verse reference should be
    made to the *Mirsád al-'Ibád* of Najm Rází, op. cit., text chapter ii of the fourth
    section, and especially pp. 77-78, translation, Second Part, Fourth Chapter, and
    especially pp. 103-104. In the *Mirsád*, in the context of the angels' surprise that
    God paid Adam, a creature of clay, greater respect than He accorded them,

Iblís penetrated Adam's body in search of the secret treasure, the jewel of love, which God had deposited in Adam's heart, after He had dismissed the angels and given Himself privacy in which to fashion Adam's heart as the chamber for this gift. Iblís could find no way into Adam's heart and returned from his quest disappointed and as if "rejected". (See also Poem CLXXIX, note 1.)

3. The reference is to the angels and, see Koran XXXIII, 72, "the heavens and the Earth and the mountains" to which God "offered the trust" which man alone bore, the others having refused to bear it.

POEM CXLIX

At dawn when the Khusrau of the East planted his flag on the
hills,
With the hand of compassion my friend knocked on the door of
the hopeful.

When before morning the state of the wheeling heavens' love
became clear,
He rose. He shot a taunting laugh at the complacents' pride.

When last night my idol got up with the intention of dancing,
He unknotted his locks and struck the beloved ones' hearts.

I in the blood of the heart that moment washed my hands of
righteousness
When his wine-measuring eye threw out the invitation to the
sober.

What iron heart taught him this ordinance of deceit,
That from the moment he emerged, he waylaid the vigil-keepers
of the night?

My forlorn heart conceived a fancy for a cavalier, but suddenly
he went.
O Lord, preserve it because it has set itself on the centre of the
squadron.

For the lustre and colour of his cheek, what a grief we've
swallowed and soul surrendered;
When his picture was first vouchsafed, it expunged the life-
resigners.

How might woollen gown clad I lasso his haughtiness,
A whisp of hair that with dagger darting skill his eye-lashes have
pierced?

The eye is on the dice of Divine Guidance and the auspicious-
ness of the fortune of the Sháh:

Grant gratification to the heart of Háfiz who has struck the omen
   of the lucky.

The King of Kings, with the victorious aura the brave of the
   Kingdom and the Faith, Mansúr,[1]
Whose unstinted generosity has mocked the clouds of spring,

From that moment when the wine-bowl was honoured by his
   touch,
Fate the cup of happiness quaffed to the toast to wine drinkers!

From his head-scattering sword victory gleamed that day
When, like the star-erasing sun, he alone struck at the legions.

Long life for him and for the kingdom ask, O heart, of the grace
   of God,
When the wheel has struck this coin of fortune in the circling of
   time.

---

1.   See Poem CXLIII, note 3.

POEM CL

Strike up a tune in harmony with which a sigh can be drawn.
Recite a verse to which a bumper of wine can be drained.

If on the threshold of the beloved the head can be laid,
The hymn of exaltation might strike the heavens.

Pliable our bent stature seems to you, but
Arrows can be shot at the eyes of foes from this bent bow.

The secrets of love-play are not confined to the dervish hospice:
The cup of Magian wine can be drunk with Magians,[1] too.

The dervish mayn't have the delicacies of the Sultan's palace;
It is a case of us and a worn-out gown from which a fire might
    be lit.

People of insight play both worlds on the chance of a look:
It is love, and the first move can be made with the soul as the
    counter.

If fortune wished to open a door to union with him,
In the hope of this, heads can be thrown on the doorstep.

Love and youth and raffishness are the sum-total of desire;
When spiritual truth's subtleties have all been gathered together,
    the ball of explanation can be struck!

Your tress has become safety's waylayer and in this there's no
    surprise:
If the highwayman be you, a hundred caravans can be waylaid.

Háfiz, by the truth of the Koran, may you come out of fraud and
    hypocrisy,
It could be that the ball of some pleasure in this world might be
    struck.

---

1.   i.e. non-Muslims; by "dervish hospice", *khángáh*, the Muslim Súfi House or
     hospice is, of course, meant.

POEM CLI

If I go after him, he kicks up a tremendous fuss,
But if I retire from the chase, he rises in high dudgeon.

And if out of desiring, like dust under his feet,
At a passing-place I fall down a moment, he's off like the wind!

And if I seek half a kiss, a hundred derisions
From the crucible of his mouth like sugar he pours out.

That deception I see in your eye
Has reduced many a reputation to the level of dust on the road.

The steeps and slopes of the desert of love are calamity's snare;
Where is the lion-heart that is not wary of the ordeal?

Ask you for a long life and patience, because the juggling sphere
A thousand games more novel than this conjures up.

Place your head, Háfiz, on the threshold of submission,
Because if you kick over the traces, Fate will kick back.

POEM CLII

No one outreaches our friend in beauty of disposition and fidelity;
Contradicting us in this matter is not for you.

Although beauty-purveyors have come showing off their wares,
No one in beauty and the salt of elegance rivals our friend.

By right of old association I swear no secret-sharer
Comes up to our unwavering, favour-requiting friend.

They might bring to the market of the Cosmos coins by the
    thousand;
Not one will come up to the coin of our Master of Assay.[1]

A thousand images issue from the reed of the Creator, but
Not one equals the heart-pleasing of our idol's image.

Alas for the caravan of protection that departed in such a way[2]
That its dust does not reach the air of the places of our abiding.

O heart be not hurt by the scorn of the envious, but be confident,
Because no evil may assail our hopeful heart.

So live that, were you to become the dust of the road, to nobody
The dust of vexation would arise through our passing by.

Háfiz burned, but I fear the elucidation[3] of his story
May not reach the ear of our august sovereign.

---

1. See Poem xi, note 1. Qavámu'd-Dín Muhammad ibn 'Alí was the Chief Assayer to Sháh Shujá'.
2. Possibly a reference to the precipitous departure from Shíráz of Sháh Shujá'.in 1364. See Poem cxliii, note 3.
3. This poem bears the stamp of a message of loyalty to the absent sovereign. The apology for its being, as it were, in code, comes in the penultimate verse, about so conducting oneself as not to raise suspicion. Even so, there is the fear that the message might not reach the ear of the Sháh. The word in this verse translated, "elucidation" is in the text as edited by Dr Khánlarí *sharh*. In a copy of Háfiz's poems from a manuscript dating 846/1442–3 AD, some 53 or 54 years after Háfiz's death, the word is *shawq*, "passion", "craving", which seems to fit the context better than "elucidation". Dr Khánlarí's text, however, is based on the authority of earlier MSS.

POEM CLIII

Whoever might have a mind to be aroused by your fresh down,
May not put a foot outside the border so long as he exists.

If I were to rise from the dust of the grave, like the tulip
The brand of passion for you would be the secret of my heart's
    core.

Where are you yourself, O peerless pearl, now
That in longing for you the eyes of men should all be sea?

From the root of every eye-lash of mine water is flowing. Come,
If you've a fancy for the brink of a stream and a spectacle.

Like my heart, step outside the veil a moment and come in,
Because another time no meeting might be offered.

May the extended curve of your tress be across my head,
Because beneath this shadow might be the steadying of a crazy
    heart.[1]

Out of haughtiness your eye does not turn towards Háfiz. Yes,
Arrogance is the property of the wanton narcissus.

---

1. See Poem 1, note 3.

POEM CLIV

I and denial of wine? What story is this?
Am I likely to have this amount of reason and self-sufficiency?

I, who night after night with harp and drum have robbed the
    Way of piety,
At this moment take the straight and narrow? What a story this
    would be!

If the ascetic doesn't take the road to debauchery, he is forgiven:
Love is a matter conditional upon guidance.

I am the slave of the Magian Elder, who saves me from spiritual
    ignorance:
Whatever our Elder does is the essence of holiness.

Until the end I was not aware of the Way of the wine-shop,
Otherwise our abstinence would not have lasted so long.

The ascetic – self regard and prayer, and I – drunkenness and
    supplication:
Well now, which of the two would you be disposed to favour?

Last night I could not sleep because of this torment that a sage
    might have said,
"If Háfiz were to be drunk there would be grounds for complaint!"

POEM CLV

The Súfí's coin isn't all purity unalloyed.
Ah, there's many a gown fit for the flames!

Our Súfí, who would be drunk on the morning litany,
Observe him in the evening when he's tipsy!

It would be good if the touchstone of the assay came into action,
For the faces of all who contain adulteration would be black with
    shame.

The daintily nurtured rich do not take the road to the friend;
Being a lover is the way of long-suffering outcasts.

How long must you suffer the grief of the base world? Ask for
    wine.
It would be a pity that the heart of the sage should be confused.

If the wine-boy's sprouting beard paints a picture like this on
    water,[1]
O many a face will be rouged with tears of blood!

The wine-seller will get Háfiz's prayer mat and gown,
If the wine be from the hand of that moon-like wine-boy.

---

1.   The allusion is to the reflection of the wine-boy's sprouting beard in the water.
    But in Persian the expression, "pictures on water", is also an idiom implying
    "evanescence", "futility". The wine-boy's sprouting beard, of course, will not
    last long. Hence the *double entendre*.

POEM CLVI

The retreat's fine if the friend is my companion.
May I not burn, but he may be the candle to the crowd!

Not for anything would I take Solomon's ring,
Which from time to time falls into the hand of Ahriman.[1]

God forbid that in the sacred enclosure of union,
The rival should be the intimate and my share invalid!

Tell the auspicious Humá[2] never to cast the shadow of glory
Over that country where the parrot is less than the kite!

What need of explaining passion when the ecstasy of the fire of
    the heart
Can be perceived through the ardour that is in the words?

Desire for your street never leaves the head. Yes,
The stranger keeps his wandering heart for his native land.

If, like the lily, Háfiz were to become of ten tongues,
Like the rose-bud, before you there'd be a seal over his mouth.

---

1. Ahriman, the Zoroastrian principle of evil: Satan. Solomon's ring was captured
    by a devil. See Poem XXIV, note 3.
2. See Poem C, note 1.

POEM CLVII

When might happy verse arouse the heart that's sad?
We recited one subtlety from this notebook and this is it.

From your ruby, if I found a protective ring,
A hundred realms of Solomon would be under my signet.

O heart, it is not necessary to be grieved by the scoffing of the
    envious.
Perhaps, when you look carefully, your good may be in it.

Whoever does not fathom this imagination-stirring pen,
Even if he were a Chinese-picture maker may his images be taboo.

The bowl of wine and soreness of heart, each were given someone:
In the circle of destiny this is how things are.

In the matter of rose-water and the rose, the decree of Eternity
    before Time was this,
That this one should be the adored of the marketplace, and that
    one kept in the cupboard.

It is not that for Háfiz being a rake has departed from the mind:
What has gone before will be until the Last Day.

POEM CLVIII

Happy has come the rose, and nothing is happier than this,
That in your hand there should be nothing but the cup.

Discover the time of the heart's cheer and understand
That not always might there be a pearl inside the shell.

Seize the moment and drink wine in the rose's garden:
In a week the rose will be no more.

O you, filling the cup full of ruby,
Grant a share to the one who has no gold.

Come, Shaikh, and in our wine-booth
Taste a wine that's not in the Sacred Pond of Paradise.[1]

Wash the pages clean if you're our classmate,
Because the science of love is in no text-book.

Listen to me and bind the heart to a beloved
Whose beauty is not decked out with jewels.

Give me wine that has no hangover, O Lord,
From which there is no head-ache at all.

The person finds fault with Háfiz's verse
Who in his nature completely lacks any kindly grace.

I by my life am the slave of Sultan Uvais,[2]
Although he doesn't remember his servant,

With his world-adorning crown, that the sun
As a diadem is not so becoming.

---

1. The Sacred Pond, *kawthar*, literally, "abundance", but also the name of the
    sacred pond in Paradise, whence in afterlife the righteous may drink of Divine
    Grace. See Koran cviii, 1, "Verily, We have given thee abundance", i.e. grace

abounding. *Kawthar* is "the inexhaustible fountain of Divine grace". See Nicholson, *Commentary on the Masnaví* (op. cit.) p. 170, on the verse in the *Masnaví*, Book I, 2734. It is this verse which Háfiz, with his reference to the pearl in the second verse of his poem, might have had in mind. In the *Masnaví* the context is that of the precious pearl of Gnosis, *ma'rifat*.

What indeed is it? It is the pearl of the Water of Kawthar,
A drop from which is the origin of the pearl.

Háfiz, however, turns the matter on its head. (It was believed that pearls were formed in the oyster shell from rain-drops secreted in the shell).

2. Sultan Uvais the Jaláyirid ruler of Mesopotamia and Ázarbáiján from 1356 to 1374 AD, was the patron of the poet Salmán-i Sávají (b. *c.*1300, d. 1376), Háfiz's contemporary at a Court to which Háfiz himself sometimes looked for favours. The two poets were evidently fully aware of each other's work. Some of Sávají's lyrics have been included by copyists in the works of Háfiz. (Cf. Poem XLII, note 2.)

POEM CLIX

The rose without the face of the friend is no good.
Without wine, the spring is no good.

The side of the meadow and walking round the garden
Without the tulip-cheek are no good.

The dancing of the cypress and the ecstasy of the rose
Without a note of the thousand[1] are no good.

To be with the sugar-lipped, well-proportioned friend
Without a kiss and a cuddle is no good.

The garden of the rose and wine is fine, but
Without the company of the friend it's no good.

Every picture the hand of reason makes,
Excepting the picture of the idol, is no good.

Life is base coin, Háfiz:
For festive confetti it's no good.

---

1. The nightingale: the thousand-noted.

The breath of the easterly breeze will be musk-scattering.
The world grown old will again be young.

The red of the Judas tree will give the jasmine a carnelian cup.
The eye of the narcissus will be looking at the anenome.

That mortification the nightingale has endured in separation's
    grief,
Will be raising a cry as far as the pavilion of the rose.

Do not find fault if from mosque to tavern I have gone:
The sermon's congregation sits long, but time will not wait.

O heart, if the pleasure of today you put off till tomorrow,
Who will be surety for the cash for the wager on lasting that long?

In the eighth month[1] do not let go the cup, because this sun
Will go out of sight until the eve of the fast-breaking feast.

The rose is precious. Count its company a boon,
Because by this way it came to the garden and by that it will go.

O minstrel, it is the gathering of intimacy. Recite a lyric and sing
    a song.
How much more will you be saying, "Like that it went and like
    this it shall be"?

For your sake, Háfiz, it moved towards existence's clime.
Be on your marks for its farewell: it'll be going.

---

1.   See Poem XLVII, note 3. The eighth month of the Muslim lunar calendar,
    Sha'bán, immediately preceeds the month of fasting, *Ramazán*.

POEM CLXI

For me, love of the dark-eyed won't go out of my head.
Heaven's decree is this and it won't be otherwise.

The rival uttered reproaches and left no room for peace;
But won't the sighs of those who rise at dawn go up to the
  circling dome?

The day of Eternity before Time nothing but licentiousness was
  decreed for me.
Every lot that on that day befell will be no more than this.

For God's sake, forgive us, magistrate, for the noise of drum
  and fife:
The harmony of the Religious Law through this incantation
  won't acquire dissonance.

Ruby wine, a place of safety, the wine-boy a kind friend:
O heart, when will your affair go better if not now?

Let my opportunity be just for this, that in secret I might practise
  his love;
Of his kissing and embrace and enclosing arms, what might I say
  when it will never be?

O eye, do not wash the image of yearning off the tablet of
  Háfiz's breast.
It is the sword-blow of the holder of hearts, and the blood-stains
  will not go away.

POEM CLXII

"The day of separation and the night of being divided from the
    friend are over" –
I took this omen and the star passed, and the trial was over.

All that loveliness and opulence autumn was deigning to show
Will at the spring breeze's coming in the end be gone.

Thank God that by the good fortune of the exaltation of the rose,
The presumption of December's wind and the prick of the thorn
    are gone.

Ask the morning of hope, that has become the devotee of the
    Invisible's veil,
To come forth, because the struggle of the dark night is over:

Those long nights of distraction due to the yearning of the heart,
In the shadow of the idol's locks have all gone.

Because of the inconstancy of the times, still I cannot believe
That by the friend's felicity the tale of woe has been ended.

O wine-boy, you have shown kindness! May your cup be full of
    wine,
Because through your good management, the hangover's
    discomfort has gone.

Although no one includes Háfiz in the reckoning,
Thanks that those unbounded and uncountable agonies have at
    last gone.

POEM CLXIII

A star shone out and became the moon of the assembly,
For our afflicted heart became the friend and solace.

My idol,[1] who went to no school and could not write a line,
With a glance became the preceptor of a hundred professors.

In hope of him, lovers' sick hearts, like the breeze,
Have become the sacrifice of the wild rose's cheek and narcis-
    sus's eye.

Now the friend seats me in the chief seat of the inn – [2]
Behold the town beggar become the prince of the party!

Love's mansion of joy now becomes restored,
Since the arch of the friend's eyebrow has become its architect.

For God's sake, wipe clean the lips of the drippings of wine,
Because my conscience has become a whisperer to itself of a
    thousand sins.[3]

Your look has measured out such a wine to mystics,
That learning has nothing to impart and reason's become bereft
    of sense.

Friends, from the way to the wine-booth turn the rein:
Why? Because Háfiz went this way and ended without a penny!

He fancied the Water of Khizr[4] and the cup of Kai Khusrau,
And became a wine-bibber of Sultán Abu'l-Faváris's.[5]

My verse is like the precious gold of existence, yes,
This copper's alchemy has become acceptable to the mighty.

---

1. i.e. the Prophet Muhammad, who was said to be unlettered.
2. Cf. *Masnaví*, op. cit., Book i, ll. 2796–7:

I came to this door the petitioner for goods.
The chief seat was mine as soon as I entered the vestibule.
I brought water as a gift for the sake of bread.
Hope of bread brought me to the chief seat in Paradise.

3. See Koran L, 15.

We have created man, and We know what his soul whispers
within him, for We are nearer to him than his jugular vein.

Also, chapter CXIV:

1. Say "I take refuge with the Lord of the people,
2. The King of the people,
3. The God of the people,
4. From the evil of the whispering, the lurking,
5. Which whispers in the breasts of the people,
6. Of jinn and men".

For Satan's whispered temptations to Adam see VII, 19 and XX, 118.
4.   The Water of Life, see Poem XL, note 1.
5.   Sháh Shujá'. See Poem XXX, note 7.

I see no friendship in anyone. What's become of friends?
When did friendship come to an end? What's happened to
    friends?

The Water of Life's become black in colour. Where is Khizr[1] of
    the auspicious foot?
The rose has changed from its own hue. What's become of the
    breeze of spring?

Nobody avows that comradeship owes the due of friendship.
What condition has befallen acknowledgers of dues? What's
    come over comrades?

This land was "the city of friends" and "the dust of the kindly".
When did kindness come to an end? What's happened to the
    city of friends?

It's years since any ruby has come out of the mine of bounty:
What has happened to the heat of the sun, the exertion of the
    wind and the rain?[2]

The ball of good luck and of magnanimity has been thrown into
    the midst.
Nobody enters the field. What's become of the mounted hockey
    players?

A hundred thousand roses have bloomed, but the song of no
    bird has arisen.
What has hindered the nightingales? What's befallen the
    thousand-noted?

Venus[3] strikes up no sweet melody. Is it that she's burnt her
    lute?
Nobody has enthusiasm for getting drunk. What's become of the
    topers?

No one knows the Divine Mysteries; Háfiz, be silent.
Of whom do you enquire, "What has happened to the wheeling
   of Time?"

---

1. Khizr, the "Green Man", from beneath whose feet verdant plants sprang.
2. Háfiz is here alluding to the popular belief that minerals were fashioned by the
    effects of the sun, wind, and rain.
3. See Poem iv, note 2.

POEM CLXV

Háfiz the recluse last night went to the wine-shop:
From thought of the pledge he went to contemplating the cup.

The adored of the time of youth had come to him in a dream.
With an old man's grey head, again he became a lover and mad.

The love-crazed Súfí who yesterday smashed the bowl and the cup,
Soon with one gulp of wine turned sensible and wise.

The Magian boy, highway robber of religion and the heart, went by.
In pursuit of that friend, he became a stranger to all else.

The fire of the rose's cheek burnt up the harvest of the nightingale.
The laughing face of the candle became the moth's catastrophe.

The weeping of morn and evening—thanks be that it never
    diminished—
A drop of our rain, into a pearl of the first water turned.[1]

The narcissus of the wine-boy chanted a spell-binding verse:
The circle of our prayer recitals became a congregation for
    incantations.

Háfiz's resting place is now the Court of the Emperor:
The heart went to the heart-keeper. The soul came to the beloved.

---

1. See the end of Poem CLVIII, note 1.

POEM CLXVI

The soul melted that the heart's affair might be ended. It wasn't.
We were scorched in this foolish desire, but it didn't come about.

Alas, that in seeking the remittance slip on the treasure of my
  desire,
I became a wreck in the world through utter longing, yet it didn't
  come about.

Pain and woe that in search of the boon of the Presence,[1]
So much did I in begging haunt the noble, but it wasn't
  vouchsafed.

In jest he said, "One night I'll be your gathering's chief."[2]
In my enthusiasm I became his humble slave, but he didn't come.

He sent a message that, "I'll join in with the sots."
Notoriety for sottishness and draining the dregs was mine, but
  he didn't come.

In the lust that in drunkenness I might kiss that ruby lip,
What blood poured into my heart as if it were a cup, but nothing
  happened.

In the street of love do not put a foot without a guide for the way:[3]
I on my own have made a hundred attempts, but to no avail.

Out of slyness Háfiz has put up a thousand artifices
In longing for that idol to be tamed, but he wasn't.

---

1. See Poem 1, note 4. The word *huzúr* can be taken to mean "the union of heart".
2. Or, "In jest one night he said..."
3. The necessity of having a guide, the *pír*, is an axiom in Sufism. Cf. Poem CLIV, third and fourth verses.

POEM CLXVII

Last night from His Excellency the Ásaf[1] came the bearer of the
  good news,
That from Solomon's Majesty the signal for merriment's come.

Make the dust of our being cement with the moisture of wine:
The time for repairing the dereliction of the mansion of the
  heart has come.

Hide my fault. You of the wine-stained gown, be on your guard,
Because he of the unsullied robe has come on a visitation here.

This endless exposition they've given of the beauty of the friend
Is one word out of thousands that have been expressed.

Today the status of every one of the fair becomes obvious
Since that assembly-lighting moon has assumed precedence:

On Jamshíd's throne, the crown of which is the ladder of the sun,
See the holy recognition when, in its insignificance, an ant
  appeared.[2]

Preserve your faith, O heart, from his mischievous eye,
Because this bow-drawing sorcery, bent on plundering has
  come.[3]

Let one defiled like Háfiz ask for grace from the king,
Because that element of beneficence for the purpose of ritual
  cleansing has come;

His assembly is an ocean. Go, find, seize the moment.
Make haste, O long-sufferer. The time for a deal has come!

---

1. Solomon's legendary minister, but here probably Muhammad Qavám'ud-Dín,
    minister to Sháh Shujá'. See Poem xi, note 1, and Poem clii, note 1.
2. The allusion to Ásaf and Solomon in the first verse is here revived. The ant saw
    the host of Solomon and warned the other ants to go into their holes in order
    not to be crushed. At this Solomon was pleased and, to which the poet alludes
    in "the holy recognition", thanked God for the good He had bestowed upon
    him. See Koran xxvii, 18–19.
3. The eye-lashes are the arrows.

POEM CLXVIII

Love of you became the root of bewilderment:[1]
Union with you became absolute bewilderment.

Many are they drowned in the state of union
Whose heads in the end also encountered confusion.

Neither union is left nor the uniter
Then, when the mind to confusion has been reduced.

Show a single heart of which, in the path of Him,
The mole[2] of bewilderment has not appeared on the cheek.

On every side that I bent my ear to,
Came the sound of perturbation's questioning.

From head to foot the being of Háfiz
In love became the sapling of bewilderment.

---

1. "bewilderment", *hairat*, which is a Súfí term for the bewilderment of the
    devout who contemplate the various manifestations of the beauty and majesty
    of the Divine, which are beyond comprehensibility in the light of reason. See
    Masnaví, op. cit., Book 1, lines 311–12:

    Who might describe the action of Him Who has no like?
    *   *   *
    Sometimes it appears like this and sometimes its opposite:
    The business of religion is nothing but bewilderment.

2. See Poem III, note 1.

POEM CLXIX

In prayer the curve of your eyebrow came to my memory:
A state occurred such that the prayer-niche came to protesting.

Of me now expect neither patience nor heart nor sense,
Because that endurance which you saw has gone by the wind.

The wine became clear and the birds of the field, drunk:
The season of falling in love and affairs well entrained has come:

I sense the fragrance of well-being from the conditions of the
     world;
The rose has brought gladness, and the morning breeze joyfully
     has come.

O bride of virtue, do not rail against luck;
Adorn beauty's bridal chamber: the bridegroom has come.

Heart-beguiling plants have all clasped on jewels
Since our heart-stealer with God-given beauty has come.

Trees that have attachment labour beneath a burden.
O happy the cypress that free of the burden of sorrow has come!

Sing, minstrel, an intoxicating lyric from the compositions of Háfiz,
That I may weep, that of the time of happiness memories have
     come.

POEM CLXX

Good news, O heart, that the morning breeze has come back.
The hoopoe[1] of happy tidings, from Sheba's side has come back.

O bird of the dawn draw out the Davidian song again,
Because the Solomon rose from the breeze of the air has come
    back.[2]

The tulip breathed the bouquet of fine wine in the breath of
    dawn.
It was heart-branded. In the hope of physick, it came back.

Where is the gnostic who might understand the lily's tongue,
That he might ask why it went and why, came back?

Courtesy and kindness God-given luck showed to me
When that stony-hearted idol to the way of fidelity returned.

My eye awaited expectantly that caravan out on the road,
Until in the ear of my heart the sound of the bell reverberated.[3]

Although Háfiz knocked at the door of estrangement and he
    broke his word,
See his grace that in peace he to our door has returned!

---

1. Cf. Poem XCI, note 1.
2. An allusion to King Solomon's riding the wind.
3. An unforgettable sound is that of the bells hanging from the necks of the
    camels and causing the deep-noted reverberation which from afar heralds the
    approach of a caravan.

POEM CLXXI

The morning breeze with felicitations for the wine-selling Elder
　　has come,
That the season of delight and enjoyment and flirting and
　　sweetness has come.

The air has turned into the breath of the Messiah, and the dust,
　　musk-letting.
The tree has turned green and the bird turned to warbling.

The breeze of spring has so lit the oven of the tulip,
That the rose-bud has become drowned in sweat and the rose
　　come on heat.

Hear me with the ear of sense and make pleasure your purpose,
Because from the voice of the Invisible this dawn this mandate
　　came to my ear.

I do not understand what the noble lily's ear heard
From the morning bird, that with all its ten tongues silent it
　　became.

Come out of distracting thoughts, so that you become concentrated,
By dint of this that, when Satan went, the Archangel came.

What place is the intimate gathering for the company of the
　　uninitiated?
Cover the cup, because the gownsman has come.

Háfiz is off to the wine-shop from the Súfí hospice:
Maybe he has come to his senses from the intoxication of
　　pseudo-asceticism.

POEM CLXXII

At dawn wide-awake luck came to my pillow.
It said, "Get up, because that sweet Khusrau has come.

Drain a cup and with mellow head stride out to look,
To see with what rites your idol has come."

O musk-pod-opening recluse, spread the good news
That from the desert of Khotan the musk-producing gazelle has
    come.

Weeping has brought back lustre to the cheeks of the scorched
    ones:
Lamentation became the lowly lover's rescuer.

The bird of the heart flutters again with desire for an eyebrow;
O pigeon, watch out! The royal falcon's come.

Give wine, wine-boy, and don't worry about friend and foe,
Because, to the gratification of my heart, this has gone and that,
    come.

When the clouds of spring saw the rule of the bad faith of the
    times,
Its tears fell on the jasmine and hyacinth and wild rose.

When the morning breeze heard the utterance of Háfiz from the
    nightingale,
Ambergris-scattering to the sweet-basil's display it came.

POEM CLXXIII

O you whose pistachio's[1] laughed at talk of candy,
I am full of longing. For goodness' sake, offer just one sugared
    laugh.

You want no tide of blood to well up from your eye?
Don't attach the heart to fidelity in the company of people's
    children.

The Túbá tree[2] cannot boast of your stature;
I'll leave this story, because the telling would spread aloft!

If you display contumely or if you utter gibes,
We are not believers in self-regarding folk.

Of the turmoil of our condition, when will that one be informed
Whose heart has never been caught in this lasso?

The market of passion has become brisk. Where's that candle-form,
For me to make my soul wild rue[3] strewn on the fire of his face?

Háfiz, if you will not abandon the ogling of Turks,
Do you know where your place is? Khwárazm or Khojand?[4]

---

1. See Poem LVIII, note 1: the allusion is to the smallness of the beauty's mouth.
2. See Poem LX, note 1.
3. See Poem CII, note 1.
4. Places in Central Asia, whence Turkish slaves and soldiers were imported into
    the lands of the Eastern Caliphate.

POEM CLXXIV

Not everyone who rouges the cheek knows what it is to be a
    heart-ravisher.
Not everyone who fashions a mirror knows what it is to be an
    Alexander.[1]

Not everyone who put his cap at an angle and impetuously
    mounted
Understands the wearing of the crown and the requirements of
    chieftainship.

Like beggars, do not you practise slavery conditioned by the hire:
The friend of his own accord knows the way of nurturing slaves.

Keeping your word is good, if you will learn,
But if not, everyone you see knows what it is to be unjust.

I staked my crazy heart, but I didn't know
That a mortal's child knows a peri's ways.

Here are a thousand points finer than a hair:
Not everyone who shaves the head knows what it is to be a
    wandering dervish.

Do not withhold your mole from the cynosure of my sight,
Because the jeweller knows the value of the peerless gem.

With stature and looks anyone who has become king of the fair
Might conquer the world, provided he knows what dispensing
    justice is.

Of the heart-winning poetry of Háfiz, he is aware
Who knows the charm of verses and composing words in Darí.[2]

---

1. See Poem v, note 2.

2. *Darí*, the dialect of (spoken) Persian current in the north-eastern Iranian regions—it has been cited as the chancery language of Bukhárá—where it was used by the first poets in Persian whose verses were preserved in written form and which date from the 9th century AD. It was used in poetry from the dawn of poetry in New Persian, the language that developed after the Arab invasion of Iran and, to a greater or lesser extent, included words of Arabic derivation. This use of *Darí* in the early development of a great canon of verse makes references to it especially evocative in terms of Persian literary culture. It was a form of the *zabán-i Fársí*, "the Persian tongue", that was called *darí* from its having been the dialect in use in Courts; the word *dar* means door or, as in the Sublime Porte, Porte, the Royal Court. That the early poets used the language of current speech in urban circles is significant and has contributed to the comprehensibility of their works down to modern times where the language which they helped to establish a thousand years ago has remained less modified than, for example, English has since the time of Chaucer.

POEM CLXXV

Whoever became the intimate of the heart has remained in the
    friend's holy precinct,
And he who did not understand this, remained in rejection.

If our heart has emerged from behind the screen, make no
    reproach;
Thank God it has not tarried behind the conceit[1] of notions' veil.

All the Súfís retrieved their clothing from being in pawn for wine.
It was our gown that was left at the vintner's.

Other gown-wearers have got drunk and it has been forgotten;
It is our story that has stayed in every mouth on the market square.

I had a dervish cloak and it cloaked a hundred secret faults.
The cloak became surety for wine and minstrel, but the pagan
    girdle[2] remained.

All the ruby wine I took from that crystal hand
Turned into a tear of sorrow and hung on the pearl-shedding eye.

Apart from my heart, that from Eternity without Beginning to
    Eternity without End has been in love,
I've heard of nobody who forever stayed that way.

I have heard no sounds sweeter than the song of love—
The souvenir that beneath this circling dome has not been lost.

The narcissus turned sick that it might become like your eye.
The elegance of this was not granted it, and it stayed sick.

One day the heart of Háfiz went to the show-place of his tresses
Intent upon coming back, but it stayed captive.

---

1. For the Súfí connotation of this concept, see R. A. Nicholson, translator, the
    Kashfu'l-Mahjúb of Hujwírí, op. cit., pp. 150, 155, and the Index under the word
    pindásht.
2. See Poem CXLII, note 2.

POEM CLXXVI

The good news has come, that the days of sorrow will not last—
Such as that has not lasted and such as this too will not last.

Although in the eyes of the friend I have become contemptible,
The rival will not forever be respected.

Since the Keeper of the Curtain strikes down all with the sword,
Nobody will stay resident in the sacred abode.

What's the point of gratitude and complaint over the scheme's
    good and evil,
When on the page of existence not a mark will be left?

They have said that the anthem of Jamshíd's assembly was this,
"Bring the bowl of wine because Jam won't remain."

O rich man, win over your poor one,
Because the hoard of gold and store of silver will not remain.

Count, O candle, uniting with the moth a boon,
Because this trafficking won't outlast the break of dawn.

On this emerald vault it has been written in letters of gold
That apart from the goodness of the generous nothing will remain.

Háfiz, do not cut off hope of the kindness of the beloved:
The expression of violence and show of tyranny will not last.

You've not written how things stand and several days have elapsed.
Where's a confidant that I may send you a message or two?

We cannot reach that exalted destination,
Unless perhaps your kindness puts forward a step or two.

Since wine has left the vat for the flagon and the rose thrown off
    the veil,
Regard the moment opportune for pleasure, and drain a cup.

Sugar mixed with the rose is no remedy for our heart.
Mix a few kisses with a taunt or two.

Pass, ascetic, by the street of the sots into safety,
Lest the company of outlaws corrupt you.

Since all the faults of wine you have recited, tell of its virtue as
    well;
For the sake of the hearts of common folk, negate not wisdom.

O beggars of the tavern, God is your friend;
Do not look for reward from a bunch of animals.

How well the Elder of the wine-shop spoke to his dregs-drainers
When he said, "Don't tell the state of the broiled heart to some
    of the raw."

In passion for your sun-bright face Háfiz has burned;
O satisfied one, spare an occasional glance for the unfulfilled.

POEM CLXXVIII

Last night as dawn broke I was salvaged from sorrow
And in that darkness of night, given the Water of Life.[1]

By the radiance of the ray from True Existence, I have been taken
    outside myself:
They've given me wine from the chalice of the epiphany of the
    Attributes.

What a blessed dawn and what a fortunate moment,
That Night of Power this fresh lease was given me;

After this, it's a case of my face and the beauty-reflecting mirror,
Because then news of the unveiling of the Divine Being was given.

If I have become gratified and happy at heart, no wonder—
I was deserving, and these as righteous alms they gave me.

That day the Voice gave me the joy of this luck,
That under that cruelty and oppression patience and steadfastness
    had been granted me.

It was Háfiz's devotion and the breaths of the risers at dawn
That gave me salvation from the bonds of the grief of the time.

---

1.   See Poem xxx, note 1.

POEM CLXXIX

Last night I saw that the angels knocked at the wine-shop's door:
Adam's clay was kneaded and cast into a wine-measure's mould:

The dwellers in the veiled sanctuary of holiness and the chastity
    of the angels' realm
Me, sifting the dust of the road, suffused with the wine of
    ecstasy.[1]

The heavens could not bear the burden of the Trust.[2]
The lot for this was cast in the name of mad me.

Establish forgiveness for the war of the Seventy-Two Sects;
Because they did not see the track of the True, they took
    fable's way.

Let there be thanks for this, that between him and me peace has
    come;
The Houris dancing have drained the cup of gratitude.

Fire is not that with the flame of which the candle laughs.
Fire is that with which the moth's harvest was set alight.

Nobody has unveiled the face of contemplation like Háfiz
Since the tress-tips of speech were combed by a pen.

---

1.   The background to these first two verses is furnished by the *Mirsád al-ʿIbád* of
    Najmu'd-Dín Rází, op. cit., in the second part of Chapter Four, on the Creation
    of the Human Frame. (English translation, op. cit., pp. 94–109.) There God's
    kneading of Adam's clay, some say for forty thousand years, is described, and
    how He deposited His Treasure of Love in Adam's heart (see Poem CLXVIII,
    note 2). The angels were amazed at God's solicitude for a creature of clay, and
    they examined Adam's form, but were unable to comprehend its mystery.
    Upon the dust of Adam, "from the cloud of munificence the rain of love" had
    been poured, and that dust become the clay out of which the "Hand of Power"
    fashioned the heart:

From the dew of love Adam's dust became clay:
A hundred upheavals and agitations came into the world.
The lament of love pierced the vein of the spirit.
One drop of blood dripped down and "heart" became its name.
(Text pp. 71–72, Translation p. 100.)

Since it was God who kneaded Adam's clay, obviously the angels of the first
hemistich of the first verse are not the subject of the verbs *besirishtand* and
zadand in the second hemistich: "kneaded" and "cast". These verbs, although in
the active form, can, as in the English, in the Persian idiom be read as passive,
"was kneaded" and "(was) cast", and should be. The angels, knocking at the
wine-shop's door alludes to the angels described in the *Mirsád* as examining the
outward form of Adam, after his clay had been kneaded and shaped, ready for
the reception of God's secret treasure.

2. Koran xxxiii, 72:

> Verily We offered the Trust to the heavens
> and the earth and the mountains, but they
> refused to bear it and shrank from it, and
> man bore it.

POEM CLXXX

Might it be that coins are taken for assaying,
So that all false monastery-dwellers are sent packing?

In my view what is expedient is that all the comrades pass
Everything up, and grab hold of the bend in the curl of a friend.

The companions would happily take the tip of the wine-boy's tress,
If the Firmament permitted them to gain some repose.

Don't parade the strength of abstinence's arm before the fair,
Because in this squadron with a single horseman they capture a
    castle.

O Lord, how bold after blood are these Turkish whelps!
Because every moment they shoot down prey with an eye-lash's
    arrow.

The dance to sweet verses and the wail of the flute are lovely,
Especially the moment in it when the hand of the beloved is
    grasped.

Háfiz, opportunists have no care for suppliants.
If possible, it is better for them to make a detour away from this
    milieu.

POEM CLXXXI

If the wine-vendor makes lawful what sots crave,
God'll forgive the sin and ward off contamination.

Wine-boy, in the bowl of impartiality dispense the wine, so that
    the beggar
May not feel a jealousy that fills the world with woe.

For us who have the pangs of love and the misery of the hangover,
Either being united with the friend or wine that is unclouded
    provides the cure.

O God, may good news arrive, of salvation from these griefs,
Provided that the pilgrim keeps faith with the Trust.[1]

Whether torment befalls you or ease, O sage,
Do not attribute them to another: God is their author.

In the workshop learning and reason have no access to,
Why does the feeble imagination express an impertinent view?

Minstrel, tune the lute to sing, "No one dies outside the
    Appointed Time,"[2]
And he who does not sing this ditty is in error.

In desire of wine life passed, and Háfiz was burned by love.
Where is the one of Jesus's breath, to make us alive again?

---

1.   For "Trust", see Koran vii, 171, and xx, 114, and xxxiii, 72.
2.   See Koran x, 50, and xxix, 53.

POEM CLXXXII

Burn, O heart, because your burning achieves things;
A midnight prayer wards off a hundred calamities.

Lover-like, bear the peri-cheek's reproaches,
Because one loving glance makes up for a hundred rebuffs.

From the kingdom as far as the realm of the Power they lift the
    veil,
Whoever attends upon the world-displaying cup.

The physician for love is Messiah-breathed and kind, but
If no pain in you he sees, for whom is he going to prescribe?

Leave matters to your God, you, and keep a cheerful heart,
Because, though the Adversary shows no compassion, God does.

I'm tired of sleeping luck. It may be that keeping awake
Might, at the time of the opening of morning, constitute a prayer.

Háfiz burned, but stole not a single fragrance from the tress of
    the friend.
Perhaps the morning breeze will act for him as guide to this
    good luck.

POEM CLXXXIII

That meddler finds fault with me for being a reprobate and in love,
Who objects to the mysteries of knowledge of the Hidden.

Look at the perfection of the sincerity of love, not at the
    shortcomings of sin:
It is whoever turns out lacking virtue that has an eye for faults.

From the fragrance of the Houris of Paradise that moment a
    scent ascends
When he makes the dust of our wine-booth ambergris for his
    breast.

The key to the treasure of felicity is the acceptance of the people
    of the heart.
Let there be no one who doubts or questions this.

The shepherd of the valley of the Blessed Mount[1] attains his
    desire that time
When with his life for several years he performs service for
    Shu'aib.[2]

Háfiz's fable makes the blood weep from the eye,
When it remembers the time of the period of youth, and old age's.

---

1.   See Koran xix, 53. Moses was called from the right-hand side of the Mount. Cf.
    Koran xx, 8 sqq.
2.   Shu'aib, Jethro: See Exodus iii, 1, which says, "Now Moses kept the flock of
    Jethro, his father in law, the priest of Midian: and he led the flock to the back-
    side of the desert, and came to the mountain of God, even to Horeb."

POEM CLXXXIV

If the bird of fortune should again fly this way,
The friend might come back, and make a compact with union.

Although profusion of pearls and jewels is no longer left in the eye,
The heart consumes blood; it might furnish a scattering.

Last night I asked, "May the ruby of his lip dispense my cure?"
The Voice of the Unseen proclaimed, "Yes it will."

No one can breathe a word of our story to him—
Unless the wafting of the dawn breeze conveys it.

I have aimed the flight of the falcon of vision at a pheasant;
He calls back; perhaps he makes a lucky swoop, and his quarry.

Where is a kind one at whose feast of merriment the afflicted
Might drain a draught and get rid of the hangover?

The city is empty of lovers. It might be that from some quarter
A man comes out of himself, and into action.

Either fidelity or news of union with you, or the rival's death:
The sport of the sphere metes out at least one of all these.

Háfiz, if not even for a day you desert his door,
He might from some hidden angle sweep by over your head.

POEM CLXXXV

The day your dusky reed remembers us,
It will gain for reward the two hundred slaves it manumits.

What would it matter if the courier from the court of Salmá[1]—
    may it be safe!—
Were to make our heart glad with a greeting?

Try it, because much desired treasure would be granted you,
Were your kindness to restore a ruin like me.

O Lord, inspire the heart of that Shírín's Khusrau,
That with compassion he might spare the head of Farhád.[2]

O at this time the glance of your love has destroyed my
    foundations,
So what schemes has it in store for another time?

Your pure essence does not need any eulogy of ours:
With God-given beauty why should an adorner be thought of?

In Shíráz we have not obtained the object of desire.
Happy the day Háfiz takes the road to Baghdad.

---

1. Salmá, like Laylá, is a name given in old Arabic poetry for a beloved, but Háfiz
   is referring to the court of Sultan Uvais-i Jaláyir (see Poem CLVIII, note 2) at
   Baghdad, which was situated in an Arabic-speaking region. Hence Háfiz uses
   the reference to Salmá.
2. See Poem LV, note 1. Khusrau was the husband of Shírín, the beloved of Farhád.

POEM CLXXXVI

Who is he who'll have the kindness to treat me with constancy?
Who on behalf of an evil-doer like me will for once do a good deed?

First, to the sound of the flageolet and pipe he might convey his
    message to the heart;
And then with a measure of wine show me fidelity.

Of the ravisher of hearts, through whom the soul has been melted
    but my heart's purpose left unattained,
To be hopeless cannot be: it could be that he'll try heart-cherishing.

I said, "So long as I have been, not a knot have I undone of that
    curl."
He replied, "I have ordered it to play fast and loose with you."

The woollen-gowned of narrow disposition has not smelt the
    perfume of love.
Out of intoxication tell him a riddle of love, that he might
    abandon sobriety.

Such a friend was hard to get for the likes of me, a beggar of no
    note;
How can the Sultan enjoy secret pleasure with an urchin of the
    marketplace?

If I experience tyranny from that tress full of twists and curls, it
    is easy:
What do bonds and chains matter to those who play the cut-purse?

The army of grief has become uncountable. I seek help from luck,
That it might be that Fakhr-i Dín 'Abd al-Sammad[1] offers consolation.

With his eye full of sorcery do not, Háfiz, engage with him,
Because that knavish drunken eye plays many a trick.

---

1.   Sayyid Enjevi Shirazi has conjectured that the person here referred to was a great
    paragon of learning and virtue who was a contemporary of Háfiz's and called
    Mauláná Baháu'd-Dín 'Abd al-Sammed Bahíabádí, who due to his outstanding
    reputation for goodness was able to escape persecution at the hands of the Sultan.

POEM CLXXXVII

Why does my cypress of the meadow show no inclination for the
  meadow?
It doesn't seek intimacy with the rose. It does not remember the
  jasmine.

The morning breeze has been perfume-anointing. For what reason
  does your pure skirt
Not make the violet-bed's dust into the musk of Khotan?

In the hope of union with you, the heart is not at one with the
  soul:
In desire for your street, the soul does not serve the body.

Once my vagrant heart entered the twist of his curl,
Because of its long journey, it does not make for its native place.

Before the bow of his eyebrow I am pleading, but
The ear is drawn back: he does not hear me.

With all the folds of your gown, I wonder at the morning breeze,
That from wafting by you it does not make the dust musk of
  Khotan!

When from the gentle breeze the violet's tresses become full of
  broken crinkles,
Alas, what memory is there that my heart does not recall of that
  breaker of promises?

Though it were all dregs that my silver-thighed wine-boy were
  pouring,
Who is it that would not make the body into a wine-bowl, all
  mouth?

Háfiz, heedless of advice, has become the slain of your fetching
  glances.
The sword is proper punishment for those who take no pains
  over speaking.

POEM CLXXXVIII

Those without awareness are bewildered by our eye-play.
I am that which I seem. The rest, they know.

The rational are the compass point of existence, but
Love knows that in this circle their heads are spinning.

The Divine concluded our compact with the lips of the
     sweet-mouthed,
We, all slaves, and that party, the masters.

We are the penniless, but our desire is for wine and song.
Ah the pity if they won't take a woollen gown for a pledge!

Boasting of love and complaining of the friend? Splendid the
     lying boast!
Such players at love as this merit desertion.

Not alone is my eye the unveiling chamber of his cheek;
The moon and the sun are also focusing on this looking glass.

The description of the sun is quite beyond the scope
     of the blind bat,
When those possessed of vision are amazed at this mirror.

Perhaps your dark eye will teach me how to act.
But otherwise, not everyone is capable of temperance and
     drunkenness.

If the Magian children become aware of our meditation,
After that will they not take as a pledge the Súfí gown?

If the breeze carries your scent to the pleasure-garth of spirits,
Reason and life, the essence of being, they will scatter.

If the ascetic does not understand Háfiz's licentiousness,
     what matter?
The devil flees those folk who recite the Koran.[1]

---

1. An allusion to the poet's sobriquet, *Háfiz*, he who can recite the Koran by
    heart from beginning to end.

POEM CLXXXIX

When they sit, the jasmine-scented lay the dust of sorrow.
The fairy-faced snatch away the heart's repose when they are
    embattled.

When to the saddle-strap of tyranny they bind hearts, they
    draw tight.
When they open the ambergris locks of loved ones, they spread
    them.

From my eye they rain pomegranate-like rubies when they laugh.
From my face when they look, they read a hidden secret.

When, in a lifetime, for a moment they sit with us, they get up!
When they rise, they leave implanted in the heart the seedling of
    desire.

When they discover the tear of those in retreat, they find a pearl.
If they know, they will not turn away the cheek of love from
    those who rise at dawn.

For the desire they conceive, like Mansúr[1] they are hanged:
When Háfiz is summoned to this Court, he is simply turned away.

Into this Presence, when the yearning bring their supplication,
    let them bring grace,
Because, if they are bent on a remedy, in pain they'll remain.

---

1.   Mansúr al-Halláj: see Poem CXXXVI, note 1.

POEM CXC

The slaves of your intoxicated eye are the wearers of crowns.
The drunk on your ruby wine are the sober.

For you the wind and for me the flooding eye have become
    telltales.
Otherwise, lover and beloved would keep the secret to themselves.

When you pass by, look from under the bending tress,
Because to the right and the left there are the tormented;

Like a zephyr blow over the violet-bed and see
How afflicted they are by your tress's tyranny.

O God-knower, go away. Paradise is our portion,
Because it is sinners who merit grace.

Not only I sing odes to that rose-cheek:
Your nightingales are in their thousands on every side.

O Khizr of the auspicious foot,[1] be you the taker-up, for I
Am going on foot, but those travelling with me are mounted.

Come to the wine-booth and make the cheek flushed.
Do not go to the cloister. There the doers of dark deeds are.

May Háfiz not be freed from those curled tresses:
The captives in your lasso are the freed.

---

1.   See Poem CLXIV, note 1.

POEM CXCI

Those who with a glance turn dust into the philosopher's stone,
Might it be that they spare me the corner of an eye?

My pain, best hidden from false physicians,
It might be they will cure with physick from the Dispensary of
    the Invisible.

Since the beloved does not lift the veil from the cheek,
Why do people give an account based on supposition?

Since the success of the issue lies not with debauchery or
    abstinence,
It were better that they left their affair to Providence.

Do not be without cognition of holiness, because at love's auction,
Those of insight deal with those they know.

Drink wine, because a hundred sins strangers commit behind
    the screen
Are better than an act of devotion that they perform in hypocrisy
    and pretence.

The coat from which comes my scent of Joseph,[1]
I fear that his jealous brothers will cut to pieces.

Today many are the dissensions going on behind the curtain,
So what will they be doing on the Day when the curtain slips?

Do not wonder if stone were to grieve at this tale:
People of the heart tell the story of the heart tellingly well.

Háfiz, uninterrupted union is not possible:
Kings pay scant attention to the state of the beggar.

---

1.   Joseph, *Yúsuf*, the paragon of beauty. For his story, see Koran XII.

POEM CXCII

If beauties practise heart-stealing like this,
They'll make holes in the faith of ascetics.

Whenever that narcissus stem comes into flower,
The rose-cheeked will make their eye a narcissus holder.

When our friend begins the ecstatic chant,
The holy angels by the Throne[1] clap their hands.

O youth of the cypress form, thwack a ball
Before the time when they make a hockey-stick of your body!

Lovers have no control over their own heads:
Whatever your command may be that they perform.

The pupil of my eye has become soaked in blood.
How can they subject man to this oppression?

Compared with my eyes, less than a drop
Those tales that of the deluge are told.

When is the festival of your cheek, so that lovers
In fidelity to you may make their lives a sacrifice?

O heart, come out gleefully in grieving, because the people of the
    secret
Achieve their gratification in the crucible of separation.

Háfiz, do not reject the midnight sigh,
So that shining like the morning your mirror[2] may be made.

---

1. 'arsh, the Throne of God in Heaven.
2. i.e. the heart which when cleansed may reflect the Divine.

POEM CXCIII

I said: "When will your mouth and lip provide my gratification?"
He answered: "Sure, whatever you say so they'll do!"

I said: "Your lip exacts the revenue of Egypt."
He answered: "In this transaction less would be loss."

I asked: "To the point of your mouth who is there that finds the
   way?"
He answered: "This is a tale told him who knows subtle points."

I said: "Do not be idol worshipping. Sit with the Eternal."
He answered: "In the street of love, both that and this are done."

I said: "The air of the wine-shop relieves the heart of sadness."
He answered: "Happy those who a single heart make glad."

I said: "Wine and the patched gown are not religiously
   ordained."
He answered: "These comprise the rite performed in the Magian
   Elder's sect."

I asked: "What profit does an old man get from the sweet ruby of
   lips?"
He answered: "With a sweet kiss they make him young."

I asked: "When will the master[1] be going to the bridal chamber?"
He answered: "The time when Jupiter and the moon are in
   conjunction."

I said: "Prayers for his good fortune are the daily litany of Háfiz."
He answered: "These prayers are made by the angels of the
   Seven Heavens."

---

1. Master, *khwájeh*, taken to be a reference to the Vazir and Chief Assayer under
   Shah Shujá', Qavám ud-Dín Muhammad (see Poem xi, note 1). When Háfiz was
   close to the Court of Shah Shujá', he must have frequently been in the com-
   pany of this Minister, to whom he makes a number of allusions. The legend is
   that in this poem Háfiz is referring to the Khwájeh's forthcoming marriage. In
   the succeeding verse, according to the commentator Súdí, Jupiter stands for
   the Khwájeh and the moon for the lady who was to be his bride!

POEM CXCIV

Preachers who make all this show in the prayer-niche and pulpit,
When they retire in private, engage in quite other pursuits.

I have a problem. Ask the assembly's wise one,
Why enforcers of repentance themselves so little repent.

It might be said that they do not believe in Judgement Day,
Because in the judge's business they practise all this falsity and
  jugglery.

I am the slave of the Tavern Elder whose dervishes
Out of needlessness put riches to shame.

O Lord, mount these upstarts on their donkeys,
Who, with Turkish groom and mule, give themselves such airs.

Angel, tell your beads at the door of the tavern of love,
Because it's inside there they leaven Adam's clay.

However many lovers his infinite beauty slays,
From the Invisible another batch will be fetched by love.

O beggar in the dervish hostel, leap up, because in the Magian
  Temple
Thirsts are quenched and hearts enriched.

Empty, O heart, the house, for it to be the Sultán's abode:
The desirous make heart and soul soldiers' resorts.

At the time of morning, a chorus was coming from the Throne.
Reason said: "It seems angels chant poems of Háfiz by heart."

POEM CXCV

Do you know what the harp and lute are saying?
"Drink wine on the quiet: allegations of apostasy are being made."

They're saying, "Do not hear or divulge hints of love";
It is a hard saying which they are expressing.

"Love's dignity and lovers' grace are being pillaged:
The young are prohibited and the old rebuked."

Outside the door we are deluded by a hundred wiles.
There is no telling what schemes are afoot behind the screen.

They're again giving the Magian Elder a troubled time—
See what these wayfarers are doing to the Guide!

A hundred honours can with half a glance be bought.
Those of beauty are falling short in this transaction.

One party by striving and effort has established union with the
    friend.
Another leaves it to Divine Decree.[1]

In short, do not rely on the constancy of the sphere,
Because this is a workshop subject to being changed.

Give wine because, when you look closely, the Shaikh and Háfiz,
The disher-out of judicial decrees and the censor of morals, all
    practise deceit.

---

1. The genuine mystic believes that union can only be sought successfully if God
   moves the seeker.

Unadulterated wine and an attractive wine-boy are two of the
    Path's snares,
From the noose of which the worldly wise do not escape.

Although I am a lover, a reprobate, a drunk, with a bad record,
A thousand thanks that in the city there are comrades without sin.

Do not set foot in the tavern other than with etiquette nicely
    observed,
Because the dwellers within it are the confidants of the King.

Harshness is not the practice of a dervish or a follower of the Way;
Bring wine, because these pilgrims are not the braves the road
    requires.

Do not look scornfully upon love's beggars:
These are beltless kings and Khusraus without the diadem.

Do not act so that a sweetheart's glitter might be desecrated,
When his servants desert and his slaves go on the run.

I'm the bondsman of the zeal of undeviating dregs-drainers,
Not that group who are in the dress of piety but black of heart.

Beware, because when the wind of the Unneeding blows,
A thousand harvests of devotional acts won't fetch half a groat.

The Portal of Love is lofty. Some zeal, Háfiz,
Because lovers do not give the way of the unzealous to themselves.

POEM CXCVII

Let it, O heart, be that they'll open the wine-shops' doors,
Undo the knot of our business tangled up in failure.

Though they shot the bolt for the sake of the self-regarding
    ascetic's heart,
Be of good cheer: for the sake of God it will be opened;

By the purity of heart of reprobates, drainers of the morning
    draught,
With the key of prayer many a closed door is opened.

For the daughter of the vine indite a letter of condolence,
So that from eye-lashes all the comrades may loosen the blood
    of sorrow;

Cut the tresses of the heart in mourning for the death of pure
    wine,
So that all the Magian's boys might undo their twisted curls.

They've closed the tavern door. O God, do not approve,
Because they'll be opening the door of deceit and subterfuge.

Háfiz, this gown you wear, see tomorrow
From under it what a pagans' belt will cruelly be exposed!

POEM CXCVIII

Now that the rose has come into the meadow, come from
    non-existence into being,
At its foot the violet has bowed its head in adoration.

Drink a cup of the morning wine to the clamour of drum and harp.
Kiss the wine-boy's curving chin to the melody of reed and lute.

In the season of the rose do not sit without wine, a beauty, and
    the lyre,
Because, like the season of its survival, it's reckoned a week.

From the mansions of sweet herbs, bright like a starry heaven
The earth has become through the lucky star and auspicious
    ascendant.

From the hand of a fair-cheeked darling possessed of Jesus's breath
Drink wine and dismiss the story of Ád and Thmúd.[1]

The world in the season of the lily and the rose has become like
    Paradise Sublime,
But to what profit when there is no abiding in it?

How the rose gets mounted, Solomon-like, on air, when
In the morning the bird enters with the psalmody of David!

Revive in the garden the rite of the Zoroastrian Faith,
Now that the tulip has rekindled the fire of Nimrod.[2]

Call for the morning cup, to toast the Ásaf of the Age,
'Imádu'd-Dín Mahmúd,[3] Minister to the realm of Solomon.

It may be that through the felicity of his patronage of Háfiz's
    coterie
All that it is asking might be found for it.

1. Two peoples punished because of refusal to obey Messengers from God. See Koran VII, 65–72, 73–79, XI, 50–60, 61–68, and other references.

2. Nimrod is not mentioned by name in the Koran, but the casting of Abraham into a blazing fire when he smashed the idols of idolatrous compatriots, for whom Ázar, Abraham's father, was an idol-carver, is described in Koran XXI, 68–69. God ordered the fire to turn cold. Commentators have identified the ruler of this people as Nimrod, who is said to have ordered Abraham to be catapulted into the vast fire because it was so hot no one could go near enough physically to throw him in. Gabriel came to the rescue and the blaze around Abraham was transformed into a fragrant flowered meadow, or, as in the account in the *Qisasu'l-Anbíya*, "Tales of the Prophets", of Abú Ishaq of Níshapúr (Tehran 1340/1960–1, pp. 51–53) of the century before the time of Háfiz, Abraham was seated on a bench beside a rill in the midst of a host of narcissi and the verdure growing round a pond. There is also the account of how the blaze turned into a bed of roses. Háfiz's play on the colour red, the red of the tulip, of wine, and of the fire, suggests (see next poem, note 2) the heart lit by the Light of the Divine—light is the Zoroastrian principle of good—and becoming rid of the dross of darkness (see the last verse of the next poem, CXCIX). For Nimrod, "The Mighty Hunter", see Genesis X, 9.

3. Khwájeh 'Imádu'd-Dín Mahmúd of Kirmán was a minister to Shah Abú Ishaq between 1343 and 1353 AD, the latter year being that in which Abú Ishaq's rule was supplanted by the Muzaffarid Mubárizu'd-Dín Muhammad, after which Imádu'd-Dín gained high office in Azerbaijan and then, in 1358 AD, he became governor of Isfahán. Dr Khánlarí attributes this poem to the time when Imádu'd-Dín was Abú Ishaq's minister in Shíráz—"the realm of Solomon". Hence this *ghazal* must be attributed to the time of Háfiz's youth. He died in 1389, so that, having in view the last year, 1353, of Imádu'd-Dín's holding office in Shíráz, Háfiz must have composed this ghazal some 36 years before his own death. See Volume II of the *Díván-i Háfiz,* edited by Khánlarí (Tehran, 1362/1982–3) p. 1248.

POEM CXCIX

Years has our notebook been in pawn for red wine—
From our lesson and prayer has been all the glamour of the
    wine-shop!

See the goodness of the Magian Elder when we the rotten drunk—
Whatever we did was, in his benign sight, beautiful!

Wash out the whole of our book of knowledge with wine,
Because I have seen the Firmament, and it was at enmity with
    me the learned.

O heart, if you are a connoisseur of loveliness, look for it in idols,
As that one said who, in the art of seeing, was sighted.

The heart like a compass was swivelling round and round,
But in that circle, spinning on a fixed point.

Because of the pain of love the minstrel was accomplishing a
    performance
Such that eye-lashes of sages were sieves for straining blood.

I opened up in gladness because, as with the rose at the edge of
    the stream,
The shadow of that tall straight cypress was over my head.

My Elder, Gulrang,[1] in respect of those gowned in blue,
Did not permit malevolence. Had he, many a tale would have
    been told!

With him Háfiz's rusted heart[2] got nowhere,
Because the honest dealer was not blind to hidden defects.

---

1.   "My Elder, Gulrang": *gulrang* literally means "rose-coloured". It is found mean-
ing this in Poem CCLVII, verse 4, and CCCIII, verse 6, but here it is the proper
name of a *Pír*, Elder or Guide, with whom Háfiz was in close association. This
fact is attested by the reference in the same verse to "those gowned in blue",
azraq-púshán. The blue-gowned followed a Shaikh who was in Shíráz at Háfiz's
time and named Shaikh Alí Kuláh, whose disciples followed their Master in the
wearing of a blue tunic with short sleeves. (See Poem CXXIX, verse 5, with the

reference to the shortened sleeve. In this poem Háfiz has this same Shaikh Alí in his sights. See also Poem cxcvi, verse 7, where the phrase is *azraq-libás*, translated as "dress of piety".) This Shaikh was the enemy of Háfiz's mentor, the Pír-i Gulrang, but Shaikh Gulrang prohibited speaking ill of the "blue-gowned" as not in keeping with Súfí manners, in which love and reconciliation are inculcated.

2. In this verse Háfiz continues the theme of his teacher discouraging malevolence in respect of the rival Shaikh. Háfiz says that he is able to see into his pupil's heart, that of the *muríd*, disciple or novice, and discern its defects. The word used for "heart", *qalb*, can also mean "coin", but this play on words is not reflected; the meaning "heart" is clearly to be preferred because Háfiz is subtly playing on the name of his mentor. Gulrang, "rose-hued", carries the invocation of the colour red. In the *Mirsád al-'Ibád* (Text, op. cit., p. 306, Translation, op. cit., p. 300), in the Seventeenth Chapter of the Third Part, which contains an exposition of the significance of different colours in the context of perceiving the Divine Light, it is stated that as "the darkness of the soul decreases, and the light of the spirit increases", a red light is witnessed. In other words, the red light betokens a heart becoming purified, cleansed, eventually to be ready to reflect the Divine. He of the rosy hue was the Knower on the path towards pureness of soul. Háfiz's heart was still defective. (Cf. Mu'ín, *Háfiz-i Shírín Sukhan*, op. cit., pp. 416 sqq.)

POEM CC

May yours be the memory of when for me there was a stolen
    glance;
The imprint of your love was legible on our face.

Let there be the memory that, while your rebuke was slaying me,
On your sugar-crunching lip was the miracle of Jesus.

Let it be remembered that, when in the gathering of intimates at
    dawn a draught was drained,
Only I and the friend were there, but God was with us.

And the memory that, when your cheek ignited the candle of joy,
This scorched heart was the moth that had no fear.

Let there be the memory that, in the party of good manners and
    restraint,
The drunkenly laughing one was the wine that was red;

When the ruby in the cup was merrily gurgling,
Between your ruby and me, let it be remembered what
    exchanges there were!

Be it remembered that, when my moon would fasten on his
    helmet,
At his stirrup the new moon was his world-traversing squire.

Let there be the memory that I was a haunter of the tavern and
    drunk,
And that what today in the mosque I lack used to be there.

Be it remembered that, through your putting them in order,
The verses of every unpierced pearl Háfiz possessed would come
    out right.

POEM CCI

So long as of the wine-shop and wine there will be the name
    and the sign,
Our head will be the dust of the Magian Elder's path.

From Eternity before Beginning, the Magian Elder's ring[1] has
    been in our ear:
We are about that which we were, and so it will be.

When you step by the head of our tomb, ask for grace,[2]
Because it will be a pilgrim shrine for the roisterers of the world.

Go away, self-regarding ascetic, because from your eye and mine
The secret of this veil is hidden and hidden it will be.

My lover-slaughtering Turk strode out today drunk —
Now what other blood from eyes will be running?

My eyes the night when because of passion for you I lowered my
    head into the grave,
Will go on looking out until the morning of the Day of
    Resurrection:

If Háfiz's luck will render help in this wise,
The tress of the Beloved will be in the hands of others.[3]

---

1. The ring of a slave.
2. In other words, to visit the tomb of Háfiz would be an act of beneficial piety.
3. This verse harks back to the third with its reference to the grace afforded by
Háfiz's tomb.

Before this for lovers you had more consideration than this:
Your profession of love for us was notorious all over the world.

At the gate of the Sháh, a beggar made a witty sally.
He said, "At every feast I go to, God is the provider."

May those nocturnal causeries be remembered when, with
    sweet lips,
There was discussion of the mystery of love and of the circle of
    lovers.

Although the beauty of the moon-faced of the assembly stole
    heart and religion,
Our debate was about the grace of disposition and the moral of
    goodness.

From the dawn of Eternity without Beginning's morning to the
    end of the evening of Eternity without End,
Friendship and love have been governed by one covenant and
    one pact.

Before the time that green ceiling and enamelled vault were
    drawn out,
For my eye's cynosure, the arch of the eyebrow of the beloved
    was the sight.

What harm would come if the shadow of the beloved fell on the
    lover's head?
We were in need of him. He was eager for us.

Forgive me if the prayer-bead's string has snapped—
My hand was on the silver-legged wine-boy's arm.

On the Night of Power[1] if I made the dawn wassail, do not chide
    me;
The friend came merry, and a cup was on the ledge of the niche.

The poetry of Háfiz in the time of Adam, within the Garden of
    Paradise,
Was the adornment of the pages of the book of the white and
    red rose.

---

1.   Night of Power, see Poems xxx, note 1, and xliii, note 2.

POEM CCIII

Let it be remembered when my abode was on your street;
The light of my eye the harvest of the dust of your door.

True as the lily and the rose, from the effect of pure association,
For me on the tongue was all that for you was in the heart.

When from the Wise Elder the heart was inditing mystical
    meanings,
Love was uttering by way of commentary what the heart found
    hard.[1]

It was in my heart that, "May I never be without the friend".
What can be done when my and the heart's striving was of no
    avail?

Much as I wandered inquiring the cause of the pain of separation,
At this proposition the expounder of reason had no reason
    whatever to offer.

For sure, the Abú Ishaqian[2] signet ring's turquoise[3]
Was splendidly brilliant, but his power speedily over;

Did you see, Háfiz, that clucking of the strutting patridge
Which was inattentive to the falcon-claws of Fate?[4]

---

1. See Rúmí in the *Masnaví* (Mathnawí), op. cit., Book 1, lines 114–115:

    When the pen was hastily scribbling,
    When it got to "love", it split upon itself;
    Reason in describing it lay down like a donkey in the mire.
    The explanation of love and lovers, love itself uttered.

2. A reference to Háfiz's early dynastic patron, the lavish, pleasure-loving Abú
    Ishaq. He was the last ruler of Shíráz and Isfahán of the House of Ínjú. After
    scarcely a decade of rule in Shíráz, he was defeated and ousted by the
    Muzaffarid Mubárizu'd-Dín Muhammad in 1353. (See Poem cxcviii, note 3.) Abú
    Ishaq fled to Isfahán, where his enemy again laid him under siege and, this
    time, captured him. In 1357 he was ignominiously executed.

3. The turquoise was highly prized among Iranians as a protection against evil and, through its magic power, promoter of the wearer's prosperity: but rulers were not advised to wear turquoise, because it was believed that their glory and power would be eliminated in the greater glory and power of the stone. (See Donaldson, *Wild Rue*, op. cit., pp. 152–153.)

4. This poem seems really to be a threnody on the fate of Abú Isḥaq, a patron whom Ḥáfiz apparently loved very much. This hemistich can be read in conjunction with historians' accounts of Abú Isḥaq's nonchalance and continued indulgence in pleasure even when the Muzaffarid's army was formidably encircling Shíráz and at its gates.

POEM CCIV

Last night your locks were our circle's theme.
Until the heart of the night, the talk was of the links of your hair.

The heart, blood-soaked from your eye-lash's arrow-tips,
Yet was eager for your eyebrow's stretched bow.

May God forgive the morning breeze that was handing in your
    message;
Did it not, there was no one else from your street we've seen.

The world knew nothing of love's terror and perversity;
The arouser of trouble in the world was your bewitching glance.

I the head-turned also used to be of those of sanity.
The twist of your black tress was the snare in my path.

For my heart to open, unfasten the ribbons of the tunic—
From the side of your breast was any opening that was mine.

In your faithfulness may you pass by the burial place of Háfiz,
Who while he left the world was still in desire of your face.

POEM CCV

Last night he was coming, and he had kindled the cheek.
Wonderful how a single glance once more inflamed the heart!

The lover-slaughtering style and the mode of upending cities
Were the garb that was stitched onto his form:

He considered the souls of lovers rue for his face,
And he had kindled his cheek for its burning.[1]

Faith's highway-robber was his tress's unbelief, and that stony heart
From his cheek had lit a torch on religion's path.

He declared, "I will slay you cruelly," but I knew
That secretly he was sparing heart-scorched me a look.

The heart hoarded much blood but it was spilled from the eye—
God! God! Who let it run to waste, but who collected?

Do not for the world sell the friend: nothing was the profit
Of those who had sold Joseph for coins not legal tender.[2]

He said, and he spoke well: "Go, Háfiz, burn the patched gown."
From whom, O Lord, had he learnt the spotting of base coinage?

---

1. Comes to mind one of the two fragments extant of one of the earliest of Háfiz's predecessors in the composition of verses in New Persian. Sometime before 862 AD Hanzala of Bádghís, said:

    > Though my friend were to cast wild rue seeds into the fire,
    > So no hurt from the eye of evil might touch him,
    > To him what use might rue and fire be,
    > With a face like fire and a mole like the grain of rue?

2. Koran XII, 20: the caravan's people "sold him at a low price, a few dirhams", when they had discovered Joseph in the well. Koranic commentators have suggested that the silver dirhams were below standard and not legal tender.

POEM CCVI

Yesterday at dawn one or two cups had chanced to come my way,
And the wine of the lips of the wine-server had tinctured my palate.

Because I was drunk, again I was wanting
To return to the fine youngster of youth's prime, but a divorce
    had intervened.

Wherever through the Path's stages we voyaged,
Separation of chastity from eye-play had befallen.

Wine-boy, hand the bowl out from moment to moment, because,
    travelling the Path,
Whoever did not come as a lover into hypocrisy had fallen.

I conceived the notion of withdrawing into a corner, away from
    that sultry eye;
The capacity of patience, on account of his eyebrow's arch, had
    run out.

Make a good report, dream-interpreter, because last night the sun
In the sweet sleep of dawn had chanced to be my bedfellow.

The time Háfiz was writing down this disjointed composition,
Into the snare of longing the bird of his aspiration had tumbled.

If out of high-mindedness Nusratu'd-Dín Yahyá[1] had not acted,
The affairs of the realm and of the faith had become disordered
    and fallen out of joint.

---

1. See Poem CXLIII, note 3, concerning Sháh Yahyá's younger brother, Mansúr, ally-
    ing himself to their uncle, Sháh Shujá', in aiding the latter to regain Shíráz in 1363
    from Mahmúd, another uncle, who had ousted his brother, Sháh Shujá', two years
    earlier. Sháh Yahyá had been put in charge of the district of Yazd by Sháh Shujá'
    in 1361–2, to thwart the designs of Mahmúd on the revenues of that important
    entrepôt district, where Háfiz had not found a prince, whom he usually praised,
    as magnanimous as he had hoped he would be—see Poem XII, note 1. It was from
    Yazd that Sháh Yahyá sought, and, in beautiful verses from Sháh Shujá', obtained
    forgiveness for having defected from loyalty. And it was from Yazd that Sháh Yahyá
    dispatched his younger brother, Mansúr, with the reinforcements that enabled
    Sháh Shujá' to regain Shíráz. It seems likely that it is to this action on Sháh
    Yahyá's part that Háfiz is alluding.

POEM CCVII

The gem in the treasury of mysteries is the same as it was.
The casket of love is under the same seal and label as it was.

Lovers comprise the keepers of the Trust's treasure;
Inevitably the jewel-raining eye is the same as it was.

Ask the morning breeze: all night until dawn-break
The scent of your tresses is for us the same soulmate as it was.

There is no seeker after rubies and pearls, but if there were,
   the sun
Would be busy working mines and quarries as ever it was.[1]

The slain by your own glance has come in pious visitation:
The poor wretch is that same ever-wakeful heart as he was.

The colour that you were hiding, of the blood of our heart,
Is as visible on your ruby lips as it was.

I said, "May your dark tress be no more waylaying."
Years have passed, yet it is of the same nature and kind as ever
   it was.

Again, O Háfiz, resume the narrative of eyes' tears of blood:
From this source still flows that same liquid as ever was.

---

1. The allusion is a double one: first, to the never-ending bounty of God, and the
    profusion of tears from the loving eye. Secondly, to the belief that the sun and
    planets influenced the formation of veins of metals and precious stones in the
    rocks of earth.

POEM CCVIII

At dawn, O Lord, what a hubbub there was in the
    wine-shop's street!
What a seething, of the adorable, the wine-server, candles and
    flambeaux!

Love's telling, which has no need of word and articulation,
In the booming of drum and wailing of reed, in chorus was in
    full blast.

In this congregation, the disputation going on
Was beyond the Seminary and propositions' proposal and
    response.

For the wine-dispenser's ogling the heart was thankful, but,
At its ill-supporting luck, not without a hint of complaint!

I made a comparison—a thousand sorcerers of Sámirí's[1] sort
At that magic-working, drunken eye would have been aggrieved.

I said to him, "Transfer a kiss to my lip."
Laughingly he replied, "Whenever was this traffic yours with me?"

An auspicious aspect is on the way from my star because, last
    night,
The moon and the cheek of my friend were face to face.

Alas, that the mouth of the friend, which held the cure for
    Háfiz's pain,
Was, at the moment for expansiveness, of narrow capacity.

---

1.   Sámirí, he who in Moses' absence duped the Israelites. See Poem CXXIV, note 1.

POEM CCIX

I saw in a sweet dream[1] that there was a cup in my hand.
The interpretation was apposite: the result, imputed to good
    fortune.

Forty years we'd endured grief and pain, but in the end,
Our restorative was at the hand of two-year-old wine.

That pod of desire which I was seeking from luck,
Was in the curl of that musky-locked idol's tresses.

In the dawn, grief's hangover had brought me to the end of my
    tether.
Luck turned favourable: there was wine in the cup.

On the steps of the wine-shop I am forever drinking the blood of
    longing.
From the board of munificence, this provision was our daily bread.

Whoever's not sown love nor of a beauty plucked a rose,
In the path of the wind would be the watcher over the tulip.

In the morning my way fell in the direction of the rose garden,
The moment when sighing and lamenting were the bird of the
    meadow's occupation.

We have heard Háfiz's heart-alluring poetry in praise of the Sháh.
Of that collection, a single verse were better than a hundred
    treatises;

That Sháh ferocious in attack, before whom the lion-seizing sun
On the day of battle was less than a doe.[2]

---

1. Súdí comments that to dream about wine was taken as a good omen.
2. Sháh Shujá' was a fugitive from Shíráz from 1364 to 1366 (see Poem ccvi, note
    1, and cxliii, note 3). See verses 8 and 9 in this poem.

That friend on whose account our house was a peri's home,
From head to foot he was a like a peri, innocent of any defect.

The heart averred, "In this city in hope of him I will remain."
The poor wight, it didn't know its friend was voyaging.

My looked-to sage was that moon which,
With courtesy of manners, had the art of a Master of Vision.

My malignant star snatched him from my grasp.
Yes, what can I do? It was the luck of the gyration of the moon.

Grant pardon, O heart, because you're a dervish, but he,
In the realm of beauty, had the head befitting a crown.

Not only from before the secret of our heart has the veil dropped
When tearing curtains down has been the habit of the Firmament.

Those times were good which were spent with the friend.
The rest has been without gain, and without news.

The banks of the brook, the roses and the green were lovely, but
Alas that this precious currency was passing!

The nightingale killed itself out of envy of this that
At dawn the rose was cavorting with the morning breeze.

Every boon of felicity bestowed by God on Háfiz,
Was owed to nocturnal prayers and the dawn lectionary.

POEM CCXI

I had a heart once, Muslims,
With which, if a problem arose, I used to commune;

When because of sorrow I was falling into a whirlpool,
With its resourcefulness, there was hope of the shore.

A heart that understood the pain, a friend observant of expediency,
This was the support of those of the heart,[1]

Was lost to me in the street of the beloved—
O Lord, what a skirt-snatching halting-place that was!

There is no virtue without privation's blemish, but
When was there any beggar more deprived than I?

Have mercy on this distracted soul,
Because there was a time it was skilled in expression;

So long as love instructed me in the art of speech,
My sayings were the witticisms of every party.

Do not say any more that Háfiz is expert in wit,
For we have seen, and his was a dyed-in-the-wool negligence.

---

1.   i.e. the Súfís, *ahl-i dil*, a phrase still current for those who share in spirituality.

POEM CCXII

In Eternity without Beginning all whom bountiful fortune has
    graced
Have for Eternity without End the cup of desire as the soul's
    intimate.

The very moment I was about to repent of wine,
I whispered, "If this branch bears fruit, it'll be remorse."

I accept that I threw over my shoulder a lily-white prayer-mat;
Would the frock stained rose-red with wine suit a Muslim?

I cannot sit in retreat without the lamp of the bowl;
The corner of people of the heart has to have light.

Be rid of the jewelled chalice. Seek the highest aspiration;
For the reprobate the most precious ruby is the juice of the grape.

Though it may seem disorderly, do not take our approach as easy
When, in this land, begging is the pride of Sultáns.

Do you, O heart, want good repute? Do not keep company with
    the bad.
Approval of evil, my dear, is proof of folly.

The intimate gathering, springtime, poetry being debated in the
    midst—
It would be churlish not to take the wine-cup from the beloved.

Yesterday a dear one said, "Háfiz imbibes wine in secret."
O dear one of mine, this is no crime! It is better it should be
    hidden.

POEM CCXIII

When the wounded are on the quest but lacking strength,
If you commit cruelty, it would not be what decency demands;

We do not expect tyranny from you, and you yourself do not
    approve
Of what should not be in the rite of Masters of the Way.

Dull that eye the water in which conveys no tears of love.
Tarnished that heart which lacks the candle of love.

Seek luck from the auspicious bird,[1] and its shadow,
Because raven and kite haven't the pinions of good fortune.

Do not find fault if I look for inspiration in the wine-booth;
Our Shaikh has said that there's no inspiration in the cloister.

When purity is absent, the Ka'ba and idol-temple are one:
In that house where there is no chastity, there is no blessing.

Cultivate courtesy and learning, Háfiz, because in the assembly
    of the élite,
All who have no manners are unworthy of the company.

---

1.   See Poem C, note 1; the Humá is referred to.

POEM CCXIV

Fate did not decree the killing of this wounded one by your sword,
Otherwise, in your cruel heart no fault would have lain.

When in madness I let go your tress,
Nothing was more fitting for me than the bondage of chains.

What special property, O Lord, has the mirror of your beauty,
That my sighs leave no impression upon it?

In confusion I raised my head to the door of the tavern:
In the chantry there was no Elder knowing you.

No form more delicate than yours grew in the field of grace.
In the world of painting there was none finer than your picture.

That I might perhaps, like the morning breeze, gain your street,
Last night apart from night-raiding weeping no harvest was mine.

O separation's burning, from you have I endured what
At your hands has left me no alternative but to be extinguished
    like a candle!

Lacking the friend, the torment of Háfiz's grief was a verse[1]
Which for nobody at all needed any commentary.

---

1. Háfiz for the word "verse" uses the word normally reserved for a verse of the
Sacred Koran, *áyat*, while, for "commentary", he uses *tafsír*, the technical word
for exegesis or commentary.

POEM CCXV

From our eye the heart's blood runs all over our face.
Do you not see what is going on in our face?

Within the heart we have hidden a desire.
If our heart goes by the wind, it goes because of that desire.

We have laid our face in the dust of the friend's path.
It would be lawful were the friend to walk over us.

The eye's tears are a torrent and by whomsoever it races,
Though his heart were of stone, still it would be moved.

Day and night our preoccupation is with the tears from the eye,
As to the reason why they might be flowing as far as the top of
     his street.

The eastern sun might tear its dress in envy
If my love-nurturing moon dons a bright tunic.

With sincerity of heart Háfiz goes all the time to the street of the
     tavern;
Like cloister-keeping Súfís, he goes out of purity.

POEM CCXVI

If I touch the tip of his tress, he flies into a rage.
And if I seek reconciliation, he resorts to reprimand.

Wretched watchers with the corner of his eyebrow he waylays
Like the new moon, but he withdraws behind the veil.

The night of wine with sleeplessness he ruins me,
But if in the day I complain, he nods off.

O heart, the way of love is full of catastrophe and affliction;
He who on this path hastens, falls.

When the wind of pride touches the top of a bubble,
Its crown of conceit tumbles into the wine.

At the door of the beloved do not barter beggary for sultanship:
Would anyone desert the shade of this door for the sun?

O heart, now you've grown old, do not flaunt beauty and
    flightiness;
It is in the world of youth that this commerce prospers.

The inky register of black hair, when it draws to an end,
Even if a hundred pickings were made, the white would not
    grow less.

You, Háfiz, are the veil in the way. Get out of the way!
Happy he who penetrates the mystery veilless.[1]

---

1.   i.e. divested of the self.

POEM CCXVII

The affair of anyone who leaves the top of your street in frustration
Will not go right and he will depart ashamed.

By the light of guidance the wayfarer seeks the way to the friend,
Because he would get nowhere if he went astray.

At life's ending, redeem in wine and the beloved the pledge:
A pity times that entirely go to waste.

O Guide of those whose heart is lost, for God's sake help!
If the stranger does not know the road, with guidance he might
    go forward.

The issue of temperance and drunkenness is to the end all
    deferred:
No one has known in what condition in the end he goes.

The caravan of which the escort is God's protection,
In good trim alights, and in glory moves on.

From wisdom's spring, Háfiz, in the palm of your hand draw up
    some liquid.
It might be that from the page of your heart the image of
    ignorance[1] will be washed away.

---

1. For "ignorance" Háfiz uses the word *jahálat*, which carries the connotation of
    "ignorance of the Faith": the state of being in the pre-Islamic paganism. In his
    selection of this word, Háfiz is suggesting that the heart needed to be cleansed
    of the images of faithlessness.

POEM CCXVIII

O wine-boy, the tale of cypress, rose and tulip is being unfolded,
And this discussion goes with the three cleansing gulps.[1]

Pass the wine, because the fresh bride of speech has attained
    beauty's limit:
On this occasion the bride's adorner has nothing left to do.

All the parrots of India might end up crunching sugar,
With this Persian candy on its way to Bengal.

See a poem's passage through time and space in the voyage
When this child of one night accomplishes the journey of a year.

See that everlasting eye of the beguiler of the devotee,
In the wake of which a caravan of enchantment follows.

For the world's caress do not desert the Way, because this old hag
Is at rest a swindler, and on the go a trickster.

Dropping beads of sweat, along he proudly comes, and on the
    jasmine's cheek
Out of shame at his face the sweat of night-dew is falling.

The breeze of spring is blowing from the flower garden of the
    Sháh,
And wine is dripping into the tulip's cup from the moisture of
    the morning.

Háfiz, on the theme of longing for the assembly of Ghiyásu'd-Dín[2]
    do not be silent;
Your business will prosper from the plaintive note.

---

1. The "three draughts", the *thaláthe-ye-ghussáleh*, said to be derived from a Greek
custom of drinking three gulps of morning wine as a digestive. Five draughts
were also customary after a meal, and seven to induce sleep. The "three draughts"
are certainly associated with the "morning draught", as a purifying agent.

2. Views have differed about who this Ghiyásu'd-Dín is, but the references in the poem to India and Bengal indicate that the poet had the Subcontinent in mind. Dr Khánlarí suggests (Vol. ıı of the *Díván*, pp. 1193–1195) that Ghiyásu'd-Dín Muhammad Sháh of the Tughlud Sultanate of Delhi and Bengal (1320–1420 AD) is meant. This would be the second Tughlud ruler, and he reigned from 1325–1351, and was known for his interest in Persian poetry, and establishing relations with other Islamic powers. But who Háfiz's "Ghiyásu'd-Dín" was remains a matter for speculation. In addition to Dr Khánlarí's suggestion, reference might be made to Dr Mu'ín's *Háfiz-i Shírín Sukhan* (op. cit., Vol. I, pp. 246 sqq.), but in his list of rulers no one bearing the name Ghiyásu'd-Dín appears. Others of the Tughluds bearing this name were chronologically either too late or too early for Háfiz to have been in correspondence with them. Dr Khánlarí's choice fits the chronology covering Háfiz's contemporaneity with Ghiyásu'd-Dín Muhammad Sháh. However, others have been suggested as candidates for the patron, or would-be patron, to whom in this poem Háfiz is referring. Reference should be made to E. G. Browne, *A Literary History of Persia*, Vol. ııı (Cambridge, 1928) pp. 285–287.

POEM CCXIX

O happy the heart that is not incessantly running after a whim,
Not ignorantly darting unto every path it's invited to!

Not to fix desire on that sweet lip were best for me,
But how can a fly not go after sugar?

Do not with tears wash out the black of my grief-experienced eye,
Because the reflection of your mole should never leave my sight.

Don't be such a flibbertigibbet, O heart, and so restless,
Because with these arts you will get nowhere at all.

No one do I see with a record more black than mine;
Like my pen, how should the smoke of my heart not come to a
    point?

Under the skirt of forgiveness cover the fault of drunken me,
Because the honour of the Religious Law does not extend as far
    as this.

I, the beggar, am desiring a cypress form
Into whose girdle no hand reaches except with gold and silver.

You who are of the virtuous perfection of another world,
It is not that my constancy and troth escape your memory, is it?

By the crown of the hoopoe do not lure me from the Way:
In its pride, the white falcon does not go after paltry prey.

Bring wine and first offer it to Háfiz,
On condition that no word passes beyond the party.

POEM CCXX

Although the town preacher won't find these words easy to
    swallow,
As long as dissembling and hypocrisy are his métier, he'll be no
    Muslim.

Learn wine-bibbing but behave humanely. Not all that clever
Is the beast that drinks wine, but does not become human.

A pure essence is needed to become the receptacle of grace.
Without it, rock and clay do not become pearl and coral.

He of the Name Most High knows His own business—rest content,
    O heart
Because by means of fraud and deceit, no devil might become
    Muslim.

I indulge in love and the hope that this noble art
May not, like other skills, be the cause of disappointment.

Last night he was saying, "Tomorrow I will give you your heart's
    desire."
O God, devise a means whereby he'll have no occasion for
    remorse;

For your beauty I seek from God a good disposition,
That on your account our heart may not again be distraught.

So long, Háfiz, as the mote lacks lofty aspiration,
It will not be the seeker of the source of the shining sun.

POEM CCXXI

I fear that tears may prove tearers of the veil over our grief,
And the secret under seal become the talk of the world.

They say that in being resigned to patience stone turns to ruby.
Yes, it does, but it does so with the blood of the liver.

I will go to the wine-shop weeping and seeking redress,
That there perhaps I might be freed from the grip of sorrow.

I have sent arrows of prayer winging on every side.
It might be that among them one will hit the mark.

O soul, recite our tale to the holder of hearts,
But not so that the morning breeze gets wind of it.

I am seized by amazement at the airs of the rival.
O Lord, let it not be that he who is a beggar becomes an object
    of veneration!

Through the alchemy of love for you, my face into gold was
    changed.
Yes, by the felicity of your grace dust does become gold.

Other than beauty many a subtlety is necessary for anyone
To become acceptable to the genius of the man of insight.

This disdain that is in the head of your tall cypress—
When can our feeble arm be round your waist?

Háfiz, when his tress-tip's musk bladder is in your hand,
Say not a word lest the breeze of the morning becomes a tearer
    of the veil.

POEM CCXXII

Were I to pick one fruit from your garden,[1] would it matter?
Were I to see clearly by your lamp, would it matter?

O Lord, within the border of the shadow of that cypress,
Were I the scorched to sit a moment, would it matter?

If at last, O Jamshíd's seal-ring of the blessed tokens,
Your reflection were to fall on my bezel's ruby,[2] would it matter?

When the town preacher prefers the love of the king and consta-
   ble,
If I choose the love of an idol, would it matter?

My reason has fled its home, and, if this is wine,
Then I've had a preview of what may happen in the house of faith.

Precious life has been squandered on wine and the beloved,
So, from the former what might come, from the latter what
   might be?

The Master[3] knew that I am a lover, but nothing happened.
If Háfiz also knew that I am such as this, what would it matter?

---

1.   The allusion is to the mouth of the beloved saying sweet things.
2.   i.e. the suitor's blood-soaked heart. Cf. Poem ccxxi, verse 2, where the ruby is
     said to be reddened by being steeped in the blood of the liver, that is to say, in
     grief; compare "eating the heart out".
3.   The poet's mentor-patron is presumably meant here.

POEM CCXXIII

Not a hint does luck vouchsafe me of the mouth of the friend.
Fortune gives me no knowledge of the hidden mystery.

I would give my soul for the sake of a kiss from his mouth.
He neither snatches that nor grants me this.

I have died of longing, but there is no way behind this veil;
Or there is, but the veil's guardian won't show me.

The morning breeze has ruffled his tresses. See the mean sphere
That in this does not give me the scope of the blowing breeze.

However much like a compass I circle the perimeter,
The circling heavens give me no entrance, like the compass
    point, to the centre.

With patience some sugar will in the end be accorded, but
The bad faith of Time will not grant me the time.

I said, "I'll go to sleep, to see the image of the friend in dreams,"
But with his groans and sighs Háfiz allowed me no peace.

POEM CCXXIV

News has arrived, happily, that spring has come and
   green sprouted.
If my allowance arrives, it will be spent on booze and roses!

The trilling of the bird has come. Where is the wine-butt?
Woe has befallen the nightingale. Who unveiled the rose?

Today pluck a rose from the moon-like wine-boy's cheek,
Now that the line of violets round the garden's face has flowered;

And so much has the Ganymede's glance possessed my heart,
That I have no strength for intercourse with anyone else.

I want to burn this ragged rose-hued gown,
Which the wine-selling Elder won't purchase for a single draught.

The marvels of the way of love, O friend, are many—
From in front of this desert's doe fierce lions have fled.

Do not in the street of love step out with no guide for the Way:
Those who on this road have not gained a guide have gone astray.

Do not complain of travail because, on the track of the quest,
He who has suffered no pain has achieved no comfort.

From Paradise's fruits what relish might find
He who hasn't bitten the apple of a darling's chin?

Help for God's sake, O guide in the sacred Way,
Because the wilderness shows no limit.

Háfiz has picked no rose out of the garden of desire;
Is it that in this field the wind of humanity does not blow?

Drink up the wine and pass Háfiz the golden cup,
Because in his kindness the king has forgiven the Súfís' sin.

POEM CCXXV

The clouds of spring have arisen and New Year's March[1] wind blown.
I want the price of wine, and the minstrel celebrating its arrival.

Beauties decked out, but I, of my purse ashamed:
The burden of love and pennilessness is hard, but has to be borne.

There is a dearth of open-handedness—my honour is not for sale:
Wine and the rose for the price of the patched gown have to be
    bought.

It might be said, by my good fortune a matter will be cleared,
    because last night
I was at prayer and the true dawn broke:

With a lip and a hundred thousand smiles the rose has entered
    the garden—
You would say it smelt the fragrance of some generous one in a
    corner.

If the hem of the frock is torn, in the world of roistering what
    does it matter?
In good repute, too, a frock must be torn.

These pleasantries I have uttered about your ruby lip,
    who uttered them?
And that high-handedness I experienced at the tip of your tress,
    who experienced it?

I do not know who shot the lover-slaying arrow at the heart of
    Háfiz.
What I do know is that from his softly delicate verses blood was
    dripping.

If the Sultán's justice does not ask the condition of the
    love-oppressed,
Recluses will have to give up expecting any comfort.

---

1. The Persian New Year is at the Vernal Equinox, 21 March.

POEM CCXXVI

If the heart lures me to musky wine, it is right,
Because the odour of goodness does not arise from feigned
    asceticism.

Worldlings, suppose all of you forbid me love,
I will do that which God the Creator commands.

Do not abandon desire of the bounty of grace, because the quality
    of the Merciful
Forgives sin and has compassion on those who love.

The heart resides in the circle of the recital of the Holy Names,[1]
    in the hope that
It might unravel a ringlet of the Friend's tress-tips.

For you who possess God-given loveliness and luck's
    bridal chamber,
What need is there of the bride's attirer to adorn you?

The meadow is delightful and the air heart-seducing, and the
    wine pure.
At this moment nothing is lacking but a happy heart.

The world is a fine bride, but beware,
Because this virgin ties the knot of betrothal with no one.

In supplication I asked, "O moon-cheeked, how would it be
If by one sugar lump from you one broken-hearted were
    comforted?"

Laughing he answered, "Do not for God's sake, Háfiz, make it right
That a kiss from you should contaminate the face of the moon!"

---

1.   The *zikr*, see Poem xxx, note 4.

I said, "I'm suffering because of you." He said, "Your suffering
    will come to an end."
I said, "Be my moon." He said, "If it comes up."

I said, "From those versed in love learn the rite of faithfulness."
He said, "This rite rarely appears in the moon-faced."

I said, "To your image I have tied the way of sight."
He said, "That is a thief in the night: it enters by another route."

I said, "The scent of your tress has made me the lost of the world."
He said, "Did you but know, it is this that would be your guide."

I said, "Happy the air that from the garden of beauty arises."
He said, "Cool the breeze that blows from the street of the
    beloved."

I said, "The sweet drink of your ruby has killed me with desire."
He said, "Perform you it its service, that it may become a
    slave-cherisher."

I said, "When will your compassionate heart purpose peace?"
He said, "Until the moment for this arises, say not a word to
    anyone."

I said, "Did you see how the time of pleasure came to an end?"
He said, "Be quiet, Háfiz, because this anguish too will end."

POEM CCXXVIII

I am intent on this, that if it turns out feasible,
I might apply myself to something so that distress might be ended.

The view from the heart is no place for the company of adversaries:
When the devil departs, the angel enters.[1]

Dealing with officers of government is the darkness of winter's
    longest night.
Call for the light of the sun. Maybe it will come;

At the door of the lordlings of the world
How long must you sit, asking when the Master will come?

Do not give up begging: you could discover treasure
Through the glance of a pilgrim[2] happening to come by.

The good and the bad have set out their wares.
On whom, then, might acceptance fall, and what catch the eye?

Nightingale lover of you, plead for long life, because at last
The garden will turn green, the rose branch will appear.

In this coop, Háfiz's imprudence is no surprise:
Visitors to the wine-booth lose their wits.

---

1. This hemistich has become a proverb. See Dihkhudá, 'Ali Akbar. *Kitáb-i Amsál
   wa Hikam* (Tehran, 1310/1931–2) Vol. II, p. 852.
2. The *sálik*, wayfarer on the Path. Háfiz uses the word *rahraví*, "traveller". The
   glance of a holy man, as, in particular, one notable anecdote in 'Attár's
   Mantiqu't-Tair demonstrates, was looked upon as highly effective as a merciful
   opening.

POEM CCXXIX

I'll not give up the search until my desire is achieved;
Either the body gets to the beloved, or the soul issues from the
    body.

After death, open my tomb and look,
Because from my heart's burning, smoke issues from the shroud.

Show your face: a whole creation is amazed and confounded.
Open your lips, that from men and women cries for help might
    arise.

Life is on the verge of expiring and yearning is in the heart.
    Because from his lips
No satisfaction comes, the soul is leaving the body.

My soul is straitened in longing for his mouth.
When from that mouth to the needy might come what they desire?

In the hope of finding your face shining in the garden,
Comes the breeze continuously round the meadow blowing.

In the troop of love's gamesters, his praise is spoken
Whenever into the assembly the name of Háfiz comes up.

POEM CCXXX

Whenever in the east of the cup the sun of wine comes up,
In the garden of the wine-server's cheeks a thousand tulips bloom.

In the face of the rose the breeze breaks the hyacinth's curls,
When from the midst of the meadow the scent of those ringlets
    comes.

The tale of the night of separation is not the lament of a state
One scintilla of which might a hundred volumes comprise;

From the upturned wheeling board of the heavens, no
    expectation can be
That without the agony of a hundred griefs a morsel might be
    dropped.

If you've the patience of the prophet Noah in the gloom of the
    deluge,
Disaster will ebb, and the craving of a thousand years come in.

The sought-after jewel cannot by one's own effort be attained;
It were an illusion that this without reliance on another comes.

If the breeze of union with you over the tomb of Háfiz blows,
A hundred thousand tulips from the dust of his corpse might
    bloom.

POEM CCXXXI

O happy the time when the friend[1] comes back,
To the gratifying of the grief-stricken the grief-dispeller comes
    back!

To meet the king of its fancy I led out the piebald eye,
In the hope that that royal cavalier might be coming back.

In expectation of his poplar arrow, the heart of the quarry is
    throbbing,
Imagining that he'll return in a mood for hunting.

I have sat the dweller at the end of his road like the dust,
In longing for this, that by this route he'll come back.

If my head is not caught in the bend of his polo-stick,
What can I say of the head, and what earthly use might the head
    turn out to be?

A heart that has committed itself to the tips of his twin tresses,[2]
Do not imagine that repose to that heart will come back.

If his waist comes back into my embrace,
My tears will no longer beat waves like the ocean on the shore.

What tyrannies have nightingales endured from December,
In the hope that once again fresh Spring will come back!

From the designer of destiny there is the hope, Háfiz,
That into your arms the cypress-like beauty will come back.

---

1.   Sháh Shujá'. See Poem xxx, note 7.
2.   The "twin tresses" are an allusion to the Prophet Muhammad.

POEM CCXXXII

If that holy bird were to fly back through my door,
Life spent would come back to my aged head.

I with these rain-like tears hold to the hope that again
The lightning streak of luck that has gone from my sight might
   come back.

He the dust of the sole of whose feet was the crown on my head,
I asked of God that he might come back to my head.

I will go in pursuit of him and, if to dear comrades
My person does not return, news of me will come back.

If I do not treat as precious the scattering from the foot of the
   friend,
For what other purpose would life's essence come back to me?

The rumour of the rose and sweet drowsing have become his
   hindrance,
Otherwise, if he heard my dawn sighs, he would come back.

From the roof of felicity I would beat the drum of fortune renewed,
If I saw that my journeying new moon were coming back.

I am desirous of the moon-like countenance of the Sháh. Háfiz,
An act of resolution, that he might in safety again shine through
   my door!

POEM CCXXXIII

Breath has expired, but gratification from you has not come—
Alas, that my luck has not emerged from slumber!

The morning wind into my eye has thrown specks of dust from his
lane,
Because into my sight the water of life has not returned.

So long as I may not hold your lofty form to my breast,
No fruit will come from the tree of my craving and desire:

Only the heart-enhancing face of our friend, otherwise,
By no means else can anything come about.

The heart that perceived an enticing inkiness has made your tress
its abode,
And from that strange endurer of calamity no news comes.

From the thumb-stall of sincerity I have let fly a thousand arrows
of prayer,
But to what profit? Not a single one hit the mark.

Háfiz, the least obligation of fidelity should be losing one's life.
Go, go, if from you this is not accomplished.

POEM CCXXXIV

I came out of the heart, but nothing is achieved.
I came out of the self, but the friend does not come in.

In this fancy, life's time came to an end, but still
The affliction of your long tresses is not abated.

In passion for the dust of your gate, so do I die
That the water of life does not enter my sight.

Many are the tales of my heart for the breeze of the dawn,
But with my luck, tonight no dawn comes.

Only by the heart-enlarging countenance of that friend,
But by no other means, can the matter come to a conclusion.

We have not sacrificed life nor goods for the friend.
Alas that not even to this extent has love's duty by us been
    discharged.

So much has the heart of Háfiz shied away from everyone,
Now it never comes out of the circle of your tress.

POEM CCXXXV

Good news, O heart, that one of the Messiah's breath has come,
From whose blessed breaths the fragrance of a certain person is
    coming.

Do not bewail the grief of being parted nor cry out, because last
    night
I took an omen and a rescuer is coming.

From the fire of the Sacred Vale[1] not only am I gladdened:
There in hope of a firebrand Moses is coming.

There's nobody at all who in the street of the beloved has not
    something to do:
In the way of desire everyone is coming thither.

No one has known the whereabouts of the beloved's dwelling;
There is just this much, that the clanging of a bell[2] is coming.

Tell the friend, if he has a mind to ask after the grief-sick,
"Go tenderly after him, because he still manages a breath";

Ask news of the nightingale of this garden, for I
Hear a lament that is coming out of a cage.

The comrade has the intention of harming Háfiz, friends;
A royal falcon's coming to hunt down a fly.

---

1. "Sacred Vale", *wádí aiman*, see Poem xxvii, note 2. The whole of this verse is a
    beautiful allusion to Koran xx, 10, and xxvii, 7. Moses sees the fire on the side
    of the Sacred Vale and goes to it to fetch a firebrand (*qabas*) for his people, but
    from the burning bush he hears the voice of God. (Cf. Zechariah iii, 2: "a brand
    plucked out of the fire".)
2. An allusion to the bells round the necks of the camels in caravans of seekers
    looking for the dwelling of the beloved.

POEM CCXXXVI

Friends, remember the nocturnal comrade.
Recall what is sincere service's due.

At the time of intoxication, the way of lovers' lamentation
Bring you to mind, to the sound of the tune of harp and cymbal.

When the boon of wine adds lustre to the wine-boy's cheek,
Invoke the memory of lovers in song and ditties.

When to the desired waist you reach out the arm of hope,
Bring you to mind meanwhile the time of our being together.

Do not suffer one moment's grief for the faithful;
Remember the infidelity of Time's revolving.

If the steed of fortune is a trifle unmanageable, yet
Remember fellow-riders caught in the lash of the whip.

By way of compassion, O dwellers in the seat of glory,
Recall the face of Háfiz, and this doorstep.

POEM CCXXXVII

Come, because the victorious standard[1] of the Pádsháh has
    arrived;
Good news of triumph and glad tidings have reached the sun
    and the moon.

The bounty of luck has thrown the veil off the face of victory.
The acme of justice has answered the army of seekers of redress.

Because the moon has come out, now the sphere wheels a happy
    circling.
The world now attains to all that the heart desires, because the
    king has come.

From the road's highwayman now safely march
The caravans of the heart and wisdom, because the Man of the
    Path has come.

The darling of Egypt,[2] in despite of jealous brothers,
Has arisen from the depths of the pit to the zenith of the moon.

Where's the Súfí of false pretentions and impious mien?
Say, "Burn, because the rightly guided refuge of the Faith has
    come."

Tell the morning breeze what in this grief has befallen my head,
From the fire of a burning heart and the smoke of sighs;

From longing for you, O Sháh, to this captive of separation
That has come which from fire to straw would come.

Do not lapse into sleep, because Háfiz the Court of Acceptance
Has reached by dint of midnight litanies and the morning lesson.

---

1.   or "the standard of the victorious Pádsháh": the name "Mansúr" means "victo-
rious", but the allusion is generally taken as signifying Sháh Shujá's nephew,
Sháh Mansúr (see Poem CXLIII, note 3). In this poem, however, the allusion is
most probably to Sháh Shujá' and therefore the word *mansúr* is being used
adjectivally and not as a name.
2.   Joseph.

POEM CCXXXVIII

Whoever from the morning breeze has breathed your pleasing
    perfume,
From a familiar friend has sensed the breath of the Friend.

For my grateful heart this was not its desert,
That from its own dispeller of sorrow it heard unmerited words.

O Lord, where is there a sharer of secrets, that at some time
The heart might describe what it saw and what things it heard?

O King of Beauty, spare the condition of the beggar a glance,
Because this ear has heard many a tale of kings and beggars.

It is with musky wine I refresh the soul's sense of smell,
Because it was the odour of hypocrisy I sniffed from the cloister's
    dervish-gowned.

We do not today secrete the wine beneath the dervish cloak:
The Elder of the House of Wine has heard these goings-on a
    hundred times.

We do not today drink wine to the sound of the harp:
Many a revolving's gone by since the wheeling vault heard this note.

I am left in amazement at whence the wine-seller heard
The secret of God which the gnostic pilgrim told to no one;

Wine-boy, come, because love cries out loud:
The person who told the tale against us, heard it also from us.

If I have been deprived of the top of his street, what difference
    does it make?
From the rose bed of Time, who has scented the fragrance of
    constancy?

The sage's advice is absolutely correct and perfectly sound.
Happy the fortune of him who with the ear of acquiescence hears;

Your duty, Háfiz, is the saying of prayer, nothing else:
Do not be questioning whether he heard or heard not.

303

POEM CCXXXIX

Bosom friends, open the knot of the tress of the friend;
It is a convivial night. By this means lengthen it.

It is the congregation of the retreat of intimacy and friends are
    gathered:
Recite the Word, "Those who disbelieve would be about to...",[1]
    and bolt the door.

The rebeck and harp say with plangent voices,
That you should lend the ear of comprehension to the message
    of those versed in the mystery.

By the soul of the friend, grief will not tear away your veil
If you place reliance on the favours of the Creator.

There is much difference between lover and beloved;
When the friend displays disdain, you make supplication.

The first advice of the Elder of the Companions is this:
"Avoid the ignoble associate;

Upon everyone who in this circle is not alive with love,
Though he is not dead, on my fatwa's[2] authority repeat the
    funeral prayer."

But if Háfiz seeks from you largesse
Assign him to the heart-cherishing lips of the friend.

---

1. Koran LXVIII, 51. Háfiz cites the first three words of the verse. They are *wa'in
    yakádu*. They mean "would be about to"; the whole verse may be translated:
    "Those who have disbelieved would be about to make you slip by their looking."
    It is a warning against enemies of the Faith who might endeavour to mislead the
    believer from the True Path. The opening words came to serve as a formula
    uttered for protection against the effects of the evil eye, or ill-wishers.
2. *fatwa*: legal decree or opinion.

POEM CCXL

Ho, O parrot,[1] speaker of mysteries,
May your beak not be empty of sugar!

May your head be ever verdant and your heart happy,
For a fine picture have you displayed, of the line of down of the
    friend.

You have spoken obscure words to the comrades:
For God's sake, from this riddle lift the veil!

Rose-water from the bowl dash upon our faces,
Because, O luck awakened, we with sleep still are drowsy.

What melody was this which the minstrel struck in a mode
Such that drunk and sober are dancing with each other?

From this opium which the wine-server has sprinkled onto the
    wine,
The comrades have neither heads nor turbans left.

To Alexander they give not a drop[2]—
This business is not attainable by force and gold.[3]

Come and hear the condition of people of pain,
In words that are few, but in meaning, a great deal.

The Chinese idol is the foe of the Faith and of hearts;
O Lord, preserve my heart and my Faith.

To the veiled reveal not the mysteries of intoxication;
Do not ask the story of the soul from a picture on the wall.

By the felicity of the luck of Mansúr Sháh,
In the composition of poems, Háfiz has become the model.

He performed the role of a master towards servitors.
O Lord, protect him from calamity!

1. With reference to note 3 on Poem 1, concerning *khatt*, the line of down encircling the face of a youth whose beard is beginning to sprout, it might here be added, since in the reference to the parrot there is a veiled reference to singing, another interpretation of the symbolism of the *khatt* is that it represents the host of angels bordering the Divine and singing God's praises.
2. When Alexander was led to the well of the Water of Life by Khizr, he was denied a taste of it.
3. Háfiz must have had in mind the Alexander legend as told, inter alia, in the context of Alexander's quest for eternal life through drinking the Water of Life, in the *Qisasu'l-Anbíyá* of Abú Ishaq Níshábúrí, op. cit., pp. 321 sqq.

POEM CCXLI

It is the Feast[1] and the end of the rose, and the friends are waiting.
Wine-boy with the face of the Shāh, see the moon and bring wine.

I had withdrawn the heart from the season of the rose, but
The zeal of perfect observers of the fast has served its purpose.[2]

Bind not the heart to the world, but ask of a drunkard
About the bounty of the cup, and the affair of Jamshíd the Mighty.[3]

I've nothing in the hand but the cash of life. Where's the wine,
That this too I may squander for the wine-server's enticing look?

Happy is a stroke of good luck, and happy a generous Khusrau.
O Lord, from the wounding eye of Fate keep him safe.

Drink wine to the poetry of the slave, because another ornament
      it gives
Your jewelled cup with this regal pearl.

From this, that you have a sin-concealing generous forgiveness,
Forgive our heart, which is a coin of base assay.

I fear that the Day of Doom neck and neck will go
Our prayer-beads and the patched cloak of the wine-bibbing rogue.

Háfiz, since the fast is over, but the rose also soon must fade,
There is nothing to do but to drink wine, because there's no
      time left.

---

1. The *'Ídu'l-Fitr*, the Feast marking the end of *Ramazán*, the month of fasting in
   the Muslim calender. In the context of this poem it is apparent that on the occa-
   sion of its composition the festival coincided with the end of the season of roses.
2. The allusion is to the abstinence imposed during the month of *Ramazán*, now over.
3. "the affair of Jamshíd the Mighty", whose glory was as ephemeral as anything
   else mundane. Cf. *Ruba'iyat* of Omar Khayyám, translated by E. Fitzgerald,
   stanza xviii:

   They say the Lion and the Lizard keep
   The Courts where Jamshíd gloried and drank deep.

POEM CCXLII

Breeze, do not refrain from passing by the home of the beloved,
And do not begrudge the lost-hearted lover news of him.

In gratitude for your having blossomed to luck's utmost wish,
   O rose,
Do not begrudge the bird of dawn and the breeze of union.

When you were a new moon, I was a contestant for your love.
Now you're a moon in full, do not begrudge a glance.

Now that your delectable lip's a fountain of candy,
Say something: do not begrudge the parrot sugar.

The world and all there is within it are mean and trifling;
Do not begrudge men of insight this trifle.

Your generous deeds the poet to the horizons carries.[1]
Do not begrudge him rations and provision for the journey.

Since you seek a fair repute, the issue is this:
Do not withhold silver and gold as the price of speech.

The fog of grief is lifting and things are looking up.
Háfiz, begrudge not this event your tears.

---

1.   The poet-encomiast can spread, and preserve for posterity, the reputation and
splendour of a patron.

POEM CCXLIII

O breeze, bring me a scent from the street of So-and-So.
I'm sick and afflicted with sorrow. Bring me comfort for the soul.

Ply this profitless heart with the elixir of desire.
In other words, bring me a hint of the dust of the door of the
　　friend.

In the ambuscade of the glancing eye, my heart is at war with itself.
From his eyebrow and darting look fetch me a bow and arrow.

In estrangement and separation and the heart's grief I have
　　grown old.
Bring me a bowl of wine from the hand of a fresh youth.

Make disapprovers also taste two or three cups of this wine,
And if they don't take it, running bring it to me.

Do not, wine-giver, postpone until tomorrow today's delight,
Or bring me the decree of protection from what Destiny has
　　recorded!

My heart came out of the veil when last night Háfiz was saying,
"O breeze, bring me a scent from the street of So-and-So."

POEM CCXLIV

O breeze, bring a breath of the scent of the dust of the path of
the friend.
Take away the heart's sadness and bring news of the heart's holder.

Speak a spirit-enlarging intimation from the mouth of the friend;
Bring an epistle of good news from the world of mysteries.

That I may fill my nose with the odour of your breeze's grace,
Bring a hint of the fragrances of the beloved's breath.

In your fidelity, the dust of the path of that dear friend
Bring, without any speck that appears from outsiders.

Bring from the Way of the friend a little dust for the blinding of
the interloper,
As a salve for this blood-dripping eye.

Rawness and simple-heartedness are not in the practice of
life-riskers;
Bring some news from the breast of that wily stealer of hearts.

In thanks for this that you, O bird of the meadow, are in enjoyment,
Bring to captives in the cage happy news of the rose plot.[1]

The palate of the soul has been soured by the patience I have
kept, lacking the friend.
Bring a palliative from that sweet, sugar-pouring lip.

It is a time that the heart has not seen the desired face.
Wine-boy, bring that mirror-like reflecting cup.

Of what worth is Háfiz's patched cloak? Stain it with wine,
And then bring him, drunk and besotted, to the head of the
marketplace.

---

1. There is a reminiscence here of the story of the parrot kept in a cage by a mer-
    chant whom, when he was going on a voyage to India, the parrot asked to tell
    the parrots of India its plight as the merchant's prisoner. See *Mathnawí*,
    Nicholson's edition, op. cit., Bk. i, Text, pp. 95–112, Translation, pp. 85–101.

POEM CCXLV

Reveal the face and obliterate my existence[1] from memory.
The harvest of the burned tell the wind to blow away.

Since we have dedicated heart and eye to the deluge of calamity,
Say, "Flood of yearning, come and from its foundations tear up
    the house."

His tress like pure ambergris, who might smell? Alas!
O vainly-desiring heart, forget it.

Instruct the breast, "Extinguish the fire-temple of Fárs."[2]
Tell the eye, "Steal the Baghdad Tigris of its pre-eminence."

No striving borne in this Way, you'll get nowhere.
If you seek the wage, pay obedience to the master.

When there is the power of the Magian Elder, the rest doesn't
    count:
Tell the outsider to go, and expunge my name from memory.

On the day of my demise grant a moment's promise of beholding,
Then carry me unentrammelled and free to the grave.

Last night he was saying, "I will slay you with the long eyelash."
O Lord, banish from his mind the thought of injustice.

Háfiz, think of the tenderness of the friend's intention.
Go from his Court: take away this complaint and crying for help.

---

1.   Cf. Mauláná Jalálu'd-Dín Rúmí, *The Mathnawí*, op. cit., lines. 3o55–3o64:

> That one came. He knocked at the door of a friend.
> The friend said to him, "Who are you, O trusty one?"
> He answered, "I". He said to him, "Go: this is not the time:
> At such a feast there is no place for the uncooked."
> The uncooked other than the fire of exile and separation.
> Who will cook? Who rescue from hypocrisy?

That poor wretch went and for a year in voyaging.
In absence from the friend was scorched by sparks of fire.
That burnt one got cooked. Then he came back.
Again he walked round the comrade's house.
He rapped the knocker on the door with great fear and deference.
Lest a disrepectful word should escape his lips.
His friend called out, "Who's that at the door?"
He repied, "At the door it is you too, O snatcher of hearts."
The friend answered, "Now since you are me, O me come in.
In this mansion there is not room for two of us."

Cf. Rúmí as quoted on p. 330 above, note 1. The word here translated "imma-
turity" is, literally, "rawness", "being uncooked", *Khámí*.

2. Háfiz (see Muʻín, *Háfiz-i Shírín Sukhan*, op. cit., p. 747) has been called the
    "kindler of the fire-temple of Fárs", in addition to being known as the *Lisán al-
    Ghaib*, "The Tongue of the Invisible". Although it is not likely that Háfiz is
    alluding to any specific fire-temple in Fárs, it might be noted that the early
    Arab historian Masʻúdí refers to a great fire-temple at Istakhr in Fárs. Here
    Háfiz was most probably referring to himself as the "fire-temple of Fárs". That
    he asks the breast to extinguish this fire-temple would not militate against this
    allusion to himself: in the very first hemistich of his poem, he asks for his exis-
    tence to be obliterated.

POEM CCXLVI

It is the Night of Power[1] and the registering of separation has
    ended.
All is well in it until the dawn's arising.

O heart, in being in love stand firm,
Because in this Path no labour lacks reward.

I will not repent of licentiousness,
Even if, with separation and stones, you hurt me.

My heart went, but I saw not the sweetheart's face.
Alas for this disdain; sighs for this scolding restraint!

O morning light of the heart, arise for God's sake,
For I am seeing dark the night of separation.

You wish for constancy, Háfiz? Be the endurer of harshness,
And for sure, what you lose on the swings you gain on the roundabouts.[2]

---

1.   See Poem xxx, note 1, and Poem CLXXVIII, note 1.
2.   Literally: "And verily there is profit and loss in commerce." The lines in italics
    are in Arabic in the original.

POEM CCXLVII

If there be life, I might again reach the wine-shop;
Another time I would do nothing but serve the sots.

Good that day when, eyes raining tears,
I go again, to splash the tavern door with the water.

In this nation there is no knowledge of the Divine.
    A reason, O God,
For me to carry my pearl to another purchaser.

Though the friend departed without recognizing the dues of old
    association,
God forbid that I should go in pursuit of another lover.

If the circle of the revolving azure vault were to be my aid,
Then I might enfold him once more, in another perimeter;

See our close-kept secret that all the time has been cried
With fifes and drums at the top of another marketplace!

My heart is seeking composure, did his saucy ogling
And that rascally forelock again permit it.

I every minute bewail pain, because every moment the Firmament
Makes to wound my heart with another affliction.

Again I say, in this conflict Háfiz is not alone:
In this desert many another has been overwhelmed.

POEM CCXLVIII

O you from whose cheeks joy is given the tulip-bed of life,
    come back,
Because, without the rose of your cheek, the Spring of life has
    ended.

If tears drip from the eye like rain, it is proper,
Because in grief for you life's span like lightning has passed.

These two or three moments when the promise of seeing is
    possible,
Accomplish our purpose, because life's dealing is not predictable;

How much longer the morning wine and dawn's sweet drowsing?
Get sober now, because life's choices are no more.

Yesterday he was going by, but spared no glance for me.
Helpless the heart that glimpsed nothing of life's going-by.

Theirs is no care for annihilation's encircling sea, whose
Life is centred on the point of your mouth;

A squadron of accidents lies in ambush on every side,
Because of this, life's horseman pulls on a broken rein.

I live, but without life. You must not think this all that surprising:
Who would count time spent in separation part of life?

Speak out, Háfiz, because on the page of the world,
This inscription will remain life's memorial from your pen.

POEM CCXLIX

Once again from the erect cypress's branch the patient nightingale
Strummed the note, "Be the eye of evil far from the rose's face!"

O rose, in thanks that you are emperor of beauty,
Do not be haughty towards lovesick, heart-lost nightingales!

I make no complaint because of your absence:
So long as there is no absence, there is no delight in presence.

If others with gladness and cheer are joyous and full of glee,
Let yearning for the idol be our gladness's substance.

If the ascetic hopes for houris and mansions,
Our mansions are the wine-shop, our houri, the friend.

Drink wine to the sound of the harp and suffer no remorse, and
   if anyone
Says to you, "You mustn't drink wine," say, "He is forgiving."

Háfiz, why do you complain of the sorrow of separation?
In separation is union and in darkness, light.

POEM CCL

The lost Joseph will return to Canaan. Do not grieve.
One day the hovel of sorrows will become a rose garden. Do not
  grieve.

The state of the grief-stricken heart will look up. Do not be
  downhearted:
And this distracted head will find itself again. Do not grieve.

For two days the wheeling of the sphere did not go our way.
The revolution's circling is not forever the same. Do not grieve.

If again the springtime of life ascends the meadow's throne,
O sweetly-singing bird, over your head draw the parasol of the
  rose. Do not grieve.

O heart, if annihilation's flood uproots the foundations of being,
Since for you Noah is the captain of the ship, at the deluge do
  not grieve.

Indeed, since you are unaware of the mystery of the Invisible do
  not despair;
Behind the veil tricks might be hidden. Do not grieve.

If out of yearning for the Ka'ba you plant your foot in the desert,[1]
If the desert thorn pricks you, do not grieve.

Although the alighting-place is full of jeopardy, and the destination
  far,
There is no road that has no ending. Do not grieve.

Our state between separation from the beloved and the
  machinations of the rival—
Everyone knows the lordly spinner of states! Do not grieve.

O Háfiz, in the corner of poverty and the reclusiveness of dark
  nights,
So long as your litany is of prayer and lessons read from the
  Koran, do not grieve.

---

1. i.e. go on the Pilgrimage to Mecca.

POEM CCLI

Let me give you a piece of advice, listen and make no excuse.
Everything the tender counsellor tells you, accept.

"In the estimation of lovers, the wealth of both worlds is but two
    groats:
The merchandise of this is trivial, and the gift of that paltry."

I want a pleasant companion and well-tuned strings,
For me to sing my pain to the dirge of notes bass and treble.

Since without our presence Eternity without Beginning's
    assignment was made,
Do not carp if it is somewhat contrary to what might be wished.

Intending repentance, I have a hundred times put the cup out of
    reach,
But the wine-boy's fetching look never fails.

Boy, into my tulip-like cup pour wine and musk,
Because the image of the mole of my idol won't leave the mind.[1]

Count a boon union with the face of the young,
Because in life's ambuscade lies this old world's deceit.

Have I not, O heart, told you, "Beware of his tress,
Because in the chain of this ring the wind is dragged along"?

Two-year-old wine and the fourteen-year-old beloved,
Enough for me is this same association with the greater and less.

My head is set on this that I will drink no wine and commit no sin,
Provided the Divine Decree of God goes according to my plan.

Bring the ruby cup and the bounteous pearl of finest water.
Tell the envious, "See the Ásafian munificence and die."

In this feasting-hall do not tell the tale of repentance, Háfíz;
Let the bow-eyebrowed wine-servers shoot arrows at you.

What place is there for Khwájú's composition or Salmán's,
When the poetry of our Háfiz is better than the fine verses of
Zahír?[2]

1. The wordplay here is on "musk" and *khál*, "mole": to say that "There is musk on the face of the moon" is to say that the moon-face of the beloved has a mole on it.

2. Khwájú of Kirmán was born in 1281 AD, was a Súfí of the Kázarúniyeh Order and wrote *qasidas* redolent of Sufism, and *masnavís*. He died in Shíráz in either 1352 or 1361. Thus he was a senior contemporary of Háfiz's, and the latter was undoubtedly influenced by his poetry. See E. G. Browne, *A Literary History of Persia*, op. cit., Vol. III, pp. 293–294, for examples of parallel passages in the two poets' work; examples much augmented by Muhammad Mu'ín, *Háfiz-i Shírín Sukhan*, op. cit., pp. 306 sqq. Similarly Salmán-i Sávejí, the poet of the Jaláyirid rulers of Western Iran and Mesopotamia, who was born *c.*1300 and died in 1376, was both contemporary and, it seems, a correspondent with Háfiz. (See Browne, pp. 296–298, and Mu'ín, *passim*.) There seems to be no doubt that Háfiz greatly respected these fellow labourers in the field of poetry, but that, though it might seem immodest, he was perfectly correct in claiming a superiority legitimately his. For he undoubtedly developed the genres in which they too were expert, to a higher degree than any of those predecessors to whom he owed a debt. As for Zahír, this was an interesting boast indeed: Zahír came from Fáryáb near Balkh in what is today northern Afghanistan. He was born *c.*1156 and travelled to many courts in northern and northwestern Iran as a panegyrist whose far-fetched conceits elicited the reproaches of Sa'dí, Háfiz's great Shírázi predecessor. Therefore Háfiz is being somewhat ironic when he says that his poetry is better than the "fine verses of Zahír": he is alluding to the intricate devices which Zahír, who died in solitude in 1201-2, deployed in eulogies of princes. Like Sa'dí (d. 1292 AD), Háfiz would be contemptuous of a distorted, over-elaborate style. He could be sometimes difficult to construe, but was always on the side of clear diction.

POEM CCLII

Show the face and say to me, "Separate the heart from life."
To the candle, flame for the moth, say, "Burn the soul away."

See our thirsty lip and do not begrudge water.
Visit your slaughtered victim's head and lift him from the dust.

Though he lacks gold and silver, do not abandon the dervish;
Tears over you count as silver, and for gold take my patched gown.

Tune the harp and prepare the reception. If there is no
    aloes-wood,[1] do not complain;
My love is the fire, my heart, the aloes. Take my body for the
    chafing dish.

Come to the chantry and throw the cowl off the head, and dance.
Or otherwise, retreat into a corner and pull the gown over the head.

Pull the wool[2] off the head and draw in the wine of purity;
Gamble silver and, for gold, take into the arms a silver-breast.

Tell the friend to be the ally, and all that's the world to be the foe.
Tell luck turn its back, and the army seize the face of the earth!

Do not be apt to go, O friend. Be a moment with us!
On the bank of the stream seek joy, and take on your palm the
    bowl.[3]

Take me as gone from the breast, from the fire, and the water of
    heart and eye:
Take my yellow pallor, my parched lip, and my tear-soaked chest.

Háfiz, deck out the feast and to the preacher say,
"Look at my congregation and forget the pulpit."

---

1. Aloes seed and aloes-wood, with the fragrant and bright up-leaping flame they
   produce, are associated with expression of joy as on a festive occasion or when
   welcoming a guest. Cf. Poem CCLV below, verse 3 and note 1.
2. "wool", *súf*, the derivation of the word "Súfí", because the Súfí's gown was of wool.
3. The generally shallow bowl or saucer-like cup were balanced by the imbiber on
   the palm of the hand.

POEM CCLIII

A thousand thanks, to my gratification I have seen you again
In the way of sincerity and purity becoming my heart's consort.

Travellers on the Way follow the road of calamity:
What distress from ups and downs has love's fellow voyager!

Better yearning for the hidden beloved than searching for the
    rival:
The breast of the lord of rancour is not privy to the secret.

What a riot there was when Fate's tiring woman decreed
He should blacken his saucy eye with coquetry's collyrium;

Thanks to this that the assembly is illuminated by you.
If injustice is done you, like the candle burn and adapt.

With half a kiss, from the people of the heart[1] buy a prayer
That will preserve body and soul from the wiles of the enemy.

Spread the rumour of love in the Hejáz and 'Iráq:[2]
The singing and the voice of the lyrics of Háfiz of Shíráz.

---

1.   The genuine Súfís. See Poem XXVI, note 1.
2.   Hejáz is where Mecca is situated. 'Iráq was Western Iran and Mesopotamia, the
     realm of the Jaláyirids (1336–1411).

POEM CCLIV

It is I who opened the eye to the sight of the friend.
What thanks can I utter, O slave-caressing fixer?

Tell the needy in affliction, "Do not wash dust off the cheek,"
Because the elixir of desire is the dust of the street of need.

With one or two drops that you, O eye, spatter,
O many a coquettish glance do you throw in fortune's face!

If the lover does not in heart's blood make ablutions,
On the authority of the mufti, the prayer is invalid.

The aim is beauty's languishing look. Were it not, Mahmúd's[1] glory
Would have no need of Ayáz's tress.

O heart, because of the difficulties of the Way do not divert
    the rein;
The man of the road takes no notice of the ups and downs.

In this illusory station grab nothing but the cup;
In this house of sport, play nothing but love-play.

From the tale-bearing breeze what profit's mine,
When in this garden the erect cypress is no sharer of the secret?

Independent of another's love though your beauty is,
I am not he who of this amorousness will repent.

How can I tell you what I experience from inward burning?
Ask this tale from the tears, because no fabulist am I.

Nahíd's[2] ghazal-singing does not take the prize
In that place were Háfiz's voice is raised.

---

1. See Poem XLI, note 3.
2. *Nahíd*, Venus, for whose assocation with music see Poem IV, note 2.

POEM CCLV

O new-sprung cypress of loveliness, how well with grace you move!
Lovers every moment have a hundred needs of your caress.

May your delicate guise be happy because in Eternity without
  Beginning,
For your cypress form the garment of elegance was tailored.

Him whose desire is the ambergris-fragrance of your tress,
Tell to burn and, like aloes-wood[1] on blazing fire, be happy too.

The moth had burning of the heart on account of the candle, but,
Without the candle of your cheek, my heart had melting.

My metal's assay is not debased by the taunts of the rival,
Even if like gold they pare me between the blades of shears.

The heart that found understanding in circumambulating the
  Ka'ba of your street,
Out of longing for this sacred precinct has no mind for the Hejáz.

Every moment in the blood of the eye's tears what avails ablution,
When my praying is uncanonical without the arch of your
  eyebrow?

The Súfí who, lacking you, last night had repented of wine,
Broke his word when he saw the door of the wine-shop open.

Like new wine, hand-clapping back to the brim of the vat went
Háfiz, who last night heard the secret from the lip of the cup.

---

1.   "Aloes-wood": See Poem CCLII, note 1. Háfiz in this line is alluding to happiness,
     however much the agony of burning; hence the use, in the English version, of
     the word "happy" for his imperative, sáz, literally, "put up with".

POEM CCLVI

Who shall spell out the state of bloodied hearts,
And ask of the heavens the blood of the vat?[1]

May it be put to shame by the eyes of wine-worshippers,
If the drunken narcissus grows again.

Whoever like the tulip was an offerer of the cup,
Because of this oppression will be washing the face with blood.

So much, in the key of its strings, has the harp expressed itself,
Cut off its hair so that it may mourn no more.[2]

Apart from the wine-vat keeping Plato,
Who else can retail the mystery of wisdom?

My rosebud-like heart will not open if
It does not smell again the bouquet of the tulip-coloured cup.

If he does not die, Háfiz will be running
Headlong round the sacred precinct of the wine-butt.

---

1. This threnody seems to have been composed during one of the periods in Shíráz in Háfiz's time when abstinence was being imposed by an orthodox regime.
2. This conceit alludes to mourners' tearing their hair as a sign of grief, an action which Háfiz parallels to fingers pulling the strings of a harp.

POEM CCLVII

Come and launch our ship into the estuary of wine:
Throw clamour and tumult into the souls of young and old.

Freight my boat with wine, O wine-boy,
For, as the saying goes, "Do a good deed, and cast bread upon
    the waters."[1]

In the way of erring I turn back from the wine-shop's street.
Out of kindness hurl me back on to the right path.

Bring a cup of that musk-scented, rose-hued wine;
Douse the sparks of covetousness and envy in the rose water's
    heart.

Although you are a rotten drunk, still perform an act of grace:
Spare this distracted, ruined heart a glance.

If at midnight you must have the sun,
Throw the veil off the face of the rosy-cheeked daughter of the
    vine.

On the day of my death, do not let them consign me to the dust:
Take me to the tavern, throw me into a wine-barrel.

When, Háfiz, the cruelty of the wheeling sphere has driven your
    heart to the end of its tether,
Shoot down the devil of miseries with the arrow of crackling fire.

---

1.   Cf. Ecclesiastes XI, I.

POEM CCLVIII

Arise and pour the mirthful water into the golden cup
Before the time the skull's cup in dust is cast.

In the end the vale of the silent is our alighting-place.
For the present, make the vault of heaven resound with
    riotousness.

By your verdant top, O cypress, when I become dust,
Set disdain aside and over this dust throw shade.

On the cheek of the darling the eye of lustful intent is not
    permissible:
On his face the reflection of the unsullied mirror[1] shine.

Our heart, stung by the snake of your tress,
For the antidote grant with your lip access to the clinic.

Know you that the estate of this cultivated patch has no
    permanency.
From the wine-cup's heart set estates on fire.

I made my ablutions with tears, because the people of the Path say,
"First cleanse yourself, then cast your eye on the pure."

O Lord, that self-regarding ascetic who only sees defects,
Throw the smoke of a sigh onto the glass of his perception.

As the rose on account of its fragrance does, tear your garment,[2]
    Háfiz,
And nimbly throw this garment into the way of that shapely form.

---

1. i.e. the purified heart.
2. There is an allusion here to the scent of the garment of the beloved, e.g. Joseph.

POEM CCLIX

Through craving for your lip my desire has still not been fulfilled.
In the hope of the cup of your ruby lip, I am still a drainer of
    the lees.

My faith went the First Day in thinking of your two tresses,
So what still has this madness got finally in store?

O wine-boy, a draught of that fire-coloured liquid, because I,
Among those broiled in his love, am still uncooked.

By mistake one night I called your hair the musk of Khotan;[1]
His hair is still slashing my body with swords.

In error one day my name passed the lips of the beloved;
People of the heart still from my name enjoy fragrance for the soul.

For a time in my retreat the sun saw the radiance of your face,
Like a shadow it is still every moment coming to my door and
    my roof.

The wine-server of your ruby in Eternity without Beginning
    gave us
The draught of a cup from which I am still reeling.

O you who said, "For ease of heart to be yours sacrifice the soul",
I have surrendered the soul to sorrow over him. There is still no
    ease.

Háfiz has penned the saga of your ruby lip;
The Water of Life is still pouring every moment from my pen.

---

1.   Khotan in Central Asia, celebrated for the musk of its deer.

POEM CCLX

My heart has been ravaged by one gypsy-like, riot-inciting,
Of promises false and a murderous disposition, and fickle.

May the sacrifice of the torn shirt[1] of the moon-faced be
A thousand garments of piety and the patched cloak of austerity.

Angels do not know what love is.[2] O wine-boy,
Call for the cup and pour wine on Adam's dust.

I am attendant on those words that kindle fire,
Not the idiom that pours cold water on leaping flame.

I am come to your Court poor and broken. A little pity,
For I have nothing to hold on to but devotion to you.

Do not delude yourself with your own sport, because the word is,
"There are a thousand schemes at the king-maker's command."

Come, because last night the Voice of the Tavern said to me,
"Rest in the station of contentment and do not run away from
    destiny."

Tie a cup to my shroud, so that on the morning of the Day of
    Doom
I might with wine rid the heart of the dread of the Resurrection.

There is no screen between lover and beloved:
You yourself, Háfiz, are your own veil. Get out of the way.

---

1. See Poem XXII, first verse, second hemistich, "Shirt in shreds...".
2. Only Man bears the Trust which entails passionate love for Him with Whom
    (Koran VII, 171) Man made the Primordial Covenant. See Poem XX, note 4.

POEM CCLXI

O breeze, should you pass over the banks of the River Aras,[1]
Press a kiss on the dust of that valley and make the breath musky.

The halting-place of Salmá,[2] for whom let there be greetings
    every moment,
You will find full of camel-driver's cries and the clanging of bells.

Kiss the litter of the beloved, then with humility present the
    petition,
That "I have burned in separation from you, O kind friend, come
    to the rescue".

I who used to call the dicta of counsellors the twanging of the
    rebeck,
Have suffered an ear-drubbing from separation, which for me is
    counsel enough.

Delight in nocturnal revels without any fear, because in the city
    of love
The night-rovers have means of access to the Chief of the Watch.

Love-play is not a matter of playing games. O heart, risk the head;
Were it not, the ball of love cannot be struck with the stick of lust.

It is through longing that the heart surrenders the soul to the
    friend's drunken eye,
Although the sober have not relinquished to anyone their
    self-control.

Parrots in the land of abundant sugar are living in delicious
    gratification,
But because of frustration the wretched fly is flapping its legs
    round its head.

If the name Háfiz should rise to the nib of the pen of the friend,
For His Majesty the Sháh this supplication of mine will suffice.

1. The River Aras (Araxes) flows from the region where the Euphrates rises. By way of Azerbaijan, it reaches the Caspian Sea. It is probable that Háfiz is, as it were, inditing this poem to the poet Kamál-i Khujandí (d. *c.*1400), with whom it seems evident that Háfiz, although his were far superior to Kamál's, exchanged *ghazals*. See Mu'ín, *Háfiz-i Shírín Sukhan*, op. cit., pp. 334–339. Kamál comes to mind in connection with the River Aras because he spent most of his time, not in Khujand where he originated, but in Tabríz, where he died. Tabríz is the capital of Azerbaijan.

2. The celebrated beauty of Arabia. See Poem CLXXXV, note 1.

POEM CCLXII

A rose-cheeked is enough for us from the rose garden of the
   world;
From this meadow that swaying cypress's shade is enough for us.

Far from me be mingling with the company of hypocrites;
Of the world's heavinesses a heavy bumper is enough for me.

The Palace of Paradise is bestowed as a reward for works;
For us, who are reprobates and beggars, the Temple of the
   Magian is enough.

Sit at the edge of a stream and see life's passing,
And for us this token of the transitory world is enough.

Look at the market of the world's cash, and at the torments of
   the world;
If this profit and loss is not enough for you, it is enough for us.

The friend is with us. What need that we should seek more?
Felicity of the company of that solacer of the soul is enough for us.

From your door, for God's sake, do not consign me to Elysium,
Because the end of your street, of space and being is enough
   for us.

Háfiz, complaint against the cup of Fate is unjust:
Disposition pure as water and flowing lyrics are enough for us.

POEM CCLXIII

O heart, well-wishing luck is a sufficient travelling companion
    for you.
The breeze of the garden of Shíráz is courier enough for you.

Do not, dervish, journey again from the dwelling of the beloved.
The voyage of spiritual truth and the corner of the hospice are
    enough for you;

Fondness for the familiar habitation and the promise of the
    ancient friend
Are sufficient for travelled wayfarers to grant your plea for
    forgiveness.

And if from the corner of your heart a grief leaps from ambush,
The sanctuary of the Magian Elder's Court is refuge enough for
    you.

Sit on the tavern bench and drink a glass of wine,
Because this amount of gaining riches and rank is enough for you.

Seek nothing extra. Take things easy:
A glass of ruby wine and a moon-like idol are enough for you.

The Firmament accords to ignorant men the reins of desire:
You are of the virtuous and of learning. For you, this is sin
    enough.

O Háfiz, there is no need of any other litany:
The midnight orison and morning reading for you are enough.

Do not habituate yourself to the favours of others.
The assent of God and the reward of the king are enough for you.

POEM CCLXIV

Who said to you, O my dear, "Do not ask us how we are,
Be a stranger and ask of no comrade's story"?

Because your compassion is all-embracing and your nature kind,
Pardon the sin not committed and do not ask the circumstances.

You wish that the mysteries of the torment of love be clear to you?
Ask the candle the story. Do not ask the morning breeze.[1]

That person who told you not to ask the dervish,
Has not a single inkling of the world of holy poverty.[2]

Do not seek payment for the quest from the ragged-cloaked in
    the chantry.
In other words, do not ask the routines of alchemy from the
    penniless.

No sensible physician's pharmacopoeia has a section on love:
O heart, grow accustomed to the pain and do not ask the
    medicine's name.

We have not perused the account of Alexander and Darius,[3]
Of us only ask the tale of love and constancy.

Háfiz, the season of the rose has arrived. Don't utter spiritual
    knowledge.
Discover what the time offers and do not ask the why and the
    wherefore.

---

1. Which has access to the beloved while suitors, and the candle poised in one
    place, do not.
2. i.e. *darvíshí*, "dervishism".
3. Alexander the Great defeated Darius, the last Achaemenid ruler, in 331 BC.

POEM CCLXV

I have suffered a pain of love of which do not ask.
Bitter lees of separation I have tasted of which do not ask.

I have wandered about the world and at the end of the affair,
Choosen a sweetheart of whom do not ask.

So much in longing for the dust of his door
Do my eyes' tears rain that, do not ask.

Last night from his mouth with my ear
I have heard words of which do not ask.

Why do you bite the lip at me, saying, "Don't tell"?
I have chosen a ruby lip about which do not ask.

Lacking you, in the hovel of my own beggary
I have suffered torments about which do not ask.

Like Háfiz, the stranger on the Way of love,
I have reached a stage, which, do not ask.

POEM CCLXVI

Do not ask how many complaints I have against his black tress;
How much on account of it I have been left ruined and deprived.

Let no one in hope of constancy abandon heart and faith:
So much remorse is mine for having done this that, do not ask.

For one draught of wine, followed by no harm to anyone,
Do not ask what trouble I am enduring from the
    uncomprehending.

O ascetic, leave us in peace, because this ruby wine
Steals heart and faith in such a way that, do not ask.

My desire was retirement and security, but
Do not ask what trials that seductive eye is plying.

The saying goes that in this Path life is melted away,
While everyone contends with, "See not this, ask not that".

I said, "Let me ask of the Firmament's ball the present state of
    play."
It answered, "Do not ask what in the curve of the hockey-stick
    I endure."

I asked him, "For the murder of whom have you twisted your
    tress?"
"Háfiz," he answered, "this story is long. By the Koran do not ask."

Come back and be the soulmate of my constricted[1] heart,
And to this burnt one be the intimator of the hidden mysteries.

Of that wine which at the inn of love is sold,
Pass me two or three goblets and say, "Let the Month of Fasting[2] be!"

When, O wayfarer of the knowledge, you have set fire to the ascetic's gown,
Make an effort and be chief of the circle of the world's lawless ones!

The sweetheart who said, "My heart is waiting for you,"
Tell, "I am on my way. Be ready with good cheer."

In longing for that life-giving ruby lip my heart has turned into blood.
O jewel-case of love, be with that same seal and stamp!

So that because of grief not a speck of dust might rest on his heart,
O flood of tears be flowing in the wake of my letter.[3]

Háfiz, who makes the world-seeing cup[4] his desire,
Say, "Dwell in the sight of Jamshíd's Ásaf."

---

1. "constricted": this alludes to the two states between which the mystic alternates, that of *qabz*, "constriction" or "contraction", and of *bast*, "expansion", "openness". The states which these two terms designate are familiar to all mystics.
2. *Ramazán*. See Poem xxv, note 1.
3. As suggested in, for example, the note on Kamál-i Khujandí and Háfiz (Poem CCLXI, note 1), poets not infrequently corresponded with each other in *ghazals*, and not only poets. Examples are recorded of rulers communicating with fellow princes in verse; Sháh Shujá' for instance. Háfiz's reference in this verse to his "letter" is interesting.
4. The allusion is to the cup of Jamshíd in which, as legend says Alexander the Great could do in his mirror, Jamshíd could view past, present, and future. For Ásaf, see Poem xxiv, note 3: were Háfiz to take up his abode in the sight of the ruler's *vazír*, that is to say enjoy the latter's patronage, then the ruler's all-seeing cup might be his.

POEM CCLXVIII

If you would be a compassionate companion, a keeper of your
    word,
Comrade in the chamber and in the baths[1] and the rose garden,

Do not give your tress's curls to be blown about by the wind:
Do not speak, saying, "Tell the hearts of lovers to be dishevelled."

If it is your wish with Khizr[2] to be seated,
Like the Water of Life be hidden from the eye of Alexander.

Singing the psalmody of love is not work for every bird;
Come and of this lyric-chanting nightingale be the
    newly-blossomed rose.

The path of service and the etiquette of performing the duties of
    a slave,
For God's sake invest in us and be Sultán.

Do not again draw the sword against a prey in the sanctuary.[3]
    Beware,
And for what you have done to our heart, have remorse.

You are the candle of the assembly. Be of one tongue and one
    heart.
Look upon the dream and the striving of the moth and be laughing.

The perfection of heart-stealing and of beauty is in eye-play;
In the art of looking be of the rarities of the age.

Keep quiet, Háfiz, and make no complaint against the cruelty of
    the friend.
Who said to you, "At the face of beauty, be distracted"?

---

1.   As in Greek and Roman times in the West, the public baths were places of
    resort and sociability.
2.   For Khizr see Poem XL, note 1, and in connection with Alexander, Poem CCXL,
    note 1.
3.   In Islamic Law, hunting and killing prey in sacred precincts is forbidden.

POEM CCLXIX

In the season of the tulip take the cup and be unhypocritical.
With the scent of the rose be a moment companion to the breeze.

I do not tell you, "Worship wine throughout the year."
For three months drink wine, but for nine be abstinent.

When the Elder Wayfarer entrusts your love to wine,
Drink and wait upon God's mercy.

If you aspire to reach, like Jamshíd, the secret of the Invisible,
Come and be lip-to-lip with the world-showing cup.

Although the world's business is, like the rosebud, folded close,
You, like the wind of Spring, be the knot's untier.

Do not look for constancy from anyone and, if you do not heed
   what is said,
Be in vain a searcher for the Símurgh[1] and the Philosopher's
   Stone.

Háfiz, do not become the disciple of the devotions of strangers,
But be the intimate of rogues who are familiar.

---

1. See Poem VII, note 1. In Súfí lore the *Símurgh* symbolises the Divine Agent, the
    Godhead, to which it is the Súfí's aspiration to return.

POEM CCLXX

Súfí, pluck a rose and give the thorn the patched gown,
And give this bitter asceticism to wine easy on the palate.

Relinquish disordered raving and mumbo-jumbo for the tune of
harp;
Give the prayer-beads and the cassock to wine and its cognoscente.

Severe austerity, that neither the beloved nor the wine-server
will buy,
Throw to the breeze of Spring among the gathering in the mead-
ow.

O chief of lovers, ruby wine has waylaid me;
Give my blood for the dimple in the friend's chin.

O Lord, in the season of the rose pardon the sin of the slave,
And let bygones be ascribed to the cypress on the stream's edge.

O he who has reached the reservoir of desire,
From that ocean bestow upon abject me a drop.

In thanks that your eye has not seen the countenances of idols,
Consign me to the forgiveness and beneficence of the Lord of All.

Wine-boy, when the Sháh drains the morning wine,
Say, "To Háfiz, the nightly vigil-keeper, give the golden cup."[1]

---

1. i.e. Háfiz who keeps the night alive with song in prayer and praise for the Sháh.

POEM CCLXXI

If the gardener must have the society of the rose for five days,
With the tyranny of the thorn of separation he must have the
    patience of the nightingale.

O heart, in the fetter of his tress do not complain of being
    roughed up:
When the wise bird tumbles into the snare, it must have
    resignation.

With such tresses and a cheek like his, let amorous ogling be
    forbidden
Whoever needs his jasmine face and hyacinth curls.

What business with prudence has the world-burning reprobate?
It is dominion's business that requires attentiveness and planning.

Relying on piety and learning is, in the Way, unbelief:
Though the wayfarer might have a hundred virtues, trust in God
    must be his.

Taunts from that Turk narcissus eye this shattered heart must
    endure,
So long as it needs that curl and that lock of hair.

O wine-boy, how long the delay in circulating the cup?
When the round falls to lovers it must be uninterrupted.

Who is Háfiz that he will not drink without the sound of the lute?
Wretched lover, why must he have so many embellishments?

POEM CCLXXII

The whole intention of the nightingale is this, that the rose be
    his beloved;
The rose, intent on how to play fast and loose with him.

That the lover should be slain is not all that heart-snatching is
    about:
The Master is the one who has room for the sorrows of the servant.

It is proper that the heart of the ruby's blood should froth in waves
At this swindle, which is spoiling its market.

The nightingale learnt to sing through the graciousness of the
    rose. Otherwise,
In his beak all these words and lyrics would not have been arrayed.

You who in the quarter of the beloved are wending your way,
Watch out. Heads get broken against his wall.

That voyager whose companions are a hundred caravans of hearts,
Wherever he is, God preserve him.

Prosperity's blessing may strike you, O heart, as felicitous, but
The tract of love is precious. Do not neglect it.

The tipsy Súfí who like so knocks his cap awry,
Two cups more and his turban will be undone as well.

Háfiz's heart has grown accustomed to the sight of you;
It is pampered by being united. Do not seek its harm.

POEM CCLXXIII

It's intoxicating wine I want, the strength of which knocks men out.
I might perhaps find respite from the world, and its wrongs and
    distractions.

Bring wine, because with the heavens' guile there is no safety,
With the caprice of Venus the harper, and their javelin-throwing
    Mars.

The despicable-nurturing sphere's table has no honeyed comfort:
O heart, wash away the bitterness and sourness of the taste of
    greed and avarice.

Throw aside Bahrám's[1] hunting lasso and raise the cup of wine,
For I have explored this desert plain: there is neither Bahrám
    nor his wild ass.

Greatness does not preclude having regard for dervishes.
Solomon,[2] for all his glory, had an eye for the ant.

Come and let me show you the mystery of Fate in pure wine—
On condition you do not reveal it to the ill-disposed and blind of
    heart.

The bow of the eyebrow of the beloved never lets Háfiz out of its
    sights,
But smiles are raised at his powerless arm.

---

1. The allusion is to the Sassanian ruler, Bahrám V (r. 420–438 AD), famous for
   courage, hunting, and amorousness. Said to have been a poet himself, his
   exploits and heroism have become legendary and figure in some of the great-
   est poets' *oeuvre*. His passion for hunting the onager, wild ass, occasioned his
   sobriquet of *gúr*, "Bahrám Gúr". As well as meaning "wild ass", however, the
   word *gúr* means "grave", "tomb". Bahrám died, mysteriously it appears, from a
   fall from his horse while ahead of his entourage he was alone pursuing a wild
   ass. He is said either to have followed it into a cave in which he disappeared,
   or, as an early narrative has it, died through being toppled into and submerged
   by a morass or swampy ditch. The two meanings of *gúr* give rise to the pun on
   "grave" and "wild ass". Bahrám's grave, is, of course, unknown, so that the wan-
   derer in the desert plain would not be able to find it, but for this translation
   "wild ass" has been chosen: it is more forceful; it implies that neither the king
   nor what he was principally preoccupied with could be discovered anymore.
2. See Koran XXVII, 18–19, for the description of how Solomon noticed the cower-
   ing ant.

POEM CCLXXIV

O happy Shíráz and its peerless situation!
O Lord, preserve it from extinction.

Ruknábád's stream, pray God a hundred times, "Let it
   not run dry,"
Because its clear water grants the life of Khizr.[1]

Between Ja'farábád[2] and Musallá,[3]
Its ambergris-mixing north wind blows.

Come to Shíráz and the bounty of the Holy Spirit
Seek from its lords of Perfection.

Breeze, of that merry, runaway, besotted darling
What news do you have? How's he getting on?

For God's sake, don't awaken me from this dream;
I am having a lovely time with his image.

Were that sweet boy to shed my blood, O heart,
Make it as lawful to him as mother's milk.

Who mentioned Egyptian sugar here,
Without the sweet ones putting it to shame?

Why, Háfiz, when you were burning in separation,
Did you not give thanks for the days of union with him?

1. See Poem III, note 3.
2. A garden resorted to for recreation.
3. A similar resort. See Poem III, note 3.

POEM CCLXXV

O Lord, that fresh laughing rose you entrusted to me,
I entrust it to you because of the eye of envy in the meadow.

Although from the street of constancy he has wandered to many
    a distant station,
May harm from the wheeling of the Firmament be far from his
    body and soul.

If, O breeze of the morning, you reach as far as Salmá's[1]
    alighting-place,
I have the expectation that you'll take a greeting to her from me.

With reverence, open the musk pod from that black tress.
It is the home of precious hearts. Do not tangle it up.

Say, "My heart has the due of fidelity to your line of down and
    mole.
Keep it with respect in that ambergris-coiled curl."

In a stage where they drink to the memory of his lip,
Base is he who retains news of himself.

From the tavern's door bartering and collecting riches is not fitting.
Whoever partakes of this liquor throws his belongings into the sea.

For whoever is afraid of affliction, the grief of love is not sanctified;
It is a case of, our head and his foot, or our lip and his mouth.

Háfiz's verses are each the key verse for the understanding of
    the lyric.
Bravo for his heart-pulling word and his language's charm.

---

1.   The legendary Arab beauty. See Poem LXXXV, note 1.

POEM CCLXXVI

When the morning breeze ruffled his ambergris-diffusing locks,
By every separated strand it touched, its soul was refreshed.

Where is the close intimate, for me by way of description to
    disclose
What the heart endures on account of the days of separation
    from him?

The morning postman took a letter of fealty to the friend,
The seal of the inditing of which was of the blood of our eyes.

Time made out of the petal of the rose a likeness of your face,
But, because of shame before you, it concealed it in the bud.

You have been afflicted, but love knew no limit:
Blessed be God for this Path which has no ending;

Perhaps the beauty of the Ka'ba[1] may ask the pilgrims' pardon,
Because the souls of the vigilant-hearted have burnt in its desert.[2]

To this shattered tent of sorrow who will bring
A sign of the heart's Joseph from the pit in his chin?

Let me take that tress-tip and give it to the hand of the Master,
That it may retrieve my redress from his deceptions and devices.

---

1. *Ka'ba* here means the abode of the beloved.
2. The desert through which pilgrims to the *Ka'ba* must pass.

POEM CCLXXVII

From me repose and strength and sense
A sweet-lipped, silver-necked idol stole;

A beauty, all agility, liveliness, like a peri,
An artful one, moon-like, a tightly-tunicked Turk,

From the heart of the fire of the passion of love for him,
Like a cauldron I am forever on the boil.

Heart at rest, I would be like an enfolding shirt,
Were I to take him like a mantle to my bosom.

If my bones were to become decomposed,
Love for him would not be forgotten by my soul.

My heart and faith, my heart and my faith he has snatched;
His breast and shoulder, his breast and shoulder, breast and
    shoulder.

Your remedy, Háfiz, your remedy is
His sweet lips, his sweet lips, sweet lips.

POEM CCLXXVIII

At dawn from the Voice of the Invisible good news reached my
 ears,
That it is the age of Sháh Shujá': wine boldly drink.

Gone that time when people of vision were withdrawing to one
 side,
A thousand utterances mute in the mouth and on the lip;

To the sound of the harp we'll tell those tales,
From the concealing of which the breast has been seething.

The domestic wine,[1] fear of the Moral Policeman[2] having been
 swallowed,
We will drink to the face of the friend and cry, "Drink up,
 drink up."

Last night on their backs from the tavern's lane they bore
 "Mister" Imám,[3]
Who'd pulled his prayer mat over his shoulder.

O heart, let me furnish you with good directions for the road to
 salvation:
Do not take pride in debauchery, but do not parade austerity.

The seat of revealing light is the luminous judgement of the Sháh.
If you seek closeness[4] to him, in purity of resolution strive.

Make only praise of his glory the daily litany of the heart.
Because the ear of his heart is the confidant of the message of
 Surúsh.[5]

Khusraus know the intricacies of the kingdom's welfare;
Do not you, Háfiz, a beggar sitting in the corner, raise your voice.

---

1. Shíráz is famous for its wines.

347

2. The *Muhtasib*, policeman of morals. See Poem XLII, note 2.
3. The high religious dignitary who is leader of the Friday Congregational Prayers. That he had pulled his prayer mat over his shoulder implies that he had become a wandering dervish.
4. See Poem I, verse 7.
5. See Poem XXXVII, note 1. *Surúsh* may also stand for the Archangel Gabriel, who brought the Revelation, the Holy Koran, down to the Prophet Muhammad. Cf. the preceding verse where the "Sháh" is apostrophised as the "seat of revealing light", the light of the epiphany.

POEM CCLXXIX

A voice from a corner of the tavern last night
Called, "Sins are forgiven. Drink wine."

The Divine Pardon performs its own purpose:
The Guardian Angel[1] causes good news of compassion to come.[2]

God's grace is more than our sin.
Why do you divulge a sealed subtlety? Keep quiet!

This raw sense to the wine-shop take,[3]
For the ruby wine to bring its blood to the boil.

Although union with him is not to effort granted,[4]
O heart, try you all that you can.

It's a case of, my ear and the curl of the friend's tress;
My face and the dust of the wine-seller's door.

Háfiz's licentiousness is not a hard sin
For the ruler's fault-concealing kindness;

Arbiter of the Faith, Sháh Shujá', he who made
The Holy Spirit the earringed slave of his command,

O King of the Throne of God, grant his wish,
And from the danger of the evil eye preserve him.

---

1. *Surúsh*: see preceding poem, note 4, and xxxvii, note 1.
2. See note 5 in the preceding poem: this could be an allusion to the descent, from God to Man, of the Holy Koran.
3. Take the worldly senses to be illuminated and lifted to the status of the divine world.
4. A reflection of the teaching developed in the school of Ibn Khafíf of Shíráz (d. 982 AD) and Rúzbihán Baqlí (d. 1209), to the effect that grace is obtainable, not through the acquired sciences of worldly learning, but through following the example of the Saints who, in their turn, follow the inspiration and example of the Prophet Muhammad. This teaching is enunciated very clearly on page 4 of Abúl-Hasan al-Daylamí's *Síratu'sh-Shaikhu'l-Kabír Abú 'Abdu'l-lláh ibn Khafíf-i Shírízí*, "The Life of Shaikh al-Kabir Abú 'Abdu'l-lláh ibn al-Khafíf-i Shírází", translated into Persian by Ibn Junayd of Shíráz (from the Arabic original), edited by Annemarie Schimmel, and published in Ankara, 1955.

POEM CCLXXX

In the reign of the error-forgiving, sin-covering Pádsháh,
Háfiz has become a flagon-drainer and the Muftí[1] a drinker of the
    cup.

The Súfí from the chantry's corner has sat at the foot of the vat
Ever since he saw that the police chief carries a pitcher of wine
    strapped to his back.

The state of the Shaikh and the Judge and their furtive drinking
At the break of dawn I enquired of the seller of wine.

He said, "It's not a matter to be mentioned even though you are
    a trustworthy confidant:
Hold the tongue and draw the veil, and drink wine."

Wine-boy, Spring is coming, but no funds for wine are left.
Have a thought, because from longing the heart's blood is on
    the boil.

It is love, and penury, and being young, and the fresh spring—
Accept my excuse and as an additional favour, conceal my sin.

Till how long are you going to stick out, like a candle, the tongue
    of eloquence?
The moth of desire has found its home. O lover, be silent.

O Pádsháh, in form and substance the likes of you
No eye has seen nor any ear heard.

Stay long enough for your youthful luck to receive
The blue gown from the old rag-clad Firmament.[2]

---

1. A learned lawyer empowered to issue *fatwas*, legal opinions, in advising judges.
2. The Firmament is evanescent. Its blue mantle, eternal. Háfiz is suggesting that
    Sháh Shujá' will receive his just reward on the Last Day.

POEM CCLXXXI

Last night a sharp-witted expert told me in secret,
"From you the secret of the wine-selling Elder is not to be
    hidden:"

He said, "Take things easy because, of its nature,
The world is hard on those who struggle hard".

And then he passed a bowl from the radiance of which, in the
    heavens
Venus started dancing while the lutists were saying, "Drink."

He went on, "Listen, boy, to my advice and suffer no anguish on
    account of the world.
I have given you a dictum like a pearl, if you are able to hear.

With the heart full of blood, show a lip laughing like the bowl
    of wine:
If a wound afflicts you, do not be like a crescendo-twanging harp."

So long as you do not become acquainted with this veil, not a
    clue will you hear:
The ear of the non-intimate is not the repository of the message
    of Surúsh;[1]

In the sanctuary of love there can be no boasting of speaking
    and hearing,
Because there all the organs must be the eye and the ear;

In the arena of those versed in subtleties, self-promotion is not
    the convention;
O man of sense, either utter words properly understood or speak
    not at all.

O wine-dispenser, give wine, because the knavery of Háfiz has
    been fathomed by
Ásaf,[2] the Lord of the Fortunate Conjunction, the forgiver of
    sins, the hider of faults.

1. Cf. Poem CCLXXIX, note 4.
2. See Poem XX, note 6; Háfiz here uses *Ásaf* in allusion to one of the ministers who were his patrons, a device which raises the ruling prince, their master, to the status of Solomon.

POEM CCLXXXII

You whose whole figure is excellent and wherever you are is happy,
My heart rejoices in your sugar-crunching carnelian lips'
    enticement.

As delicate as a fresh rose petal is your person;
As fine as the cypress in the meadow, your stature.

Sweet are your wheedling and cajolery. Comely your line of down,
Your mole. Your eye and its brow, beautiful. Your form and
    height, superb.

Because of you the garden of my imagination is full of pictures
    and paintings;
My heart's sense of smell by your trefoil-sifting tress is perfumed.

In the path of love self-obliteration's torrent cannot be evaded;
In the desire of you, joyous have I made my heart.

I would die before your eyes, because, in this infirmity,
With your lovely cheek they make my pain felicitous.

Although in the wilderness of the seeking, danger lurks on
    every side,
The heart-surrendered Háfiz progresses bravely under your
    protection.

POEM CCLXXXIII

Happy the water's brink, willow's foot, poetic genius, a fair friend;
Happy a heart-stealing sweet companion and a rose-cheeked
    wine-server.

O here's to the happy turn of fortune that knows the value of a
    moment!
May your enjoyment be congenial when a happy time is yours.

All those who from passion for a heart-snatcher have a laden heart,
Tell to scatter wild rue upon the fire, that they may enjoy a happy
    outcome.[1]

The bride of nature I bejewel with solicitude for a virgin.
May it be that by Time's design a benign idol into my hands
    might fall.

Consider the night of companionship opportune and do the
    heart's happiness justice,
Because a ray of moonlight is heart-enkindling and delightful the
    margin of the tulip-bed.

By the blessing of God, in the cup of his eye the wine-boy has wine
That makes the reason drunk and leaves a sweet desire.

Life has passed, Háfiz, in negligence. Come with us to the
    wine-shop,
So that the free wheeling lovely ones may teach you some nice
    trick!

---

1. See Poem ccv, note 1.

354

POEM CCLXXXIV

His moon-like cheek is the sun of beauty and grace,
But he hasn't any love or constancy. O God give him them!

My sweetheart is an angel, but an infant, and one day for fun
He will cruelly kill me, but in the eyes of the Law bear no sin.

I have a fourteen-year-old idol, sweet and nimble,
Who, by the soul of the earringed slave, is a moon of fourteen
    nights.

The smell of milk like sugar issues from his lip,
Although blood drips on account of his eye's sly glance.

It were best for me that I take care to keep my heart away from
    him,
For he has experienced neither good nor evil[1] and would not
    take care of it.

In pursuit of that newly-blossomed rose where, O Lord, has our
    heart
Gone, that in this lapse of time I have not seen it?

I would give my life thankfully if that unique pearl's
Resting-place were to be the shell round the eye of Háfiz.

If my heart-gaining friend smashes the army's centre[2] so,
The king will quickly take him as personal sword-bearer.

---

1. Reflected here is the innocence, albeit seemingly at times heartless (see the
   second verse above), of prepubescent youth, a degree of purity and freedom
   from worldly contamination recognized and extolled in Iran's ancient
   Zoroastrianism; and also reminiscent of Wordsworth's "Intimations of
   Immortality".
2. *qalb*, which also means "heart", hence there is a pun involved here.

POEM CCLXXXV

My heart has escaped, but I the dervish am incurious
About what has befallen that head-turned prey.

For my own faith I am trembling like a willow,
The heart at the mercy of the bow of an infidel eyebrow.

Let me approach the street of the tavern, my head bowed and
  weeping,
Because for what I have accomplished I am overwhelmed with
  shame.

Neither the life of Khizr nor the dominion of Alexander survive—
Do not, dervish, contend against the vile world;

Let me preen myself on that saucy, salvation-slaying eyelash,
That on its point flicks a wave of the Water of Life.

From the sleeve of physicians a thousand drops of blood might
  trickle,
If by way of examination they place a hand on my wounded heart.

Háfiz, you are the slave. Do not complain against friends:
A condition of love is not complaining over less and more.

Not the hand of every beggar, Háfiz, attains to that jewel.
Bring as your offering a treasury greater than the treasure of
  Korah.[1]

---

1. See Poem V, note 3. Háfiz uses the name *Qárún*, the *Korah* of the Old
Testament. (see Numbers xvi, 1, and *passim*). He is mentioned three times in the
Koran: xl, 24, xxix, 38, and xxviii, 76–82. He is the symbol of worldly boasting
and pride in the possession of worldly wealth, but here Háfiz is merely allud-
ing to the vast amount of treasure which he is being asked to offer in order to
attain to that "jewel".

POEM CCLXXXVI

We have tried our luck in this town.
From its engulfing danger our goods must be withdrawn.

By so much biting of the hand and the sighs I heave,
To my body, torn and scattered like a rose, I have set fire.

Sweet last night was the nightingale when it was singing—
On the branch of its bush, the rose opened wide its ears—

Singing, while that sulky friend sits
So resentful at its luck, "O heart, be glad!"

If events' polluting wave upsurging reaches to the heavens' height,
Still the mystic would not wet his clothes with the water, nor
    his fortune.

You would that the sometimes hard sometimes soft world pass
    you by?
Pass you from your own slighted promises and harsh denials.

O Háfiz, if the object of desire were forever in one's grasp,
Would Jamshíd still from his throne be so far?

POEM CCLXXXVII

I swear by the splendour, honour and glory of Sháh Shujá',
That over rank and riches I have no quarrel with anyone.

The house wine is enough for me. Bring the Magian wine.
The comrade of wine has arrived. Farewell to the friend of
    repentance!

For God's sake, in wine wash my tattered robe,
Because in that posturing I sense no hope of good.

See how, dancing to the chord of the harp, goes
The one who used to forbid listening to music!

Spare a glass for lovers in thanks for this boon,
That I am the willing slave of you, the obeyed Pádsháh.

We are thirsty for the favour of a draught from your cup, but
Boldness we are not showing. Trouble we are not giving.

Virtue does not buy time, but other than this I have nothing.
Where might I go to barter in this unsaleable merchandise?

May God not separate the forehead and cheek of Háfiz
From the dust of the audience hall of the grandeur of Sháh Shujá'!

POEM CCLXXXVIII

When in the morning from the chamber of the palace of novelties
The candle of the East casts its rays over all sides,

The heavenly sphere draws a mirror from the horizon's pocket
    and in it
Reveals the face of the world in thousands of guises.

In the corners of the pleasure dome of the Jamshíd of the heavens,
Venus tunes the organ to the refrain of the dervish chant.

The harp strums arpeggios asking, "Where has the disapprover
    gone?"
The bowl falls to gurgling, "Where has the prohibiter gone?"

See the deposition of the wheeling. Take up the glass of joy,
Because in every outcome this is the best of states.

The dangling locks of the darling of the world are all twists and
    tricks;
Those versed in the spirit seek no disputation on this thread's tip.

If you are after worldly advantage ask long life for the Khusrau,
For he is a being munificent, liberal in doing good;

The manifestation of Eternity without Beginning's Grace, and
    the light in the age of hope,
The compendium of deeds and wisdom, the life of the world,
    Sháh Shujá'.

In fidelity to your love, among the fair I am as well established as
    a burning candle,
Sitting the night out in the street of reprobates and those who,
    candle-like, risk their heads.

At the hand of grief over you, my patience's mountain has
    turned soft as wax,
Since in the fire and water of love for you I melt as a candle does.

The thread of my patience has been snipped by the snuffer of
    yearning for you,
Even as in the fire of love for you I am laughing like a candle.

If the bay steed of my rose-coloured tears had not been galloping,
How might my hidden secret have become like a candle, a light
    for all to see?

In the midst of fire and water, so hot-headed for you
Is this distressed, tear-raining heart of mine, guttering out like
    a candle.

Without your world-adorning beauty my day is like night,
With the perfection of your love I am nothing but wasting away,
    like a candle.

O proud youth, one night make me proud by union with yourself,
That from your candle-like eye my portal may be lit.

As in the morning one moment with the sight of you is left me,
O sweetheart show the cheek so that I may, like a candle, let life
    splutter out.

In the night of separation send me the passport to union,
Otherwise like a candle with its burning I will make a world burn.

Strangely has Háfiz taken into his head the fire of love for you.
With the water of the eye, how might I put out the heart's fire, as
    if it were a candle?

POEM CCXC

If fortune gives help, I will grasp the hem of his garment in my
    fingers.
If I get hold of it, what joy! And if he kills, what an honour!

From no one has this heart of mine, so full of hope, any generous
    profit,
Although words are carrying my story all over the place.

Because of the curve of your eyebrow no victory has been mine.
A pity that in this crooked fancy precious life has been wasted!

When will the eyebrow of the friend become captive to my vision?
Nobody from this bow on the mark has shot the arrow of desire.

How long must I fondly nurse love for stony-hearted idols?
These unworthy sons do not remember the Father.

Intending asceticism I sat in withdrawal's corner,
    but it is marvellous
How from every side a Magian child attacks me with fife and drum.

Ascetics are without awareness, but sing the song and tell it not.
The magistrate is a dissimulating drunk. Give wine and be not
    afraid.

See the town Súfí. Since he consumes the dubious morsel,
May his crupper be extended, the well-foddered beast!

If, Háfiz, you plant a foot with sincerity in the Path of the Family,
The grace of Najaf's Magistrate[1] will be your escort on the journey.

---

1.   The exalted 'Alí, the Prophet's son-in-law and cousin, is buried in Najaf, in
what is today 'Iráq. In addition to being for Shí'í Muslims most sacred, it is to
'Alí that many Súfí Orders trace back the lines of their *Pírs*, Guides. "The
Family" is the Holy Family of the Prophet Muhammad, prominent in which
was, of course, 'Alí. Shí'í Muslims always pray for "The Prophet and his
Family": his "Household".

The tongue of the pen has no head for speaking plainly about
    separation,
Otherwise I would elucidate separation's story for you.

We are companions of the squadron of imaginings, and the fellow
    riders of patience,
Yoked to separation's burning and consorted with absence's grief.

Ah, the pity for my life's span which, in hope of union,
Has reached its end, but the time of being apart has not.

The head I in boasting rubbed against the summit of the
    rolling sphere,
For the pay-off I have fixed on the threshold of abandonment.

How can I again spread wing in desire of union,
When the bird of my heart has shed its feathers in separation's
    nest?

Now what is the remedy when, in the ocean of grief, into a
    whirlpool
The skiff of my patience has fallen, blown by the spinnaker of
    absence's regret?

Not much was wanting for my life's bark to founder,
Because of the billows of passion for you, in the limitless sea of
    separation.

Upon my soul how might I pray for union with you when
My body has become the proxy of Fate and my heart,
    the guarantor of separation?

When the Firmament saw my head caught in the collar of love,
It bound the neck of my patience with the cord of being separate.

Far from the friend, in the fire of longing my heart was turned
    into a kebab.
Forever at separation's board do I drink the liver's blood.

If, Háfiz, with the step of yearning this Path were trodden to
the end,
No one would have placed in parting's hand the reins of
separation.

POEM CCXCII

The abode of security, unadulterated wine, the kind companion,
Were they to be available to you, O what a blessing!

The world and its affairs are all nothing within nothing;
A thousand times have I found this point to be true.

Woe and pain that until this time I did not know
That the alchemy of happiness is the friend, the friend.

Go to a place of safety and count as opportune Time's reprieve,
Because in life's ambush highway robbers lie.

Come, because repentance of the idol's ruby and the laughter of
    the bowl
Is an illusion that reason does not attest.

Although the hair breadth of your waist does not reach the likes
    of me,
My heart is happy thinking of this slender vision.

The depth of the sweetness that you have in the dimple of
    your chin,
Not a hundred thousand profound thoughts can encompass.

Although my tears are the colour of carnelian, what wonder
When the seal of my signet ring is your carnelian-like ruby?

Laughingly he replied, "Háfiz, I'm the slave of your genius."
See to what an extent he takes me for a fool!

POEM CCXCIII

If you drink wine, sprinkle a draught on the dust.
What is there to fear in a sin from which the benefit goes to
   someone else?

Go and with all you have got, drink. Have no regret,
Because without any, Fate wields the sword of death.

By the dust of your foot, O my tender-cherishing cypress,
On the day of death do not remove your foot from off my dust.

Whether a denizen of hell or of heaven, whether a man or an angel,
In the religion of all, abstinence is apostasy from the Path.

The engineer of the Firmament the road of the six-sided world
So contrived that from under the snare of the pit there is no
   way out.

The guide of the daughter of the vine marvellously waylays the
   path of reason.
Till the Day of the Resurrection may the vine's trellis not fall
   down!

Happy you went from the world by way of the wine-shop, Háfiz.
May the prayer of people of the heart be the bosom companion
   of your pure heart!

POEM CCXCIV

Were a thousand enemies to attempt my destruction,
If you are a friend to me, of enemies I have no fear.

Hope of union with you keeps me alive.
Did it not, from being apart from you I would be every moment
    in fear of death.

From breath to breath, if I did not scent your fragrance on the
    wind,
From moment to moment in grief for you like the rose I would
    be tearing my collar.

On account of the vision of you can my eye close in sleep? Never!
Can my heart be patient in absence from you? God forbid!

If you inflict a wound, it's better than another's salve.
And if you administer poison, it is better than another's antidote.

My killing by the blow of your sword is our everlasting life,
Because my soul would delight in being your sacrifice. *

Turn not the rein because, if you strike me with the sword,
I'll make my head a shield and not take my hand from your
    saddle-strap.

You as you are, how might every sight behold?
Everyone perceives according to their capacity for seeing.

Háfiz will become precious in the eyes of men the time
When on the dust at your door he lays the face of meekness.

---

*   Italicised verses are in Arabic in the original.

POEM CCXCV

O you on whose lip the due of hospitality's salt my scarred heart
    holds,
Keep it, because I am going. May God be with you!

You are that chaste pearl of which, in the World of Holiness,
Speaking well should be the theme of angels' divine praise.[1]

If there is any doubt of my sincerity, apply the test;
Nobody knows pure gold's assay like the prayed-to touchstone.[2]

You had said, "I'll get drunk and grant you two kisses."
The promise has run out, but we've not seen two kisses nor one.

Open the laughing pistachio nut[3] and pour out sugar—
Do not cast people into doubt about your mouth.

I'll smash the sphere's wheel to bits if it turns contrary to my
    desire.
I am not the one to suffer being abased by the wheeling dome.

Since you will not allow Háfiz access to his own,
O competitor, from his breast at least step back a pace or two.

---

1.   The role of the angels in heaven is to praise the Almighty.
2.   "prayed-to touchstone" because alluded to is probably the Black Stone in the
     Ka'ba for which the phrase *mihak-i zarrín*, "touchstone of gold", is used.
3.   The mouth.

POEM CCXCVI*

O northern breeze, be you of good cheer.
Because for me the time of union is coming.

What news have you of Salmá,¹ and from the place of the mimosa-tree?
Where are our neighbours, and how are they?

The banquet hall is left empty of
The comrades and the brimming bumper;

Obliterated the dwelling after prospering;
How it is, inquire of the debris.²

Now that the night of separation has cast its shadow,
What will the night-rovers of the imagination be up to?

The tale of love is seamless:³
It is the tongue of speech that's cleft.

Our Turk⁴ spares not a glance for anyone.
Alas for this pride, loftiness, and grandeur.

In beauty of perfection, you have attained your desires.
God avert from you the Eye of Perfection!⁵

O Háfiz, how long love and patience?
Sweet is the lovers' lament. Lament!

O messenger from the place of safety, God protect you!
Welcome, welcome, come, come.

---

* Italicised verses are in Arabic in the original.
1. The legendary Arab beauty. See Poem LCXXXV, note 1.
2. Salmá's dwelling. The verse is in the form of the opening, the *nasíb*, "erotic prelude", of a typical Arabic *qasída*, "ode" or "purpose poem", usually beginning with lamentation over the debris of the deserted camp which the departed beloved and her people have abandoned. The poet is inspired by seeing remains which remind him of the beloved from whom he has become separated.
3. Love is inexpressible in words.
4. Sháh Shujá': see Poem XLVIII, note 2.
5. The Eye of Perfection means the Evil Eye: to be perfect is to risk nemesis.

POEM CCXCVII*

*I sniffed the sweet breath of friendship and looked out for union's
    lightning streak.*
Come, for am I dying for your scent, O breeze of the north.

*O camel-driver with your shanties urging on the friend's camels, halt
    and alight,*
Because in longing for beauty, to me patience is not beautiful.

The story of the night of separation is better left
In thanks for this, that the day of union has thrown off the
    curtaining veil.

When the friend has a mind for peace and is asking pardon,
In every circumstance can the jibes of the rival be overlooked.

Come, for the rose-spattering veil of the eye's seven screens[1]
I have adorned with elegant patterns from imagination's
    workshop.

Other than in the imagination your mouth is not in my
    constricted heart;
Let no one be like me, running after the unrealisable vision.

As an expedient do I show vexation with the beloved,
Otherwise no one seriously displays weariness with his very life.

Killed by love for you, Háfiz has become an outcast.
Pass by our dust, because our blood is lawful to you.

---

*   Italicised verses are in Arabic in the original.

1.   The allusion is to the seven screens by which the Supreme Beauty is shielded
    from the mortal eye. The poet has a Sultán's tent screens in mind, which were,
    as suggested in the following hemistich, elegantly decorated with flower
    designs of the kind known as *qalamkárí*, literally, "pen-work". Such patterned
    textiles are still available in Iran for curtains, bedspreads, tablecloths, etc.

POEM CCXCVIII

Possessor of the world, Nusratu'd-Dín,[1] the perfect Khusrau,
Yahyá ibn Muzaffar, just ruler of the world,

O your Islam-sheltering Court[2] has opened
On the face of the earth a window for the soul and a door for the
heart.

Honouring you is incumbent on the soul and sense, and obligatory.
Your largesse to beings and places is abundant and universal.

The day of primordial Eternity from your reed a black drop,
That was to be the answer to problems, fell upon the face of the
moon;

When the sun saw that black mole, in its heart it said,
"O would that I were that fortune-favoured Hindu slave!"

O Sháh, because of your festivities the Firmament is dancing
and singing.
Do not remove the hand of joyousness from the skirt of this
chanting;

Drink wine and spare the world: by the tress of your lasso
The ill-wisher's neck has become captive in chains.

The wheeling of the heavens all at once is on the course of justice.
Rejoice, because the tyrant gets nowhere.

Háfiz, the pen of the Pádsháh of the World is the apportioner of
bread:
Do not needlessly worry about your sustenance.

---

1. Nusratu'd-Dín Yahyá, son of Sharafu'd-Dín Muzaffar and nephew of Sháh
Shujá' and Sháh Mahmúd, was given sovereignty of Fárs by Tímúr before that
conqueror returned to Central Asia after his first incursion into the vicinity of
Shíráz in the winter of 1387 (some two years to the month before Háfiz's death).

Tímúr returned in 1392 and in 1393 had practically all the surviving Muzaffarid princes put to death, Yahyá included. The poem, presumably written for the occasion of Sháh Yahyá's appointment as Tímúr's deputy in the ruling of Fárs, is expressive of the joy that must have been felt when, on account of troubles nearer home, Tímúr the Lame was forced in February 1388 to return to Samarqand, his capital, after he had appointed Sháh Yahyá governor of Shíráz. It was not long before Sháh Yahyá's brother, Sháh Mansúr, made Sháh Yahyá a fugitive and himself assumed control of Shíráz, which he retained until defeated and slain on Tímúr's second invasion, in 1393.

2. This might be taken as alluding to the paganism of Tímúr and his soldiery.

POEM CCXCIX

In the time of the rose I became ashamed of repenting of wine.
May no one be ashamed of improper conduct!

Our propriety is all a snare in the Way and I through this luck,
I am not ashamed of the darling and of the wine-boy in any
    way at all.

May it be that, out of goodnaturedness, the friend is not offended
    by us,
Because I am tired of questions, and ashamed of the answer.

Of the blood that last night issued from the socket of the eye,
We were ashamed in the sight of sleep's nocturnal passers-by.

It is allowable if the drunken narcissus's head has drooped:
It has been abashed by that eye full of the airs of reproachful
    disdain.

It is a lifetime since we have not turned a cheek from your
    threshhold.
With the help of the grace of God, of this doorstep no shame
    is mine.

You are more handsome-visaged than the sun, and thank God that,
Because of you, I am not shy of the face of the sun.

The water Khizr knew veiled itself in darkness[1] because of this,
That by the genius of Háfiz and this flowing verse it was put to
    shame.

It hid its face in the veil of the shell because of this,
That the pearl of the first water was shamed by his excellent poetry.

---

1.   The spring of the Water of Eternal Life, which was situated in a dark place.

POEM CCC

If to your street the opportunity of arriving were mine,
With the good fortune of union with you my outlay might gain
  its reward:

Those two fetching hyacinth curls have borne tranquility away
  from me.
Those two collyriumed narcissi have deprived me of repose.

Since from the pearl of your love the heart has lustre,
May it, whatever events arise, stay clear of misfortune's rust.

I, broken by adversity, might find life
That moment when, by the sword of longing for you, I am slain.

O soul and O heart, what fault have I committed in your presence,
That the devotion of heart-lost me is not acceptable?

Since I, with neither wealth nor gold nor strength, through your
  door
By no means have any way of coming out or going in,

Where should I go, what should I do, how should I proceed,
  what remedy apply,
When beaten I am by grief and the tyranny of Fate?

Grief for you found no place more ruinous than my heart,
When it dismounted to abide in that constricted abode.

Put up with the pain of love, Háfiz, and be silent:
Do not divulge the secret sign of love to the party of the rational.

POEM CCCI*

In describing those good qualities, at each point I made
Everyone listening exclaimed, "God, what a richly talented speaker!"

Restlessness and love at first seemed easy to come by.
In the end, in gaining those excellences my life was consumed.

I asked, "When will you forgive my ineffectual soul?."
He answered, "That time life is no intervening obstacle."

On the gibbet's height Halláj[1] this subtlety nicely sings:
"From the Sháfi'í[2] they do not inquire the likes of this proposition."

I have given the heart to a friend, a cheeky, flirtatious idol,
Of an agreeable nature, commendable morals.

In the very act of keeping the recluse's corner my eye shot off
    the Way
And now, like the intoxicated, I've reeled in the direction of your
    eyebrow.

A hundred times I have witnessed Noah's deluge in the outpouring
    of the eye,
But from the tablet of my heart your image has never been effaced.

O friend, Háfiz's arm is an amulet against the misfortune of
    the evil eye.
O Lord, let me see it hanging from your neck!

---

*   Italicised verses are in Arabic in the original.
1.   Mansúr al-Halláj (see Poem CXXXVI, note 1), the ecstatic mystic put to death in Baghdad in 309 AH/922 AD, allegedly for exclaiming *ana al-Haqq*, "I am God". For the Súfís he represents the path of *sukr*, ecstatic intoxication, in contrast to the way of *sahv*, sobriety.
2.   A *Sháfi'ite* of the way of *sahv*, would be a follower of 'Alí 'Abdu'l-Alláh ash-Sháfí (b. 767 AD, d. 820 AD). He was the great rationalist and Traditionalist who established the principles (*usúl*) of Muslim Jurisprudence, the *usúl al-fiqh*, based on analytical rational application of the Sunna, example, of the Prophet, and on the Koran, to the exclusion of the personal ecstasy of the individual as a valid ground on which to postulate intuition of the Divine in a process in which reason had no part.

POEM CCCII*

Glad news that peace has alighted on the mimosa tree.[1]
Praise be to God, announcer of these ultimate favours!

Where is that happy report that has given the happy news of this
  victory,
That at its feet I might scatter my life as if it were silver and gold?[2]

With the Sháh's return to this rare alighting-place,
His foes' attack is consigned to the pavilion of oblivion.

For sure the treaty-breaker is reduced to defeat;
Among people of understanding verily are pledges inviolable;

He was looking for clemency from the cloud of hope, but
His searching eye gave out nought but tears.

He fell into a Nile of grief. The sphere mockingly cried,
"You have repented now, but gained no advantage from repentance."

Wine-server, since the friend is moon-cheeked and of the people
  in the secret,
Let Háfiz drink wine, and let the Shaikh and the jurisprudent do
  so as well.

---

*   Italicised verses are in Arabic in the original.
1. See Poem ccxcvi, note 2 (the dwelling of the beauty, Salmá). Here the allusion
    is to Shíráz, the capital of Sháh Shujá', to which it appears that he has safely
    returned from successful warfare against refractory tribal groups.
2. An allusion to scattering coins on the track of the bearer of good news.

POEM CCCIII

Love's dalliance and youth and ruby-coloured wine,
The intimate gathering and sympathetic comrade and wine
   unending,

The wine-server sweet-mouthed and the minstrel sweet-voiced,
The companion of pleasant ways, of good fame the bosom friend,

A darling the envy of the Water of Life for beneficence and purity,
A sweetheart the envy of the full moon for beauty and comeliness,

A feasting hall[1] heart-easing like the palace of the
   highest paradise,
A rose bed surrounding it like the garden of the Abode of Peace,

The ranks of well-wishing sitters and the stewards courteous,
Friends who know the mysteries, and friend-gratifying partners,

Wine rose-coloured, sharply bitter, easy on the palate,
It is accompanying sweetmeats from the idol's ruby lip while it is
   the conveyor of undiminished carnelian,

The wine-boy's glance, a drawn sword for pillaging the senses,
The tresses of the beloved, the snare spread for trapping the heart,

A knower of subtleties, a wit like Háfiz of the sweet utterance,
An exemplar of generousity, world-illumining like Hajjí Qavám[3] —

Whoever does not want this companionship, for him happiness
   of heart is destroyed,
And he who does not seek this gathering, to him life is unlawful.

---

1.   Háfiz is providing a picture of a typical convivial assembly of guests being
entertained to wine and music. They would be seated round the room, min-
strels and singers of verse performing in front of them. This verse is reminis-
cent of the wonderful description in the great *qasída* in honour of Abú Ja'far
Ahmad ibn Muhammad ibn Khalaf of Sístán, composed by the poet Rúdakí
(d. 940–1 AD), in which the poet describes the court of the Sámánid ruler Nasr II

ibn Ahmad (r. 913–942 AD), on the occasion of a victory celebration. Rúdakí speaks of the courtiers sitting in ranks according to the dignity of their positions in the Court, and being served by Turks:

> Each shining like a two-week-old moon,
>
> Each having a garland of myrtle placed on his brow,
> The lips of each, ruby wine, and their curls and tresses, fragrant flowers;
>
> The wine-server an idol uniquely fair among beauties,
> Child of a Turkish Princess and of the Turk Kháqán.

In accordance with the convention whereby the poets of Persia learnt hundreds of the verses of their predecessors by heart as part of their training, if for no other reason, Háfiz would indubitably have been familiar with this great ode, and, equally indubitably, must have had it in mind when he composed the verse about the heart-easing feasting hall, and the following verse, to which this note is applied.

2.   See Poem XI, note 1.

377

POEM CCCIV

Hail auspicious-footed bird of the happy message,
Harbinger of goodness, what news?

Where is the friend? Which the way?
O Lord, may this caravan have Eternity without Beginning's
    grace for escort,

Because by it the enemy has been ensnared and the beloved
    reciprocated desire.
What has beset me and my beloved has no end; whatever has no
    beginning receives no conclusion.

Since the tress of the holder of the heart demands the pagan
    girdle,
Go away, O Shaikh: the dervish gown is unlawful for our body.

The bird of my spirit that was singing from the Lote Tree[1]
The grain[2] of your mole in the end cast into the snare.

For my feverish eye sleep would not be becoming—
How might he with an incurable disease sleep?

For heart-lost me you show no pity. I said,
"This is my plea and, you there, there will be times anon."[3]

The rose has taken gracefulness beyond any limit. Out of
    kindness show your cheek.
The cypress preens itself and that is not agreeable. You, for God's
    sake, show your graceful gait.

If Háfiz has a penchant for your eyebrow, this is fitting:
Men of eloquence do make their abode in the prayer-niche's
    corner.

1. Lote Tree: "The Sidra tree of the Boundary" near which the Prophet Muhammad was visited by the Angel of the Lord (Gabriel), who began to reveal to him the news of the Lord which was not to be disputed. See Koran, in an amazingly moving passage, LIII, 1–18. The Sidra is the *Zizyphus jujuba* of Linnaeus, the prickly plum; but cf. the Texas buckthorn, *Condalia obtusifolia*.

2. In Islamic tradition, it was a grain, not an apple, which occasioned Adam's fall from grace.
3. The threat of retribution and remorse is implied, although, as the third verse says, the situation has no ending.

POEM CCCV

I am the lover of the youthful, happy, freshly blooming face,
And of God I have asked in prayer the joy of this affliction.

I am a lover, a wastrel, and a roving eye, and I speak plainly,
So that you may know with how many virtues I am adorned.

I am visited with shame for my sullied gown,
Which I have embellished with patches with a hundred guileful
    artifices.

Burn well, O candle, in grief for him, for behold,
I too have girded my loins and risen to this same occupation.

With such a trial as this my employment's gains were lost.
With sorrowing I have added to what I have squandered from
    the heart and soul.

Like Háfiz I go to the tavern, my garment ripped open;
It may be that the newly blossomed heart-snatcher will pull me
    to his breast!

POEM CCCVI

Come back, wine-boy, because I want your ministrations;
I am eager for service and praying for a good turn of luck.

As the bounty of the bowl lit with luck is yours,
Light up the way out of the darkness of my confusion.

Although in a hundred ways I am immersed in an ocean of sin,
As soon as I became acquainted with love, I am of those
    deserving mercy.

Do not censure me, O sage, for profligacy and having a bad name,
Because this was preordained in the book of my fate.

Drink wine, because to be a lover is not by personal acquisition
    or choice:
This gift came as my creation's legacy.

I who in all my life have not chosen to journey from my native
    land,
From the love of seeing you am eager for travel.

Sea and mountains in the way, and I, wounded and weak—
O Khizr of the auspicious foot,[1] give strength to my resolution!

Outwardly I am far from the door of the fortunate mansion of
    the friend,
But in heart and soul I am of the dwellers in the Presence.

Háfiz will surrender his life before your eyes:
This is my dream, if life gives me time.

---

1. According to legend, verdure sprouted wherever Khizr (the Green Man) placed
   his foot.

POEM CCCVII

Last night the languishing of your eye deprived me of power,
But by the grace of your lip I conceived the form of the soul.

My love for your musky line of down is not a thing of today:
For a long time I have been intoxicated by this cup's new moon.[1]

From my constancy this point happily emerged, that despite
     oppression,
I have not at the end of your street given up the quest.

Do not look for prosperity from me, the haunter of the tavern,
Because ever since I existed I have confessed the service of
     wastrels.

In the Way of Love, a hundred dangers lie that side of mortality,
Lest you would say, "My life ended, I am saved."

After this what care should be mine of the ill-aimed arrow of the
     envious,
When I have hooked on to the bow of the beloved's eyebrow?

For me a kiss on the jewel-casket of your carnelian is lawful,
Because, for all the sorrow and injustice, I have not broken fideli-
     ty's seal.

The high degree of the learning of Háfiz had ascended to the sky.
Yearning for your lofty box-tree stature has brought me low.

A military idol put my heart to the sack and departed—
Alas if the king's benevolence does not rescue me!

---

1.   i.e. the beloved's face partly revealed from shadow, and reflected over the rim
    of the cup. See Poem cccxi, verse 6.

POEM CCCVIII

Apart from this that I have lost my faith and understanding,
Come, tell what advantage I have gained from love of you.

Although longing for you has thrown my life's harvest to the wind,
By your dear foot's dust I swear I have not broken my pledge.

Although like a mote I am miniscule, behold the power of love,
How in desiring your face I have become linked to the sun!

Bring wine because it is a lifetime since I with no apprehension
    or fear
In the nook of safety for the sake of pleasure have sat.

If, O preacher of counsel, you are of those who are sober,
Do not write words on dust, for what is the point? I am drunk.

How for the sake of the friend might I raise my head from the
    shame
That no worthy service has come from my hand?

Háfiz burned, but that heart-caressing friend never said,
"Let me send him a salve for I have wounded his heart."

POEM CCCIX

Lest it should ruin me do not give your tress to the wind.
Lest I be undermined do not lay the foundation of coquetry.

Light up your cheek, to disengage me from the petals of the rose.
Lift up your stature, to free me from the cypress.

Do not become the talk of the town so that I am not driven to
    the mountains:
Do not display the disdain of Shírín lest you make me Farhád.[1]

Do not drink wine with others so that I do not consume liver's
    blood.
Do not lift the head in pride so that my cry does not reach the
    heavens.

Do not make your tresses into a curl so that you do not put me
    in fetters.
Do not add lustre to your face lest you destroy me.

Do not like the Firmament shift about so that Háfiz you do not
    slay.
Come to heel so that auspicious fortune might do me justice.

Do not be the candle in every gathering, otherwise it is me you
    will burn.
Do not drink to every party so that I may not drink in memory
    of you.

Do not be the friend of strangers so that you do not rob me of
    yourself.
Do not grieve over others so that you do not make me unhappy.

Have mercy on wretched me and come to my rescue,
Lest my cry for help reaches the door of Ásaf.[2]

God forbid that Háfiz should turn his face away because of your
    tyranny:
From that day that I have been in bondage to you, I am free.

1. Desperate because of his unrequited passion for Shírín, the legendary lover Farhád went out into the desert and the mountains, wildly wandering.
2. The Chief Minister: as Háfiz's protector, it might be he who would carry Háfiz's complaint of neglect to the Sháh, his master.

POEM CCCX

I speak openly and am happy-hearted at what I say:
I am the slave of love and free of both worlds.

I am the bird of the Holy Rose Garden. What description shall I
    give of separation:
Of how I have tumbled into this snare of accidents?

I was an angel and my home was the highest Paradise.
Adam brought me into this temple of the abode of desolation.

The shade of the Túbá,[1] gratification from the Houri, and the
    brink of the Pond[2]
Went from my memory in desire for the end of your street.

On the tablet of my heart there is nothing but the alif[3] of the
    friend's stature.
What can I do? The Master has taught me no other letter.

No astrologer has recognized the star of my lucky fortune.
O Lord, under what horoscope was I born of mother-earth?

From the time that I became the earringed slave of the tavern
    of love,
Every moment a fresh sorrow comes to me with a "May it be
    blessed!"

The pupil of my eye drinks the blood of the heart and it is right
    to do so:
For what else have I given the heart to the darling of the people?

Cleanse the face of Háfiz with the tress-tip dipped in tears,
Otherwise this perpetual flood will wash my foundations away.

---

1. The Túbá tree, a tree in Paradise. See Poem LX, note 1.
2. *Hauz*, the pond (or river) of abundance, *kawsar* or *kawthar*. See Poem CLVIII,
    note 1.
3. The first letter of the Arabo-Persian alphabet, "l".

POEM CCCXI

You see me and at once increase my pain.
I see you and every moment my fondness becomes greater.

Of my condition you do not ask. I do not know what your
    intention is.
You make no attempt to effect my cure. Is it that you do not
    understand my pain?

The way is not this, that you dump me in the dust and pass on.
Do the passing by, but still enquire of me, so that I may become
    the dust on your path.

I will not withhold my hand from the hem of your garment
    except in the dust, and even then,
When you are going over my dust, my dust will seize your hem.

By love for you my breathing is stifled. How long will you show
    disdain?
You have destroyed me, yet you do not say, "Requiescat in pace."

One night in the darkness among your tresses I found my heart;
I was beholding your cheek and again drinking from the new
    moon of the crescent cup:[1]

All at once I drew you to my breast and your locks were entangled
    in twists.
I put my lip on your lip, and sacrificed heart and soul.

Be gentle toward Háfiz. Tell the enemy to go and give up the ghost;
When I see warmth from you, what fear is mine of the ineloquent?

---

1. The lips of the beloved.

POEM CCCXII

I followed the creed of the reprobates for years
Until by the decree of wisdom I locked up cupidity in prison.

Not on my own did I travel the path to the nest of the 'Anqá:[1]
I completed this stage with the bird of Solomon.[2]

I, contrary to custom in the quest for desire's assuagement,
Obtained composure from those scattered tresses.

Cast, O treasure of desire, a shadow over my scarred heart,
Because in madly wanting you I have laid waste this house.

I repeated that I would not kiss the wine-server's lip, but now
I am biting my lip over why I heeded those who do not
    comprehend.

Temperance's planning or drunkenness's is not in my hand or
    yours:
That which the Sultán of Eternity without Beginning said "Do",
    I have done.

From the grace of Eternity without Beginning I am expecting the
    Elysian garden,
Although I have so often acted as doorman at the tavern.

That my aging head cherishes the society of Joseph,
Is the wage for the patience that in the heart of sorrows I have
    endured.

No háfiz[3] in the arch of the prayer-niche enjoys
This prosperity that I by the power of the Koran have done.

If for a *diván* of lyrics I am seated in the seat of the mighty, what
    wonder?
I have performed the Sahib *Diván's*[4] service for years.

1. *'Anqá*, the mythical, inaccessible bird also called *Símurgh*.
2. The hoopoe, *hudhud*, the messenger between Solomon and the Queen of Sheba (see Koran xxvii, 20 sqq. Cf. I Kings x.) It seems that Háfiz had 'Attár's *Mantiqu't-Tair*, "Speech of the Birds", in mind. The birds set off in quest of the Símurgh, the hoopoe acting as their guide and encourager.
3. *háfiz*, one who, as Háfiz's sobriquet shows he could, can recite the whole of the Koran from memory.
4. *Sahib Díván*: it is not precisely known which of Háfiz's patrons or protectors is intended here; the Sahib Díván, Head of the Chancellery, was a high government official. However, the fact that Háfiz was appointed teacher of Koranic exegesis under the patronage of Hajjí Qavám, makes it seem that a reference to the latter may have been intended while a note of gratitude was being struck in this verse. Hajjí Qavám as Keeper of the Seal (see Poem xi, note 1) could be considered Head of the Chancellery.

POEM CCCXIII

Last night I was waylaying the passage of sleep with a torrent
of tears.
I was engraving on water[1] a picture in memory of your line of
down.

The eyebrow of the friend in my sight and the patched gown
burnt,
I was raising a cup to the memory of the prayer-niche's corner.[2]

For me to view, the face of the idol was revealing the splendour
of a bride unveiled,
And from afar I was implanting a kiss on the splendour of the
moon in full.

My eye on the wine-boy's face and my ear on the harp's continuo,
I with eye and ear took an omen[3] from this conjunction.

Until daybreak I was limning in the busy workshop of the
sleepless eye
A picture of the imagined vision of you.

Every bird of thought that from the top of the branch of speech
took flight,
Again I stroked with the violin bow of your dangling locks.

To the accompaniment of this ghazal, the wine-boy was taking up
for me the cup;
I was uttering this song and quaffing the pure wine.

Háfiz's state was happy and I for good luck took an omen
For the long life and happy fortune of lovers.

---

1. The phrase "to write on water", of course, means to attempt the impossible, or
   to act in vain, but Háfiz here also has the "torrent of tears" in mind.
2. The eyebrow of the friend.
3. It is still a practice in Iran to take an omen (*fál*) from the *Díván* of Háfiz. The
   analogy is taking *sortes Virgilianae*.

POEM CCCXIV*

Although I have become old, wounded of heart and feeble,
Whenever your face is remembered, I become young.

Thanks to God that whatever I asked of him,
To the utmost of my desire I was satisfied.

O young rose bush, enjoy luck's fruits, because
In your shade I have become the nightingale of the garden of the
  world.

At first, of the see-saw¹ of my existence I had no inkling.
It was in the school of grief for you I became conversant with
  such distinctions.

Fate consigns me to the tavern,
However much I have been that or this.

I am not old in years and months: it is the faithless friend
That, as does life, passes me by; it is because of this I have
  grown old.

The door of True Meaning was opened to my heart from that day
That I became one of the dwellers in the Court of the Magian
  Guide.

On the high road of eternal fortune to the Throne of Fortune,
With the bowl of wine I achieved the hearts of friends'
  gratification.

From that time your eye's incitement hit me,
From the evil of the last of Time I was safe.

*Last night the Guardian gave good news saying, "O Háfiz,
Come back, because I have gone security for your sin's forgiveness."*

---

* Italicised verses are in Arabic in the original.
1. i.e. up or down, good or bad, saved or rejected.

POEM CCCXV

In the eye's weaving mill I drew the image of your face;
No idol with your appearance have I heard of or seen.

Although in seeking you I ride as swiftly as the north wind,
The dust of your strutting cypress form I cannot reach.

It was your reproving eye and heart-enticing neck
That put me like a wild deer to flight from mortals.[1]

Because of longing for the fountain of your sweet drink, what
    drops I have shed!
Because of the ruby of your wine-selling, what frustrating
    coquetry I have bought!

With the fetching look, what arrows you have shot at my
    wounded heart;
At the end of your street, what a burden of anguish have I borne!

O breeze of the morning, from the street of the friend bring a
    speck of dust,
Because from that dust I have scented the smell of the blood of
    wounded hearts.

A breeze like a rosebud from his street passed over my head,
So that at his fragrance I tore the veil off the blooded heart.

In the night of your tress I attached no hope to the day of my life:
From heart's desiring I dismissed expectation of the circulating
    of your mouth.[2]

I swear by the dust beneath your foot and the light of Háfiz's eye,
That without your cheek from the lamp of the eye I have seen
    no light.

---

1. Drove me to the deserts and mountains as Farhád's love of Shírín drove him
    into the rocky wilderness.
2. As wine would be circulated among guests.

POEM CCCXVI

Who might I be that near that benevolent heart I should pass?
O you the dust of whose door is a crown on my head,
    what kindness you show!

O ravisher of hearts, tell who it was that taught you courtesy to
    the slave,
For I could never ascribe this idea to those about you.

O holy bird, make aspiration the escort for my journey,
Because the way to the destination is long and I am new to
    travelling.

O breeze of the dawn, convey my homage,
Saying, "At the time of your dawn prayer do not forget me."

Show me the way to the private retreat that henceforth I
May drink wine with you and not again suffer the stress of the
    world.

Happy that day when from this staging post I pack up my traps
And it is from me that comrades ask news of the end of your street.

O Háfiz, it is fitting if, in quest of the jewel of union,
I make the eye an ocean of tears and plunge into it.

The dignity of verse is exalted and world-captivating. Speak,
That the Ocean King[1] might fill your mouth with pearls.

---

1. The ruler of Hormuz, anciently the Persian Gulf's emporium for trade with India and the Far East, was in the hands of Qutbu'd-Dín Tahamtan (d. 1347) and his son and successor, Turánsháh. In addition to being an important trading post, Hormuz was a rich source of Persian Gulf pearls. Ibn Battuta. *Travels, 1325–1354*, translated by H. A. R. Gibb (Cambridge, 1962) Vol. II, pp. 400 sqq. gives a description of Hormuz and its rulers, based on two visits he made to that island. He especially, and, in the context of Háfiz and Sufism, significantly mentions the dervish garb which Tahamtan constantly wore, even when giving audience. He also alludes to eminent Súfís resident on the island. Háfiz did not visit Hormuz (see Mu'ín, op. cit., pp. 156–157); as (see Poem XII, note 1) he implies, he received gratuities from its king, though he had not seen him. The ruler of Hormuz was known as the "Ocean King". It was the practice to fill a gratifying poet-eulogist's mouth with precious stones as a reward.

POEM CCCXVII

You are like the morning and I am the candle in the dawn
   chamber.
Give a smile and see the soul, how I am surrendering it.

The brand of your unbridled tress on my heart is such that
When I pass away, my tomb will turn into a bed of violets.

To the threshold of hope for you I have opened the gateway of
   the eye,
That you might spare me a glance. Have you yourself cast me
   from sight?

How might I thank you, O grief's battalion? God protect you,
Because, yes, in the time of desertion you do not leave my side.

I am the slave of the pupil of my eye that at blackheartedness
Rains a thousand drops when I reckon the pain of my heart.

At every glance our idol displays lustre, but
No one sees these enticing looks I am seeing.

If over the dust of Háfiz the friend should pass as the wind does,
In longing, in the heart of that narrow place, the grave, I would
   rip up the shroud.

POEM CCCXVIII

My poverty burdens me,
Because by the lofty-statured I am put to shame.

Perhaps a chain of hair might come to my rescue.
Otherwise I shall give myself to madness.

Enquire the fluctuations of the revolving dome from my eyes,
Because from nightfall to day I am counting the stars.

I kiss the lip of the bowl in thanks for this,
That it has informed me of the mystery of Time.

Very grateful am I to my arm,
Because I lack the strength of an injurer of men.

If I offered a prayer for vendors of wine,
What would it matter? I would be rendering kindness's due.

I have a head like the drunken Háfiz, but
I live in hope of the favour of that headman.

You will not be raising me from the dust
Even were I to rain gems instead of tears.

Although because of his tress my business has been beset by a
    tangle,
Nevertheless I have the hope of an opening because of his
    kindness.

Do not impute the ruddiness of my face to joy. Like the
    wine-bowl,
From my cheeks the blood of the heart gives out a reflection.

The minstrel's mode will make me lose self-control.
Woe if because of this, within this mode audience is denied me.

I am the poet of the magic that, with the speech's fascination,
Rains from the reed of the pen candy and sugar.

We set out into this wilderness with a hundred hopes.
O Guide of my strayed heart, do not desert me.

As I am unable to see you passing with the speed of wind,
Whom might I ask to utter a few words to my friend?

At the telling of the tale of him, the eye of luck dropped asleep.
Where a breeze from Providence, to wake me up?

I have become the watchman over the sanctum of the heart,
In order to let no reverie other than of him get behind its veil.

Last night he was repeating, "Háfiz is all show and hypocrisy."
In my business, apart from the dust of his door, with whom a
    better way?

POEM CCCXX

If the dust on the sole of the idol's foot were to lend me a hand,
I would trace a dusty line on the slate of my sight.

If, in quest of the soul, his edict[1] were to reach me,
That very moment like a candle at one breath I would be
    extinguished.

Though my friend does not put the base coin of my heart to
    the test,
Yet on his path from my eye I count out coin of legal tender.

Do not shake the dust of me off the hem of your garment,
    because after me,
Not even the wind can from this door blow my dust away.

I am drowned in hope of your embrace, but there is the hope
That by the wave of my tears I might be carried to the shore.

Today do not divert the head from my fidelity, but think
Of that night when out of grief I lift my hand in prayer.

Your brace of black tresses[2] for the comforting of lovers
Granted a settlement but left me unsettled.

O wind bring me a breeze from that wine,
That by its fragrance it might cure my hangover.

Háfiz, since to me his ruby lip is precious life,
May it be a life for me the moment I am about to give life up.

---

1.   That the word *parváneh* means both "moth" and "edict" or "decree" presents
the poet with the opportunity to indulge in a pun which introduces the under-
lying note of the candle and the moth, but which cannot be imitated in the
vocabulary of another language.
2.   The Prophet Muhammad is depicted as having two dark tresses hanging down
either side of his face: there is an allusion here to his Message, the news of
God's compact with Man, the Koran.

POEM CCCXXI

In the hidden recess of close companionship I have a sweet idol,
Because of whose tress and cheek I am beside myself.

I am a lover and a reprobate, and a loud-voiced[1] imbiber of wine,
And all these honorifics are mine because of that fairy-like houri.

If you will take a step into the rogues' nest,
I have some unadulterated wine, and nice titbits of poetry to go
    with it.

If in this fashion you keep me without means,
With morning sighs I will keep your tresses tousled.

And if like this the bluish patina of the friend's young beard
    sprouts,
I shall be keeping a pale face painted by a wash of gory tears.

Bring the dart of a glance of the eye, and the halter of a tress,
    because I
Am embattled with my wounded, disaster-struck heart.

O Háfiz, since the grief of the world and its joy are transient,
It is better I keep my own heart cheerful.

---

1. Uproarious, but while the implication is a drinker of wine who is unafraid of being
   known as such, Háfiz is also alluding to his role as a poet, see the reference in the
   next verse to poetry as the sweet titbit that accompanies unadulterated wine. note
   also the contrast between the "hidden recess" and openly drinking wine.

POEM CCCXXII

I have a compact with the beloved that so long as I have a soul in
    my body,
I will hold the lovers of his street as dear as my life.

I seek the purity of the mind's inner sanctum from the candle
    of Chigil,[1]
I have radiance in the eye and light in the heart from that moon
    of Khotan.[2]

When to my heart's satisfaction and desire I have harvested an
    intimate privacy,
What care should I have on account of the evil-mouthed of the
    assembly?

In my abode I have a cypress in whose stature's shade
I enjoy freedom from the cypress of any garden and the box-tree
    of any meadow.

Although I might have a hundred armies of beauties laying
Ambushes for my heart, Praise and Thanks be to God, I have an
    army-routing idol!

It is fitting that through his ruby signet ring I boast myself a
    Solomon:
Where the Great Name[3] is, what have I to fear from Ahriman?

Hey O Wise Elder, do not because of the wine-shop find me at
    fault,
Because in deserting the cup I would have a word-breaking heart.

For God's sake, O prying rival, tonight close your eyes a while,
Because I to his silent ruby lip have a hundred secret words to tell.

When I am proudly strutting in the rose bed of his acceptance,
    Praise be to God,
I have no partiality for tulips and wild roses, nor the petals of the
    narcissus.

Háfiz is become notorious among intimates for being a sot, but
Why should I be sorry when in the world I have
       Qavámu'd-Dín Hasan.4

---

1. Chigil, see Poem LI, note 1. The Chigil is in the eastern basin of the Syr Darya (Jaxartes). Its people were noted for beauty—hence Taráz, one of the Chigil centres, is also alluded to as the source of beautiful people. Rúmí in the *Mathnawí* (op. cit., II, line 314) speaks of the "beauty of Chigil" in a line which Háfiz most probably had in mind and certainly would know:

    What do you, O glass-hearted, know of the sorrow of patience—
    Especially patience for the sake of that Beauty of Chigil?

    Again (III, line 4131), Rúmí refers to Chigil as a source of comeliness in people:

    That which made the sugar cane's heart and soul sweet,
    And that from which a speck of dust gained the form of Chigil.

2. Khotan in the same eastern region of Central Asia, west of Tibet and China, is, of course, mentioned by Persian poets as the source of the musk extracted from the musk pod of the deer. Both the Chigil and Khotan areas were centres whence slaves were brought into the Eastern Caliphate of Islam.

3. Solomon's signet ring had the Name of Almighty God engraved on it so that it endowed him with power over birds and beasts, and also *dívs*, devils. Ahriman is the name of principle of Evil in Zoroastrianism.

4. See Poem XI, note 1. The Keeper of the Seal to Abú Ishaq Ínjú and Háfiz's patron. Qavám died in 1353, when Háfiz was still a young man.

POEM CCCXXIII

Were he to kill me by the sword, I would not restrain him,
And were he to shoot me with an arrow, I'd take it as a favour.

Tell the bow of our eyebrow to let go the arrow,
That I might die by your hand and your arm.

When the sorrow of the world knocks me off my feet,
What but the cup might come to my rescue?

Come out, O sun of the morning of hope,
For in the hands of the night of separation I am captive.

Respond to my cry for help, O Elder of the tavern:
Make me young with one draught of wine, for I am old.

By your curls last night I swore
That I would not lift my head from your feet.

Burn this worn-out cassock of piety of yours, Háfiz,
Because though I might become fire, in it I would not take.

POEM CCCXXIV

Do not shoot an arrow from the tip of your eyelid at my heart,
That I should die in front of your languishing eye.

The taxable portion of beauty lies within the bounds of
    perfection—
Give me the alms-tax, because I am wretched and impoverished.

Fill the cup, because in the realm of love,
Though I am old, I am the one in the world young in luck.

So full of the friend did the cavity of my breast become,
Thought of self vanished from it.

Let there be nothing but the reckoning for minstrel and wine,
If my recording angel's pen records any word.

In this Tumult when no one is answerable for anyone,
I by the Magian Elder will be treated with courtesy.

O ascetic, how, as if I were a child, can you deceive me
With the apple of the Garden and the honey and the milk?

I have made an agreement with the wine-sellers,
That on the Day of Sorrow I should take nothing but a cup.

I am that bird whose song each evening and dawn-break
Is rising from the roof of the Throne of God.[1]

Like Háfiz I have His treasure[2] in my bosom,
Although the adversary regards me as poor.

Happy that moment when the oblivion of drunkenness
Grants me freedom from king and minister!

---

1. *'Arsh*, the Throne of God, see Koran IX, 130, "He is the Lord of the Mighty
    Throne", also VIII, 52, and XX, 4, and *passim*. But Háfiz is alluding to the state of
    being beyond any form or phenomenon: of being in the most exalted state of

the sempiternal spiritual world. (See Rúzbehán Baqli Shírází, who lived between 1128 and 1209 AD, and in his *Kitáb-i 'Abhar al-'Áshiqín*, "The Jasmine of the Love's Faithful", ed. Corbin and Mu'ín, published for the Bibliothèque Iranienne, Tehran and Paris, 1958, pp. 4–14 for the Persian text, and pp. 112–126 for the French translation.)

2. "His treasure": see Poem cxlviii, note 2 for the important allusion here to God's special insertion of His secret in the heart of Adam when he created Man.

POEM CCCXXV

At the time of homesick strangers' evening-prayer, when
    weeping I begin
To start my story with the wailings of the distressed,

Remembering my homeland and the friend, so grievously do I
    weep
That I cast any fashion for travel out of the world.

I am of my beloved's country, not the territory of aliens.
Preserver from terror, send me back to comrades!

O companion on the Way, for God's sake, some help, for me
Again to hoist my standard in the street of the tavern.

How might good sense take account of my old age,
When once more I am playing love's game with a child idol?

Apart from the easterly breeze and the north-easterly nobody
    knows me:
My darling, I have no sharer of secrets but the wind!

The air of the house of the friend is our Water of Life;
Morning breeze, fetch me a breath of the dust of Shíráz.

My tears fell and brought my fault to the fore:
Of whom can I complain? My tale-bearer is of the home.

To the harp of Venus I heard that at daybreak she was singing,
"I am the slave of sweetly-cadenced, sweet-voiced Háfiz."

POEM CCCXXVI

If again I might find access to the curl of your two locks,
What heads as if a ball I'd knock with your polo-stick!

Your tress is long life for me, but there is not
In my hand a hair-tip of this longevity.

O candle, issue the decree for my comfort, because tonight,
From the fire of the heart, before you like a candle I am melting.

That moment when with a laugh like a flagon's gurgle
   I surrender life,
I want the drunken ones with you to offer a prayer for me.

Since the prayer of corrupted me is no prayer,
In the wine-booth on this account my burning and melting do
   not diminish.

Whether in the mosque or tavern your image appears,
Of your two eyebrows I make the prayer-niche and the bass
   viol's bow.

Were you one night to illumine our retreat with your cheek,
Like the morning I would raise my head over the world's horizons.

Laudable would be the outcome of toil on his Path,
If life were surrendered on account of passion for Ayáz.[1]

To whom, Háfiz, may I tell the sorrows of the heart when at
   this time
Nothing but the wine-bowl is fitting to be privy to my secret?

---

1.   Ayáz, see Poem XLI, note 3. For "laudable", "praiseworthy", the poet uses the
    epithet *mahmúd*, thus by means of a pun getting the name of Ayáz's famous
    lover, Sultán Mahmúd, into the same verse as that of Ayáz.

POEM CCCXXVII

If once more I may chance to pass into the Magian tavern,
Straight away I'd stake all the harvest of gown and prayer-mat.

If today like ascetics I knock on repentance's door,
Tomorrow the wine-shop's cashier will not open the door to me.

But if blitheness lends a hand, like the moth
Only to that candle-cheek will be my flight.

If, embracing me like a lyre, you will not grant the wish of my
    heart,[1]
From your lips, gratify me as you would a flute with a moment's
    breath.

I don't desire the society of houris: it would be the height of sin,
If, having your image, I were to make approaches to another.

I will not relate to anyone what has happened to my blooded
    heart,
Because, apart from the sword of yearning for you, I've no one in
    whom to confide.

The secret of yearning for you would have stayed hidden in my
    breast,
If the tear-raining eye had not let it out.

Bird-like out of the cage of dust I became a creature of air,
In the ambition[2] that perhaps the falcon might make me its prey.

If on Háfiz's body there were heads so many as every one of his
    hairs,
Like your long tresses I would throw them all down as far as
    your feet.

---

1.   i.e. with sweet words.
2.   *havá'í*, but there is a pun here: the word also means, "flighty", "licentious",
    "debauched", etc.; also, "fancy", and "ambition".

POEM CCCXXVIII

Where the good news of union with you, for me to rise from
    desiring life?
I am the holy bird and would rise from the snare which the
    world sets.

By the love of you I swear that if you call me a slave of yours,
I would rise above wanting mastery of the Cosmos.

O Lord, from the cloud of guidance cause rain to fall,
Before like a mote of dust I float upwards.

Sit at the head of my tomb with wine and minstrel,
That at the scent of you, I dancing might from the grave arise.

Get up and show your tallness, O idol of sweet movements,
So that, like Háfiz, I might rise above minding life and the world.

Although I am old, draw me one night into your embrace,
That at break of day I might get up young from your side.

POEM CCCXXIX

I am the lover of the cheery face and heart-alluring hair.
I am crazy for the languishing eye and wine unadulterated and
    pure.

In being a lover there's no escaping long suffering and the
    burning.
I am standing like a candle. Don't make me afraid of fire.

I am a man of Paradise, but on this voyage
Now I am the captive of love for moon-like youths.

If luck would help me to take my traps from these regions,
The locks of the houri would be sweeping the dust off my carpet.[1]

Shíráz is the mine of the ruby lip and the quarry of beauty.
I am the penniless jeweller. For this reason I am perplexed.

So many an intoxicated eye have I seen in this city,
O God, I swear that now I will not touch the wine, yet still be
    merry.

You said, "Relate one subtlety from the mystery of the Covenant
    of Eternity without Beginning."
"That time when I have drained two cups, I will tell you!"

Háfiz, the bride of my genius has a wish for bridal array.
I have no mirror. Therefore, I heave a sigh.

---

1. Alluding to Koran LV, 54, and LVI, 33, where it says that the righteous are rewarded
   in Paradise "reclining on carpets" and on "carpets raised".

POEM CCCXXX

Why should I not be after setting out for my own country?
Why not be dust at the end of my friend's lane?

When I cannot bear the misery of being alien and away from
home,
Let me go to my own city and be my own prince.

I shall be of the sharers in the privacy of the royal pavilion of
union:
I shall be of my own king's slaves.

As life's outcome cannot be foreseen, this at least is best,
That the day I die I should be with my idol.

Of deeply slumbering luck's dealing and business gone awry,
If I have any complaint, let me keep it to myself.

To be a lover and reprobate was always my boast;
Let me go on being engaged in my own occupation.

May it be that the grace of Eternity without Beginning, Háfiz, will
be the shower of the Way.
If it is not, until Eternity without End, of myself I shall be
ashamed.

POEM CCCXXXI

When the image of your face passes by the rose bed of the eye,
The heart comes to the eye's window in pursuit of the sight.

Come, because for your arrival's offering, ruby and pearl
I am drawing from the treasure house of the heart to the
    treasury of the eye.

I see no look-out a fit resting-place for you;
From the world there is me, and this destined corner of my eye.

At dawn my flowing tears were bent on exposing me,
Had not the blood of my liver been stopped by the skirt of my eye.

The first day I espied your cheek, the heart was declaring,
"If any harm comes, my blood be on the eye's neck!"

Last night, in hope of good news of union with you, till dawn
I placed the lighted lamp of the eye in the path of the wind.

For humanity's sake, do not strike Háfiz's pain-stricken heart
With the heart-piercing, man-overthrowing arrow-point of the eye.

POEM CCCXXXII

Although from the heart's fire I am seething like a vat of wine,
My lip sealed, I am swallowing the blood and am silent.

To desire the lip of the beloved is to attempt one's life.
Look you at me who in this predicament am striving with my soul.

When might I get free of the heart's distress when every moment
The blackness of an idol's tress plants a slave's ring in my ear?

God forbid, I am not a believer in my own devotion;
This is as far as it goes, that from time to time I drink a bowl.

My hope is that, in spite of the enemy, on the Day of Requital
The abundance of His forgiveness will not load me with sin.

My father[1] sold the Garden of Paradise for a couple of grains of
    wheat.
Why should I not sell the garden of the world for a barley-grain?

My wearing the patched cloak is not out of excessive religion:
I am donning a covering for a hundred hidden sins.

I who only want to drink from the clearest wine of the vat,
What should I do if I did not hear the word of the Magian Elder?

If in this way the assembly's minstrel captures the mode of love,
At the time of hearing, Háfiz's verse will deprive me of sense.

---

1. i.e. Adam.

POEM CCCXXXIII

Were I to be mindful of persecutors' reproof,
The rite of drunkenness and wastrelism would get nowhere
  with me.

The asceticism of reprobrates newly initiated is of no worth.
Why should I, the most notorious in the world, contemplate virtue?

Call bankrupt me, king of the hare-brained,
For the reason that in all the world I am the most wanting in sense.

Paint a mole on the forehead with the blood of my heart,
So it might be known that I, your sacrifice, am of infidel faith.[1]

Show some trust, and for God's sake, leave me alone,
So that you might not realise what in this patched gown a
  non-dervish I am.

O wind, convey my blood-raining poem to that friend,
Who, with a black eyelash, has stabbed my jugular vein.

What have I, whether I drink wine or not, to do with anybody?
I am the guardian of my own secret and the spiritually
  perceptive of my own time.[2]

---

1. As it were, considering that it is a Hindu practice to paint a spot on the fore-
   head, a Hindu.
2. In Sufism, *vaqt*, "time", has the additional connotation of the mystic's time with
   God. Háfiz might be claiming that he is the *'árif*, "spiritually perceptive", of his
   day; equally he is implying that he is observant of his times or states in the Súfí
   sense.

POEM CCCXXXIV

The dust of my body is becoming the veil in front of the face of
    the soul.
O happy the moment when from off that face I cast the veil aside!

A cage like this is unworthy of a sweet singer like me.
I will go to the rose bed of Paradise, because I am the bird of
    that Garden.

It is not clear why I came, where I was;
Pain and woe, that of my beginning and end I am unaware.

How can I make my circuit in the space of the World of Holiness,
When, in the enclosed world of contrivance, I am tied to the
    plank of my body?

If from the blood of my heart the scent of yearning comes,
Do not be surprised: I am the musk pod of the fellow sufferer of
    Khotan.

Have no regard for my candle-like gold-laced tunic of Taráz,[1]
Because hidden under my shirt the burnings are.

Come and from him snatch away Háfiz's being:
With your being, nobody will hear from me, "I am."

---

1.   For Taráz, see Poem CCCXXII, note 1. Also, see note 2 for a reference to Khotan.
    It was inevitable that Háfiz should follow his reference in the preceding verse
    to Khotan with one to a tunic from Taráz, which, in addition to its fame for
    beautiful people, was noted for its exquisite textiles.

POEM CCCXXXV

After forty and more years I am still boasting
That of the servitors of the Magian Guide I am the least.

Through the favour of the wine-vendor's kindred affection never
Has my cup been left empty of pure and luminous wine.

In love's ranking and the luck of reprobates sincerely staking
  their all,
My seat at the inn remains always the dais of honour.

In my case, for draining the dregs do not think ill:
The garment's got sullied, but I am clean.

I am the falcon on the wrist of the ruler. O Lord, in what a way
Have they forgotten my fondness for my perch!

A pity, that a nightingale like me, now in this cage,
With this mellifluous tongue should be as silent as the lily.

The air and water of Fárs[1] take wonderful care of the down
  and out!
Where a fellow voyager, that I might pull my tent up from this soil?

How long, Háfiz, must you drain the cup from underneath the
  patched gown?
At the Khwája's banquet, I'll throw the veil off what you do;

The august Turánsháh[2] who heaps favours upon me—
Gratitude for his gifts is the collar round my neck.

---

1. The province of which Shíráz is the capital.
2. Turánsháh is the "Khwája", "Master", mentioned in the preceding verse. He is
    taken to be Jalálu'd-Dín Turánsháh, the last *vazír* of Sháh Shujá' and a great
    patron of Háfiz, who alludes to him in a number of his poems. He was *vazír*
    from 1364–5 AD to the year in which Sháh Shujá' died, 1384, and for a short
    while under his successor until, disgraced and injured, he died in 1385. There
    was, however, also Turánsháh ibn Qutbu'd-Dín Tahamtan, the king of the
    island of Hormuz between 1347 and 1385–6. This ruler was one of those to
    whom Háfiz alludes, and to whom he often expresses gratitude for gifts (See
    Poem cccxvi, note 1). But the general consensus among Iranian scholars is that
    the Khwája Turánsháh was the *vazír* already mentioned in this note. (See
    Mu'ín, op. cit., pp. 255–259 and *passim*.)

POEM CCCXXXVI

It is a lifetime that I am daily stepping out on the quest,
Every moment thrusting into good repute the hand of intercession.

Without my love-kindling moon see how I make my days pass:
I spread a snare on a path. For bait I thrust a bird into it.

Where is Aurang[1] the lover, Gulchihreh the rose-cheeked? Where
    the picture of love and constancy,
Now I've wagered my all on being a lover?

I know that this blood-spraying sigh I heave every morning and
    evening
Will bring grief to an end and lend colour to the story;

That perhaps I might find news of the shade of that cypress,
From all sides I sound the note of love at any sprightly strider.

Although aware that the ease of the heart does not bestow the
    heart's desire,
An ideal picture I draw; an omen of perseverance cast.

Notwithstanding that I am absent from him, and, like Háfiz,
    repentant of wine,
In the assembly of the spiritual still from time to time I quaff a
    bowl.

---

1.   Aurang is the name of a celebrated lover; Gulchihreh was his beloved.

POEM CCCXXXVII

Without you, O striding cypress, what should I be doing with a
    rose and rose plot?
Why pull a hyacinth tress? What would I do with the lily cheek?

Alas that for fear of the ill-wisher's reproach, I did not see your
    face;
My face is not like a mirror, of iron.[1] What can I do?

Go away, admonisher, and do not blame lees-drinkers.
The Orderer of Fate does this. What can I do?

When the lightning streak of jealousy so leaps from the ambush
    of the Invisible,
You command what I of the burned harvest am to do.

When the king of the Turks[2] approved and threw me into the pit,
If Tahamtan proves no rescuer, what can I do?

If the fire of Túr[3] lends no help to a lamp,
What might I make the remedy for the Valley of Sinai's dark night?

Háfiz, my hereditary home is the most exalted Paradise.
Why should I make my nest in this ruined halting-place?

---

1.   Mirrors were made of polished metal.
2.   The king of the Turks; here most probably Sháh Shujá', but Afrásiyáb, ruler of
    Turán and enemy of Iran, is implied because of the mention of Tahamtan in the
    next hemistich. Tahamtan was Rustum, Iran's champion against Afrásiyáb as
    told in the *Sháhnámeh* of Firdausí. Also, as Háfiz might have been at outs, as he
    often was, with his "king of the Turks", it might be that he was appealing to the
    generosity of Tahamtan, the name adopted by the King of Hormuz.
3.   Túr, Sinai, see Poem xxvii, note 2.

POEM CCCXXXVIII

I'm not the reprobate to abandon the darling and the cup!
The moral police's chief knows that I rarely act like this.

I, who time and time again have censured repenters,
Would be mad were I to repent of the wine of the time of roses.

When the morning breeze has washed the clustered rose petals
    with the water of grace,
Call me cross-grained if I keep my eyes on the lesson-book.

The tulip a taker-up of the cup, the narcissus drunk, but for me,
    debauchery's repute;
I have plenty to answer for. Whom, O Lord, shall I make the judge?

Love is the pearl-grain and I am the diver, and the sea is the tavern.
I have plunged in there. Let us see how I bob up.

I am a poor and dust-stained beggar, yet let there be shame at
    my ardour
If I wet my garment with water from the spring of the Sun King![1]

I who in beggary hold in my hand a royal treasure,
What expectation have I of the wheeling of the base-nurturing
    sphere?

Draw back the rein a moment, O my city-upsetting Turk,
So that I might from tears and cheek fill your path with gold and
    pearls.

Last night your ruby lip was offering Háfiz enticement, but
I'm not the one to believe these fables from him.

---

1.   See the next verse.

POEM CCCXXXIX

O idol, how can I cope with the sorrow of love for you?
Till when in grief for you must I make the night loud with wailing?

The heart that is crazed is beyond being able to heed advice,
Unless I make a chain for it out of the tip of your tress.

With your tress the whole of my distraction,
Where my ability to relate all in each detail?

Alas, that which in the time of your absence I have suffered,
It is not feasible for me to write in one letter alone.

The time when my desire is to see my darling,
In my sight I fashioned the likeness of your fair cheek's picture.

If I knew that by this means union with you would be granted,
I would gamble away heart and religion and make a profit.

Distance yourself, preacher, from me and stop your
    futile muttering—
I am not the one again to lend an ear to lies.

There is no hope, Háfiz, of righteousness out of depravity.
Since such is Fate, what can I do about it?

POEM CCCXL

Let me make the eye an ocean and scatter patience over the desert,
And in this operation, fling my heart into the sea.

From the constricted heart of a sinner I heave a sigh,
Which I throw on to the crimes of Adam and Eve as fire.

I have been hit by the arrow of the Firmament. Give wine that
    drunk,
I might throw a knot into the fastening of the Twins'
    constellation's waist.[1]

I pour a draught of wine on this mutable throne:[2]
I cast the harp's resonating bass note at this blue enameled vault.

The substance of the heart's happiness is there where the keeper
    of hearts is.
I am making the effort that perhaps I may launch myself there.

Lift the veil,[3] O sun-capped[4] moon,
So that, like your tresses do, I might let the passion-afflicted
    heart drop at your feet.

O Háfiz, to rely on Time's passing days is to be careless and in
    error;
Why then should I postpone the pleasure of today until tomorrow?

---

1.   The *tarkash-i jauzá*, "Gemini's quiver". This constellation resembles a quiver in shape. It is as if Háfiz were dismissing the zodiacal influence in the light of the precedence of love over the phenomenal: *láhút*, divine nature, over *násút*, the human or worldly.
2.   In astrology Gemini is one of the four signs of the Zodiac associated with mutability, adaptability; the others are Virgo, Sagittarius, and Pisces.
3.   In a poem that contains more than one astrological allusion, it might be noted that the word here translated "veil", *burqá*, also means either the seventh, the fourth, or the first heaven. Háfiz would be thinking in terms of the seventh.
4.   *khurshíd kulah*, "sun-capped", is used as a nickname for a beauty crowned with red hair. Could it but be known, Háfiz might have had a favourite redhead in mind.

POEM CCCXLI

I declared last night I would rid the head of longing for his cheek.
He said, "Where the chains for me to control this mad man?"

I called his stature a cypress. He drew back from me in anger.
Friends, my idol takes offence at the truth. What am I to do?

I uttered an unweighed subtlety. Forgive me, O stealer of hearts.
Deign a little wheedling, that I might turn genius into balanced
    verse.

On account of that innocent, delicate nature I bear a wan face.
Pass a bowl, wine-boy, for me to rose tint the cheek.

O breeze of Salmá's dwelling, for God's sake till when
Must I rummage round the campsite and make a River Oxus of
    the debris?[1]

I who have traced the track to the treasure of the friend's infinite
    loveliness,
After this may make Korahs of a hundred beggars like myself.

O moon of the fortunate conjunction, remember the slave Háfiz,
That I might pray for the felicity of that daily-waxing beauty.

---

1. For Salmá see Poem CLXXXV, note 1, for reference to this symbol of the beloved.
The campsite debris is imitated from Arabic love poetry, in which odes open
with reference to the remains of the departed paragon's former campsite.

POEM CCCXLII

Intent on repenting at dawn I said, "I'll take an omen for luck."
Repentance-shattering Spring's on the way. How can I manage?

I must say frankly, I cannot see
Comrades drinking wine with me looking on.

In tulip-time, physick me
If I step aside from the midst of the banquet of merriment.

Because of the face of the friend, desire in me has blossomed
    like a rose.
I impute the head of the enemy to hard stone.

I seat an idol as a Sultan on the throne of the rose.
I make him a collar and bracelet of hyacinth and jasmine.

I am a beggar of the wine-shop, but, see, in the time of
    drunkenness
I flirt with the Firmament and pass sentence on the stars!

Laughing like a rosebud, to the memory of the king's assembly
I raise the cup, and in longing tear my clothes.

I who have means of livelihood from the gold of the royal tribute,
Why should I blame the wine-bibbing sot?

Háfiz has grown tired of secret wine-drinking.
To the clamour of pipe and lute, I will make his secret public.

POEM CCCXLIII

God forbid that I in the season of the rose should abandon wine!
I boast of intelligence—when would such action be mine?

Where's a minstrel, that all the harvest of asceticism and learning
I might make to the raising of the boisterous notes of harp and
     flute?

Now I've sickened of the disputation of the Schools
Let me a while again take up attendance upon wine and the
     beloved.

Where the morning's courier, that the complaints of the night of
     separation
I might lay before that auspicious aspect and lucky foot?

When was there fidelity in the realm of Time?
Bring the wine bowl that I might recite the tale of Jam, Ká'ús
     and Kay.[1]

I'm not afraid of the Black Book, because on Resurrection Day,
With His abundant grace I'll settle a hundred of these accounts.

This borrowed life the Friend entrusted to Háfiz,
One day I might see His face, and this life surrender.

---

1.   Ancient, and some legendary, kings whose glory time eclipsed.

POEM CCCXLIV

It has been a while that I am rendering the wine-booth service;
In the frock of poverty doing the work of the blessed ones;

Till the time when I might entice the elegantly strutting partridge
    into union's snare,
I am lying in ambush and looking out for the opportune moment.

Our sermoniser lacks the scent of the True. Listen, because this
I also say in his presence—I make no slander in secret.

I am running to the friend's street rising and falling like the breeze,
And asking of companions on the Way the support of spiritual
    purpose.

No more than this will your street's dust put up with our
    importunity:
O idol, you have shown kindnesses. I abate the importuning.

The heart stealer's tress is the snare in the Way, and his glance,
    temptation's arrow;
Remember, heart, the sundry counsels I am making yours.

Veil the eye of the caviller, O generous overlooker of sin,
From these bold sallies I make in the corner of seclusion.

I am the Koran-reciting Háfiz in the congregation; at a party the
    drainer of dregs.
See the mischief, how I am playing verbal tricks on people!

I am not abandoning love, nor the darling, nor the cup.
I have repented a hundred times, but will do so no more.

The paradisial Garden, the shade of the Túbá tree, the Houris'
    palace,
I do not equate with the dust of the street of the friend.

The people of insight's proposition and teaching are a hint;
I have uttered an allusion and I'm not repeating it.

News of my own head will never be mine
So long as in the wine temple's midst I do not raise it.

The admonisher scoffingly cried, "It's forbidden: do not drink
    wine."
I replied, "Sure, but it is not to every ass that I listen."

Angrily the Shaikh said to me, "Go, abandon love."
No need for quarrelling, brother, I won't.

For me it is absolute piety that aloft on the pulpit's steps
I am not fondling and ogling the beauties of the town!

Háfiz, the threshold of the Magian Elder is the abode of fortune.
I will not give up kissing the dust of this door.

POEM CCCXLVI

With black eyelashes you have pricked a thousand holes in my
faith.
Come so that out of your languorous eye I might pluck a legion
of pains.

Hey there, companion of the heart from whose memory your
friends have gone,
May no day be mine that a moment I sit forgetful of you.

This world is old and lacks foundation. Save us from this
Farhád-slayer
Whose deceit and treachery have made me weary of sweet life.

From the fire of separation's heat, I was like a rose drowned in
sweat.
Bring, O night-capturing wind, a breeze from that wiper-away[1] of
my sweat.

I see the passing and the lasting world as the sacrifice to the
darling and the wine-boy,
Because I see the world's sultanate as love's uninvited guest.

If the friend prefers another to me, he's the judge.
May it be unlawful to me if I prefer life to the friend.

The nightingale has sung, "Good Morning." Where are you
wine-boy? Get up,
Because the vision of last night's dream has my head in turmoil.

The night of departure too, I'll leave my bed for the palace of
dark- and wide-eyed Houris,
Provided that at the moment of surrendering life you are the
candle at my pillow.

The dictum about desiring that has been recorded in this narrative
Is indeed void of error because Háfiz dictated it to me.

---

1. The allusion is to the tresses of the beloved brushing away moisture from the face.

425

Right now I perceive the requirement of the times in this,
That I move my traps into the wine-booth and contentedly settle
   down;

Save cup and book no friend nor intimate will be mine,
That I may see as little as possible of false comrades from the
   world.

I have boasted so much of righteousness beneath a stained gown,
I am put to shame by the wine-boy's cheek and the bright-hued wine.

Let me seize the wine-bowl and be far from hypocrites;
In other words, let me prefer pureness of heart to the world;

In freedom from creatureliness, like a cypress I would raise my
   head,
If it chanced that I might pluck my skirt clear of the world.

The dust of tyranny lies on my heart. Do not, O God, allow
My sun-reflecting mirror to be dimmed.

Whether I am a tavern roisterer or the Háfiz of the town,
This is what I have to offer, and I am less than it.

Alas for my straightened breast and the weight of grief for him!
My puny heart is not the man for this heavy load.

I am the Ásaf of the Age's slave. Do not divert my heart from
   the Way,
For were I to breathe a word about the wheel of Fate, it would
   seek revenge of me.

POEM CCCXLVIII

Should it be in my power to sit with my sweetheart,
I would be drinking wine from the cup of union and plucking a
   rose from the garden of delight.[1]

The bitter Súfí-burning wine will obliterate my foundation;
O wine-boy, place your lip on mine and snatch up my sweet life.

Perhaps in this desire I shall go mad for, night until day,
I am talking to the moon; seeing a peri in my dreams.

When every speck of dust the wind brought bore a bounty from
   your largesse,
Call to mind the slave's condition, for I am an ancient servant.

Your lip gave sugar to the drunkards, and your eye wine to the
   hungover.
Out of excess of asceticism, I am neither of these, nor of those.

Hear from me the conundrum of drunkenness and debauchery,
   not from the preacher,
Because nightly I with goblet and bowl am the intimate of the
   Moon and the Pleiades.

Not of everyone who's cast a pattern of verse are the words
   agreeable to the heart.
It is I who am capturing the rare partridge, because my falcon's
   swift,

And if you don't believe go and ask the painter in China,[2]
Because Máni is after a copy from the nib of my musk-dropping
   pen.

Fidelity and speaking the truth are not the accomplishments of
   everyone;
I am the slave of the second Ásaf, the Glory of the Truth and of
   the Faith.[3]

1. The cheek of the friend.
2. Mání the 3rd-century AD Mesopotamian-Iranian heresiarch, legendary for his skill as a painter, which is associated with his sojourn in China.
3. Jalálu-l Haq wa'l-Dín a Minister to Sháh Shujá', Khwája Turánsháh. See Poem cccxxxv, note 2.

POEM CCCXLIX

I see the light of God in the Magian Tavern.
Behold this marvel, from where I see such a light!

O King of the Hájj,[1] don't give me your airs and graces,
    because you
See the house, but I see the Master of the house.

I want to make an opening in the musk pod of the idol's tresses.
The thought is a far cry—as if I were to visit Cathay!

Burning of the heart, flowing of tears, sighing at dawn, the
    night's lament—
I experience them all through the sight of your grace.

The highway robber of my imagination is every moment a vision
    of your face.
To whom can I tell what things I am seeing behind this veil?

No one has experienced from the musk of Khotan and
    musk bladders of China
What I experience from the morning breeze every morning.

Friends, do not fault Háfiz's eye-playing,
Because I see him as belonging to your loved ones.

---

1. The commander of the annual Mecca Pilgrimage.

POEM CCCL

For the time's misery, of which I see absolutely no end,
The only remedy I see is wine as red as the Judas tree blossom.

I have no desire to give up attending the Magian Elder,
For I see that to do so would not be for my own good.

In this hangover nobody offers me a drink,
See, not one in the town do I find a person with a heart.[1]

Do not calculate pleasure's ascent from the sun of the cup.
I do not see the time's horoscope amenable to this.

A lover is the emblem of people of God. Keep to yourself,
Because in the Shaikhs of the town I do not see this sign.

The trace of his hair-like waist to which I have committed the
     heart,
Do not ask of me, when in the midst I am unable to see myself.

Once your stature left the rivulet of my sight,
In place of the cypress I see only flowing water.

A thousand pities for these two bedazzled eyes of mine
That, with a brace of mirrors, I do not clearly see his face.

It is a case of me and the vessel of Háfiz's poems, because in this
     ocean
I see no other heart-grabbing cargo of speech.

---

1. *ahl-i dilí*, "one of heart", but the allusion is to the *Ahl-i Dil*, i.e. Súfís.

POEM CCCLI

Happy that day when I go from this ruined stopping place.
I seek the soul's repose and I'm going in pursuit of the darling.

Although aware that the stranger might not get anywhere,
I am proceeding by the perfume of that dishevelled tress.

With ailing feet and a powerless heart, like the breeze
I move in longing for that swaying cypress.

Of the terror of Alexander's prison[1] my heart sickened.
Let me pack my bags and go to the realm of Solomon.[2]

In his way, if going must be like a pen with the tip of my head,
With wound-enduring heart and weeping eye will I go.

I vowed, should I one day emerge from this grief,
I would go to the wine temple in glee and singing a song;

In desiring him, like a dancing mote
To the lip of the source of the dazzling sun I would go.

The Arabs have no sorrow for the grief of the heavy laden;[3]
O Persians, some help that I may go happily and with ease,

And if like Háfiz I do not follow the route out of the desert,
I will go in the companionship of the party of the Ásaf of the Ages.

---

1. A style used of the city of Yazd, the only city Háfiz is known definitely to have ever left his native Shíráz to visit, and where, see Poem xii, note 1, he was very dissatisfied and unhappy.
2. i.e. Shíráz.
3. There is a covert allusion here to the sufferings of the pilgrims to Mecca as they cross the Arabian desert. Desert Arabs often made short work of stragglers; see the next verse for a distinct reference to the desert, and not being a straggler in it.

POEM CCCLII

If from this house of exile I may go homewards,
When I go there again, I shall go learned and wise.

If from this journey I reach my native land in safety,
I have made a vow that straight from the road I'll go to the
    wine-shop;

To relate what in this travelling and wayfaring has been revealed
    to me,
With harp and wine-cup I will go to the dervish
    assembly-place's door.

Were those acquainted with the Path of love to drink my blood,
I'd be a nobody if complaining I approached the stranger.

After this it will be a case of my hand and the idol's chain-like
    tress.
How much and how long must I go in pursuit of the crazed
    heart's gratification?

If again I see the curve of his prayer-niche-like eyebrow,
I will kneel in gratitude and proceed in acknowledgement of
    favour.

Happy that moment when, like Háfiz, in friendship for the Vazír,
I go from the wine-booth to the garden lodge with a merry head
    and the friend.

POEM CCCLIII

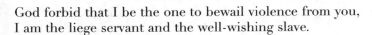

That one who made me like the dust of the road the trampled on
    of tyranny,
I kiss the dust and ask forgiveness of his foot.

God forbid that I be the one to bewail violence from you,
I am the liege servant and the well-wishing slave.

I have tied a trailing votive rag[1] of hope to the curl of your tress.
May it not be that this begging of mine curtails the tress!

I am a mote of dust, but in your lane my moments are joyous—
O friend, I am afraid lest a breeze should suddenly blow me away.

I am the Súfí of the World of Holiness's cloister, but
The abode now assigned to me is the Magian Temple.

At dawn the wine-shop's Elder handed me the world-seeing cup,
And with that mirror informed me of your beauty.

With me let the wayside beggar get up and come to the wine-booth,
That in that circle you might see what lordly rank is mine.

Drunk you passed by and of Háfiz had no thought.
Woe if my sigh should snatch the skirt of your loveliness!

I liked it when at sunrise the Khusrau of the East was saying:
"In spite of all this sovereignty I am Turánsháh's[2] servitor."

---

1. The poet is alluding to the tying of votive rags to such objects as a sacred bush
near the shrine of a saint, or to the railings round a saint's tomb, with prayers
for something desired, and a vow to make an offering if the desire is satisfied.
2. In all likelihood the famous minister to Sháh Shujá' mentioned in Poem
CCCXXXV, note 2, and CCCXLVII, note 3.

Seeing became possible, and kissing and hugging too.
I thank luck, and Time as well.

Go away, ascetic, because, if my star is in the ascendant,
The bowl is in my grasp, and the tress of the darling too.

We do not blame anyone for debauchery and drunkenness.
Idols' ruby lip is a delight, and wine pleasant on the palate too.

I give you good news, O heart. The Censor[1] is no more,
And the world is full of wine, and of wine-drinking paramours too.

Gone the time when the eye of evil was on the watch from an
    ambuscade.
The foe has withdrawn from the midst, and the tear from the
    breast too.

To give the heart over to distraction is not a clever move.
Seek to be concentrated, and bring the cup too.

On the dust-spattered of love spill a draft from his lip,
That the dust might turn ruby-coloured, and musk-bearing too.

Since all existences are alive through hope of you,
O sun, do not withhold your shadow from us either.

Since the lustre of the lily and the rose is the brimming over of
    your bounty,
O cloud, rain grace upon dusty me too.

Háfiz has been caught in you locks. Fear God —
And the retribution of the Jamshíd-powered Ásaf too:

The Burhán-i Mulk va Dín[2] by the power of whose ministry
The age became prosperous and the sea opulent too.

The ball of Earth was snatched up in his stick of justice,
And this toppled over the encompassing blue dome too:

The nimbly managed rein of your resolution has brought into
    motion
The firm centre loftily orbiting, too.

To the memory of his luminous judgement, in the morning, heaven
Sacrifices its life, and scatters the constellations too,

So that, as a result of the Firmament and the style of his time,
Is the change of years, months, autumn and spring too.

May the palace of his glory not be empty of chiefs,
And of cypress-bodied, rose-cheeked wine-servers too.[3]

1. The *muhtasib*, generally taken to be the way in which Háfiz alluded to the
    orthodox Sunnite Mubárizu'd-Dín Muhammad Muzaffar deposed and blinded
    by his son Sháh Shujá' in 759 AH/1357 AD. Hence it might be feasible to date this
    poem from the year of the "Censor's" deposition. He had closed wine-shops
    and smashed wine-vats. See further note 2 below.
2. Burhán-i Mulk va Dín, "Proof of the Realm and the Faith", Burhánu'd-Dín
    Fathulláh, Mubárizu'd-Dín's *vazír* until the latter's removal, after which this
    powerful minister was tortured to death. Some historians record this as hap-
    pening two months after the fall of Mubárizu'd-Dín. As Háfiz in verse 4 says
    that the "Censor" was no more, does this allusion to the minister mean that he
    survived his master's dethronement for two months, so that he would still be
    active when Háfiz composed what has been seen as an encomium of him. In
    spite of the deposed ruler's lack of attention to Háfiz, it appears that
    Burhánu'd-Dín protected the poet with his patronage. See Mu'ín, op. cit., Vol. II
    p. 627, and Khánlarí, *notes on Personalities*, p. 1245 in Vol. II, of the *Díván*.
3. Interestingly, in these last verses eulogising the Minister and especially the last
    verse Háfiz plays in the mode of early Persian poetical poems of praise, with no
    "mystical" overtones. The last verse could have been composed by Rúdakí, who
    died in 940–1 and who was at one stage of his life prominent in the court of the
    Samanid ruler Amír Nasr II, who ruled in Transoxania from 914 to 943 AD.

POEM CCCLV

My pain is due to the friend, and the cure too.
The heart has become his sacrifice, and life too.

Those who say that a certain something is better than beauty,
Our beloved has this, and that too.

We are telling the tale veiledly, and
It shall be told with cunning too.

Both worlds are one single light from his face —
I have told you this openly, and again secretly too.

May that one be remembered who, intent on our own blood
Broke the tress, and the Covenant too.

There's no relying on the working of the world,
And certainly none on the wheeling of the sphere either.

As the felicity of the nights of union has come to an end,
The days of separation will pass too.

The Censor knows Háfiz is a lover,
And the Ásaf of the realm of Solomon too.

The lover is not afraid of the judge. Bring wine;
And he does not even fear the rescript of the Sultan either.

POEM CCCLVI

We, tipplers with no regrets, have yielded the heart.
We are sharers of the secret of love, and intimates of the
    wine-bowl.

Against us often has the bow of blame been drawn,
From the moment our affair was shown up by the eyebrow of the
    beloved.

O rose, last night you have drawn out the brand of the morning
    cup;
We are that tulip which was born with a brand.

If the Magian Elder were too weary of our repentance,
Say, "Make the wine pure, because we stand contrite."

Matters progress because of you. Spare a glance, O Guide of
    the Way,
That you may render me justice; but we have fallen from the Way.

Do not see the tulip-like wine and the cup in the forefront of
    things.
See this brand-mark that we have impressed on our blooded heart.

You inquired, "What's all this colouring and fancy, Háfiz?"
Do not call it devious patterning: we are simply that same
    tabula rasa.

POEM CCCLVII

A hundred times have we laid our face in the dust beneath your
    foot:
I have put aside the falsity and hypocrisy of people.

We have not imposed on the feeble heart the weight of the world.
Rather, we have reposed this business in attachment to a single
    hair.

The arch and portico of the college and the learning's
    propositions and arguments
We have deposited on the path of the cup and sun-faced wine-boy.

We have not conquered the realm of well being with an army.
Not by strength of arm have we established the throne
    of sovereignty.

What game does the eye of the beloved keep up till dawn, that we
Should have placed our foundation on a bewitching glance?

Lacking soothing grace from his narcissus, the head racked by
    the hangover
I have laid like a violet[1] on the knee.

In hope of the festival of union, like watchers out for the moon,[2]
I have placed the eye of seeking on the crescent of that eyebrow.

They ask, "Where, O Háfiz, is your distracted heart?"
We have placed it in the rings of that twist of curls.

---

1. Violet is the colour of mourning.
2. The allusion is to the watchers for the moon that signals the end of *Ramazán*,
    the Muslim month of fasting, which ends with the Festival of the Fast-break-
    ing, *'Ídu'l-Fitr*, on the first of the Arabic month of *Shawwal*.

POEM CCCLVIII

It is a lifetime since I turned to the way of grief for you;
Since I put on one side the pretence and dissimulation of people.

We have cast the reputation of several generations of ancestors
    of good name
Into the way of the bowl and sun-faced wine-server.

We are the sober and sensible who on the heart's arms and legs
Have imposed the chains and fetters of tresses' curls.

Deign some hint, because the two eyes of hopefulness
Have I fixed on the corners of that eyebrow's curve.

Also I have resigned the soul to two magic narcissi.
The heart too, have I placed on those two dark hyacinths.[1]

It is a lifetime since we, in the hope of a sign,
Have placed an eye of seeking on those two eyebrow corners.

You said, "O Háfiz, where is your distracted heart?"
We have put it in the rings of that curled hair.[2]

---

1. The allusion is to two locks of hair growing down both sides of the face.
2. Lest it should be thought that some mistake has occurred, this verse is in fact
   an echo of the last verse of the preceding poem.

POEM CCCLIX

We have not come to this door in pursuit of pomp and rank.
We have come here for refuge out of adversity.

We are voyagers through the stations of love and from
    non-existence's frontiers.
We have traversed all this way as far as the country of being.

We saw the fresh green sprouting of your down, and of the
    Garden of Paradise;
We became engaged in the quest for this heliotrope.

With a treasure such that the archangel Gabriel[1] became its
    treasurer,
We have come begging to the door of the abode of the Sháh.

Where, O ship of Divine Guidance, is the anchor of your
    indulgence?
For in this sea of munificence we have got drowned in sin.

Honour's lustre is going. O sin-hiding cloud, bring rain,
For in the register of deeds our record has become black.

Throw away this woollen gown, Háfiz, because we
Have come in pursuit of the caravan with the fire of sighs.

---

1. The allusion is to Gabriel's role as the bringer of the Revelation to the Prophet
Muhammad; a Revelation, the Koran, which Háfiz, as a *háfiz*, had memorized,
and in the exegesis of which he was a teacher.

POEM CCCLX

I have the Magian Elder's fatwa, and an old saying it is,
That wine is forbidden where there is no intimate friend.

I will tear up this robe of hypocrisy. What am I to do?
The companionship of the unsympathetic is to the spirit
    excruciating torment.

So that the lip of the beloved might perhaps let spill a draught
    over me,
It is years that I have been haunting the wine-shop's door.

Maybe the long years of my service have escaped his memory.
O dawn breeze remind him of the Covenant[1] of old.

Were you after a century to pass over my dust,
My decayed bones from the clay would raise their head dancing.

First the heart-stealer snatched from us the heart with a
    hundred hopes;
Apparently the kindly nature does not forget the Covenant.[2]

Tell the rosebud, "Because of failure do not be of a straitened
    heart,
For from the breath of morning and the spirits of the breeze
    help will be yours."

Thought for your own welfare, O heart, lay at another door:
No physician's ministrations make the lover's pain any better.

Acquire the pearl of divine gnosis to bear away with yourself:
The estate of gold and silver is the portion of others.

The snare holds tight unless God's grace becomes the ally;
Otherwise, Adam would not take the lead over the accursed Satan.

If, Háfiz, neither silver nor gold is yours, what does it matter?
Be thankful. What is there better than the grace of speech's
    richness and a temperament serene?

1. The Covenant between God and Adam, signalled by God's question to Adam, "Am I not your Lord?" See Koran VII, 171.
2. See the note above: God asked Adam to confirm that He was his Lord. In this hemistich, Háfiz palliates the boldness of the second hemistich of verse 4, but it was not unusual for Súfí poets to address God with a kind of bold, bantering impudence—such as might pass between lovers.

POEM CCCLXI

Get up so that we might seek an opening at the wine-shop's door:
Let us sit in the path of the friend and be on the lookout for a
    boon.

For the journey to the holy precinct of union we lack the
    pilgrim's provisions.
Perhaps through begging at the vintner's door we might get some.

Our stained tears are running, but
For conveying them to him we are looking for one pure of heart.

Let the relish of the brand-mark of grief for you be forbidden
    our heart,
If for the violence of the tyranny of your love we seek redress.

The spot of your mole cannot be stamped on vision's tablet
Unless from the pupil of the eye we seek black ink.

With all its soul the heart desired a loving sign from your
    sweet lips.
With a smile of sugar[1] your lips replied, "It's a higher bid we're
    looking for."

So long as the melancholy-tinctured heart must have a perfumed
    prescription,
We seek a receipt from your fragrance-spreading down.

Since other than in a joyful heart grief for you is not to be found,
In hope of sorrowing for you we seek a joyous heart.

How long, Háfiz, must you sit at the College Gate?
Arise, because it is from the wine-shop's door we seek a revelation.

---

1. The allusion is not only to sweetness, but to the teeth behind the lip like lumps
   of white sugar.

POEM CCCLXII

We were expecting help from comrades.
What we were assuming was completely wrong.

Till the time when the tree of friendship might bear fruit,
We are off now, but we have sown a seed.

Bandying words is not the dervish style.
If it were, we have some old scores with you.

Your eye's sly look has the feint of war.
We make a mistake: we take it for peace.

The beauty of your rose bush was not of itself heart-enkindling:
We cast the spell of devotion over it.

Subtleties have passed, but no one complained:
We did not damage the dignity of respect.

He said, "You yourself surrendered to us the heart, O Háfiz:
We have not sent anyone the tax-gatherer."

POEM CCCLXIII

Why, when we have invited drunkards, in us do you seek virtue?
At the rolling of your drunken narcissus eye we bade propriety
    farewell.

Open the door of the wine-shop, because the dervish hospice
    offered nothing.
Whether or not you believe it, this was the problem and we have
    spoken.

I have fallen down overcome because of your eye, O wine-boy, but
Any disaster that comes from the beloved I give a thousand
    welcomes.

I described your stature as a tall tree, but great was the shame
    produced
As to why we made this comparison and uttered this slander.

If you do not forgive me, you will suffer remorse in the end.
Bear this truth in mind, how in the way of service we have spoken.

My vitals have, like a musk pod, turned into blood, but this was
    the least I deserved;
The retribution of one who in error mentioned China[1] in relation
    to his tress.

You, O Háfiz, have turned into fire, but it has not caught on with
    the friend—
On account of the rose's bad faith, you'd say we've been talking
    to the wind.[2]

---

1. The land of rare and beautiful novelties.
2. i.e. in vain.

POEM CCCLXIV

In the interest of the wine-shop we have laid down our gains:
The harvest of prayer we have laid out along the path of the
    beloved.

This brand which we have seared onto our mad heart
Can set on fire a hundred learned ascetics' threshing corn.

The Sultan of Eternity without Beginning granted us the
    treasure of the grief of love
As soon as we set our faces towards this desolate halting place.

I will give the love of idols henceforth no access to the heart:
I have implanted the seal of his lip on the door of this abode.

There can be no more hypocrisy under the patched gown;
In such a way as this have we in debauchery fixed its foundation.

How will this battered ship plough on when, after all,
We have dedicated life to obtaining this peerless pearl?

God be thanked that, like us, he whom we have set up
For wisdom and nurturing sense,[1] was heart-lost and outside
    religion.

Like Háfiz we were content with an illusion of you;
O Lord, what a beggarly and out of the way aspiration we
    established!

---

1.   i.e. the Magian Elder.

POEM CCCLXV

Let us go by the street of the wine-shop
As, for the sake of a draught, of that door we are all in need.

On Day One, when we boasted of licence and love,
The condition was that we should follow only the path of this
    Way.

The place where Jamshíd's throne and dais go by the wind,
It is no good if we pine with sorrow. It is better that we drink wine.

So long as it may be that no hand can reach his waist,
We are seated ruby-red in the blood of the heart.

Preacher desist from counselling the love-crazed, because we,
With the dust of the street of the friend have no interest in
    paradise.

As in the mystic ecstasy and the dance Súfís are pre-eminent,
So we also might likewise whirl the arms in deceit.

From your potion's draught dust discovered pearl and ruby.
Poor wretches we who before you are less than dust!

Since, Háfiz, there is no attaining the battlements of Union's
    Palace,
Let us go on with the dust of this door's threshold.

POEM CCCLXVI

Get up so that we might take the Súfí gown to the tavern:
Take ecstatic outpouring and ejaculations of the possessed to the
   market of superstitions.

Let us, by way of a novelty brought from a distant voyage,
Take to the wild wandering calendars[1] the Bistámí[2] cloak and
   rapturous exclamations.

Since all reclusives seize the morning cup,
Let us to the door of the Exemplar of private prayers[3] bring the
   morning harp.

That Covenant we concluded with you in the Auspicious Vale,[4]
Let us, like the "let me see" – saying Moses, take it to the
   Appointed Place.[5]

Let us beat the drum of your fame from atop the Throne's
   battlements;
Carry to the roof of the heavens the banner of your love.

Tomorrow on Resurrection's field we will carry the dust of your
   street
On the crown of the head as a boast.

If in our way the ascetic plants the thorn of reproach,
Into the gaol of retribution we will carry him out of the rose
   garden.

May we be ashamed of our stained woollen cloth,
If to "virtue" and "munificence" such as this we ascribe the name
   of acts of grace.

If the heart fails to understand the value of time[6] and achieves
   nothing,
For this harvest of times may we bear great shame.

From the ceiling of this vaulted dome temptation rains. Get up,
That in the wine-shop we might take refuge from all evil.

In the wilderness of desire how long must be being lost?
Let us ask the way. Perhaps we'll trace great endeavours.

Háfiz, do not at the door of every rapscallion squander your
    honour's lustre;
Better we take our want to the Arbiter of Needs.

---

1. In Persian, *qalandar*, which denotes wandering, often in bands, ecstatic and utterly antinomian dervishes, notorious for devil-may-care and sometimes lewd behaviour.

2. *Bistámí*: an allusion, as startling as it is interesting, to the celebrated Súfí Abú Yazíd (Báyazíd) of Bistám. He died in either 877–8 AD or six years earlier. His mystical preaching and practise were of the *sukr*, intoxication, type as opposed to the *sahv*, sober kind. It seems as if Háfiz is attacking the *sukr* school of Sufism, in spite of his own unconcealed distrust of reason and denial of its efficacy where the Way of Love is concerned. But he might be criticising false Súfís who used *sukr* as a cover for obnoxious and excessive conduct. The reference to a "voyage" prepares us for the reference to something from Bistám, which is situated in Khorásán far from Shíráz. *Rah-ávard*, suggests a gift brought from a distant land.

3. Háfiz is contrasting *munáját*, discrete, well ordered, private orisons, with *shath*, mentioned in the first verse above, translated "ecstatic outpouring". Its plural is *shathiyyát*, sayings often as gnomic as they are rapturous, and a type of mystical utterance for which Rúzbihán Baqlí (522–606 AH/1128–1209 AD) was famous, and of which a book of his is extant and has been edited by H. Corbin, Tehran & Paris, 1966. Rúzbihán preached for half a century in Shíráz where he established a *ribát*, Súfí hospice. His Order survived through several generations of his family, until, in fact, Háfiz's own time. The founder won the soubriquet of the "ecstatic doctor", even in his lifetime. He was certainly of the *sukr* kind of mystic, but Háfiz again might have been condemning him less than later sanctimonious, hypocritical followers who exploited his name and perverted his doctrine. God knows best.

4. The Wádí Aiman, "Auspicious Vale", see Poem XXVII, note 2. The oath or "Covenant", is the primeval oath between God and Man. See Koran VII, 171. See Poem XX, note 4. But here, of course, the actual covenant referred to is that between God and Moses, the Vale being where Moses had his encounter with God, see next note.

5. "Appointed Place", for which Háfiz here used the Koranic term *míqát*, for Moses's meeting place with God. See Koran VII, 139 and Poem XXVII, note 3. (The word *míqát* also means a place in the vicinity of Mecca where the pilgrims don the *ihrám*, and thus prepare themselves for the rituals of the pilgrimage.) Moses asked to see God.

6. See Poem XX, note 1, for the mystical significance of time, *vaqt*, in a Súfí context.

POEM CCCLXVII

Come that we may scatter roses and fill the cup with wine,
Split the ceiling of the Firmament and dig out a fresh foundation.

If the army which sheds the blood of lovers excites regret,
I and the wine-boy will mount a joint raid and uproot it.

For the Judas blossom red wine we will add rose water to the
cup.
For the perfume-diffusing breeze onto the chafing dish we will
throw sugar.[1]

Since, minstrel, a melodious lute is in your hand, sing a tuneful
ditty,
That clapping our hands we might sing a ghazal and in dancing
let ourselves go.

Whip up our dust, breeze, as far as that lofty threshold.
It might be that I cast a glance at the face of the Sháh of the fair.

One boasts of reason. Another braids[2] ecstatic ejaculations.
Come so that we might cast these differences before the Judge.

If you want the Paradise of Eden, come to the wine-shop with us.
One day we'll throw you from the wine-vat's foot into the Pond
of Kawthar.[3]

They do not pursue the knowing of verse and singing well in
Shíráz.
Come, Háfiz, so the we might betake ourselves to another realm.

---

1. Sugar which, besides providing additional sweetness, will make the fragrant
   flame burn up more lustily, as it would if aloes where thrown onto it.
2. To braid or weave ejaculations which are supposed to be spontaneous is a
   contradiction that illustrates the falsity of the ejaculations.
3. See Poem CLVIII, note 1.

POEM CCCLXVIII

Come Súfí that we might tear off the cloak of hypocrisy,
And draw the line of cancellation through this tissue of fraud.

We'll stake the dedication and free offerings of the chantry as
    the price;
We'll drag the gown of false sanctimony through the tavern's
    waters.

The secret of Fate, that is hidden behind the veil of the Invisible —
Drunkenly we'll snatch the veil from before its cheeks.

Tipsy we'll leap out and from the Súfís' banquet,
Plunder wine and pull the beauty to our breast.

We will indulge in pleasure and, if not,
We'll be slain by disappointment the day we drag life's chattels
    to another world.

Where a fetching glance from beneath his eyebrow, so that, like
    the new moon,
We might play the ball of the sphere in the golden hockey-stick's
    bend?

Tomorrow, if the Garden of Rizván[1] is not granted us,
We'll drag youths[2] from the Seventh Heaven to the gate, and
    Houris from the Garden.

Háfiz, it is not within our bailiwick so to boast;
Why should we any more overstep the mark in obedience?[3]

---

1. *Rizván*, the Guardian of the Garden of Paradise. See Poem L, note 1.
2. "youths", *ghilmán*. Háfiz uses this word which occurs in Koran LII, verse 24,
    where it designates the attendants who "as if they were hidden pearls" wait on
    the righteous in Paradise.
3. Literally, "why draw your foot further from beneath the blanket?"

POEM CCCLXIX

Friends, it is better that at the time of the rose we strive for
　　pleasure.
This is the word of people of the heart; let us heed it with our life.

There is no generosity in anyone and the time of joy is fleeting.
The remedy is this, that we sell the prayer-mat for wine.

There is a pleasant, gladness-bestowing air. O God, send
Some delicate form for us to drink rose-red wine to his face.

The organ player of the Firmament[1] is the highway robber[2] of
　　people of virtue.[3]
How might we not lament over this frustration, and why not cry
　　out loud?

The rose is boiling over with blossom and we have not doused it
　　with a drop of wine.
Inevitably we are on the boil, with the fire of sorrow and desire.

From the cup of the tulip we draw imaginary wine.
May the Eye of Evil be far, because, lacking minstrel and wine,
　　we are confused.

To whom, Háfiz, can this wondrous state be told, that we
Are nightingales which, in the season of the rose, are silent?

---

1. Venus.
2. "highway robber", *rahzan*, but this word can also mean "musician", literally, "striker of strings", or "melodies".
3. For Venus ought to protect the virtuous, but she betrays them too: the music of the Súfí circle attracts the attention of the hostile. In Islam the strictly orthodox consider music taboo.

POEM CCCLXX

One night we will lift up our hands and utter a prayer.
From somewhere we will find a remedy for the grief of separation
    from you.

The ailing heart is beside itself. Friends, help,
So that we might fetch a physician to it and effect a cure.

The root of gladness has dried up. Which is the way to the tavern,
That in that climate we might grow and flourish?

He who with no cause took offence and struck me with the
    sword, and went,
Bring him back for God's sake, for us to know some serenity.

In lust's way, because of which our breast has turned into an
    idol-temple,
We will let fly the arrow of a sigh and mount an attack.

Seek help from the heart of profligates O heart, but if not,
Dire is the task. God forbid we make any mistake.

The bird of the puny maw's shadow is of no avail:
Search for the auspicious shadow of the Humá.[1]

My heart has fallen out of tune, Háfiz. Where is there the right
    cadence,
So that from his speech and lyrics we might create melody and
    song?

---

1. See Poem C, note 1, for this fabulous bird of good fortune.

POEM CCCLXXI

We speak no evil and incline to no falsity:
We put nobody into mourning nor do we make our own gown
    blue.[1]

We indite no deceptive cipher on the pages of learning's
    notebook.
We do not append the mystery of the Divine to the margin of
    fraudulently disputatious sheets.

The fault of the poor and of the rich is by and large bad:
In this it is best we practise no evil at all.

The heavens splinter the ship of lords of virtue.
Best is this that on that somersaulting ocean we place no reliance.

If the Sháh does not reverently drink the draught of the licentious,
We will have no respect for his pure filtered wine.

Likewise if an envier spoke and a comrade was hurt,
Say, "Be of good cheer, because we do not lend an ear to fools."

If, Háfiz, the enemy speaks in error, we will not catch him out:
But if he speaks truthfully we have no quarrel with the truth.

---

1.   Blue is the colour of mourning but see Poem cxcix, note 1, for the blue gowned
    dervish Order in Shíráz, which Háfiz apparently derided. While blue is the
    colour of mourning it is perhaps significant that this reference to the "blue
    gown" follows that in the preceding hemistich to "falsity" and speaking evil.

POEM CCCLXXII

I am tipsy and saying very noisily
That I am seeking the breeze of life from the cup.

Let the moroseness of asceticism accord with the look of the
    hangover:
I am the disciple of the dregs-draining party of the
    happy disposition.

If the Magian Elder does not open the door to us,
On which door should I knock? From where seek a cure?

Do not in this meadow reproach me for growing on my own:
As nurture is granted me, so I grow.

Do not see the Súfí hospice and the tavern in the foreground;
God is witness that, wherever he is, I am with him.

The dust of the Way of Seeking is the elixir for waxing daily better;
I am the slave of the fortune of that ambergris-perfumed dust.

Out of passion for the languorous narcissus eye of the tall form,
I am like the tulip drooping with the cup at the edge of the stream.

I became notorious for dizziness when the curl of the friend
Drew me like a ball into its hockey-stick bend!

Bring wine because, by the decree[1] of Háfiz, from a pure heart
With the brimming over of the cup we may wash away the fog of
    hypocrisy.

---

1.   i.e. fatwa.

POEM CCCLXXIII

I have said many times and will say one time more
That I the lost do not of myself run this course:

As if I were a parrot I have been kept the wrong side of the
    looking-glass—
What the Master of Eternity without Beginning said, "Say,"
    I say.[1]

Whether I am the thorn or whether the rose, there is an Adorner
    of the field;
It is by that power by which he plants me that I grow.

Do not, friends, censure heart-lost crazy me—
I have a jewel and am seeking the possessor of perception.

Although the colour of wine does not go with the
    particoloured[2] gown,
Do not fault me, because I wash away the colour of hypocrisy
    with it.

The laughter and tears of lovers belong somewhere else:
In the night I am singing, but at break of day, I am moaning.

Háfiz said to me, "Do not sniff the dust of the wine-tavern's door."
Say, "Cast no blame, for I am smelling the musk of Khotan."

---

1.   The expression meaning "the parrot the wrong side of the looking-glass",
    alludes to a parrot being put before a mirror while an instructor from behind it
    teaches the parrot to speak, which the parrot does imagining that he himself
    must be speaking the words on his own since he cannot see the instructor.
    Read "instructor" with a capital "I" and Háfiz's point becomes clear.
2.   The word translated "particoloured", *mulamma'*, besides meaning "variegated",
    "particoloured", etc., can also mean "hypocritical". See next hemistich.

POEM CCCLXXIV

Although we're the slaves of the Pádshá,
Kings of the realm of the morning hour[1] are we.

Treasure[2] up the sleeve, but nothing in the purse,
The world-seeing cup, but we are dust on the road.

Sober in the Presence, but drunk in folly,
The ocean of Unity, yet we are drowned in sin.

When luck's darling deigns a glance,
We are the mirror for his moon-like cheek.

Every night for the Shá of alert fortune
We are the guardian of the crown and the casque.

Say, "Take advantage of our zeal,"
Because you are asleep, but we are on the look-out.

Shá Mansúr[3] is aware that we,
Wherever we direct our zeal,

Make a shroud out of blood for enemies:
On friends we confer the mantle of victory.

Let there be no false colouring in us:
We are the tawny lion, and the black adder too.

Tell them to repay Háfiz's debt;
You have owned up to it and we are witnesses.

---

1. "the morning hour", prayers uttered during which are said to be answered, so
   that the devotee who utters them becomes acceptable to the court of the
   Divine.
2. The inference is that we have spiritual knowledge, *ma'rifat*, but this is in contrast
   to our being without material goods. In the next hemistich, the contrast is further
   elucidated.
3. See Poem CXLIII, note 3.

POEM CCCLXXV

When you come, over the wounded utter a recital of the Fatiha;[1]
Open the lips because the ruby of your lip confers life on the
    injured.

To him who came to ask after me, and read the Fatiha and departs,
Say, "One moment," so that I may send the spirit after him.

O you who are a physician for the hurt, scan the surface of my
    tongue,
Because this breath and this sigh from my breast are the burden
    of the heart on the tongue.

Although on account of love fever made my bones hot and
    then abated,
Unlike the fever, the fire of love does not abate in my bones.

Because of your mole, the home of my heart is in its fire;
Because of your two eyes, my eye has been pierced and put out
    of action.

With the water of the two eyes reduce my heat, and take
My pulse, to see whether it shows any sign of life whatsoever.

He who has conferred the never-ending glass on me for the sake
    of keeping me alive,
Why does he keep on taking my specimen glass to the doctor?

Háfiz, your poetry has granted me a dose of the Water of Life!
Forget the doctor: come and study my medicine's prescription.

---

1. *Fatiha*: the opening chapter of the Koran recited by mourners visiting the
    bereaved, and on other occasions of grief, dismay and expression of sympathy.

POEM CCCLXXVI

However much I told the doctors my ailment,
They had no cure for poor wretched strangers.

The seal is no longer on the jewel-case of love[1] —
O Lord, may the wish of rivals not be gratified.

That rose, every moment in the power of a gust of wind,
Tell, "Be ashamed for the nightingales' sake."

We told our secret pain to the friend:
Pain cannot be hidden from physicians.

O Lord, grant immunity, for the eyes of lovers
Again to see the countenance of the beloved.

O benefactor, how long will it now finally be
That at the feast of your bounty we are left among the non-sharers?

Háfiz would not have become the lunatic of love
If he had listened to the advice of those with a sense of fitness.

---

1. The jewel-case of love has been tampered with by rivals aiming to alienate the
   beloved from the speaker of the verse. The lips are implied, as the casket of
   speech.

POEM CCCLXXVII

I burn on account of your disengagement. Give up cruelty.
Separation has become our bane. O Lord, avert banefulness.

On the blue-grey steed of the heavens the moon is showing off.
Get astride Rakhsh,[1] for the moon to come to its setting.

For the rape of reason and religion, stride out drunkenly;
Set your hat at a jaunty angle on your head and, like a clown,
    wear your cloak open at the front.

Let your tight curls cascade down, that is to say, to spite the
    hyacinth
Round the meadow twirl a scented chafing dish as does the breeze.

O light of drunkards' eyes, I am all expectation;
Caress a doleful harp and a cup, or make it go the rounds.

Since on your cheek time inscribes a lovely line,
O Lord, divert from our friend any evil inscription.

Háfiz, of the fair-looking other than this amount no luck is yours.
If this is not to your satisfaction, change the decree of Fate!

---

1. The celebrated horse of Rustam, the champion in Iranian legend. The word
can, however, be used for any horse of good points and noble mien, and it can
also mean "the sun", a fact which obviously lies behind Háfiz's use of the word
in this context.

POEM CCCLXXVIII

O Lord return that musky deer to Khotan,
And that straight swaying cypress to its meadow.

Caress our stricken heart with a gentle breeze.
In other words, restore to the body that precious soul that has
    left it.

Since by Your command moon and sun travel to their stations,
Fetch back also to me our moon-faced friend.

In seeking the Yamanite ruby[1] the eyes have turned to blood.
O Lord, return that shining star to Yaman.

Go auspicious bird of the blessed influence,
Take word of the crows and kites back to the 'Anqá![2]

The word is this that without you we have no desire for life.
Listen, O news-bearing messenger, and take word back.

Him whose proper home was Háfiz's eye,
As is to be wished, send back from the foreign to his native land.

---

1.   The play is on redness: ruby, blood. The gem for which Yaman was noted was
    agate, but Háfiz has promoted the object of his desire to ruby. In the next
    hemistich, Yaman refers to Shíráz, as did Khotan, etc., in the first verse.
2.   The fabulous bird also in Persian called *Símurgh*.

POEM CCCLXXIX

For God's sake hobnob less with wearers of the patched gown:
Do not hide your face from inopulent sots.[1]

There is under that cloak plenty of corruption.
O happy the time of the wine-vendors' gown!

You are of a delicate disposition and unable to bear
The moments of 'gravitas' of a handful of the dervish-gowned.

Come and from these fraudsters' cheating, turn to see
A cup of the blood of the heart and a harp plaintively wailing.

Since you have got me drunk, do not sit veiled.
Since you have given me wholesome liquor, do not make me
    drink poison.

I have seen no sign of suffering in these so-called Súfís.
May the pleasure of the dregs-drinkers be of the pure sort.

Beware the warm heart of Háfiz:
His breast is like a boiling cauldron.

---

1. The genuine as opposed to false Súfís.

POEM CCCLXXX

The Sháh of tall box-tree forms, Khusrau of sweet mouths
Who with his eyelashes breaks the centre of all rank-smashers,

Passed drunkenly by and on dervish me threw a look,
And said, "Hey lamp and eye of all sweet of speech,

How long must your purse be empty of silver and gold?
Become my slave and all silver bodies enjoy!"

You are not less than a mote. Do not be degraded. Practise love,
So that whirling now this side up, now that, to the private chamber
    of the sun you might arrive.

Do not rely on the world and, if you have wine in the cup,
Drink the joy of Venus brows and those of tender limbs.

My wine-measuring Elder—may his soul be glad—
Said, "Shun association with promise-breakers."

Of the breeze in the tulip-field at dawn I asked,
"For whom are all these gory shrouds the martyrs?"

It answered, "You and I, Háfiz, are not in this secret.
Tell the tale of ruby wine and the sweet mouthed.

Take the hem of the garment of the friend in your hand and
    forswear the foe:
Be the man of God and pass safe from Ahriman."[1]

---

1. The Zoroastrian principle of Evil: the arch-opponent of Good.

POEM CCCLXXXI

In hope of your fragrance,[1] every moment like the rose
From top to bottom I tear the clothing off my body.

You would say the rose had seen your body so that
In the garden like men drunk it shredded the clothes it wore.

Because of the hold of your sorrow, my life is hard to bear,
Yet it was with ease you stole the heart from me.

On hearsay from enemies you dropped the friend;
No person becomes enemy to a friend.

Your body in its dress like wine in a glass;
Your heart in the breast like iron encased in silver—

O candle, drop bloodied tears from your eye,
Because the burning of your heart has become clear to everyone.

Do not so act that the liver-searing sigh from my breast
Like smoke from a chimney should arise.

Do not break my heart and throw it under foot,
Because it has its dwelling at your tress's tip.

Since Háfiz has fastened his heart to your tress,
Do not trample down in this way his endeavour.

---

1. This paraphrase, "in the hope of your fragrance", contrives to combine two
    meanings of the word *bú:* "smell", and "hope".

POEM CCCLXXXII

The banner of the Sultan of the Rose has sprung up from the
    margin of the meadow.
May his arrival, O Lord, be blessèd for cypress and jasmine.

In his own abode this royal accession was toward,
For now everyone can be seated in his proper place.

Through the beauty of yours give the signet ring of Jamshíd the
    good news
That the Great Name[1] has retrieved it from the grasp of Ahriman.

For Eternity without End may this house be prosperous, from
    the dust of
Whose threshold the wind of Yaman[2] every moment blows with
    mercy's scent.

From all "Chronicles of Kings"[3] the might of Pashang's son[4] and
    his world-conquering sword
Has become the story of the assembly.

The Circling Heavens' piebald polo pony has been broken in
    beneath your saddle;
O kingly knight,[5] you have superbly entered the field. Strike a
    ball!

Your sword is the running water in the channels of the kingdom;
Plant you the tree of justice. Dig up evil wishers' roots.

After this there'd be no surprise if, with your sweet
    nature's fragrance,
From the plain of Ízej[6] the musk pods of Khotan were to arise.

Reclusives in retreats are on the look-out for the joyous splendour.
Push your cap askew and unveil the cheek.

I took counsel with intelligence. It said, "Drink wine Háfiz."
Ho there, wine-boy, give wine as the counsellor instructed.

465

O breeze, submit to the wine-server at the feast of the Atábak7
The request that he may grant me from that gold-scattering
   cup a drink.

---

1. "Great Name", see Poems ccxx, note 4, and cccxxii, note 6. The allusion here is
to Solomon's ring—Jamshíd is equivalent to Solomon in Iranian mythology—
and its theft by the *dív* and how it was miraculously restored after the *dív*, i.e.
"Ahriman", the principle of evil, disguised as Solomon had ruled for forty days.
See also Poem xxiv, note 3.

2 See Poem xlix, note 2 and the *hadíth* of the Prophet Muhammad, "Lo, I feel the
breath of the Merciful from the direction of Yaman."

3. "Chronicles of Kings": The Chronicle which at once springs to mind is the
Sháhnáma (Book of Kings) of Firdawsí (d. 1020–1 or 1025–6). But Háfiz has it in
the plural, and this might be related to his seeming to praise Afrásíyáb in this
intriguingly complex verse.

4. "Pashang's son" was Afrásíyáb the descendant of Túr the son of the ancient
Iranian hero Feridún and therefore of Iranian descent, although he became king
of Iran's bitterly hostile northern neighbour Túrán. It seems odd to see a Persian
poet apparently praising Afrásíyáb, for whom bitter imprecations are generally
preserved: Firdawsí apostrophizes him as Iran's diabolically evil destroyer. In
view of Háfiz's seventh verse, it is interesting that Afrásíyáb is accused of bringing,
not only fire and sword, but drought to Iran, whereas the object of Háfiz's praise
in this poem is lauded for establishing running waters in his kingdom by the
lustre of his sword. So to which Afrásíyáb does Háfiz allude in his reference to
the son of Pashang? There are ancient references which do give Afrásíyáb credit
for playing the role of Iran's liberator from the evil Zainigav ("Follower of the
Lie"), but by Firdawsí's time the threat of Turkish inroads into northern Iran
might perhaps have contributed to the demonization of the regions north of the
Oxus and their inhabitants, mistakenly identified with Túrán and Turanians,
ruled by a thoroughly wicked King who constantly threatened Iran with
destruction. Yet even Firdawsí lets his villain remind us that he had once rid Iran
of the *Tázíyán anjuman*, "the Arab host". This allusion might be taken as a hint
at the ancient story of Afrásíyáb defeating Zainigav. (see *Sháhnáma*, edited by
Khaleghi-Motlagh, Costa Mesa, CA, 1990, Vol. II, p. 92, line 322). It is interesting
that Háfiz, uses Firdawsí's word for "host", *anjuman*, which can also mean
"assembly"; the Afrásíyáb he is alluding to seems to have symbolized a benign
power which rid the realm of enemies. However it may be, in likening his
patron to Afrásíyáb it is probable that Háfiz was once again remembering the
ancestry of Sháh Shujá', whose descent on his mother's side from the Qará-
Khitay Qutlugh Khan Buráq Hájib of Kirmán might be considered "Turanian".
(See Poem xxx, note 7).

5. The reference to a "kingly knight" seems to clinch the supposition that Háfiz
was speaking of his patron-prince, Sháh Shujá', hence the "Turanian" ethos
evoked in the preceding verse.

6. Opinions may differ but this place reference could be to the ancient Elamite
centre in the southern-facing folds of the Zagros mountains and situated on old
routes westwards from Shíráz and those north to Isfahán and south to Ahwáz.
What is today known as Ízeh is situated on a high marshy plateau bordered by

steep rocks which in summer kick out great heat. Not the most hospitable of grounds for the musk deer of Central Asia, a region from which Ízeh is sufficiently remote.

7. Once again Háfiz echoes Turkish associations. The word *Atábak* literally means "Father-Chief". It was the title assumed under the Saljuq Turkish rulers of Iran (1037–1157 AD) for the Saljuq Princes' Tutor-Guardians, who often usurped their youthful wards' domains. The Atábaks of Luristán ruled from Ízej (Ídaj), mentioned in the preceding note, from about 1155 to 1424 AD; they would provide an example of the title in use in an area close to Shíráz. But the Atábak of the Poem must have been, of course, much nearer home. The overall impression derived from these references to Ízej is that it was hostile to Shíráz at the time.

POEM CCCLXXXIII

What than thought of wine and the cup will there be better
Till we see what the end of it all is going to be?

When there are no days left, how long can the sorrow of the
    heart be endured?
Say, "No heart and no days be," what will there be?

Tell the impatient bird to swallow its yearning, because on it
What will be the mercy of him who sets the trap?

Drink wine. Abide no sorrow. Take no advice from blind
    precedent-followers—
What credit will the mutterings of the crowd enjoy?

The wages of your toil are surely best spent gratifying desire.
Do you know what the end for the ungratified will be?

The Elder of the Wine Temple last night was telling a riddle—
From the line on the cup,[1] what the end will be—

"With drum, harp and song I have led the heart of Háfiz astray."
So what will be the punishment of reprobate me?

---

1.   The wine bowl or cup was as often as not inscribed with verses, often quatrains
    like those attributed to Omar Khayyam.

POEM CCCLXXXIV

Do you know what good luck is? To see the face of the friend;
To prefer beggary in his street to being an emperor.

To give up life is easy, but
Soulmates can only with difficulty be cut off.

With a heart contracted like the rose's folded bud I will go to
    the garden,
And there for recognition's sake rend a shirt.

Sometimes like the breeze I will whisper hidden mysteries into
    the rose's ear.
Sometimes to the secrets of love-play from the nightingale I
    will listen.

First do not give up kissing the lip of the beloved:
In the end, of biting your own hand and lip you will grow tired.

Count being together a boon because, when from this
    two-doored stopping-place
We go, there will be no coming together again.

You would say Háfiz has vanished from the memory of Sháh
    Mansúr.[1]
Of looking after the poor, O Lord remind him.

---

1.   See Poem CXLIII, note 3.

POEM CCCLXXXV

I'm the one who is the talk of the town for love-making.
It is I whose sight is not polluted by looking at evil.

In wine-worshipping I have cast my image on waters for this,
That I might destroy the scheme of worshipping the self.

We practise fidelity and put up with blame and are happy
Because in our Way[1] to be dismayed is to be heathen.

"What is the way to salvation?" I asked the Magian Elder.
He called for a cup of wine and said, "Keeping the secret."

Learn love for the cheek of the fair from the line of down of
    the friend,
Because it is good to sport in the environs of the fair one's cheeks.[2]

What, gazing on the garden of the world, does the heart desire?
With the pupil of the eye to pluck a rose from your cheek.

We will turn the reins from this congregation to the wine-shop,
Because it is imperative not to listen to sermons from those who
    do not practise what they preach.

I am trusting in the mercy of your tress-tip, but otherwise,
What does trying avail if there's no allurement from that side?

Kiss nothing but the lip of the beloved, Háfiz, and the wine-
    bowl's rim,
Because it is a sin to kiss the hands of the sellers of asceticism.

---

1. Here Háfiz uses the Súfí technical term for "Way", *taríqat*.
2. This is a highly religious poem. The down symbolizes the environs of the
    Divine.

POEM CCCLXXXVI

O you of the moon-aspected face, the fresh Spring of beauty,
Your mole and strip of down the centre of grace, and beauty's
    meridian,

Hidden techniques of sorcery in your sultry drunken eye,
In your disordered tress, beauty's fixity manifest.

From goodness's mansion no moon like you has shone,
From beauty's flowing brookside no cypress with your stature
    has sprung.

The age of heart-ravishing with the grace of your beauty has
    become joyful.
With your elegance beauty's time has been blessed.

Because of your tress's snare and the grain of your mole
In the world no single bird of the heart is not left beauty's prey.

With ever-lasting tenderness may the nurse¹ of nature
With all its heart be gently nursing you in the bosom of beauty.

The violet is fresh and moist round your lip because
It drinks the water of life from the fountain of beauty.

Háfiz has given up hope of seeing your equal:
There is no one but you in the land of beauty.

---

1. Dr Khánlarí's reading is *falak*, which also means "firmament", "the heavens",
   etc., but it can also mean "nurse", and indeed in some MSS the word *dáyeh*,
   "nurse" is given instead of *falak*.

POEM CCCLXXXVII

Veil the rose petal with musky hyacinth,
That is to say, hide the cheek and devastate a world.

Radiantly open the sleepy drunken narcissus eye,
And out of jealousy make the sprightly narcissus drowsy with
    sleep.

Spill beads of sweat from your face and make the garden borders
As full of rose water as are the glass cups of our eyes.

The season of the rose, like life's, has hastened on—
Make haste wine-boy to circulate the rose-red wine.

Smell the scent of the violet and take the tress of the darling.
Look upon the hue of the tulip, and address yourself to wine.

As you have the habit and rite of lover-slaying,
Drain the cup with enemies and subject me to scolding.

Open your eye like a bubble upon the face of the cup,
And the foundations of this abode make comparable to a bubble's.

Háfiz is seeking union by way of prayer.
O Lord, have the prayers of the broken-hearted answered.

POEM CCCLXXXVIII

It is morning. O wine-boy, fill the cup with wine —
The sphere's wheeling brooks no delay. Make haste.

Before the vanishing world tumbles into ruin,
With the bowl of rose-red wine ruin us.

From out of the east of the bowl the sun of wine has risen —
If it is pleasure's provender you're after let sleep go hang.

The day when the Firmament makes jugs of our clay,
Be sure and make the flask of our head full of wine.

We are not the man for puritan austerity, repentance, ecstatic
    ramblings;
Speak to us with a bowl of clear wine.

O Háfiz, worshipping wine is proper conduct.
Get up and fix resolution on what is proper.

POEM CCCLXXXIX

Come through the door and light up our darkened room:
Make fragrant the air of the gathering of men of the Spirit.

Heart and soul I have surrendered to the beloved's eye and its
    over-arching brow.
Come, come and behold the arch and the eye.

The star of the night of separation gives out no light.
Come you onto the palace roof and provide the lamp of the moon.

Tell the treasurer of the Elysian Garden to make of the dust of
    this assembly
A novel gift on behalf of Paradise, and aloes for its chafing dish.

The meddling of the carnal spirit produces many a tale. Wine-boy,
Do not fail in your duty: pour the wine into the cup,

And if the jurist counsels, "Do not play at love,"
Hand him a cup and tell him to wet his brain.

Since in the field the darlings are inferior to your beauty,
Give the jasmine a tender look and prink yourself before the pine.

Because of this gore-pleated turban and patched gown I am in a
    most sorry state.
With one Súfí-murdering wink turn me into a crazy wandering
    hermit.

After serving pleasure and after the love of the moon-faced,
Include in your deeds learning the poems of Háfiz by heart.

POEM CCCXC

O light of my eye, a word, listen:
"When your cup is full, drink and give to drink."

The venerable in speech speak from experience and, I tell you,
When you grow old, boy, take care to heed advice.

The power of love does not chain up the man of sense;
You desire the tress of the friend? Get rid of sense!

None of the rapture of drunkenness is granted you by beads and
    the gown.
Seek inspiration for this purpose from the vintner.

The musical instruments[1] have been smashed and of merriment
    no apparatus remains.
Draw out a dirge O harp. O drum, bang out your booms.

The evil promptings of Ahriman are not wanting in the path of
    love.
Come forward and turn the ear of the heart to the message of
    Gabriel.[2]

May your bowl, server of wine, not be empty of clear wine—
Spare a generous glance for me the drainer of dregs.

When in your gold-spangled robe you tipsily pass by,
Spare the wool-clad Háfiz one devotional kiss.

---

1. The words for "musical instruments" are "instrument" *barg*, and "musical"
navá. *Sáz* is the word translated "apparatus", but all these words are susceptible
to punning in meanings related to provisions, sustenance and so forth.
2. Gabriel, *Surúsh*, see Poem xxxvii, note 1 and clxxi, verse 6, and cclxxviii, note 4.
The Message of the Archangel Gabriel was the Koran, the Divine Revelation
which he delivered to the Prophet Muhammad; and of which Háfiz was a
reciter and teacher.

POEM CCCXCI

Cast one enticing look and break magic's bank;
Break the market of Sámerí.[1]

Let the world's head and turban be thrown to the wind.
In other words with a sweetheart's panache push your cap over
    your ear.

Tell the tress to leave off playing the hard-to-get mode.
Tell the eye to rout oppression's army centre with a single flash.

Come strutting out and snatch from everybody the ball of beauty:
Put the Houri in her place and tarnish the lustre of the Peri.

Capture the lion of the sun with the eye of a doe.
Reach the bow of Jupiter with your curving eyebrow.[2]

When with the breathing of the wind the hyacinth-tress is
    perfume-sifting,
You with a tress-tip of ambergris spoil its value.

When, Háfiz, the nightingale shows off its eloquence,
By giving tongue in pure Persian debase the price of the
    nightingale.

---

1. See Poem cxxiv, note 1 and E. M. Butler, *The Myth of the Magus* (Cambridge, 1948,
   79 and 93) p. 73–83, for Simon Magus, reputed founder of a type of dualistic
   gnosticism. He was seen as an arch heretic and the worker of wicked magic. His
   legend and his being confused with the Samarian of Koran xx, 90 (cf. the
   Samarian image of the calf in Hosea xiii, 5 and 6) might have informed Háfiz's
   references to Sámerí in his poems; references of which there are three.
2. In zodiacal terms the mansion of Leo is the "Lion of the Sun"; that of
   Sagittarius, the "bow of Jupiter".

POEM CCCXCII

My tall one of the enticing eye-play and wily contrivance
Has cut short the prolix tale of my asceticism.

O heart, you have seen at the end of old age, of austerity and of
    learning—
What falling for the sight of my bewitching coquette has done
    to me.

I said I would hide the signs of being in love under the gown of
    hypocrisy.
The tear was the talebearer and made my secret public.

The friend is drunk but does not remember drinking partners.
Let my needy-cherishing wine-boy be spoken of well!

O Lord, when will that breeze blow in whose gentle air
Scenting his kindness might become my salvation?

At present in weeping I am casting a design on water;
How long will it be before my evanescent figure becomes mated
    with the real?

I fear for the ruining of faith because the prayer-niche
Of your eyebrow steals away the Presence of my prayers.

I, laughing at myself, am weeping like the candle,
To see what to stony-hearted you my burning and writhing
    might do.

As, ascetic, nothing comes of your praying,
So it is with my nightly drunkenness, and my secret, and
    neediness.

Háfiz has burned with sorrow. O breeze, report his condition
To the friend-nurturing, foe-melting Sháh.

POEM CCCXCIII

When I am dust in his way he shakes the hem of his robe free
    of me.
And if I say, "Return me my heart," he turns his face away from me.

Like a rose he shows everyone his bright hued face,
But if I say, "You should hide it", he hides it from me!

I asked my eye at least to have a good look at him.
It replied, "Is it a stream of blood you want from me?"

He, thirsting for my blood, and I for his lip, so how it will turn out,
I snatching satisfaction from him, or he, the price from me?

If in front of him I gutter out like a candle, he laughs like the
    morning at my distress.
And if I am pained, his sensitive heart is pained because of me.

If, like Farhád's,[1] my life in bitterness expires, no matter,
Of me many a sweet legend will remain.

Friends, I have sacrificed my life for his mouth. See
How over a slight matter[2] he withholds himself from me.

Háfiz, shut the book, because if the lesson of passion is in this
    mode,
In every corner love will be reciting an incantation from me.

---

1.   An allusion to the legend of the celebrated love of Farhád and Shírín, and
    Farhád wandering stricken in the wilderness unrequited and to die of love. Háfiz
    manages to get both the name Farhád and Shírín into this verse, the former as a
    name, the latter as the adjective, "sweet", qualifying "legend".
2.   An allusion to smallness of the mouth, which was considered beautiful.

POEM CCCXCIV

Let me recount a heart-delighting subtlety: "See the mole on
    that moon-face.
See soul and reason bound by the chain of that curl."

I rebuked the heart: "Do not be of a wild disposition, wandering
    in the plain."
It replied, "Look at that lion-capturing eye and the allurement of
    that gazelle."

The ring of his tress is the morning breeze's pleasure dome.
See the souls in it of a hundred men of the heart, bound by
    one hair.

Sun-worshippers have no regard for our sweetheart.
For God's sake, O you blamers, do not look at appearances: look
    at that face.

His heart-stealing tress has put the neck of the breeze into
    bondage.
See the Indian jugglery against desirers.

Of him in quest of whom I have gone beside myself,
Nobody has seen or will see the equal. Look in every direction.

If Háfiz is lamenting in the corner of the prayer-niche it is right—
O blamer, look at that eyebrow's curve for God's sake!

Turn not, O Firmament, your destiny away from the aim of
    Sháh Mansúr.
See the keenness of the sword. Look at the strength of the arm.

POEM CCCXCV

Drink the ruby wine and look upon the moon-browed face:
Contrary to the religion of those, see the beauty of these.

Under the patched gown they keep burglars' tackle;
See these mean beggars' plundering!

They disdain the harvest of both worlds;
See the airs and graces mendicants and gleaners give themselves!

The friend is not unknotting the musky eyebrow.
See the longing of people of the heart, but see the coquetry of
    the precious one!

From no one do I hear the Covenant of Love being repeated;
See the constancy of associates and of boon companions!

To be the captive of love is the means of my release.
See the prudent mind of those with foresight!

Love's scouring clears away the dust on the heart of Háfiz;
See the brightness of intention in the pure and in those of clean
    religion.

POEM CCCXCVI

Be for sparing the ranks of the debauched a look better than this.
Better than this make your passing by the wine temple's door.

In respect of me this kindness which your lip would deign
Is ever so good—but a trifle better than this?

To him whose care unties the knot of the toils of the world,
Say, "In this subtle complexity spare attention better than this."

If to that beloved youth I give not the heart, what am I to do?
The Mother of Time owns no son better than this.

My admonisher asked, "What merit has love other than grief?"
O Wise Master, go: what merit is better than this?

When I say, "Drain the cup and kiss the wine-boy's lip,"
Listen my dear, because no other may tell better than this.

The reed of Háfiz is the sweet fruit of the sugar cane. Gather it,
Because in this garden you will find no fruit better than this.

POEM CCCXCVII

By the life of the Elder of the tavern and in gratitude for his favour,
There is nothing in our head but the wish to serve him.

Although Paradise is no place for sinners,
Bring on the wine, because I am reliant on his zeal.

May the lamp of the lightning flash of that cloud be luminous,
That struck our harvest with the fire of his love.

Bring wine, because last night the Angel of the World of the
    Invisible[1]
Gave the good news that the bounty of His mercy is for all.

If you find a skull on the threshold of the wine-booth,
Do not kick it, because His intention is not to be fathomed.

Do not view drunken me with the eye of contempt:
There is no sinning and no abstinence without His willing.

Háfiz's shabby gown is forever in hock for wine;
Surely his clay was of the tavern's dust.

Our heart has no inclination for abstaining or penitence,
But for the sake of the good name of the Master and the lucky
    aura[2] of his favour, I will try.

---

1. *Surúsh*: see Poem cccxc, note 1.
2. Háfiz uses the word *farr*, which might indicate a reference to a ruler, specially
   as it governs the word *dawlat*, which can mean "governance", "power", etc.; *farr*
   was the lucky aura that accompanied sovereignty.

POEM CCCXCVIII

He said, "Have you come out to see the spectacle of the new moon?
For the moon of my eyebrows shame on you. Go away.

It is a lifetime your heart has been of the captives of our tress.
Do not be neglectful of protecting your own comrades' side.

Do not offer the fragrance of reason for the duskiness of our curl:
In this a thousand musk pods go for a ha'penny."

In this old tillage, the seed of constancy and of love
Will be made clear at the time when the harvest season comes.

Bring wine, wine-boy, for me to tell you a riddle
About the mystery of the anciently shifting stars and the new
    moon.

The shape of the moon's crescent every month end shows
The crown of Síyámak[1] and the helmeted cap of Zú.[2]

The Magian Elder's threshold, Háfiz, is the refuge of fidelity;
Repeat the tale of love to him and from him hear.

---

1. Síyámak, son of the first man and ruler in Iranian legend, Kayúmars. Síyámak
    was slain by a *dív* and his son Húshang succeeded Kayúmars.
2. Zú was the son of Tahmásp. As related in the *Sháhnáma*, after Afrásíyáb had killed
    Nawzar, as a substitute for the latter Zú was elected king of Iran because possessed
    of royal virtue and worthy of the royal aura, *farr*. The "riddle" alluded to in the
    preceding verse is the ephemeral character of worldly pomp.

POEM CCCXCIX

I saw the green meadow of the Firmament and the sickle of the
new moon.
I remembered my own sowing and the time of reaping.

I said, "O luck, you were sleep and the sun has come up."
It answered, "In spite of all this, do not despair of the
foreordained."[1]

On the night of departure, go to the heavens like the Messiah,
So that from your lamp a hundred rays might reach the sun.

Do not rely on the star, the sneak-thief of the night, because
It was this trickster that stole the throne of Kay Ká'ús and the
belt of Kay Khusrau.

The ear may be heavy with earrings of ruby and gold,
But beauty's season is transient. note the warning.

From your mole may the Evil Eye be far, because on the
chequer-board of beauty
It has moved a pawn by which the moon and the sun lost the
wager.

Tell the heavens not to deck themselves out in all this pomp,
because in love
The moon's harvest would fetch one barley corn, and the cluster
of the Pleiades, two.

The fire of hypocritical asceticism will burn up the grain heap of
the Faith;
Throw off the woollen cassock, Háfiz, and go.

---

1. "foreordained": the Turkish commentator, Súdí, suggests that the word *sábiqeh*,
here translated "foreordained", may be related to the *hadíth*, *Sabaqat rahmatí
ghazabí*, "My compassion outruns My wrath". Thus an acceptable paraphrase for
sábiqeh might be "the overriding mercy." So much for Súdí, but there is evidence
in the works of some mystics for the word *sábiqeh* being used to indicate what is
foreordained. I owe Dr Annabel Keeler gratitude for pointing this out to me.

POEM CCCC

O sun, the mirror-holder to your beauty,
O black musk, the turning chafing dish of your mole,

I washed the courtyard of the palace of the eye, but to what avail?
Because this corner is not fit for your images' squadrons.

O sun of beauty, you are at the zenith of grace and tenderness.
Until the Resurrection, O Lord, may no setting be yours.

Lovelier than your picture not again has fashioned
The seal engraver of musky eyebrows such as yours.

In the curl of his tress, how, heart, can you be so sad
That the morning breeze said your life was in turmoil?

The scent of the rose has arisen. Enter by the door of
    reconciliation.
The augury of our fresh Spring is the auspicious cheek that is
    yours.

So that the heavens might become our bond slaves,
Where is there a saucy look from your crescent-moon-like
    eyebrows?

So that I might return to the presence of luck offering felicitation,
Where the glad news of the coming of the festival of union
    with you?

This black spot that has become the pivot of light,
In vision's garden-plot is a reflection of your mole.

In the Master's presence which hardship should I plead:
The nature of my neediness, or your being offended?

The heads of the crowd, Háfiz, are numerous in this lasso.
Do not indulge distorted ambition: it is not within your reach.

POEM CCCCI

O you the dust of whose path is the Chinese musk pod's blood
    money,
The sun, nursling of the tuft of your cap's shade,

The narcissus takes ogling beyond limit. Stride boldly out
O soul, sacrifice to your dark eye's gleam.

Drink my blood: with beauty such as this no angel
Could find it in his heart to record any sin on your part.

You are the cause of the sleep and repose of the people of the
    world.
Consequently the brink of my eye and my heart have become
    your resting place.

Every night I hold my brief with each and every star,
Because of longing for the glitter of your moon-like cheek.

All comradely friends have become separated from each other.
We remain, and your felicity-harbouring door-step.

Háfiz, entertain no hope of regard: in the final reckoning
The smoke from your sighs will set the harvest of sorrow on fire.

POEM CCCCII

O you whose height the cloak of sovereignty fits,
From the jewel[1] of whose majesty the regal crown has its sparkle,

Every moment the sun of victory has its ascendance,
From your Khosrovian diadem, your moon-face.

The sun in heaven might be the sun and the eye of the world,
But its light-giving eye is dust beneath your foot.

Everywhere becomes the bridal chamber of the bird of good
    fortune
Where the sphere-piercing Humá[2] of your canopy casts its shade.

In the canons of the Law and demonstrations of philosophy, with
    their thousand variations,
Not a single point has your sage mind ever missed.

The Water of Life drips from the eloquent beak of
Your sweet-tongued parrot, that is to say, your sugar-cracking reed.

What Alexander sought but destiny withheld from him[3]
Was a draught of your life-bestowing cup's pure liquid.

In Your Majesty's sanctuary there is no need to express need:
To your brilliant understanding no one's secret stays hidden.

Of enslavement in your presence Háfiz boasts
In hope of your life-sparing, world-pardoning forgiveness.

---

1. "jewel", but the word so translated, *gawhar*, can also mean "stock", so that a
   pun is implied whereby the line could be read as reference to a ruler's noble
   origin, the gem that gives sparkle to the crown; the allusion might once again
   be to the maternal ancestry of Sháh Shujá'.
2. See Poem C, note 1.
3. Alexander asked Khizr (see Poem XL, note 1) to lead him to the spring of the
   Water of Life, but to drink of it was not vouchsafed him (see Koran XVIII, 59–81,
   and 82–97).

487

POEM CCCCIII

The twist of your musk-diffusing curl makes the violet writhe.
Your heart-expanding laughter rips the rose bud open.

O my rose of the grateful air do not sear your very own nightingale
That in pure sincerity nightly the whole night through pleads
    for you.

I who was surfeited by the utterance of angels,
For your sake suffer the gossiping of a world.

Love of your face my natural disposition, my heaven the dust of
    your door,
Love of you my destiny, my comfort your contentment,

The beggar's patched gown has treasure up its sleeve—
Whoever has been your beggar soon attains to sovereignty.

The royal gallery that is my reflecting eye, is the resting-place for
    your image:
It is a place of prayer. O my Sháh may your abode never lack you.

From my head the tumult of the wine of your love goes that
    moment
This desire-drowned head becomes the dust at your palace gate.

Your cheek, especially in beauty's Spring, is a delightful meadow;
Háfiz of the sweet utterance has become your harmonious bird
    of song.

See the power of love when in its pride and glory,
Your beggar disdains the crown of a Sultan.

Although the robe of austerity and the wine-bowl do not go
    together,
I contrive all this imagery for the sake of your amusement.

POEM CCCCIV

Because of the bow of that eyebrow I have a blood splashing eye;
On account of this eye and that eyebrow, the world will be full of
　　trauma.

I am the slave of the eye of that Turk whose face, in the sleep of
　　intoxication,
Is a many-coloured parterre of roses; whose eyebrow is a musky
　　canopy.

With this yearning my body has become a crescent moon — with
　　his musky bow-shaped cipher,[1]
Who might be the moon, to show in heaven's vault an eyebrow?

Rivals fail to notice when every moment from that eye and forehead
A thousand sorts of message that eyebrow brokers for us.

To the soul of the secluded in retreat, his brow is a marvellous
　　flower-bed,
On the border of whose jasmine plot the eyebrow is proudly
　　promenading.

With beauty such as this, of Houri and Peri nobody again will say,
"This one has an eye such as that, and that, an eye such as this."

You the heathen hearted close not the veil of your tresses, but I
　　am afraid
That the niche of that heart-snatching eyebrow might become
　　the focus of my praying.

Although Háfiz was a clever bird in practising suitorship,
Yet still that eyebrow's bow with the arrow of a glance brought
　　him down.

---

1. The allusion is to royal and official ciphers inscribed at the top of the margin of
documents to give them validity. These ciphers were splendid achievements of
calligraphic art, the twirls and lines of the letters being twisted into the shape
of a bow. Reference might be made to Poem xi, note i; Háfiz might be referring
to Hájji Qavámu'd-Dín Hasan, the "Keeper of the Seal".

POEM CCCCV

The line of down round the cheek of the friend, by which the
    moon has been eclipsed,
Is a pretty ring, but there is no way out of it.

The eyebrow of the friend is the prayer-niche of the nook of
    felicity.
Rub the cheek there and ask your need from him.

Draught-drinker of the court of Jamshíd, keep your heart pure,
For the world-seeing cup[1] is a mirror of which, beware![2]

The Súfí took me out of the Way of love to the temple of wine.
See this smoke by which my record has been blackened.

Tell the demon of sorrow, "Do your worst":
I have found my refuge from him with vintners.

Hold, wine-boy, the lamp of wine in the path of the sun.
Say, "Light the torch of morning-time from it."

On the daily register of our deeds sprinkle water;
Maybe the records of sin can be expunged from it.

Háfiz, who has put right the harmony of the assembly of lovers,
May the courts of the banqueting house never be without him!

This fantasy in which the town beggar indulges,
Might there be a day when the Pádsháh remembers him.

---

1.   i.e. the cup of Jamshíd.
2.   From the magic cup no impurity is hidden.

POEM CCCCVI

The rosebud of delight is blossoming. Where the rose-cheeked
    wine-server?
The breeze of spring is blowing. Where the relish of wine?

Each new rose bloom recalls a rose-cheek, but
Where the ear, to hear what is said? The eye for contemplation,
    where?

The assembly of the feast of pleasure lacks the aroma of desire
    attained.
Where, O sweet breath of the moment of dawn, the musk pod of
    the friend's tress?

For me unbearable is a rose's boasting of beauty—
I am plunged in longing's agony. For God's sake, where the
    longed for idol?

Arise! At daybreak the candle has boasted of your cheek:
The tongue of a foe has gone too far. Where a flashing dagger?[1]

He said, "Is it that you want a kiss from my ruby lip?"
I have died of this desire, but where the power and the option?

Háfiz might in speech be the keeper of the treasure of wisdom,
But where the chanter of the grief of mean-spirited destiny?

---

1.   i.e. candle snuffer.

Messenger of the truthful give news of our friend.
Tell the warbling nightingale how the rose is.

For this poor fellow tell the tale of that Lord of Hosts:
To this beggar repeat the story of the Pádsháh.

Do not be worried. We are the intimates of familiarity's private
    chamber.
Let the known comrade receive the word of the friend.

When those twin musk-laden tress-tips got enmeshed together,
What had they in mind for us? For God's sake, tell.

Tell everyone who said that the dust of his path was not collyrium,
"Declare this matter as clearly resolved, as our eyes show."

Be quick. The report of holders of spiritual insight is about to be
    revealed.
Go, ask a riddle. Then come and recite a version.

Last night with my weeping, the bird of the meadow was sobbing.
Are you, O breeze, uninformed of what happened in the end?
    Please tell.

If you should again pass by that door of good fortune,
When you've made your obeisance and presented a prayer, say;

"In the path of love there is no difference between rich and poor.
O Pádsháh of beauty, spare a word for the mendicant."

Tell the man who is forbidding us the tavern
To repeat in my Elder's presence this injunction!

That wine which in the jug ravished the Súfí's heart with its
    coquetry,
When in the cup will it be flashing an amorous glance? Say, O
    wine-boy.

If, Háfiz, access to his gathering is granted you,
Drink wine and, for Goodness sake, drop hypocrisy.

POEM CCCCVIII

Delicious the amber-breathing breeze, incense of the heart's desire,
That out of hoping for you at the breaking of morning arose.

O bird of auspicious aspect,[1] be the guide on the Way,
Because in yearning for the dust of that doorway my eye has
    turned to water.

In memory of my emaciated existence, drowned in heart's blood,
Look you at the gloaming's horizon and see the new crescent of
    the moon.

It is I, breathing in your absence. Ah, the shame.
Will you perhaps forgive? But if you do not, no sin has forgiving.

In the Way of love, the dawn from your friends learned
How longing ripped open the black hair shirt.

The day I depart the world, out of love for your face
Instead of grass from my tomb the red rose will bloom.

Do not too early lay your tender heart open to weariness of me:
Your Háfiz has only just this moment said "In God's name."[2]

---

1. An oblique allusion to the *Mantiqu't-Tair* of 'Attár, the bird being the hoopoe,
chosen as the guide of the birds in their spiritual quest as described in 'Attár's
allegory. The hoopoe's "aspect" is distinguished by a crest of feathers, the
crown awarded it by Solomon for having been his messenger to the Queen of
Sheba.
2. In other words, has only just started complaints against his beloved. *Bismillah*,
"In God's name" is the opening phrase of the Koran; in a *jeu de mots* Háfiz
might have been alluding to his own profession as a reciter of the Koran.

POEM CCCCIX

From the ruby[1] the heart wants, my pleasure is never ending.
Praise to God, my quest is gratified.

Headstrong fortune, hold him tight to the breast.
Now take the golden chalice, now the ruby of the heart's desire.

Pagan Elders and aberrant Shaikhs
Have made a legend of us for licentiousness.

We have repented of the ascetic's profession,
And may there be God's forgiveness for the carrying-on of the
     devotee.

Beloved, how might I describe separation to you?
And I and a hundred tears, a soul and a hundred sighs.

May no unbeliever experience the sorrow
The cypress has experienced on account of your stature, the
     moon, because of your face.

Passion for your lip has made Háfiz forget
The evening lesson, the morning litany.

---

1. i.e. lip.

POEM CCCCX

If sword blades swish in the moon-faced's street,
Our neck is ready. It is God's decree.

I too am informed of the requirements of piety,
But for luck gone astray, what is the remedy?

Me a debauchee, and a lover, and then, repentance?
God forbid! God forbid!

We are not much given to recognizing Shaikh and Preacher.
Either give a bowl of wine or cut the cackle.

Patience is bitter. Life is fleeting.
Would that I could know how long it'll be before our coming
    together.

Your sun-face has cast no reflection on us.
Alas the face of the mirror! Alas for your heart![1]

Why, Háfiz, if you desire union do you complain?
For you there must be the drinking of blood, in and out of season.

---

1.   The reply to the charge that the sun-face has cast no reflection on us is, in
    effect, that the mirror of the heart is not clean enough to receive the divine
    reflection.

POEM CCCCXI

Better than everlasting life, union with him.
O Lord, give me that, for it is best.

He struck me with a sword, but I told nobody:
The secret of the friend is best kept from the enemy.

One night he was saying, "Nobody in the world has set eyes
On better than the pearl of my ear."

O heart, be forever the beggar in his street,
For the reason that everlasting felicity is best.

Do not, ascetic, give me the invitation to Eternal Paradise:
This dimpled apple of the chin is better than that orchard.

Branded a slave, to die at this door,
By his soul I swear is better than the kingdom of the world.

The dust of the rose which became the despised of our cypress
Is better than the blood of the crimson Judas tree.

For God's sake ask my physician
When this disability will get better.

Do not, young man, spurn the counsel of the aged:
The Elder's judgement is better.

The utterance, in the mouth of the friend, a jewel,
But the utterance of Háfiz is better than it.

POEM CCCCXII

You have suddenly cast aside the veil. What is it you're after?
Drunkenly you have rushed out of the house. What is it you're
    after?

Your tress surrendered to the breeze, your ear at a rival's command,
So you have accommodated all and sundry. What is it you're after?

You have become king of the fair but the looked-to of beggars.
You have misprized the worth of this rank. What is it you're after?

Was it not my hand into which at first you put your tress?
But again you have thrown me over. What is it you're after?

It was your words that gave a hint of your mouth, your girdle, the
    secret of your waist.[1]
Yet you unsheathed the sword against me.[2] What is it you're after?

Everyone scanning the number on the dice of love for you,
You ended up cheating everyone. What is it you're after?

When, Háfiz, into your straitened heart the beloved descended,
You failed to empty the abode of all else. What were you after!

---

1.   Alluded to is, of course, the smallness of the mouth and the slenderness of the
     waist.
2.   The poet has not divulged the beloved's mouth and waist—words and the gir-
     dle did that—so why should he be penalised?

POEM CCCCXIII

The doorway of the Magian's house[1] has been swept and
    watered.
The Elder was ensconced and inviting young and old.

To wait on him all the tipplers girded themselves,
But the crown of his cap had thrown a canopy over the clouds.

Bowl and goblet's lustre drowned the light of the moon.
The cheeks of the Magian's children robbed the sun.

For all her thousand graces the bride of luck in that bridal
    chamber
Put fresh curls in her locks and on rose petals dabbed rose water.

With the noisy jostling and rowing of pert handsome boys,
Sugar lumps are breaking, jasmine petals falling, rebecks jangling.

I made my salaam and with a smiling face he said,
"O befuddled with drink, bankrupt, wine-besotted,

Who what you have done, through weakness of will and
    judgement, would do?
You deserted the house of treasure. You pitched your tent
    among ruins.

I fear union with wakeful fortune[2] may not be granted you,
Because lying in luck's embrace you fell sleep."

The Firmament is Sháh Nusrat al-Dín's[3] groom of state—
Come, look, an angel has held the stirrup for him.

To enhance its dignity, wisdom, inspirer of the invisible,
Has thrown a hundred kisses from the height of the Throne to
    his threshold.

Come, Háfiz, to the wine-temple for me to present to you
The thousand ranks of those whose prayers have struck home.

1. An allusion to the tavern.
2. References to luck being either wakeful or sleeping are common in Háfiz and of a convention which extends very far back in Persian literature and is based on the ancient personifying of fortune as, rather like his Guardian Angel, an individual's companion, who, when awake, ensures his good luck, but when asleep, exposes him to adversity. In this verse Háfiz personifies fortune—in whose embrace it was possible to lie—and reverses the idea of sleeping fortune to make the object of fortune's concern asleep instead.
3. See Poem ccxcviii, note 1 (also ccvi, note 1).

Still drowsy with sleep I went last night to the tavern door;
The gown has been soiled, the prayer-rug stained with wine.

The magian child of the vintner came chiding.
He said, "Wake up you drowsing wanderer.

Wash and launder yourself clean. Then boldly stride into the inn,
When this temple will not be polluted by you.

How long, desiring the lips of sweet lads, will you
Stain the jewel of the spirit with liquid ruby?

Pass in chastity the stage of old age and do not
Make the robe of honour of the elderly tainted like the gaudy
    robe of youth.

Those who know the path of love have in this deep sea
Drowned and yet not been sullied with water.

Be clean and pure and come out of the pit of nature,
Because no cleanliness does dust-infected water give."

I said, "O soul and O world, the rose's record book is not
    blackened
If in the height of spring it has got stained with pure wine."

He replied, "Do not, Háfiz, foist riddles and conceits on your
    friends."
Ah the pity of this charm, besmeared by all sorts of blame!

POEM CCCCXV

Disdainfully retracting his skirt so as not to sully it, he was passing
  by in gold-sequined linen.
A hundred of the moon-faced tore at brocaded collars in envy
  of him.

From the heat of wine, the margins of his cheek exuded sweat,
Like night dew dropping on the petal of a rose.

His soul-enlarging ruby, born of the water of grace;
His blithely striding box-tree form daintily nurtured;

His utterance eloquently sweet, stature loftily lithe,
Face courteously heart-alluring, almond-shaped eye attractive,

See his heart-enticing ruby, heart-thrilling laughter,
And see him delicately treading and that unhurried pace.

This black-eyed gazelle has escaped our net.
How, friends, our heart so shunned, can we cope?

Take care so far as you can not to hurt men of insight:
The world, O chosen comrade, knows no constancy!

How long from those heart-seducing eyes must I suffer your
  displeasure?
One day deign one inviting glance, O light of both our eyes!

If your noble heart is offended because of Háfiz,
Come back, for we have repented of what has been said, and
  heard.

I wrote a letter to the friend straight out of the burning of my
    heart.
I said, "In separation from you I have known an endless
    Doomsday."

Of lacking the beloved my eyes in a hundred ways bear witness;
Its tears not the only ones.

No success was mine however much I tried;
Whosoever has tried the tried rues the day.

I asked of a doctor the circumstances with the friend.
He said, "Torment in distance. Peace in proximity."

"If I haunt your street," I said, "blame accrues."
"By God, who has known love without it?"

Now Háfiz has become a suitor, for the sake of the sweet soul, a
    bumper,
And may its relish be a bowl of munificence.

POEM CCCCXVII

For the lamp of your face the candle has become the moth.
Because of your mole, my own condition is of no concern to me.

Sense, once keeping the love-crazed in control,
Because of the scent of your locks has itself gone mad.

The candle yielded its life to the breeze at the glad message
The moment the royal rescript reached it from the candle of
    your face.

If at the fragrance of your tress life goes by the wind, what does
    it matter?
For the beloved, precious souls by the thousand are the ransom.

On the fire of his cheek, instead of wild rue
Who than his dark mole has seen a better grain?[1]

Stricken with jealousy last night I collapsed,
When I saw my darling in the embrace of a stranger.

What schemes we set on foot, but to no profit.
With him our cunning wiles turned into silly pranks.

For the sake of the roundness of the lip of the friend, the
    covenant is
That my tongue shall tell no tale but that of measures of wine.

Recite no dicta of College and the Dervish Hospice, because
Háfiz's head has once more become filled with lust for wine.

---

1.   An allusion to the practice of scattering rue seeds on fire to ward off evil or as
    a sign of welcome, etc.

POEM CCCCXVIII

At dawn, hung-over after the night, when
I seized wine to harp and bells,

Of wine I prepared scrippage for reason
Sent packing out of existence's town.

The darling of the wine-seller threw me a look
That immunised me from the tricks of Time:

From the bow-eyed wine-boy I heard,
"O butt of the arrow of scorn,

Like its cummerbund, from that waist you will have no advantage
If yourself you see in the middle.

Go. Set this snare for some other bird:
The 'Anqa has its nest far above."

Intimate friend, minstrel, wine-server, all in one is he;
Imagining water and clay is to miss the point.

Grant the ship of wine so that we may safely come over
This ocean of the unseen shore.

Our existence, Háfiz, is a riddle,
Probing which is deception and falsity.

POEM CCCCXIX

You who have come with long tress-chains,
May yours be the chance to have become the cherisher of the
    crazed.

Do not show a moment's disdain—reverse your habit:
You have come to ask after lords of indigence.

In your height I revel, whether in truce or war;
Whichever, playing the flirt has become you.

In ruby lips you have mingled fire and water—
May the Evil Eye be far now you have become so nice a conjurer.

Blessings on your tender heart because, in requital,
You have come with humble craving to those you have slain.

What does my asceticism weigh with you who, to plunder my
    heart,
Drunk and raving have stormed the sanctuary of the Secret?

He said, "Once more your gown is wine-stained, Háfiz.
Have you returned from the rite of that sect?"

POEM CCCCXX

Do not be separated from me, because you are the light of my eye.
The beloved of the soul and comforter of the dejected heart
   are you.

Lovers will not let go of the hem of your garment:
Their garb of restraint has been shredded by you.

Because of the eye of your luck may no harm befall you
On account of your having attained in stealing hearts the utmost
   perfection.

O Mufti of the Age, you forbid me love of him.
Since you have not beheld him, I hold you forgiven.

That reproach, O Háfiz, the friend gave you—
Is it that you have overstepped yourself?

POEM CCCCXXI

Come wine-server. The tulip's cup has been filled with wine.
How much more this sanctimonious lisping? Till when, pointless
    ravings?

Pass on from pride and disdain — Time has witnessed
The folding up of Caesar's mantle, and Kay's cap knocked off.

Come to your senses because, look, the bird of the meadow has
    got drunk.
Wake up because, watch out, the sleep of oblivion is on the march.

With poised grace you, the fresh branch of Spring, wave from
    side to side.
May the onslaught of the wind of winter not reach you.

There is no relying on the pity of the sphere and its playing fast
    and loose;
Alas for those who from its guile have felt safe.

Tomorrow the wine of the Sacred Pond[1] and the Houri are ours,
But today there is the moon-faced wine-boy and the wine-bowl
    too.

The morning breeze fetches memories of the days of youth.
An opiate for the soul, that takes sorrow away, grant, O child!

Do not regard the pomp and the sultanship of the rose, because
The carpet-spreading breeze scatters all its petals under foot.

In memory of Hátim Tay[2] present the two-pint bumper,
So that we may role up the black record of misers.

From the wine that gave beauty and charm to the Judas tree
Sweetness of disposition drips in the sweat from his cheek.

Take the seat of the noble into the garden because, like slaves in
    attendance,
The cypress is standing, and the reed ready to serve.

Háfiz, of your eloquent deceit's magic the tale has reached
As far as the borders of Egypt and China, the frontiers of
    Byzantium and the district of Rayy.[3]

---

1. "Sacred Pond" *kawthar* the pool in Paradise. See Poem LXVI, note 2.
2. Hátim Tay, the Arab chieftain, legendary for his splendid hospitality which did
    not stop at the slaying of a favourite mare, to provide a meal for guests who had
    come from afar to purchase that celebrated mare. Hátim al-Tá'í was known as a
    poet, but the *Díván* under his name is of dubious authenticity. The generosity of
    his gestures made him the type in literary reference, of the knightly Arab. Thus
    he inspired romantic tales and allusions, especially in Persian and Turkish liter-
    ature. An historical personage, he lived in the second half of the 6th century AD.
3. The ancient Rhazes, a city in central Iran.

POEM CCCCXXII

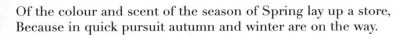

How might I cure you when, to the notes of the nightingale and
    the dove
You do not drink wine? The ultimate remedy is burning.

Of the colour and scent of the season of Spring lay up a store,
Because in quick pursuit autumn and winter are on the way.

When the rose has thrown aside the veil and the bird struck up
    its hoo, hoo,[1]
Do not lay aside the cup. What are you up to?

Being a hoarder of an heir's inheritance is blasphemy
According to the word of minstrel and wine-boy, and the decree
    of drum and fife.

When the Water of Life is yours, do not die thirsty:
"Die you not. By water everything lives that is."[2]

On the entrance gate of the Garden of the Mansion it is written,
"All who have bought worldly glamour, woe be upon them."

There is no generosity left; I am ending my speech. Where's the
    wine?
For the joy of the spirit give it, and for the soul of Hátim Tay.[3]

No miser knows the fragrance of God. Come Háfiz,
Take the cup and practise generosity. I'll go surety for you.

---

1. *hoo, hoo*, here represents a bird's cooing or sobbing, but, as *hú* is the spelling
    which Persian gives, the poet is afforded a pun: *hú* is the word for "he" and con-
    stantly uttered among Súfí's as the pious ejaculation, "He!", that is, God.
2. A saying in Arabic which used often to be found on wells and public drinking
    places.
3. See preceding poem, note 2.

POEM CCCCXXIII

I am kissing his lip and consuming wine:
I have discovered the water of life.

To no one can I tell his secret,
Nor can I bear to see anyone with him.

The cup is kissing his lip, but drinking blood.
The rose is looking at his cheek and sweating with shame.

Pass the bowl of wine and spare Jamshíd not a thought—
Who knows when Jamshíd was, and when Kay?

O moon minstrel, strike up a tune on the harp.
Finger its chords that I might cry out because of it.

Hold your tongue a moment, Háfiz:
Listen to the tale of the tongueless from the reed.[1]

---

1. Háfiz here echoes the opening verses of the *Mathnawí* of Rumi:

> Listen to the reed, how it is telling the tale,
> It is complaining of separation—
> "Ever since I was cut out of the reed-bed,
> Men and women have lamented because of my notes.
> I want a heart struck asunder by the grief of absence,
> That I might tell what the pain of desire is like."

(For the text see Nicholson's edition of the *Mathnawí*, Vol. 1, p. 3.)

POEM CCCCXXIV

I am drunk on the cup of love. Boy, give some wine.
Fill the cup. Without wine the party has no glitter.

The description of his moon-like face does not fit the mode;
Tune the right harmony, minstrel. Pass some wine, wine-boy.

My figure has become the door-knocker so that henceforth
Your guardian cannot again drive us from this door to some other.

In expectation of your face, it is a case of us and hope for a
    certain day.
In the dalliance of union with you, a case of us and a dream's
    wild fancy.

I'm drunk on those two eyes. Where is there a cup?
I am ill because of those two rubies. Am I, then, unworthy of an
    answer?

Why, Háfiz, do you give your heart over to imagining beauties?
When are the thirsty quenched by the gleam of a mirage?

O you who have thrown a veil of musky down over the moon,
You have performed a kindness—you have cast a shade over the
    sun.

What then will the radiance and colour of your cheeks do to
    us?
At present you're merely sketching the colourless outline on
    water.

Bravo! You have whacked away the ball of beauty from the
    beauties of Khallukh.[1]
Be after the cup of Kaikhosrau[2] since Afrásíyáb you have
    overthrown.

Everyone in some fashion has risked love for the candle of your
    cheek;
Moths from among them you have plunged into fluttering agony.

I am rotten with drunkenness, but do not spurn my adoration:
In the hope of requital it was you who plunged me into this
    employment.

You have secreted the treasure of your love into our shattered
    heart;[3]
Over this desolate corner you have cast the auspicious shade of
    luck.

Beware of the lustre of that cheek, by which you have made lions
Thirsty lipped, and have wiped out heroes.[4]

The wakeful you have robbed of sleep and then, with dream
    images,
Thrown suspicion on the army of sleep's night prowlers.

In the bridal chamber for one single glimpse you threw off the
    veiling of the cheek,
And out of shame threw Houri and Peri behind the veil.

From the world-revealing cup drink wine, because, on Jamshíd's throne,
From the cheek of the darling of desire you have cast aside the veil.

Through the intoxicated narcissus's beguilement and the wine-worshipping ruby
You have plunged Háfiz the secluded recluse into wine,

And in order to make the heart a prey, you have thrown round my neck a tress's chain,
Like the noose of Khusrau, the Lord of necks enslaved,

Ruler of the splendour of Darius, O you who the crown of the sun
Have cast down from the height of glory to the dust of the doorstep,

Nusrat al-Dín Sháh Yahyá,[5] you who the foe of the kingdom
With the blow of the fire-like sword have rendered naught.

---

1. Khallukh: a region in Central Asia famed for the beauty of its "amiable" and "sociable" inhabitants, in what *Hudúd al-'Álam* "Regions of the World", translated and explained by V. Minorsky (Oxford and London, 1937) p. 97, a Persian Geography of 982 AD, describes as "the most pleasant of the Turkish lands".
2. Kaikhosrau, one of Iran's ancient legendary rulers, who eventually conquered Afrásíyáb, who was slain. Háfiz frequently shares with his audience the Iranian folk memory expressed in the *Sháhnáma* of Firdawsí.
3. Apparently an allusion to the *Mirsád al-'Ibád*, op. cit. (Poem III, note 4), Text, p. 74, Translation, p. 103, "and the jewel was the jewel of love". God had declared that only "Our Majestic Presence or the heart of Adam" would be a fit treasury for this jewel. There is also a description (Text, p. 68 sqq., Translation 96 sqq.) of how God secreted His treasure in the heart of Adam, and see Translation, p. 115 for the "shattering" of that heart.
4. Literally, "thrown on the water", a metaphor for elimination. It occurs again in the last hemistich of the final verse, where it is translated "rendered naught".
5. See Poem CCXCVIII, note 1.

Don't tell the contentious the mysteries of love and intoxication,
So that unenlightened he may die in the pain of self-worship.

Despite weakness and disability, be as hale as the morning
    breeze:
On this Path infirmity is healthier than fitness.

So long as you observe learning and reason you'll abide without
    insight.
Let me tell you something: stop seeing yourself and you'll be
    saved.

On the beloved's threshold don't worry about the heavens
Lest you fall from the zenith of glory to the dust of lowliness.

Become a lover, otherwise the business of the world will be over,
The intended plan of being's workshop undeciphered.

In the teaching of the Way immaturity[1] signals unbelief.
Oh yes, the road to felicity is agility and nimbleness.

How can there be cowering in safety's corner
Once your narcissus eye intimates the riddles of intoxication to us?

I had seen the troubles which arose that day
When out of scorn you for a time did not consort with us.

Although the thorn shortens life, the rose craves pardon for it;
With drunkenness's savour wine's bitterness is easy to digest.

Súfí, measure out the cup. Háfiz, take heed of the flagon.
O you of the meanness of austerity, till when your greed?

1. Cf. Mauláná Jalálu'd-Dín Rúmí, *The Mathnawí*, op. cit., lines. 3055–3064:

> That one came. He knocked at the door of a friend.
> His friend said to him, "Who are you, O trusty one?"
> He answered, "I". He said to him, "Go: this is not the time:
> At such a feast there is no place for the uncooked."
> The uncooked other than the fire of exile and separation.
> Who will cook? Who rescue from hypocrisy?
> That poor wretch went and for a year in voyaging.
> In absence from the friend was scorched by sparks of fire.
> That burnt one got cooked. Then he came back.
> Again he walked round the comrade's house.
> He rapped the knocker on the door with great fear and deference.
> Lest a disrespectful word should escape his lips.
> His friend called out, "Who's that at the door?"
> He repied, "At the door it is you too, O snatcher of hearts."
> The friend answered, "Now since you are me, O me come in.
> In this mansion there is not room for two of us."

Cf. Rúmí as quoted on p. 330 above, note 1. The word here translated "immaturity" is, literally, "rawness", "being uncooked", *Khámí*.

POEM CCCCXXVII

Had that perfumed line of down written us a letter,
The wheeling vault would not have crumpled up our existence.

Although separation carries the fruit of union,
Would that the world's Landlord had not sown this seed!

Forgiveness is the coin of him who in the here and now
Has friendship like a Houri's and a palace like a Paradise.

Not I alone have turned the heart's Ka'ba into an idol temple;[1]
At every single step there is a Christian cell and a fire-temple!

In the tavern of love no ease can be enjoyed;
Since the pillow is not of gold, let us make do with a brick.

Do not for the Garden of Eram and the pomp of Shaddád[2] give
   up
One bowl of wine, one luscious lip, the edge of a single meadow.

O knowing heart, how long must there be the anguish of a base
   world?
It is a pity that from beauty it should become the lover of ugliness.

It is the pollution of the world that is the stain on the Dervish
   gown.
Where is a follower of the Path, a man of the heart,
   of pure disposition?

Why has Háfiz let go the tip of your tress?
Such is fate. What could he have done not to let it go?[3]

---

1. A provocatively blasphemous statement, making the sacred focus of Muslim prayer, the Ka'ba, into an idol temple; one of the Prophet of Islam's first and most famous acts on conquering Mecca was the destruction of the idols housed in its Ka'ba, which until the success of his mission had been the repository of idols.
2. The Garden of Eram, and Shaddád: see Poem LXVI, note 1.
3. The human being is at the mercy of fate, yet the purpose of his creation is to escape from it to God.

POEM CCCCXXVIII

O you of whose street a story of Paradise is the tale,
Of whose face the beauty of a Houri is the reading,

Beside your ruby lip the breaths of Jesus a trifle,
And for your mouth's sweetness, the Water of Life a metaphor,

It is a case of every fragment of my heart and a saga of sorrow,
Each moiety of your qualities and a miracle of compassion.

How, were you not endowing the rose with your scent,
Would it have been the censer of the assembly of the spiritual?

In yearning for the dust of the door of the friend we have burned.
O breeze of the morning, remember, for you have afforded no
    support.

O heart, with learning's trivia life slipped from your grasp;
Capital a hundredfold you had, yet made no profit.

The smell of my kebabed heart has spread over far horizons.
May the fire within likewise be distance-spanning;

If in the blaze the vision of his cheek should lend a hand,
Come wine-server, because of the Inferno there would be no
    complaint.

You know what from this suffering and sorrow Háfiz is after:
An inviting look from you, and from the Chosroes a favour.

POEM CCCCXXIX

Salmá[1] with her twin forelocks took my heart captive
And daily my soul is crying out to me.

On heart-lost me have mercy for God's sake
And in spite of my enemies unite with me.

You who pour scorn on loving Salmá
Ought for a start to have looked upon that fair face.

Like mine your heart should entirely be
Drowned in love in the ocean of lovingness.

There is no other way, consume the grief of this heart you must,
Otherwise you will experience what for you has no joy.

O idol, in the despair of passion for you
We have reposed our trust in the lord of slaves.

If you have observed a single act of discourtesy,
By way of asking pardon we will make amends.

In the curl of your tress Háfiz's heart has fallen
Into jet-black darkness, but God is the Guide.

---

1. Salmá: see Poem CLXXXV, note 1. For a poem which is a *tour de force* as a blend of
   hemistiches in Arabic, Persian and the dialect of Shíráz it is perhaps appropriate
   that Háfiz should have chosen the name of a legendary beloved among the Arabs
   as the name of the beloved he is addressing. The 'twin forelocks' brings to mind
   the Prophet Muhammad.

POEM CCCCXXX

In a dream last night I saw that a moon had risen,
From the reflection of whose face the night of separation had
    come to an end.

The interpretation? The voyaging friend is coming back.
Would that he entered my door as soon as can be!

Of sweet remembrance, my wine-boy of blessèd omen
Who with goblet and bowl was continually entering the door!

It were happy if in sleep he saw his own country,
So that the recollection of its society might show him the way
    to us.

If Eternity without Beginning's boon came to hand through
    force and gold,
The Water of Khizr would have been the lot of Alexander.[1]

May the days be remembered when, from the roof and by the door,
Every moment a message and letter from the heart ravisher
    would come.

When would your keeper have found so much scope for tyranny
If one night a single victim had got as far as the ruler's gate?

What do those unversed in the Path know of love's delight?
Seek one of an oceanic heart, bold in perfection.

He who pointed you in the direction of stony-heartedness,
Would that his foot struck against a boulder!

If someone else had written in the style of Háfiz,
By the genius of the art-cherishing Sháh he would have been
    accepted.

---

1. See Poems XL, note 1 and CCXL, note 1.

POEM CCCCXXXI

At dawn I was repeating the tale of yearning.
Word came, "Trust in lordly favours.

Morning prayer and sighs in the night are the key to the treasury
    of the sought;
Go by this way and in this manner so that you might join the
    Keeper of Hearts."

The pen lacks the tongue to divulge the mystery of love,
And beyond the limits of narration is the description of the
    desiring.

Bravo, O Egypt's Joseph, kept busy by the cares of a ruler.
Ask of the father where in the end a son's love went.

The wanton old world has no pity in its nature.
What do you seek in loving it? Why give it any devotion?

A Humá bird[1] as exulted as you—desiring bones is a pity:
Alas for that shadow that you have spread over the unworthy!

If in this market place there is any profit, it is to the contented
    dervish.
O God make me the beneficiary of dervishism and blessed
    contentment!

Do not surrender the heart to beauties, Háfiz. See all those
    betrayals of trust
Which the Turks of Samarqand visited on the people of
    Khwárazm.

To the poetry of Háfiz of Shíráz they are dancing and pirouetting,
The dark eyes of Kashmír and the Turks of Samarqand.[2]

1. The *Humá* is the fabulous bird whose shadow cast over kings ensures their good fortune. This sacred bird was supposed to eat no flesh or carrion, but only bones. Háfiz suggests that his beloved was too exulted even for this, the bones in this instance being the "unworthy" mentioned in the next line. Cf. Poem C, note 1.

2. With reference to the Khwárazmians and Samarqandi Turks in the preceding verse, and again the latter in this verse, in the facsimile of his notes on the *Díván* of Háfiz, graciously published by his son, Dr Qásim Ghaní explains these references partly on the authority of the historian 'Abdu'r-Razzáq of Samarqand (d. 1482 AD) in his *Matla' al-Sa'dain wa Majma' al-Bahrain*, "The Rising of the Two Stars of Fortune and the Confluence of the Two Seas". Abdu'r-Razzáq indicates that in these verses Háfiz was alluding to Tímúr's conquest of Khwárazm in 781/1379–80 AD. Tímúr (Tamburlane) had his capital at Samarqand, whence his troops sorely pillaged and laid Khwárazm (Khiva) waste.

POEM CCCCXXXII

What would it have mattered if the heart of that friend had
    been kind?
Because if he had been such as that, our state would not have
    been such as this.

If Fate had held me exulted and dear,
The dust of that threshold would have been my seat of honour.

What chance of union? I do not even see him in my dreams.
Since the former were not to be, would to God the latter were!

I might have asked how much the breeze from the friend's curl
    is worth,
If for every hair-tip I had a thousand lives.

O lord, how might the royal rescript for my ease of heart have
    come amiss,
If it bore the seal of immunity from fortune's evil?

Would that like a teardrop he had emerged from behind the veil,
That both my eyes had been under his order's command.

If the circle of love had not been inaccessible,
Head-twirling Háfiz would have been like the point at its centre.

POEM CCCCXXXIII

By his soul, if my life were at my disposal,
It would be the least of his slaves' offerings.

If my heart had not been caught in his tress,
How, in this dreary dustbin, might I have abided?

In every quarter of the horizon, like the sun in the heavens in
    face he is without equal.
Would that, alas, in the heart there were a single particle of
    kindness!

I asked what was the price of the dust on which he trod.
Would precious eternal life suffice?

O that like a shaft of light he might enter my door,
So that my two eyes might be under his doom!

Confessing to enslavement by his stature the cypress might have
    become
Had it, like the noble lily, ten tongues.

When would Háfiz's lament have come into the open,
If he had not been of one voice with the dawn-singing birds?

POEM CCCCXXXIV

If like a cypress you were one moment to stride into a garden of
    roses,
Out of envy of your face every rose would know the pang of a
    thorn.

Because of the apostasy of your tress, it is a case of every coterie,
    a tumult;
Because of the sorcery of your two eyes, every corner and someone
    afflicted.

Like my luck, do not, O beloved's drunken eye, fall asleep,
Because from every direction the sigh of the wakeful is in pursuit.

The scattering of the dust of your path is the coin of my soul,
Although for you the currency of the soul has no rating.

O heart, sing not of the heart-entrappers' tresses —
When you are morbidly minded, how can anything go your way?

My head went, yet at no time did this business reach a conclusion.
My heart shrivelled, yet you had no heart's anguish.

I said to him, "Come into the circle's centre like the compass
    point."
Laughingly he replied, "Aye Háfiz, what compass is this?"

POEM CCCCXXXV

It is a city full of delights, in every direction, an idol.
It is, friends, the invitation to loving, if you'll make an effort.

No youngster does the eye of the world see fresher than this.
No idol lovelier than this falls into anyone's hands.

Who could have seen a body when he is created of spirit?
Let no speck of dust from those created of dust be on his garment.

Why drive a shattered one like me from your presence,
When my utmost expectation is a kiss or a hug?

The wine is unadulterated. Hasten! The moment's right. Seize it.
Who entertains hope of a fresh spring in another year?

In the garden, comrades, like the lily and the rose,
Each is raising a cup to the memory of the face of the beloved.

How can I unravel this knot and show this sore?
A pain, but a sharp one. A trial, but a hard one.

Every thread of Háfiz's hair is in a saucy one's grasp.
To say the least, to be able to settle in this country is difficult!

POEM CCCCXXXVI

Whatever in the world is desired, you possess.
What sorrow do you possess for the state of the weak and helpless?

Of your slave demand heart and soul and take them instantly,
Because command over the noble is your prerogative.

Slenderness of middle leaves you no waist, but I marvel how all
    the time
In the midst of the bout of beauties you are playing the referee.[1]

The page of your face brooks no painting because
You have a line of dark down over ruddiness.

Drink wine, because you are always merry and witty,
Specially now, when you have a head mellow with wine.

Do not more than this punish and abuse our heart.
Do whatever you are capable of: the choice is yours!

If a hundred thousand arrows of violence were at your command,
You would have them in your bow aimed at the life of wounded
    me.

Forever endure the contumely of the guardians and the envy of
    the jealous,
Because, if a kind friend is yours, it is easy.

If one moment union with the friend should chance to be yours,
Go to, because you have whatever is the world's desire.

Háfiz, when in your lap you carry off a rose out of this garden,
Why bother about the shouting and complaining of the gardener?

---

1.   "referee", literally, "holder of the middle": the word-play is on the word, *míyán*,
    "middle".

POEM CCCCXXXVII

Breeze, you bear the fragrance of that musk-scented tress.
Because you have his perfume, stay as a precious memento.

If you treat it well, my heart, in which is the jewel
Of the mysteries of beauty and love, could be surrendered to you.

To those agreeable qualities no exception can be taken,
Save only that extremely quick-tempered guardians are yours.

How, O rose, can the note of the nightingale be grateful to you,
When to nonsense-prating birds you bend the ear of sense?

My head got intoxicated with your draught. Here's to you!
Tell me, from which vat is what you have in the cup?

O stream-adorning cypress, do not brag of a head exalted:
Were you to encounter him, you'd hold your head bowed in shame.

To boast like the sun of kingdoms of excellence
Becomes you, because you have moon-faced serving lads.

You alone can get away with parading a coat of beauty,
Because like the rose you enjoy all the adornment of colour and
    scent.

Do not, Háfiz, search in the recesses of the hermit cell for the
    jewel of love.
If you want to make the quest, step outside.

POEM CCCCXXXVIII

Come, cease plying this vendetta against us,
For the obligation of old association is yours.

Take a little advice, because this pearl is far better
Than that jewel you keep in the treasury.

Come, for God's sake, to the rescue of the bankrupt toper,
If you have any of last night's wine left.

Yet how should you, who hold the mirror to the sun and moon,
Reveal your cheek to the licentious ones?

O Shaikh, speak no ill of the debauched, rather, look out,
You might be making Divine Mercy your foe.

Are you not afraid of the fiery inflamability of my sigh?
You understand? It is you who have a woollen gown![1]

No verse more excellent than yours, Háfiz, have I seen,
By the Koran you have in your breast I swear it.

---

1.   Ready to catch fire from the fiery sighs.

POEM CCCCXXXIX

O you who keep your abode in the street of taverns,
When you have the cup in your hand, you are the Jamshíd of
    your age.

O you who with the tress and the cheek of the friend pass the
    night and the day,
May the chance befall that yours are sweet evenings and sweet
    mornings!

O breeze, those burned on the Path are waiting to see
If, the journey made, you bring word from that friend.

From the laughing brim of the cup I catch the bouquet of the soul.
Take a sniff, Mister, if you have any sense of smell for it.

If by you a stranger seeks a name, what does it matter—
You who today in this city have a name?

A grain of good delight is your green-sprouting mole, but
O dear, what a snare you have baited at the edge of the meadow!

Many a dawn prayer will be for your life's protection—
You who have a vigil-keeping slave like Háfiz.

POEM CCCCXL

You who take as lawful the separation of friends,
Who keep your enthralled far from your breast,

Rescue with a drop of cold water the thirsty in the wilderness now,
For the hope you have in this Way to God.

O darling soul, you ravished my heart and I forgave you, but
Look after it better than you look after me.

We will tolerate other comrades drinking our cup,
If you hold it permissible.

No tilting ground for you, O fly, is the majestic Símurgh's[1]
    precinct.
You will be a nuisance to us and lose your own reputation.

Through you own fault you have been excluded from this door.
Of whom do you complain and why keep calling for help?

Promotion, Háfiz, is sought from kings through service.
No duty performed, of favour what hope have you?

---

1. *Símurgh*: see Poem VII, note 1, and CCLXIX, note 1.

POEM CCCCXLI

It is a while you have kept us on the look out.
Sincere friends you do not keep in the condition of others:

On me not a corner of the eye of your approval has been opened.
Is this the kind of regard you have for men of spiritual insight?

Since the morning breeze has recited the page of your beauty to
    rose and nightingale,
You have all clamouring and tearing their apparel.

Better you cover the forearm since for hennaing,
You keep your hand dipped in the blood of the heart of those
    full of virtue.

O you in the patchwork robe who seek the savour of the Presence,
Some eye you've got for a mystery from those who have no clue!

O eye and lamp, since you are the narcissus in vision's garden,
Why do you bear a grudge against me the heart-stricken?

The jewel of Jamshíd's bowl comes from the mine of another
    world.
You are rummaging for it in potter's clay.

You, O heart, are the very father of experience, so with what
    purpose
Do you hope for love and loyalty from these sons?

Although debauchery and depravity are our sins entirely,
A lover has observed that it is you who force the slave into them.

Do not, Háfiz, pass the day of bliss under punishment;
What is it you are expecting from the transitory world?

POEM CCCCXLII[1]

The heavens gave you good help on the day of trial,
So how will you be rendering thanks and what gratefully bringing?

In the street of love royal pomp has no purchasers.
Consent to slavery and give evidence of servitude.

Him who has fallen—but whose hand God has grasped—
Tell, "Let it be upon you, that you may know the grief of the
    fallen."

Enter, wine-boy, my door with tidings of joy,
To remove from my heart for a moment the sorrow of the world.

On the highway great is the danger of rank and eminence:
Better you breast this steep slope lightly burdened—

Sultan and the worry of an army, anxiety over treasure and crown;
Dervish and a heart unfearful, the quiet retreat of hermits—

May I, if it is allowed, utter one Súfí saying?
"O light of the eye, peace is better than war and empire."

Attainment of what is desired is on account of concentration
    and zeal:
By the Sháh dedication to good. By Divine Grace, victory.

Do not, Háfiz, wash the face clean of the dust of poverty and
    contentment,
Because this dust is better than the operation of alchemy.

---

1. The late learned 'Abdul Rahím Khalkhálí, in his *Háfiz Námeh* (Tehran, 1941) p.
    34, cites two histories written near Háfiz's time for evidence that this thoughtful
    poem, redolent as it is of warning, celebrated the conquest of Shíráz after the
    death of Sháh Shujá' in 1384 AD, by his son Zainu'l-'Ábedín, who for more than
    a month had to fight for his patrimony. His reign lasted only until 1387 AD;
    Háfiz's poem, indeed, is sufficiently full of premonition for it to seem that he
    read troublous times all too accurately.

POEM CCCCXLIII

In order to carry off some bliss demonstrate discipleship:
Man and Peri are uninvited guests to the intoxication of love.

If you are not endowed with vision, do not look for union:
The bowl of Jamshíd in moments of sightlessness yields no
    gain.

Make an effort, my good Sir, and do not lack love's share.
Nobody buys the slave with the defect of lack of virtue.

How long wine drinking in the morning and gratitude for sleep
    at the break of day?
Strive in the craving of midnight for pardon, and in weeping at
    dawn.

Come and with the capital of beauty buy sultanship from us,
But do not in this transaction be negligent, for you might
    know regret.

The prayers of reclusives can avert disaster.
Why not from a corner of the eye spare us a glance?

By your withholding and enfolding I am confused. What remedy
    can I effect?
You are neither before the eye nor absent from sight.

A thousand souls have burned because of this jealousy,
That you are the candle each morning and evening in a different
    assembly.

As by every news I get another door to amazement is opened,
It will be a case hence forward of me and drunkenness, and the
    position of taking no notice.

Come, because, if you examine the world's condition as I have
    known it,
You will drink wine and suffer no sorrow.

Because of the blessedness of Háfiz's devotion there is hope that again
   I might see Laila in conversation on a moonlit night.[1]

Who will take the message from me to His Excellency the Ásaf,[2]
"Learn two hemistiches of mine in Persian verse:

'On the head of beauty let not the diadem of rulership be aslant,
Because you are the adornment of luck, worthy of dominion and a head crowned'"?

By the scent of your tress and your cheek are coming and going
The perfume-dispensing morning breeze and the rose with its display.

---

1. This hemistich—it might be a quotation—is in Arabic.
2. Ásaf: see, e.g., Poems XXIV, note 3, XLIX, note 3, and L, verse 12 and note 3. This line in italics is in Arabic in the original.

POEM CCCCXLIV

You who are all the time vain of yourself,
May be excused if you have no love;

Do not hobnob with the love-crazed,
Because it is for profoundest reason you are famous.

There is none of the intoxication of love in your head.
Go away. You are drunk on the juice of the grape.

For lovers the pallid face and heavy sigh
Are the physick for affliction.

Háfiz, put your name and honour aside.
Since you have a hangover, search for a cup of wine.

POEM CCCCXLV

The airs of a New Year's[1] breeze are coming from the street of the
    friend.
If from them you want help, light the lamp of the heart.

If like the rose you hold a piece of red gold, for God's sake
    spend it on pleasure,
Because passion for hoarding gold plunged Korah[2] into many
    an error.

I am uttering curtained words. Burst rose-like out of your bud,
Because the rule of the Commander of the New Year is five
    days only.

I have wine pure as the soul, yet the Súfí takes exception to it.
O God, let no intelligent man be unlucky a single day!

What is the granting of the Way of satisfaction?
    Abandoning self-gratification.
The cap of sovereignty is what from this renunciation you will
    stitch.

I do not understand what the turtle dove's lament by the edge of
    the stream is for;
Perhaps it too, as I have, has some sorrow every night and day.

Your sweet friend has become separated. Now, candle, abide alone,
Because, whether you put up with it or whether you burn, this is
    the decree of heaven.

Go into the garden, to learn love's complexities from the
    nightingale.
Come into the assembly, to learn from Háfiz the composing of
    lyrics.

---

1.   In Iran this is the vernal equinox and a spring festival of great importance.
2.   The Korah of the Old Testament, Qárún of the Koran. See Poem v, note 3 and
    L, note 2.

POEM CCCCXLVI

Life has gone by in fruitlessness and being led astray,
Give me wine, boy, that you might reach old age.

In this city what sweet souls have known contentment?
Falcons of the Path in the halting-place of a fly!

With heart blood-soaked like the musk pod must be happy
All who have reached world fame through musk-laden speech.

Spread the wing and sing from the Túbá tree.[1]
It would be a pity, a bird like you captive in a cage.

The caravan has moved on, but you, asleep in an ambush on the
  track?
Woe for so much deafness to all this ringing of the bell![2]

Light flashed from Mount Sinai and I perceived it—
Let me bring a blazing brand for you.[3]

So that, like an incense burner, we might for once seize the
  darling's hem,
I have placed my soul into fire, to raise a fragrant exhalation.

How much Háfiz do you out of desire run hither and thither!
May God make the access to you easy, my sought-after.

---

1. A tree in Paradise. See Poem LX, note 1.
2. The bell rung to signal the caravan's dawn departure.
3. This verse is in Arabic and derived from the story of Moses, Koran xx, 8 and 9.

POEM CCCCXLVII

It is the coming of spring. Try to be happy-hearted in it,
For many a rose might blow again, but you will be under the sod.[1]

From behind the curtain the harp is giving you the same
    advice, but
It is when you are right for it that preaching profits you.

Now I am not telling you with whom to sit and what to drink.
If you are smart and bright, you yourself will know.

Every leaf of the book in the meadow tells of a different state.
It would be a pity if you were neglectful of the state of all.

Although the Path from us to the friend its full of terror,
The going is easy provided you know the stages of the Way.

Worldly care can extravagantly filch your life's coin,
If night and day in this tricky business you are involved.

If, O Háfiz, help from high luck is yours,
You will be the prey of that darling of sweet parts.

---

1.   There is a good example here of Háfiz's word-play. For "under the sod" he says
     "in the clay". The Persian word for clay is *gil*. The Persian word for rose is *gul*.
     In the Persian script both these words have the same outline, *g* and *l*, the short
     vowel not being expressed.

POEM CCCCXLVIII

I have tried a thousand times for you to be my friend,
To be the granter of my excited heart's desire,

To become the lamp for my nightly wakeful eye,
The comforter of my hopeful heart.

Since Khusraus of elegant grace indulge their slaves,
You among them be my liege lord.

If of that carnelian mouth—my heart gory through its enticing—
I complain, please be the keeper of my secret.

In the meadow where idols grasp lovers by the hand,
Were this possible for you, you might be my idol!

To me the sun's ray would be meagre prey,
If for once a gazelle like you were to be my quarry.

If you do not pay the three kisses you have made my ration
From your two lips, you will be in debt to me.

For myself I contemplate this desire, that one midnight
Instead of a lap full of tears you should be in my embrace.

Although the Háfiz[1] of the town, I am not worth a bean,
Unless out of your kindness you be my comrade.

---

1. *Háfiz*: it means "protector", "guardian", as well as "one who knows the Koran by heart". It was because he was one of the latter that Háfiz became known as Háfiz. In this verse it can mean "keeper of the town", or "the town's Koran-knower". Cf. Poem CCCXLVII, verse 7.

POEM CCCCXLIX

O heart, that moment when you are drunk on rose-red wine,
You are with all the pomp of Qárún[1] without gold or treasure.

In the halting place where paupers are given the highest seats,
I expect you to be greater in rank than all.

In the peril-beset way to the abode of Laila,
For the first step the condition is that you be Majnún.[2]

Love's central point I have shown you. Beware not to be neglectful.
Otherwise, when you look you will find yourself outside the circle.

The caravan has moved on, you drowsing, left to face empty desert.
How will you proceed? From whom ask the way? What are you to
    do? How will you fare?

You seek the crown of kingship? Show your inward essence,
Whether you are of the stock of Jamshíd and Ferídún.[3]

Drain a bumper of wine and throw a draught above the
    heavens[4]—
How long, how long must your vitals be at the mercy of the times?

Háfiz, make no complaint of poverty because, if this is your verse,
No one of a happy heart would like to see you sad.

---

1.   See Poem ccccxlv, note 2.
2.   Majnún was Laila's legendary lover. Maddened by love for her, his name,
    Majnún, as an epithet means "mad".
3.   Ferídún, the legendary ruler who, helped by the blacksmith Káveh, rid Iran of
    the tyrant Zahák.
4.   The verse means that, when draining a bumper the libation is poured over the
    heavens, not onto the ground: the heavens and their influence are overcome.

POEM CCCCL

This lovely line you draw across the rose-cheek—
You draw the line across rose petals and the rose garden.

My sanctuary-keeping tears in their inward treasure-store
Behind the seven shutters of the eye, you pull out into the
    marketplace.

The sluggishly moving such as the morning breeze, by the
    perfume of a tress
You sweetly drag in chains and fetters into motion.[1]

To the memory of that wine-coloured lip and drunken eye,
    every moment
Are you drawing me from my retreat into the wine-booth.

You have declared, "Your head shall be tied to our game-hanging
    saddle-strap."
Provided you can bear the burden of the load, it will be no
    hardship.

Given your eye and eyebrow, how can I control the heart?
Alas for that bow which against afflicted me you draw!

Come back for me to repulse the Evil Eye from your cheek,
O fresh rose which from this thorn withdraws its skirt.

What more, Háfiz, do you want of the luxuries the sphere has
    to offer?
You have wine's relish and you pull the curls of the sweetheart.

---

1.   i.e. the self-denigrating poet.

POEM CCCCLI[1]

Since Suleimá[2] alighted in 'Iráq,[3]
From her separation I endure what I endure.

Camel-driver of the friend's litter,
My yearning has been drawn towards your caravan's passengers.

Throw sense into the Zindeh River[4] and take to wine,
To the wassail of 'Iráqian youths.

Come wine-boy, and present me with a brimful bumper of wine:
God give you to drink from a blissful bowl!

Recall youthfulness to my memory,
Hearing the harp, with the wine-boy's dancing.

Give the wine left over so that, drunk and merry-hearted,
I may squander on friends what is left over of life.

My heart is turned to blood from not seeing the beloved.
Indeed a horror is the time of separation!

Life's springtime in your sanctuary's meadow—
God shield you, O season of meeting.

Be at one with well-wishers a moment:
Count occasions of harmony a blessing.

Opportunities for being united passed, but we did not notice.
Sing, Háfiz, lyrics of separation.

After you, my tearful eyes—do not scorn them,
For from brooks are deep oceans formed.

---

1. This poem, in common with the next three, is a blend of whole verses, or of hemistiches, in either Arabic or Persian.
2. The affectionate diminutive of Salmá.

3. 'Iráq: central and western Persia—roughly co-terminous with the ancient Media—is what, besides today's Iraq, this geographical term would mean for Háfiz, as it does for many Iranians still.
4. That central and western Iran, rather than the Tigris-Euphrates basin, was what Háfiz had in mind, is shown by this reference to the "Zindeh Rúd", *Záyandeh Rúd* (River), which flows through Persian 'Iráq's notable city of Isfahán.

My tear ducts in flood, I wrote the tale of my longing.
Come because, in grief lacking you, I have become ready to expire.

Much in yearning have I beseeched my two eyes,
"O Salmá's halting-places, where is your Salmá?"

A weird event, an episode strange,
I the slain practising forbearance, my slayer the complainer.

To whom might it occur that he should find fault with the purity
of your garment?
For you are as pure as the dewdrop that drips on the petal of a
rose.

From the dust beneath your foot, the lily and rose's lustre
The Pen of Creation bestowed when It wrote Its inscription in
clay and water.

Ambergris-scattering the morning breeze has become. Get up,
server of wine,
And fetch me the wine with a kick, perfumed and clear.

Get rid of sloth and win the prize, because the proverb has
become current:
"Alertness and alacrity are the provision for followers of the Way."

Without your noble qualities no sign of the world would have
remained. Yes,
It is from your countenance I perceive my life's indications.

What rhetoric can Háfiz bring to bear for describing your beauty,
When, like the Divine Attributes, you are beyond comprehension?

POEM CCCCLIII

O mouth, you are like a casket of pearls.
O Lord, how fitting has the line of the new moon round it become!

Nicely does the imagining of union with you delude me now.
See what an image this imagined form sports itself as.

Heart lost, eye brimming with blood, body broken, soul expired—
In love the causes of astonishment follow one another with no
    let-up.

Give wine for, although I comprise the world's register of sin,
How might one despair of the Everlasting Grace?

Bring a bowl, wine-server, and drag me out of the retreat,
So that I might wander from door to door, a tavern-haunter
    without a care in the world.

If you are intelligent and smart, don't let go of four things:
Keeping on the safe side, unalloyed wine, the beloved, and a
    private place.

Since in no state is the scheme of the wheeling of Time ever
    constant,
Do not complain, Háfiz, so that for the present we may get on
    with wine-drinking.

The cup of the heart is pure in the time of the Ásaf of the Age.
Get up and give me to drink of delicious wine clearer than
    limpid water.

The realm has gained pride through his good fortune and diligence.
O Lord, may this rank and grandeur be everlasting;

The illuminator of the throne of dominion, mine of power and
    majesty,
Proof of the kingdom and religion, Abú Nasr son of Abú'l-Ma'álí.[1]

1. Burhánu'd-Dín Fathulláh Abú Nasr son of Abú'l-Ma'álí, was the *vazír* of Mubárizu'd-Dín Muhammad (1313–1357 AD), father of Sháh Shujá', who in 1357 deposed and blinded his father, when Burhánu'd-Dín was dismissed, to die, probably under torture, soon after. See Poem CCCLIV, note 2.

POEM CCCCLIV

The peace of God so long as night follows night
And two- and three-stringed lutes reverberate,

On the vale of the Arák tree¹ and the one who is in it,
And on an encampment at the crooked place above the sand,²

I am the prayer for the strangers of the world,
And I pray constantly and without intermission.

O heart, do not lament, because in the chain of his tress
Any disordered condition is completely composed.

Of ardent longing I am dying. Would to God it were known—
Where the word of the bringer of tidings of union?

O God, every stage which he makes his destination,
Keep him with Your unending grace.

And at all times my comfort is love for you,
And in all states my comforter, remembrance of you.

By your line of down a hundred fresh beauties are added.
May your life be a hundred glorious years!

Until the Resurrection may the black spot of my heart
Never be empty of longing and passion for you.

Congratulations for that Designer of Power
Who round the moon draws the line of a crescent.

Where might I find union with a king such as you,
I of the name of a reckless wastrel?

It is necessary for you to be, and otherwise easy would be
Loss of the stock of dignity and of material goods.

God is informed of what Háfiz's intention is;
Knowledge of God is my sufficiency for my begging.

1. A tree found in Arabia and of which twigs are used to clean the teeth and gums.
2. These Arabic verses or hemistiches imitate the traditional opening of the Arabic erotic and eulogistic *qasída* (ode), of which the beginning is traditionally an allusion to the departed beloved's last halting-place; the remains of the beloved's deserted encampment, *manzil*.

POEM CCCCLV

Like my love your beauty's art has assumed a perfection.
Be happy for this, that the beauty of the former has no decline.

It is unimaginable that in reason's depicting
A similitude in any way better than this should come.[1]

Life's happiness would be attained for us with you
If ever in our life one day were to be a day of union.

That moment when I might be with you, one year would be a day,
And that moment when I lack you, the twinkling of an eye is a year.

O beloved, how might I in a dream see the image of your face,
When through a dream my eye sees only a reflection?

Take pity on my heart, because on account of love for your fair
    face,
My feeble person has become as thin as the crescent moon.

If, Háfiz, it is union with the friend you desire, do not complain:
There must of separation be endurance more than this.

---

1.   The point is that it is a matter of the heart, not reason.

POEM CCCCLVI

One morning I went to pluck a rose.
Suddenly the voice of a nightingale reached my ear.

Like me the poor wretch had been afflicted by love for a rose,
And in the meadow was sounding a cry for help.

From moment to moment I was wandering in that meadow and
    garden,
Meditating on that rose and the nightingale,

The rose turned the mate of beauty and the nightingale,
    companion of love,
The one without any change, but that, suffering alteration.

Since the song of the nightingale affected my heart,
I became as if no endurance remained in me.

Many a rose comes into bloom in this garden, but
No one gathers a rose from it without the injury of the thorn.

From this orbiting cosmos, Háfiz, harbour no hope of joy.
It has a thousand faults, but not a single grace.

POEM CCCCLVII

This patched gown that I own is better in pawn for drink,
And this idiotic book of texts, better drowned in good wine.

Since for all that I took care, I have ruined my life,
Tumbling down into the corner of a tavern is best.

Since from dervishism to observe expediency is far,
A breast filled with fire and with it two eyes filled with tears
    are best.

The condition of the heart of the world-renouncer I will tell
    nobody,
Because were I this tale to tell, with harp and viol it were best.

So long as the Firmament's motions have neither head nor tail,
Desire for the wine-boy in the head and wine in the hand is best.

From a sweetheart like you, yes, the heart I do not retrieve:
If I suffer torment, at least from that twisted tress it is best.

Now you have grown old, Háfiz, come away from the wine-bothy;
Drunkenness and lust in the time of youth are best.

POEM CCCCLVIII

Of that wine of love, from which the apt become the inept,
Although it is the Month of Abstinence,[1] bring a cup.

Days have gone by since he of the shank of one of box-tree tallness
And of the arm of the silver-limbed grasped the hand of
    wretched me.

O heart, although the fast is a precious guest,
Consider its company a gift, but its going a boon.

In this season no wise bird flies to the door of the conventicle,
Because a snare is laid in the congregation of every sermon.

Of the ill-disposed Puritan I do not complain. The sequence is
    this,
That when a dawn breaks, an evening falls not far behind.[2]

If my friend strode out to enjoy the meadow,
Take, O courier breeze, a message from me to him:

"Might it be that the comrade who imbibes wine night and day
Should recall a drainer of the dregs?"

If, Háfiz, an Ásaf of the Age fails to render your heart its due,
Because of self-indulgence, to attain your wish will be hard.

---

1.   i.e. *Ramazán*, the ninth month of the Muslim year when all Muslims are
    enjoined by the Faith to fast from dawn till sunset.
2.   An allusion to the duration of the fast from early dawn until the sun disappears
    in the evening.

POEM CCCCLIX

From me, a beggar, who will take a message to kings,
To say, "At the feast of the lees-drinkers, two thousand Jamshíds
    rate a single cup"?

If that wine were immature, but this comrade mature,
One immature would be a thousand times better than a
    thousand mature!

O Shaikh, don't with rosary beads throw me off the Path:
When the bird happens to be smart, it falls for no snare.

Ruined I have become and of ill fame, but I am still hopeful
That, by the devotion of dear ones,[1] to a good name I might
    attain.

You who boast of alchemy cast a glance on our counterfeit coin,
Because we have thrown down a snare, but lack any bait.

Whither might I take my complaint, to whom tell my tale,
That your lip was our life, but no constancy was yours?

Marvel at the fidelity of the beloved who deigned no concern:
Neither by letter a message, nor in a scribble a greeting!

I have a mind to serve you. Buy me, please, and do not sell,
Because seldom does a slave like me fall into felicity.

Let the arrow of the eyelash fly and shed the blood of Háfiz,
Because nobody exacts revenge of such a killer.

---

1. "dear ones", *'azízán*, refers to fellow (and genuine) Súfís. The expression *'azíz*,
    "dear one", is used among the brethren.

POEM CCCCLX

Fragrances of the airs of the meadow of the blessed ones came
    and increased my desire.
May my precious life be the dust of sacrifice at the friend's door!

To hear the friend's message is bliss and salvation—
Who for me will be my greetings' bearer to Su'ád?[1]

Come to the stranger's supper and see the water of my eye,
Like clear wine in a Damascus glass.

If a bird of good augury sings in praise of the possessor of the
    Arák tree,[2]
Then my dove's cooing will not be absent from her garden.

Not long is left before the time of separation from the friend will
    come to an end.
From the heights over the beloved's dwelling I have espied
    tent tops.[3]

Happy the moment when you enter and in greeting I say to you,
"You have come with an auspicious coming; have alighted at an
    auspicious alighting-place.

Far from you I have been and become melted away to resemble
    the crescent,
Even as I have not seen your moon-like face in its fullness."

And were I to be bidden to Eternal Paradise yet not a keeper
    of my bond,
May my spirit not be happy nor I enjoy my repose.

There is the hope that by good luck I might soon see you—
You become gleeful in giving orders and I, in slavery.

Like a string of pearls of the first water is your choice verse, Háfiz,
Which, the moment of grace, outstrips the verse of Nizámí.[4]

1. The hemistich is in Arabic, so an Arab legendary beloved is invoked.
2. See Poem CCCCLIV, note 1.
3. The beloved is on the move.
4. A proud boast indeed, Ilyas ibn Yúsuf Nizámí of Ganja (d. 1209 AD) was the per-fecter of 'the epic of paragons of love'; the romantic epic in Persian literature.

POEM CCCCLXI

The breast is wracked with pain. O for a soothing unguent!
Because of loneliness the heart's at the end of its tether. For
    God's sake, a companion!

Who from the swiftly shifting sphere may look for any comfort?
O wine-boy, give me a cup, for me to know some ease a moment.

Get up so that we might give that Samarqandí Turk our heart,
Because from his airs desire for Múliyán's[1] stream keeps coming.

I said to a clever wit, "Regard these states." He laughed and
    replied,
"A tough time. An amazing business. A world turned upside down."

In the well of patience I burned for the sake of that candle of
    Chigil.[2]
The king of the Turks[3] disdains our condition. Where a Rustam?

In the game of the Path of love, safety and repose are a calamity.
May that heart be scarred that in pain for you wants a salve!

In the street of licentiousness, the self-satisfied and
    self-indulgent has no access.
It requires a world-burning voyager, not a raw one knowing no
    sorrow.

No real brave comes to hand in the world of dust;
Another world must be made, and an Adam anew.

What price Háfiz's tears before the unneedfulness of love,
When in this deluge the Seven Seas seem a drop of dew?

---

1. See E.G. Browne, *Translation of the Chahar Maqála*, (Four Discourses) *of Nizámí
the Prosodist of Samarqand*, op. cit., pp. 33–35, 113–114, and 121–122, note xvi.
Alluded to is a celebrated *qasída*, in the rhyming letter "y", as is this *ghazal* of

Háfiz. The *qasída* (ode) was composed by the poet Rúdaqí (d. 940–1 AD). Rúdaqí was at the court of the Samanid Amír Nasr II ibn Ahmad (reigned 913–942 AD), a patron of poets and the learned. The story is of the vexation of the Amír's entourage, eager to return to their homes and families, when the Amír loitered over a year in the region of Herát. The courtiers urged Rúdaqí to compose a poem which would so excite the Amír's homesickness that he would at once strike camp and return to his capitals, Bukhára and Samarqand, on the other side of the river Oxus. The poem worked: the Amír on hearing it rushed out without riding boots and leapt on a nearby guard-horse as soon as he heard the lines:

> Hope for Múliyán's stream is coming;
> The scent of the kindly friend is coming.

The stream was in a pleasance and resort near Bukhára, its water derived from the River Oxus. Háfiz is hinting at the attractiveness of the Turks of Transoxania. See also *Chahar Maqála*, ed. Mu'ín (Tehran 1955–7) pp. 52 sqq.

2. See Poem LI, note 1, and cccxxii, note 1.
3. There is a double allusion here, firstly to Afrásíyáb, whom the Iranian champion, Rustam, defeated on behalf of king Kaikhosrau (see Poem ccccxxv, note 2). Secondly, perhaps to Tímúr.

Who from the snatcher of hearts will bring me the courtesy of a
    note?
If he is still exercising kindness, where is the courier of the breeze?

I made a comparison and on the Path of love, the disposition of
    reason
Resembles a dewdrop that leaves a shape on the surface of the sea.

Come because, although my gown is in pawn to the wine-shop,
Not a farthing of any religious endowment will you find in my name.

Why, for a single sugar-cane of his, do they not buy that one
Who from the reed of a pen has poured a hundred sugar-
    offerings?

My heart sick of hypocrisy and trying to hide what everyone knows—
Better that at the door of the wine-shop I raise a flag!

Come, because those who comprehend what Time implies,
    would sell
Both worlds for a single cup of pure wine and the company of
    an idol.

The rites of love are not uninterrupted pleasure nor sybaritic living.
If you are our companion, imbibe the poison of grief.

The roadside quack does not understand the pain of love.
O dead of heart, go away and fetch one Messiah-breathed.

I am not making any complaint, but the cloud of the mercy of
    the friend
Spared those of the thirsty livers not one drop.

The narrative of how and why, O heart, makes the head ache.
Seize the cup and from your life rest a while.

Worthy of your dignity, O Sháh, there is nothing in Háfiz's power,
Save only for a nightly prayer and morning supplication.

POEM CCCCLXIII

I praise God for the Sultan's equity,[1]
Ahmad Shaikh Uvais son of Hasan Ilkání,

Khán son of a Khán and Sháhansháh of Shahanshahid descent,
He of whom it would be fitting were you to call him the soul
    of the world,

In your good fortune the seeing and unseeing have reposed
    confidence,
Welcome, O you who are worthy of such God-given grace!

If the moon were to rise without your command, it would be
    dashed in two:
The good fortune of Ahmad, and a miracle divine.[2]

The splendour of your luck steals the heart from both Sháh
    and beggar.
May the Eye of Evil be remote, for you are both a soul and one
    beloved.

Twist your forelock like a Turk, because in your horoscope
Are a Kháqán's magnanimity and the endeavour of a Chinghíz
    Khán.[3]

Although we are far away, yet in a toast to you are we raising
    the cup.
On the spiritual journey there can be no distant staging-post.

From the clay of Párs[4] for me no rosebud of gratification has
    blossomed;
Bravo for the Tigris of Baghdad and a fine-flavoured wine!

The head of the lover who mayn't be dust at the door of the beloved,
When might release be his from the torment of a head distraught?

O breeze of dawn, bring the dust of the door of the friend,
So that Háfiz might make the eye of the heart luminous through
    him.

1. The Jaláyirid or Ilkanid Sultan of Baghdad and Ázerbá'íján and regions in eastern Anatolia. He was the son of Hasan-i Buzurg, Hassan the Large, who in 1336 AD established the Jaláyirid dynasty. Shaikh Uvais ruled from 1356 to 1374 AD, and was a patron of the arts. Háfiz alludes to him twice by name in his *Díván*; see Poem CLVIII, note 2.

2. *Ahmad*, which Háfiz uses as an allusion to Ahmad Shaikh Uvais, is a variant of the name Muhammad, thus Muhammad the Prophet is also alluded to. The implication is that for any action to be initiated without the command of this puissant Jaláyirid Sultan, would be an affront to God and to the Prophet. Apocalyptic, in fact, for Koran LIV, 1, has:

   The Hour has drawn near, the moon has been split.

   a verse which is taken to refer to the phenomena of the Last Day, but which also, because of the next verse:

   But if they see a sign, they turn away and say,
   'Magic continuous'.

   has been commented upon as indicative of a miracle accorded the Prophet when unbelievers had demanded a miracle from him. Hence Háfiz's reference both to good fortune and a divine miracle.

3. An allusion to the Jaláyirids' Mongolian and Central Asian origins.

4. Párs, the province, Fárs, to which Háfiz belonged and of which Shíráz is the capital.

POEM CCCCLXIV

So far as you are able, take advantage of the time:
If you only knew, O soul, the fruit of life is in this moment.

For favour-granting the wheeling dome holds life forfeit.
Try hard to seize from fortune some measure of gratification.

Hear the advice of lovers and from the door of jollity return,
Because all this is not worth the distraction of an ephemeral world.

Breathe not a word to the Puritan about the wild side, because
To the unconfidential physician the condition of a hidden pain
    cannot be told.

When, gardener, I pass away from this place, be it unlawful to you
If you plant in my plot any cypress other than the friend.

Do not, O sugar-mouth, scorn the prayer of vigil-keepers.
The Solomonic seal-ring is under the protection of a certain
    Name.[1]

My precious Joseph has vanished. Pity, O brothers,
For from grieving for him wondrous have I beheld the state of
    the old man of Canaan.

The vat-smasher ignores this value which a domestic article
Like the pomegranate-rubicund ruby might have for a Súfí.

You go but your eyelashes shed people's blood.
O beloved, you travel fast. I fear that you might grow weary.

I withheld my heart from the dart of your eye, but
Your bow-containing eyebrow steals it by sauciness.

Concentrate the distracted heart of Háfiz with one act of kindness;
O you, your curl's twist the seat of concentration for the
    dispersed.

A taste for wine will kill the remorseful ascetic.
O sagacious one, do not do anything that brings remorse.

If, O stony-hearted idol, you have no regard for us,
To the Second Ásaf I will present my case.

---

1.   See Poem ccxx, verse 4, and cccxxii, note 3.

POEM CCCCLXV

I am desirous of you and I know that you know,
Because you both see the unseen and read the unwritten.

What does the utterer of blame understand of what passes
    between lover and beloved?
The sightless eye sees not, especially hidden mysteries.

Throw the tress aside and make the Súfí jump up and down
    and dance,
That from every patch in his robe you might scatter idols by the
    thousand.

The accomplishment of the affair of desirers is that
    heart-binding eyebrow.
Sit a moment, for God's sake. Loosen the frown from the forehead.

The angel in prostration before Adam[1] resolved to kiss the
    ground beneath you,
For something more than a human style did he find in your beauty.

The kindler of the lamp of our eye is the breeze from beauties'
    tresses.
May never, O Lord, this gathering know sorrow because of the
    wind of distraction!

O alas, the nocturnal joy that passed in sleep at dawn!
O heart, you do not know the value of time save the time you
    despair.

To be disgusted by fellow voyagers is not the way of a caravaneer:
With recollection of the reign of ease endure the hardship of
    the halt.

Imagining his tress's circle beguiles you, Háfiz.
Watch out lest you rap on the door-knocker of unattainable felicity.

---

1.   See Koran II, 32: "We said to the angels, 'Prostrate yourself to Adam.'" Cf. Koran
    VII, 10.

POEM CCCCLXVI

People said, "You're the second Joseph."[1]
When I looked carefully, in truth you are better than that.

Sweetly smiling you are sweeter than I can say,
O Khusrau[2] of the Fair, for you are the Shírín of any age.

Your mouth is not to be likened to a rosebud;
There never was a rosebud of this narrowness of mouth.

A hundred times over you have repeated, "I will grant you
   satisfaction from this mouth."
Why are you all tongue, like the noble lily?

You said, "I will grant you gratification, but will take your life."
Grant my desire I fear you will not, but take my life you will.

Your eye makes the shaft of poplar wood penetrate the shield of
   the soul.
Who has witnessed a sultry eye with so strong a bow as this?

Him whom for a single moment you exile from your own sight,
You wipe away from the eyes of men as you would a tear drop.

---

1. For the beauty of Joseph, which caused the ladies in Egypt to describe him as
   "nothing but a noble angel", see Koran XII, 31.
2. The historical Khusrau II Parvíz (r. 590–638 AD) was one of Iran's Sassanid
   rulers and famous for having a mistress, Shírín, of whom Farhád was the
   unsuccessful suitor, tricked into dying by a ruse devised by his royal rival.
   Shírín as an epithet means "sweet". In getting both the name of the emperor
   and that of celibrated associate into the same hemistich, Háfiz is deploying a
   rhetorical device of a kind characteristic of the rules of Persian poetry.

POEM CCCCLXVII

Breeze of blessedness's morning, with that sign you know
Blow by so-and-so's street, at that time you know.

You are the courier of the seclusion of the secret and eyes are on
    the lookout for you;
Out of humanity, not to order, move as you know how.

Say, "My feeble soul is beside itself. For God's sake,
From your spirit-reviving ruby lip give that which you know."

These two words I have written in such a way that another could
    not comprehend.
You too in the way of your kindness read them the way you know.

For us the image of your sword is the story of the thirsty and water.
You have made your captive. Slay as you know how.

How might I not tie hope to your gold-braided belt?
There is, O idol, a particularity in that waist that you know.

In this affair, Háfiz, Turkish and Arabic are one.
Explain the story of love in that tongue which you know.

POEM CCCCLXVIII

Two gracious friends and two large measures of mellowed wine;
Freedom from care, a book and a corner of a meadow—

I would not surrender this station for either this or the next
    world—
Although some congregation might be after me every moment—

Because whoever has given contentment's treasure for the world's,
Has sold Joseph of Egypt for the cheapest price.

Come, because the possibilites of this workshop are not
    diminished
By the asceticism of one like you, or the depravity of one like me.

See in the mirror of the cup the artistic skill of the Invisible,
For no one can recall at any time such a wonder.

On account of the whirlwind of events, there is no seeing
Whether in this field there were a rose or whether a jasmine.

Because of this pestilential gale that has blown in the direction
    of the garden,
It would be a marvel were there the scent of a rose or of a
    jasmine here.

Try, O heart, to be patient, for God does not leave
Such a precious seal-ring in the hands of a devil.[1]

The constitution of the cosmos, Háfiz, has been ruined in this
    calamity.
Where is there a wise physician's consideration and the judgement
    of a Brahman?

---

1.   The theft of Solomon's magic signet ring by a devil is being alluded to; see
    Poem xxiv, note 3. But here the precious ring means Shíráz, known as the
    Takht-i Sulaimán, Throne of Solomon. Shíráz has been ruined by a calamity, but

its enthralment to a devil is not to endure: God does not leave the precious ring in the hands of such. Háfiz seems to be alluding to the invasion of Fárs by Tímúr (Tamburlane) in the winter of 1387 AD when, called back to Transoxania because of the aggression of his rival the ruler of Khwárazm (Khiva), Tímúr had quickly to abandon the investment of Shíráz and march north. He allotted Shíráz to the Muzaffarid prince, Sháh Yahyá. If the poem refers, as it seems almost certainly to do, to these events, it would have been composed precisely two years before Háfiz's death in December 1389 AD. If Háfiz was born in about 1325–6 AD, he would have been in his early sixties.

POEM CCCCLXIX

Drain a deep bowl of wine,
To uproot grief from the heart with it.

Keep the heart open like the wine-cup:
How long must it be stoppered like a bottle?

Once you take a deep draught of selflessness,
The less you will boast of your own egotism.

Be like stone beneath the foot, not like the cloud riding the sky.
You are nothing but a dye mixer and the stain of corruption.

Devote the heart to wine and manfully
Break the neck of abstinence and hypocrisy.

Get up and, like Háfiz, make an effort so that
Perhaps you might throw yourself at the beloved's feet.

POEM CCCCLXX

It is morning and hail is dripping from a wintry cloud.
Get the morning draught ready and hand out a bumper.

I have fallen into the sea of I-ness and self-regard. Bring
Wine, for it to release me from me-ness and self-obsession.

Drink the blood of the cup, because its blood is lawful.
Be busy wine-bibbing, because it is something worth doing.

Be to hand, wine-server, because sorrow lurks in ambush for us.
Minstrel keep this same tune that you are strumming.

Give wine since to my ear the harp has bent down and said,
"Be merry and listen to this bent old man."

Wine-boy, to the health of the reprobates' unneeding, give wine
That you may hear the voice of the singer, He who knows no need.

POEM CCCCLXXI

O you who in killing us know no compunction,
You consume profit and capital and have no respect of persons.

Those pain-afflicted possess a deadly poison:
To attempt the life of this tribe is to court danger. Better not to
    try it.

When with one sidelong glance of the eye our sickness can be
    removed,
It is no part of justice for you to withhold the cure.

Since in hope of you our eye is a sea, why
Do you not make a trip to the seashore, to have a look?

The report they have made, of every hurt from your benevolent
    disposition,
Is the word of interested parties. You do not commit them.

O ascetic, if in front of you our darling displays loveliness,
Ask of God only for wine and the beloved.

O Háfiz, make your prostration to his mihráb-like eyebrow,[1]
For only there can you offer any prayer of sincere intention.

---

1.   See Poem LXX, note 3.

POEM CCCCLXXII

To free yourself from sorrow listen to this pithy saying:
"If you look for unauthorised rations, you will drink blood."

At the end of the affair, you will become cup-makers' clay.
At present have a thought for the cup, to make it full of wine.

If you are of those sons of Adam whose fancy is Paradise,
Gratify yourself with such mortals as are of fairy stock.

Presumptuously to occupy the seat of the mighty is not possible,
Unless you get all the necessities of mightiness ready.

O sovereign of the sweet-mouthed, rewards can be yours,
If you spare a look in the direction of forlorn Farhád.

Alas, when will your heart receive grace's endorsement,
Unless you cleanse scattered imagery from off the page?

If, Háfiz, you were to refer your accomplishment back to the
    Munificent,
O how much would you revel in God-given luck!

O breeze of the morning, perform the bidding of Khwájeh
    Jalálu'd-Dín,[1]
That you may make the world full of jasmine and the noble lily.

---

1. The allusion is to Khwájeh Jalálu'd-Dín Turánsháh, *vazír* under Sháh Shujá'
    from 1364-5 AD to the latter's death in 1384. See Poem ccccxxv, note 1.

POEM CCCCLXXIII

O heart you do not pass by the street of love.
You have all the equipment ready, but you do not do anything:

The polo-stick of desire in the hand, but you do not hit the ball;
Such a falcon on the wrist, but you do no hunting.

The cup genial and full of wine, but you throw it into the dust:
You take no thought for the affliction of wine-sickness.

In the sleeve of your desire musk pods by the hundred are
      wrapped,
But none do you sacrifice for the curl of the friend.

This blood that surges on your account in our vitals,
You disdain to use as rouge for the cheek of the beloved.

Because of this the breath of creation has not turned musky,
That like the morning breeze you do not pass over the dust of
      the friend's street.

I fear that you will not bear off the gauntlet of the rose from this
      field,
Because you will not tolerate a thorn from its rose plot.

Go, Háfiz, because if all are performing service
At the court of the friend, will not you sometime?

POEM CCCCLXXIV

At dawn a traveller in a certain territory
Was repeating this riddle to a companion:

"Wine, Súfí, becomes clear after
It has completed a forty-day period in a cask.

If the finger be not a Solomon's,
What special property does the seal of the signet ring offer?"

God abhors that patched gown a hundred times,
In the sleeve of which there are a hundred idols.

Although gallantry is a name without a sign,
Are you still submitting your need to some coquette?

May the reward, O owner of the harvest, be yours,
If a little pity you show to one single gleaner.

Hearts have become darkened. May it be that from the Hidden
A lamp might give light for a solitary.

No aspiration has any high hope,
Nor any heart a cure, nor any faith a pang;

Although quick-temperedness is the way of the beautiful,
How would it be to put up with at least one of the grief-stricken?

Show the way to the tavern, so that I might ask
Someone with foresight the outcome of my condition.

Not for Háfiz attendance at classes and in retreat.
Not for the learned knowledge of the Real Truth.

POEM CCCCLXXV

But might not you be sitting infatuated at the edge of a
    pool?
If so, every enticement you see, you see all from yourself.

By the God of whom you are the chosen slave,
Let it not be that you prefer anyone to this ancient
    servitor.

The Khusrau of those with moon-like faces, modestly and
    respectfully deferred to you.
Bravo for you who a hundred times merit such.

What can I do if I do not exercise patience against the tyranny of
    your keeper?
No recourse is lovers' but humbleness.

Wonderful in your grace, O rose, that you sit by the thorn!
Apparently in this you perceive the expediency of the time.

If with integrity I keep faith, there is no fear:
Heart-surrender is easy if infidelity is not in its wake.

Hear a disinterested comment from a sincere slave:
"O you, cynosure of the great of the seers of the True,

Regret visits me that you should stride out to enjoy the spectacle
    of the meadow,
When you are more lovely than flowers and sweeter than a
    wild rose.

On right and left you may see the bubbles floating up from my
    tears,
If you pause a moment within sight of the eye.

One abstemious like you of the chaste heart and pure
    disposition,
It is better you do not consort with evil men."

The flood of these flowing tears has washed away patience from
    the heart of Háfiz.
Strength to endure has reached its limit. O see you the pupil of
    my eye!

You, with this delicacy and heart allure, O source of pride,
Deserve the banquet hall of a Khwájeh Jalálu'd-Dín.[1]

---

1.   See Poem ccccLXXII, note 1.

POEM CCCCLXXVI

Wine-boy, there are the shadows of clouds. It is spring and the
  bank of a stream—
I won't tell you what you are to do. If you are a man of the heart,
  you will tell yourself.

No hope of sincerity will issue from this scheme. Get up,
In clear wine wash the stained gown of the Súfí.

The world is by nature rotten. Do not count on its beneficence.
O veteran in experience of the world, expect no constancy from
  the mean.

Open the ear, because the nightingale is calling out loud,
"Khwájeh, be guilty of no shortcoming. Sniff the rose of divine
  grace."

In thanks for this, that you have reached another Spring
Plant the root of goodness and seek the Way of Truth.

You seek the face of the beloved? Make the mirror worthy,
Because never does the rose red or white bloom out of iron
  and brass.

I will give two pieces of advice. Listen and profit a hundredfold:
Enter by the door of pleasure, but do not run the track of
  opprobrium.

You have declared, "From our Háfiz rises the scent of hypocrisy."
Congratulations on your breath, that you so well got wind of it.

POEM CCCCLXXVII

Last night the nightingale, warbling in Pahlaví[1] from the cypress
    branch,
Was reciting the lesson of the Stages on the Way of Spiritual
    Meaning.

It was saying, "Come, because the rose has displayed the fire
    which Moses saw,
So that from the bush the subtlety of the Oneness you might
    hear."

The birds of the garden are rhymesters and composers of witty
    sayings,
So that the Khwájeh might drink his wine to odes in Pahlaví.

Pleasant the time on the mat of beggary but sleeping in safety:
This luxury is not the lot of the throne of a Chosroes.

Jamshíd took from the world nothing but the legend of the cup:
Take care not to bind the heart to worldly trappings.

Hear the marvellous tale of luck turned upside down:
"Us the friend has slain with the breaths of a Jesus."[2]

With its sultry look your eye has ruined the homes of men.
May you not be taken with wine, because drunk there's no
    holding you.

How well spoke the aged farmer to his son:
"O light of my eye, you only reap what you have sown."

Perhaps the wine-server gave Háfiz an extra measure,
Because Maulaví's[3] turban-pleats are awry!

---

1. The language of pre-Islamic Sassanid Persian: the nightingale, regularly appear-
    ing in spring, is constant and retains the ancient tongue. Cf. Fitzgerald's *Ruba'iyat
    of Omar Khayyam*, stanza XVI:

And David's lips are lockt; but in divine
High-piping Pehleví, with 'Wine! Wine!
 Wine!
  Red wine!' — the Nightingale cries to the Rose
That sallow cheek of hers to incarnadine.

2.   The breaths of spiritual truth are the breath of life, with which the beloved has killed us that we may live.

3.   In the first verse the implication is that the bird is in fact reciting the *Maqámát-i Ma'nawí*, "Stages on the Spiritual Way to the Truth". Jalálu'd-Dín Rúmí (d. 1273 AD) composed the great exposition of Sufism, the *Mathnawí-ye Ma'nawí*. (See R. A. Nicholson's text and translation, published in the E. J. W. Gibb Memorial Series, 1925.) Háfiz appears to have had this work very much in mind, a supposition which seems to be borne out by the use of the word *maulaví* in the last hemistich, for Jalálu'd-Dín Rúmí is most often referred to as "Maulaví", the Master, although, with a double entendre, Háfiz in this hemistich arrogates to himself this honorific. Nonetheless, he is at the same time bringing out the background to his poem.

POEM CCCCLXXVIII

You without the news, strive to be its possessor.
So long as you are not a wayfarer, how can you be a guide?

In the School of the Truths, before one versed in love,
Hey son, make an effort to become one day a father.

Like the valiant of the Path, cleanse your hands of existence's
    copper,
To discover love's alchemy and turn it into gold.

Sleeping and eating have distanced you from your proper rank.
You will come into your own when you get above sleeping and
    eating.

Were the light of God's love to fall upon your heart and soul,
By God, you would be finer than the sun in heaven!

Be drowned in the ocean of God a moment. Do not suppose
That by so much as a hair you will be wet from the waters of the
    Seven Seas:

From head to foot all the light of God will be yours,
Once, headless and footless, you are on the path of the Lord of
    Glory.

If the countenance of God should become the object of your sight,
From then on no doubt will remain that you are the master of
    insight.

When the foundations of your being are turned topsy-turvy,
In the heart do not suppose that you will ever again be on top.

If, O Háfiz, you have a mind for union,
At the door of the virtuous you must become dust.

POEM CCCCLXXIX

At dawn the voice of the tavern in wishing me well
Said, "Come back, because in this court you are an old habitué.

A draught from us drink like Jamshíd, so that of both worlds'
    mystery
The beam of light from the world-seeing cup might inform you."

Footloose rascal dervishes are at the tavern door,
Who the imperial diadem take and give;

Beneath the head a brick and on the crown of the Pleiades a foot—
See the hand of power, and the rank-holder's office!

It is a matter of our head and the door of the wine-shop, of
    which the roof,
For all its wall is lowly, has risen as high as the Empyrean.

Without the company of Khizr[1] do not attempt this stage:
There are darknesses. Be on your guard against going astray.[2]

If, O heart, on you is conferred the sovereignty of poverty,
Your least province will be from the Moon to the Fish.[3]

You do not know how to entertain poverty? Do not reliquish
The dais of mastership and the assembly of a Turánsháh.[4]

Háfiz of crude greed, be ashamed of this narrative.
What have you done that you should demand the two worlds as
    its wage?

---

1.   Khizr, the Green Man. See Poem xl, note 1, and other references.
2.   For the Súfí, submission to the leadership of a Guide, *Pír*, is essential.
3.   i.e. the whole cosmos.
4.   See Poem ccccLxxii, note 2.

POEM CCCCLXXX

O you in whose face the lights of kingship are manifest,
A hundred divine wisdoms hidden in your thinking,

Your pen, may God bless it, on the Realm and the Faith
With a single drop of ink has opened a hundred springs of the
    Water of Life.

For Ahriman[1] the Great Name's light does not shine:
Kingdom and the seal-ring belong to you. Order whatever you
    desire.

Whoever evinces doubt of the glory of Solomon,
Birds and fishes mock his intelligence and wisdom.

Although occasionally the falcon might flaunt a crown,
The birds of the Mountain of Qáf know the etiquette of royalty.[2]

The sword to which out of its bounty heaven gives lustre,
Might on its own seize the world, without obligation to any army.

With regard to friend and foe, your pen writes discriminatingly
The phylactery for the preservation of life, and the incantation,
    "May your life be short!";

You whose element is a creation compounded of honour's
    greatness,
And your fortune, in safety from the assault of ruin,

Were a single flash from your sword to fall on quarry and mine,
It would give the red-faced ruby the colour of straw.

O king, it is a lifetime that my cup has been devoid of wine;
Behold the petition of the slave, and, from the police officer, the
    violence.

I know your heart would pity vigil-keepers' misery
If you inquired from the breeze at dawn after my condition.

Bring, wine-boy, some liquid from the tavern tap,
For me to wash gowns clean of a conventicle's conceit.

In the stead where the lightning stroke of sin scorched Adam the
     pure,
How might the pretension of sinlessness befit us?

Since, Háfiz, the king from time to time mentions your name,
Do not show offence at your luck. Come back asking forgiveness.

---

1. The devil which stole the magic ring of Solomon is, of course, alluded to, but
   see Poem cccclxviii, note 1: Háfiz is once again alluding to the ruler of Fárs
   with Shíráz his capital.
2. The allusion is to the mystical allegory, the *Mantiqu't-Tair* ("The Speech of the
   Birds"), composed by Farídu'd-Dín 'Attár (d. *c*.1221 AD); but it is also and
   primarily to the Koranic origin of the phrase (Koran xxvii, 16) where Solomon
   is said to have known the "speech of the birds", *mantiqu't-tair*. Hence the allu-
   sion to the birds mocking anyone who doubted Solomon's glory. The birds of
   the Mountain of Qáf were the birds who in 'Attár's allegory sought the King
   Bird, the *Símurgh*, whose residence was on the Mountain of Qáf, which sur-
   rounds the world.

POEM CCCCLXXXI

In no Magian Temple is there anyone so distracted as me,
My gown in one place in pawn for wine, my book somewhere else.

The heart that is a royal looking-glass is speckled with dust;
From God I seek the comradeship of one of clear vision.

I have accomplished my repentance at the hands of a wine-selling
    idol,
That never again without the face of a banquet-adorner should
    I drink wine.

From the eye to the hem of my garment I have diverted streams,
    so that
It might come to pass that one of lofty height may be seated in
    my lap.

Launch the ship of wine, because, lacking the cheek of the friend,
Out of the sorrowing of the heart each corner of my eye has
    become an ocean.

Perhaps to its tongue the candle will bring the secret of this
    subtlety,
But, if not, the moth will not be concerned with words.

Do not grieve if the narcissus boasts of beauteousness of eye:
People of vision do not go after those who are blind.

Do not mention another to me, the worshipper of the beloved,
Because beyond him and the bowl of wine I have no care for
    anyone.

How pleasing to me came this tale, that at dawn
By the wine-temple's doorway, to fife and drum a Christian was
    repeating:

"If this is to be a Muslim, that Háfiz professes,
Alas if on the heel of today there is any tomorrow!"[1]

1. In the *Habíbu's-Siyar*, "The Friend of Biographies", the historian Khwándamír (d. 1534 or 1536 AD), mentions this poem and a certain detail of Háfiz's life. Háfiz had fallen into disfavour with Sháh Shujá' because, after the latter had criticized Háfiz's poems as being too diverse in subject matter to accord with the rules of rhetoric, Háfiz had retorted by claiming that, while no verses of Sháh Shujá''s and others of his contemporaries ever went beyond the gates of Shíráz, his own were celebrated to the farthest horizons. Sháh Shujá', disgruntled with Háfiz, noticed the last verse of this poem and took it as denying the possibility of there being a Day of Judgement, belief in which is incumbent upon Muslims. Jealous members of the religious establishment were not slow to develop the Sháh's interpretation of the verse and issue a *fatwa* to the effect that to cast doubt on the event of the Day of Judgement was *kufr*, unbelief. Háfiz was perturbed, so Khwándamír 's narrative continues. He had recourse to a notable divine who was passing through Shíráz on his way to Mecca: Mauláná Zainu'd-Dín Abú Bekr. The Mauláná advised Háfiz to insert a preceding verse in which the observation about "tomorrow" contained in the last verse, the *'maqta'*, was put into the mouth of a Christian. It was proverbial that a Muslim who repeated a heretical comment by an unbeliever would not himself be culpable. See *Habíbu's-Siyar* (Tehran, 1953–4) Vol. III, pp. 315–316. The work was completed between 1520 and 1524 AD, some one hundred and thirty to one hundred and thirty-five years after Háfiz's death.

POEM CCCCLXXXII

I have had my eye on the eyebrow of a moon-faced;
I have conceived somewhere taking a fancy to one with newly
    sprouted down.

I the dervish have yielded the reins of my heart to someone
Who because of crown and throne has not a care for anyone.

My head is no longer at my command. Through expectation my
    eye has burned
In yearning for the head and eye of an adorner of the assembly.

Excellent the notion that the charter for my dalliance with love,
From that eyebrow with the small bow has flourished into a full-
    blown royal cypher.[1]

My heart is troubled. I will set fire to the patched cloak.
Come, look, because it will be quite a spectacle.

At the time of 'a certain event', make our coffin of cypress wood,
Because we will depart with the brand of one of lofty stature.

At that stage where with a glance the beautiful unsheath the blade,
Regard not as extraordinary a head tumbled at feet.

What do separation and union matter? Seek the approbation of
    the friend,
Because any desire of him other than him would be a pity.

For me, for whom, because of his cheek, the moon is in the
    night chamber,
How can there be any consideration for the twinkling of a star?

Out of love the fish would bring up pearls for confetti scattering
Were you to launch Háfiz's book[2] of poems onto the sea.

1. A small bow-shaped flourish at the top was a feature of the cypher endorsing a patent as contrasted with a *tughrá*, the complete royal cypher inscribed in the upper margin of a document and making it a royal mandate of more weight than one endorsed by order of someone less than the sovereign, in which case the bow-like flourish would be smaller.
2. The word translated "book" is *safíneh*, which also means "ship". See Poem CCCL, verse 9, where *safíneh* also means "book" or "collection", as of poems.

POEM CCCCLXXXIII

Greeting, like the sweet fragrance of friendship,
To that pupil of a luminous eye.

Greeting, like the light of world-renouncers' hearts,
To that candle of the place of piety's seclusion.

I see nobody of the comrades in his seat.
My heart has been harrowed by grief. Wine-server, where are you?

Do not turn away from the street of the Magians, for there
The key is sold to the solution of problems.

Where do they sell the Súfí-knock-out wine?
For at the hands of hypocrisy's austerity I am in torment.

In such wise have friends sundered the bond of association,
You would say no friendship at all ever was.

The bride of the world, although she is passing fair,
Takes the practice of inconstancy beyond any limit.

If it has any steadfastness, my wounded heart
Will seek no physic from those with stony hearts.

Greedy carnal spirit, if you would leave me,
I would exercise plenty of sovereignty in beggary.

Allow me to teach you the alchemy of felicity:
Separation, separation from evil fellowship.

Do not complain, Háfiz, of the injustice of wheeling Time—
What, O slave, do you know of the Divine Dispensation?

POEM CCCCLXXXIV

O Emperor of beauties, any redress for the sorrow of being alone?
Without you the heart is at the end of its tether: it is time you
   came back.

Not forever does the rose of this garden stay fresh.
Help the weak at the time when you are able.

Last night I was complaining of your tress to the wind.
It whispered, "You err. Go beyond this melancholy meditation."

A hundred dawn breezes dance there to the tress's chain—
These are the competitors; O heart, beware not to attempt the
   impossible.

Longing and a sense of separation have so distanced me from you,
That patience's strength will elude my power.

To whom, Lord, might uttering this point be fitting, that in the world
That roving beloved shows his cheek to none?

O wine-boy, without your face not a single hue graces the roseplot.
Cause your tallness to stride out, for you to lend adornment to
   the garden.

O the pain for you, my cure on the bed of unsatisfied desire!
And O memory of you, the retreat of my intimate solitude!

Within the compass of fate we are the compass point of assent.
Kindness is what you intend. Command what you command;

Self-opinionatedness and self-conceit are not in the world of
   vagabondage:
In this Order, self-regard and self-approval are apostasy.

My heart is bloodied by this azure circle. Hand out the wine,
For me in a blue glass goblet to solve this enigma.

Háfiz, gone is the night of separation. Come is the sweet odour
   of union.
O lovesick lover, may your joy be blessed.

POEM CCCCLXXXV

If, O heart, you escape from that pit in the chin,
Wherever else you go, you will soon come out in sorrow.

Be on your guard because, if you listen to the prompting of
    appetite,
From Rizván's[1] garden, like Adam out you will go.

If thirsty-lipped you come away from the well of life,
It is right that with a waterdrop heaven should not come to the
    rescue.

Like the morning's rising I give up my soul in longing for the
    sight of you;
May it be that, like the shining sun, you enter through my door.

Like the breeze, how long must I furnish you with the breath of
    devotion,
That like the rose you might burst from the bud joyous and
    laughing?

In the dark night of your absence, my life has been ready to
    expire.
It is time that, like the resplendent moon, you arose.

From my eyes I have laid the dust at your door with two hundred
    streams
On the chance that you, like the poised cypress, might come
    striding forth.

Do not be anxious, Háfiz: that Joseph of the moon-face
Is coming back and you will come out of the hut of sorrow.

---

1.   *Rizván*, the gardener and custodian of Paradise. See Poem L, note 1.

POEM CCCCLXXXVI

Call for wine and scatter the rose. What are you asking of destiny?
The rose at dawn asked this of the nightingale, "What are you
    saying?"

Take the bench into the rose garden, so that, from the sweetheart
    and the wine-server,
You might snatch the lip, might kiss the cheek, might drink wine,
    might smell the rose.

With the gait of the tall box-tree striding, set out for the garden,
So that the cypress from your stature might learn heart-enticing.

Let us see to whom your smiling rose bud will give luck;
O graceful rose twig, for whose sake do you grow?

Since the candle of beauty is standing in a draught of wind,
Hold on to the excellence gleaned from the candle of a lovely face.

Today, when your marketplace is full of the hubbub of purchasers,
Find and lay up some treasure from the stock of goodness.

That curl, of which every ringlet holds a hundred Chinese
    musk pods,
Would be fine if its perfume were from sweetness of disposition.

In the rose garden of the king, every bird enters with a song;
The nightingale with harmonious warbling, Háfiz with the
    chanting of a well-wishing prayer.

Appendix I

Notes and Definitions on Certain Words and Symbols used in the Poetry of Háfiz

but: idol. The beloved is often referred to as an idol. It should be noted that Shabistarí in the *Gulshan-i Ráz* makes it clear that the idol, so long as it is not worshipped on a phenomenal level, is "the evidence of love and unity", and, in its real being, "is not vain".[1] It is a manifestation of Being. Hence idol-worship is the quest for admission to comprehension of "unification". According to the Súfí doctrine expounded by Shabistarí, in addition to idols, the Christian *zonnar*, girdle,[2] and Christianity itself are all acceptable in Sufism provided they are seen as, not part of phenomenal unreality, but of true Being. Reference may be made to Háfiz (Poem LXIV) where he says:

> In love there is no difference between the Súfí hospice
> and the tavern:
> Wherever it is, there is the ray of the face of the beloved.
>
> The place where the cloister's business is given lustre,
> There is the chantry of the monk and the name of the cross.

chashm and *lab*: eye and lip. It is said that on account of His eye sickness and intoxication arise, and from His ruby (lip) non-being beneath Essential Being. The Súfís believed that Koran xv, 25, "so when I have formed him, and breathed my spirit into him" implies the constant efflux of Being by which all things subsist; the robe of Being thrown over the nakedness of non-being. According to Láhíjí, this is what Shabistarí has in mind.[3] Shabistarí goes on to say:[4]

> On account of His eye, souls are intoxicated and over-hung:
> By His ruby, souls are all overcome.

---

1. *Gulshan-i Ráz*, under Question 15, Whinfield's Persian text and English translation, couplets 865–869. (Note also a new translation into English by Robert Darr, entitled *Garden of Mystery*, Cambridge 2007.)
2. Ibid. couplets 885–930.
3. For Láhíjí's comment, see Whinfield's translation, p. 73 note 3.
4. *Gulshan-i Ráz*. couplet 747.

And:[5]

> From Him every glance is a snare baited with grain.
> And because of him every corner of the eye has been
>   turned into a wine-shop.

> With a glance he puts the world of creaturely being to the sack.
> With one kiss he restores it,

Sentiments which are a repeated theme in the lyrical poetry of Háfiz as the power of the beloved's eye and lip is extolled, or lamented.

khál: mole or "beauty spot", which is the point of Unity, described in Láhíjí's Commentary on the *Gulshan-i Ráz* as the "hidden Ipseity", single in itself, but embracing all phenomena.[6] Shabistarí says that the mole is:[7] The centre which is the basis of the revolving circumference.

> From it comes the line of the circle of both worlds,
> And from it the line of the spirit and heart of Adam.

kharábát: tavern or any desolate place. Persian cities were very often fringed by ruined suburbs deserted because of the failure of irrigation to provide their occupants with water or for other reasons. In these desolate places were wine bothies, secret drinking dens, hence their soubriquet of *kharábát*. In Súfí poetry, having due regard to the definition above of the centrality of wine-bibbing as a metaphor for transcending the self, the significance of the "tavern" will be obvious. As Shabistarí says:[8]

> Becoming a tavern-seeker is escape from the self.
> Self-absorption is unbelief even if the self be "pious".

---

5. Ibid. couplets 751–752.
6. The commentary to which Whinfield refers is the *Mufátihu'-I'jáz fí Gulshan-i Ráz*, "Keys to the Wonders in the Description of the Rose Garden of Mystery", by Shaikh Muhammad Láhíjí of the year 879 AH/1484 AD. (On the mole, see Whinfield, p. 77 note 2.) Reference may also be made to the selections from the *Gulshan-i Ráz* published in Tehran in 2003 by Husain Muhu'd-Dín Ilahí Qumshehi, which contains a (not, unfortunately, complete) list of definitions used by Shabistarí.
7. *Gulshan-i Ráz*. couplets 791–792.
8. Ibid.couplet 839.

Notice has been given you from the tavern
That "unification is the abrogation of attachments".

The tavern belongs to the world of no similitude:
It is the place of reckless, "free-for-all" lovers!

The tavern is the nest of the bird of the soul;
It is the threshold of no contingency.

The haunter of the tavern is desolate in desolation,
For in his desert the world is a mirage.

rukh and *khatt*: cheek and down. As Shabistarí expresses it, the cheek is "the theatre of Divine Beauty", and the down is the brink or vestibule of Almightiness.[9] *Brink* is a satisfactory rendering of the Persian *janáb*, because by the word "down" is meant the line (indeed, the word used for it in Persian is *khatt*, which means "line") of soft hair girdling an adolescent male's cheek and signalling the first sprouting of his beard. It is frequently referred to as a mark of beauty. Shabistarí goes on to say that:[10]

The down's become the green bed of the world of the soul.
Hence it has been named "the abode of life".

"The abode of life" is an allusion to Koran xxix, 64, in which the distinction is drawn between the triviality of the "nearer life" and the "abode of the Hereafter" which "is life indeed". Shabistarí continues his meditation on *khatt* by pointing out that, in the spirit world, down is the first emanation of plurality that veils the face of unity. He says:[11]

One person has seen His down as belonging to the beautiful face:
My heart sees His face in its down,

by which he means that one may see the phenomenal world and infer from it the Real, while another sees the Real in all that he beholds.

---

9. Ibid. couplet 780.
10. Ibid. couplet 782.
11. Ibid. couplet 787.

sháhid: beauty, a person who by divine grace possesses beauty. The word is derived from the Arabic verb (*shahada*) meaning "to testify", "to bear witness", also "to suffer martyrdom"; it could also mean "a witness". The extended meaning to gracefulness or beauty of person, or simply a beautiful person, or the darling, is attested by a number of eminent expounders of Sufism as Súfí usage intended to show that a beautiful person can be taken as the surrogate for God, or Divine Beauty: it can either be used to refer to the beloved with a small "b", or the Beloved with a capital "b". As Shabistarí says, the epiphanies of the Divine Verity are the *sháhid*, the *sham'*, candle, and *sharáb*, wine, "for the Divine Verity is manifested in all forms". He continues, "Wine and the candle are the ecstatic apprehension and light of the discerning".[12] Once the veil of the self is obliterated, Shabistarí says, "the Divine Beauty is hidden from no one".[13] The Divine Beauty was the beam of the light of spirits and the sparks that lit the heart of Moses, while his wine was the fire and his candle the burning bush. The Divine Beauty is referred by Shabistarí to Koran LIII, 18: "Verily, he (Muhammad the Prophet) saw one of the greatest signs of his Lord."[14] The conception of *sháhid* here expounded dates back to long before Shabistarí's time. Reference can be made to Ahmad-Alí Rájaní Bukhár'í, *Farhang-i Ash'ár-i Háfiz*, "The Dictionary of Háfiz's Poems", Tehran, 1364/1984, pp. 361–366, in which a useful bibliography of early Súfí works' definitions of *sháhid* is provided, with apposite quotations.

sharáb or *mey*: both words used for wine. In the same passage in which Shabistarí defines Divine Beauty and the Candle, he speaks of wine, which he instructs the seeker of the Súfí Way to drink as it is "the dying of the self", so that for a while in drinking it, the neophyte might find preservation from the sorrow of the self:[15]

> Drink wine so that it may release you from yourself;
> That it may cause the being of the drop to reach the ocean.

in other words the drop, freed from its phenomenal limitation.

---

12. Ibid. couplets 839–843.
13. Ibid. couplet 807.
14. The reference is in couplet 810.
15. Ibid. couplet 813.

zulf: tress or curl. In the *Gulshan-i Ráz* (see Whinfield text and translation, beginning at couplet 764), Shabistarí waxes lyrical when he comes to describing the *zulf*. He begins by saying:[16]

> The tale of the tress of the Darling is very long:
> What might be proper to say about it, for here is a mystery?

> Don't ask me the story of the twisted curl:
> A chain leading mad lovers captive.

> Last night I spoke clearly about His stately form:
> The curl's tip told me to shut up.

> Crookedness conquered its straightness:
> Hence, the road of the seeker became twisted.

> All hearts have been enchained by it:
> Through it all souls are driven wild.

and so on, in terms that make it tempting to continue reciting; but a couplet from Háfiz might be taken as saying all that need be said about the lock, curl or tress dropping over the face of the adored, sometimes like a hockey stick drawn across the face of the moon. In the Háfiz's Poem x, verse 7, he has:

> For the heart's bird the quarry of composure had fallen
> into the snare.
> You loosened a tress from our net. Our prey was gone!

Shabistarí continues to point out that the clay of Adam was leavened the moment it caught the perfume of "that amber-scented curl".[17] which Láhíjí explains in terms of Adam's having received the faculty of displaying all the Divine attributes.[18]

Shabistarí concludes:[19]

> My heart was harrowed on account of His curl,
> For it keeps my burning heart from His face.

---

16. Ibid. couplets 763–767.
17. Ibid. couplet 776.
18. For Láhíjí's comment, see Whinfield's translation, p. 75 note 4.
19. *Gulshan-i Ráz*. couplet 779.

Appendix II

Háfiz and Free Will

There has been much controversy concerning the question of whether Háfiz was a predestinarian haunted by Fatalism. Indeed, much in Persian poetic literature has seemed to lend itself to a fatalistic interpretation. But in this regard it seems clear that Háfiz must, as it were, be exonerated.

As a preliminary to the process of doing so, due regard has to be paid to the Koran. Sura xci is about Allah's omnipotence. It describes how the day reveals His splendour, and the night veils Him, and the witness of "a soul and what formed it, And implanted in it its wickedness and its piety. Prospered has he who purifies it, Failed has he who corrupts it" (verses 1–10). Sura iv, 81, makes the contrasting statement: "The good which has fallen to thy lot is from Allah, the evil which has befallen thee is from thyself; We have sent thee (Muhammad the Prophet) as a messenger to the people; Allah is sufficient witness."[1]

It will be noted that these two Koranic citations are apparently contradictory. As J. B. Mozley says in his *Treatise on the Augustinian Doctrine of Predestination* (2nd edn, London, 1878), on p. 253:

> Every reader of S. Augustine is familiar with a certain view of the nature of evil, to which he constantly recurs, and which he seems to cherish in his mind as a great moral discovery, a fundamental set-off and answer to the great difficulty of the existence of evil, and the true and perfect mode of extricating the Divine attribute of Power from the responsibility of permitting it,—the position, viz. that evil is nothing—*nihil*. God was the source; and as being the source of, included and comprised, all existence. Evil was a departure from God. Evil, therefore, was a departure from existence. External to God, it was outside of all being and substance; i.e. was no-being or nothing.

---

1. Bell's translation; Arberry has: "Whatever good visits thee, it is of God; whatever evil visits thee is of thyself. And we have sent thee to men a messenger; God suffices for a witness." Pickthall has: "Whatever of good befalleth thee (O man) it is from Allah, and whatever of ill befalleth thee, it is from thyself."

Towards an explanation of the apparent Koranic contradiction, also to be noted is Mozley's remark on p. 37: "The truth of absolute predestination cannot be stated without contradiction to the Divine justice and man's free agency. It belongs, then, to that class of truths which does not admit of statement. It is an imperfect truth—that is, a truth imperfectly apprehended by us. .... The intellect stops short and rests in suspense." But according to Súfí perception, "suspense" is avoided: even as Mozley himself points out in the passage given *in extenso* above, for the Súfí the problem of evil was solved by the postulation that, whereas God creates, indeed *is*, the only real Being, which is good, evil is a part of non-being: it has no share in the Divine Order. As Shabistarí says, in Whinfield's translation (couplet 871), apropos an idol:

> Know that God almighty is its creator,
> From good whatever issues is good.
> The existence which is there is goodness entire,
> If there be evil in it, that is from "other".

"Other", i.e. *ghair*, by which is meant the unreal realm of "non-being". And so the argument may proceed. But more to the point where Háfiz is concerned, with his frequent allusion to, for example, his debauched and drunken condition as having been his destiny from the day of his creation, Shabistarí provides transparent clarification. He plays on Koran LXXVI, where in verse 21, describing the delights promised the righteous in Paradise, the words occur, "their God gives them to drink a pure draught". In the next hemistich Shabistarí asks what this "pure draught" is. He answers that its "purity" resides in the process of becoming cleansed of the self. It is this act in his creation to which Háfiz is referring: on his creation the Almighty poured into him the wine which purifies him from the self: his is the free poetic mind, the broad-ranging imagination of the poet that is capable of encompassing the Divine element in the universe. Shabistarí continues with the remark that "The moment, when we shall quit ourselves, is most happy: the moment when we shall be most rich in utterest poverty" (Whinfield's translation), where, as Láhíjí points out in his Commentary on the *Gulshan-i Ráz*, "The Rose Garden of Mystery", we are poor by effacing the self and enriched by union with the Divine (see Whinfield's translation, p. 68 and footnotes). Háfiz had no notions of "suspense" in relation to his destiny: his Shabistarían, high-Sufistic comprehension of the One-ness and All-ness of the Divine left him in no doubt of how he was destined to be. It did not include any resort to a therory of the "nothingness" of a non-Being "other" than the reality of God: God created all, which must include the erring self; but it was this self that was subject to being predestined to suffering—and to the escape from it in the wine-shop. This is the truth which Háfiz realized and continually expressed.

Appendix III

While it is not intended to discuss the history of Persian Sufism or Sufism and Háfiz—the latter topic is touched upon in the Introduction—there is one quotation it seems desirable to offer because it indicates how characteristic of the Persian mind was the Súfí attitude towards the phenomenal world as contrasted with the world of eternal verity. The idea that the former was only a mirage in contrast to the sole reality of the latter is seen expressed in a totally non-Súfí context by one of the earliest recorded Persian poets in the New Persian language. Rúdakí, who died in 940 AD, has a poem that begins:

> Live joyously with the black-eyed happy ones,
> For the world is nothing but a fantasy and hot air.

Incidentally, it is interesting how a poem by Emily Jane Brontë of 1846, and one of the great mystical poems in the English language, encapsulates so much of the burden of Shabistarí's *Gulshan-i Ráz*: [1]

> No coward soul is mine,
> No trembler in the world's storm-troubled sphere!
> I see Heaven's glories shine,
> And Faith shines equal, arming me from Fear.
>
> O God within my breast,
> Almighty ever-present Deity!
> Life, that in me hast rest
> As I, Undying Life, have power in thee!
>
> Vain are the thousand creeds
> That move men's hearts, unutterably vain;
> Worthless as withered weeds,
> Or idlest froth, amid the boundless main
>
> To waken doubt in one
> Holding so fast by thy infinity,
> So surely anchored on
> The steadfast rock of Immortality.

---

1. *The Complete Poems of Emily Brontë*, ed. Philip Henderson, London, 1951, pp. 246–247.

With wide-embracing love
Thy spirit animates eternal years,
Pervades and broods above,
Changes, sustains, dissolves, creates and rears.

Though earth and moon were gone,
And suns and universes ceased to be,
And thou wert left alone,
Every Existence would exist in thee.

There is not room for Death,
Nor atom that his might could render void
Since thou art Being and Breath,
And what thou art may never be destroyed.

Bibliography

Aminrazavi, Mehdi. *Suhrawardí and the School of Illumination.* London, 1997.

Arberry, A.J. *Classical Persian Literature.* London, 1958.

'Attár, Faríd al-Dín. *Tadhkirat al-awliyá*, "Memoirs of the Saints", ed. R.A. Nicholson. London, 1905.
Mantiqu't-Tair. Tr. Peter Avery, *The Speech of the Birds.* Cambridge, 1998.

Binning, R.B.M. *A Journal of Two Years' Travel in Persia, Ceylon, etc.* London, 1857.

Briffault, Robert. *The Troubadours.* Bloomington, IN, 1965.

Brontë, Emily. *The Complete Poems*, ed. Philip Henderson. London, 1951.

Browne, E.G. *Literary History of Persia.* Cambridge, 1928.

Butler, E.M. *The Myth of the Magus.* Cambridge, 1948.

Dawlatsháh. *Tadhkiratu'sh-shu'ará*, "Memoirs of the Poets", ed. E.G. Browne. London, 1901.

al-Daylamí, Abu'l-Hasan. *Síratu'sh-Shaikhu'l-Kabír Abú 'Abdu'l-lláh ibn Khafíf-i Shírází*, "The Life of Shaikh al-Kabir Abú 'Abdu'l-lláh ibn al-Khafíf-i Shírází", Persian tr., "Ibn Junayd of Shíráz" (from Arabic), ed. Annemarie Schimmel. Ankara, 1955.

Dihkhudá, 'Alí Akbar. *Kitáb-i Amsál wa hikam.* Tehran, 1310/1931–2.

Donaldson, Bess Allen. *The Wild Rue.* London, 1938.

Elgood, Cyril. *A Medical History of Persia.* Cambridge, 1951.

Encyclopaedia Iranica. New York, 1982–.

The Encyclopaedia of Islam, new edition. Leiden, 1960–2004. Articles: "Ahmad-i Jám"; "al-Halláj"; "'Irákí"; "Suhrawardí".

Firdawsí. *Sháhnáma*, ed. Djalal Khaleghi-Motlagh. Costa Mesa, CA, 1990.

Furúzánfar, Badí' al-Zamán. *Ahádíth-i Masnaví.* Tehran, 1324/1944–5.

Ghaní, Qásim. *Táríkh-i 'asr-i Háfiz.* Tehran, 1321/1942.

Háfiz, Shams al-Dín Muhammad.

Editions of the Díván:
Díván-i-Háfiz, I: *Ghazaliyyát*, "Collected Lyrics of Háfiz, I: The Lyrics", ed. Parvíz Nátíl Khánlarí. Tehran, 1362/1983–4. (The basis of this translation.)
Díván-i Ghazaliyyát, ed. Khalil Khátib Rahbar, Tehran, 1374/1995.

English translations of lyrics from the Díván:
Díván, ed. and tr. Wilberforce Clarke. Calcutta, 1891.
The Poems of Shamseddin Mohammed Hafiz of Shiraz, ed. and tr. John Payne. Villon Society, 1901.

Poems from the Díván of Hafiz, tr. Gertrude Bell. London, 1928.
Fifty Poems of Hafiz, tr. A.J. Arberry. Cambridge 1947; several times reprinted.
Thirty Poems from Háfiz, tr. Peter Avery and John Heath-Stubbs. London, 1952; Cambridge, 2006.
Hudúd al-ʿálam, "Regions of the World", tr. V. Minorsky. Oxford and London, 1937.
Hujwírí. *Kashfuʾl-mahjúb*, tr. R.A. Nicholson. London, 1936.
Ibn Battuta. *The Travels*, tr. H.A.R. Gibb. Cambridge, 1962.
Isfahání, Jamál al-Dín. *Díván-i Ustád Jamál al-Dín*, ed. Vahíd-i Dastgirdí. Tehran, 1320/1941–2; 1362/1983–4.
Jámí, ʿAbd al-Rahmán. *Nafahát al-uns*, ed. Mahmud ʿAbidi. Tehran, 1370/1991–2.
Jávíd, Háshim. *Háfiz-i jávíd*, "The Eternal Háfiz". Tehran, 1375 /1996–7.
Khalkhálí, ʿAbd al-Rahím. *Háfiz-náma*. Tehran, 1320/1941.
Khayyam, Omar. *Rubáʿiyyát*, tr. Edward Fitzgerald. Numerous editions.
Khurramsháhí, Baháʾ al-Dín. *Háfiz-náma*. Tehran, 1366/1987.
Khwándamír. *Habíb al-siyar*. Tehran, 1333/1954–5.
Láhíjí, Muhammad. *Mafátíh al-iʾjáz fí sharh-i Gulshan-i Ráz*, ed. Kaywán Samíʿí. Tehran, 1337/1958.
Manúchihrí. *Díván*, ed. Dabirsiyaqi. Tehran, 1326/1947–8.
Muʿín, Muhammad. *Háfiz-i Shírín-sukhan*. "Háfiz of the Sweet Discourse". Tehran, 1370/1991.
Nasr Allah, Munshi. *Kalíla wa Dimna*. Ed. Mujtabá Mínuví. Tehran, 1343/1964–5.
Níshábúrí, Abú Ishaq Ibráhím. *Qisas al-anbíyá*, "Tales of the Prophets", ed. Habíb Yaghmá. Tehran, 1340/1961–2.
Nizámí al-ʿArúzí Samarqandí. *Chahar Maqála*, "Four Discourses", ed. Muhammad Muʿín. Tehran, 1334–6/1955–7. Trans. E.G. Browne, *The Chahar Maqála (Four Discourses)*, Cambridge, 1921.
Pascal. *Pensées*, ed. Ernest Havet. Paris, 1881.
Qazvíní, Mirza Muhammad. Article in Yádgár, vol. 1, 9 (Tehran, 1323/1944), pp. 69–78.
Quiller-Couch, Sir Arthur. *On the Art of Writing*. Cambridge, 1916.
Rávandí, Muhammad b. ʿAlí b. Sulaymán. *Ráhat al-sudúr*, ed. Muhammad Iqbal. Leiden, 1921.
Rází, Najm al-Dín Dáya. *Mirsád al-ʿibád*, ed. Muhammad Amin Ríyáhí. Tehran, 1351/1972; 1986. Tr. Hamid Algar, *The Path of God's Bondsmen*. Delmar, NY, 1982.
Rúmí, Jalál al-Dín. *Masnaví-yi maʿnavi*. Ed. and tr. R.A. Nicholson, *The Mathnawí of Jalálu'd-Dín Rúmí*. London, 1925.

Kulliyát-i Shams yá Díván-i kabír, ed. Badí 'al-Zamán Furúzánfar. Tehran, 1345/1966–7.

Rúzbihán Baqli. *Kitáb-i 'Abhar al-'Áshiqín*, "The Jasmine of the Love's Faithful", ed. Henry Corbin and Muhammad Mu'ín. Tehran and Paris, 1958.

Rypka, Jan. *History of Iranian Literature*, ed. Karl Jahn. Dordrecht, Holland, 1968.

Sa'd, Mas'úd. *Díván*, ed. Rashíd Yásamí. Tehran, 1318/1939.

Sa'dí. *Kullíyyát*, "Complete Works", ed. Muhammad 'Alí Furúghí. Tehran, 1363/1984–5.

Schimmel, Annemarie. *Mystical Dimensions of Islam*, Chapel Hill, NC, 1975.

Shabistarí, Mahmúd. *Gulshan-i Ráz, The Mystic Rose Garden*, Persian text with English trans. and notes, ed. and tr. E.H. Whinfield. London, 1880; new tr. Robert Darr, *Garden of Mystery*. Cambridge, 2007.

Súdí. *Sharh-i Súdí bar Háfiz*, "Commentary on Háfiz", Persian tr. (from the Turkish original) by 'Ismat Sattárzáda. Tehran, 1341/1962–3.

Thompson, Francis. *The Hound of Heaven*, in D.H.S. Nicholson and A.H.E. Lee, ed., *The Oxford Book of English Mystical Verse*. Oxford, 1917, pp. 409–415.

Virgil. *The Aeneid, Verse Translation. by John Dryden*, ed. Robert Fitzgerald. New York, 1965.

Zákání, 'Ubayd. *Díván*, ed. 'Abbás Iqbál. Tehran, 1332/1952.